YO-CCT-600

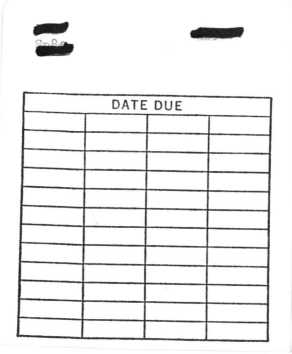

FACTS, WORDS AND BELIEFS

International Library of Philosophy
and Scientific Method

EDITOR: TED HONDERICH

A Catalogue of books already published in the
International Library of Philosophy and Scientific Method
will be found at the end of this volume

FACTS, WORDS
AND BELIEFS

by
Timothy L. S. Sprigge

NEW YORK
HUMANITIES PRESS

Published in the United States of America 1970
by Humanities Press Inc.
303 Park Avenue South
New York, N.Y. 10010
ⓒ *T. L. S. Sprigge 1970*

SBN 391 00069 1

LIBRARY OF CONGRESS CATALOG CARD NO. 77–114143

Printed in Great Britain

CONTENTS

v

CONTENTS

vi

PREFACE

Each of us believes many things to be the case. At any particular moment in our lives only a minute fragment of all that we believe to be the case can have any sort of presence in our consciousness. Still, such fragments as are present pose us this problem. How can a few stray images, muttered words or whatever, which run through our minds somehow constitute (as surely they can do) our envisagement of some situation perhaps remote in time and place from our present position? Most of this book is devoted to an attempt to formulate this question rather more precisely than has been done in these few words and to make some suggestions regarding the right way of answering it. From a practical point of view the moments when we somehow envisage the nature of some situation which we believe to exist may not be of any great importance. Our belief in the existence of these situations may be largely regarded as lying in some sort of adjustment of our behaviour to them which will be useful, if the situations really exist, from the point of view of survival and comfort. These moments of conscious envisagement of such absent situations may be rather a sign of such successful adjustment than a factor in bringing it about, and hence of no practical value in themselves. From what might be called a spiritual point of view, however, they are all important. If knowledge has any sort of intrinsic value apart from its utility from the point of view of survival and comfort, it must surely lie in those moments when one does consciously envisage some aspect of the world more or less as it really is. To try to understand the nature of those moments is to try to understand all that is of spiritual value in knowledge.

Though this is the main theme of this book, it will not be

broached for many chapters. For it will be better approached after we have sought clarity on certain matters to do with ontology and theory of meaning. The first two parts of this book, entitled 'Ontological background' and 'Semiotic background' respectively are not, however, put forward solely to serve as backgrounds for what I have called the main theme. They are also intended as contributions to ontology and semiotics in their own right. It seems suitable to present these contributions, such as they are, to those subjects in association with my discussion of believing, as my discussion of believing will to quite an extent presuppose, or otherwise link up with, my ontological and semiotic opinions.

It is to be hoped that this is not a very original work, for on the whole the more original a philosophical theory is the less likely it is to be true. It seems to me that the philosophers who have influenced me most (other than solely by way of negative reaction) are: William James, George Santayana, G. E. Moore, Bertrand Russell, H. H. Price,[1] and A. J. Ayer, not to mention the traditional British empiricists. To have pointed out in many cases where an idea derives from one of these would have been to have offered the reader a somewhat impertinent lesson in the history of philosophy in English, of which he probably stands in no need.

I should like to dedicate, and hereby do dedicate, this work to my wife Giglia, who has been intended by so many of my more delightful mental acts.

T.L.S.S.

---

[1] Since completion of my work on this book, a masterly new book (*Belief*, Allen & Unwin, 1969) by H. H. Price has been published dealing with many of the same themes as are discussed here. I much regret that I did not have the benefit of familiarity with this work in composing my own, which, however, is somewhat different in approach and aim. In Price's terminology, the main theme of Part Three of my book is an analysis of assenting to a proposition. This phrase, however, does to my mind rather carry the suggestion with it that a proposition is first presented to one as a mere 'idea' and that after consideration one gives one's assent to it, whereas in the cases I am particularly thinking of, some state of affairs is envisaged as really existing from the start. Price's phrase also has the disadvantage from my point of view that it includes the word 'proposition'. On the whole, then, I still feel justified in my use of the word 'belief' after suitable explanations have been offered.

Part One

ONTOLOGICAL BACKGROUND

I

SENSE-DATA

A treatment of the philosophy of perception is not among the main purposes of this work, yet my views on this subject do much to set the terms in which my discussion of other issues is couched. It is unfortunate that my views, though in conformity with those of many wise philosophers, some of them still living and philosophically active, are of a kind rather often condemned as outmoded and disproven. What is objected to is not so much any solution I might offer to what seems to me to be the problem of perception, as the very terms in which I set it. For me the problem of perception concerns the answer to these two questions. First, what view is implicit in the thought of the ordinary man as to the relation between the material things he perceives and the sense-data immediately present to him when he does so? Second, is this view correct, and if not, what alternative view may be substituted for it? My answer to the first question is given in the main text, and some hint of my answer to the second. (See the later part of this chapter and Chapter XII, sections 2 and 7.)

These questions can only properly be posed if it is proper to distinguish two factors in each case of perception, first, the sensing of a certain sense-datum, second, the putting some interpretation upon this sense-datum of a kind such that, if it is correct, or at least correct enough, the two factors together will constitute perception of some material thing.

There are many different ways of exhibiting the propriety of this distinction. The essential thing is to show that it is proper to draw a contrast between the sense-datum experienced and the material thing perceived, for if this distinction is granted there will not probably be much quarrel over the assertion that perception is a matter of the putting a certain interpretation upon the sense-datum which connects it in some way – to be elucidated when the problem of perception proper is discussed – with a material thing.

There is often talk of arguments for the existence of sense-data, but as I see the matter this is really somewhat misleading. Arguments for the existence of things of a certain kind must start from premises which assert the existence of things already admitted to exist. One who grasps the concept of a sense-datum will not accept that it is instantiated, *on the basis of argument*. Moreover the presentation of arguments for the existence of sense-data has often suggested that some hitherto unacknowledged fact is being established, and that the philosopher has something to say which is a novelty to common sense. Such is not my view of sense-data. The contrast I wish to draw between sense-data and material things aims simply to make more precise and explicit a contrast which in effect we all implicitly recognize anyway. We can make the contrast in such particular everyday cases as demand it in an *ad hoc* terminology which is adequate for ordinary cases; but fails to brings out the generality of the contrast involved.

Trying to point out to someone the propriety of a certain distinction is quite different from trying to prove a conclusion on the basis of certain premises, and there is no question of argument in any proper sense. The phrase 'argument from variation' may be used for certain considerations I shall now mention as apt for bringing home the distinction between sense-data and material objects. This 'argument' appeals to much the same facts and possibilities as are sometimes marshalled under the heading of 'the argument from illusion', but it differs from the latter in the form which has been under so much attack in recent years in ways which make most of those attacks quite irrelevant.

What then do I mean by the argument from variation? This argument sets out from such familiar facts as that if I look at a white wall without sunglasses on, and then look again with sunglasses on, while all will admit that there has been no change in the character of the wall, there has been a change in the appearance of the wall. It is quite natural to elaborate on this by saying that though the wall has not changed colour, the appearance has done so, but one should be careful not to assume that 'colour' is here used univocally, for good reasons can be given for denying this. There is, indeed, no way of saying what the change in the appearance is which cannot be objected to by philosophers with an axe to grind, for the description of appearances is usually done in an *ad hoc* and unmethodical manner. I content myself therefore with simply insisting that the appearance has changed, and that the wall has not, at least not in any way relevant to the perceptual situation. If one thing has changed in a thus relevant way and another thing has not changed, it is a logical inference that the two are not identical. We may point out, that for our purposes it does not matter if in saying that the appearance has changed what I mean is that one appearance has given way to another or if I mean that some one thing called the appearance has changed its character. Either case equally suffices to establish a contrast between the wall and the appearance it presents to me at any time, provided no one attempts to say that one of these appearances is the wall itself and the other is not. I think it would be rather absurd to say that the appearance the wall presents when looked at without sunglasses really *is* the wall, but that the appearance it presents when looked at with sunglasses is not the wall, though doubtless if one had to be picked out as really being the wall, that would be the one. It would be absurd because all that happens is that the medium through which the light waves travel is somewhat different in each case, and it is hard to see how this can make such a vast difference to the intimacy of my relation to the wall. The question is not, of course, which appearance is a better guide to the character of the wall, but whether it is possible in certain cases to elude the ontological distinction between appearance and thing. Anyway, were anyone to take this eccentric step of saying that one of these differing appearances really is the wall one would have to ask him to consider cases where the appearance an object (itself unchanging) presents, varies very slightly from one case to another, in a certain series, as where one views it from gradually changing positions, and ask him whether he can really suppose that any of these appearances has such a special status as to be picked out as being the object itself.

I say that this argument starts out from familiar facts and it may be said quite correctly that it hardly moves away from them. This does not represent a deviation from my intention, for all I am really concerned to do is to remind people of the contrast we all quite naturally make between changes in the appearance a thing presents us with and changes in the thing itself, and that the first by no means always requires that there has been a change in the second. No one doubts that a thing may present us with a different appearance according to our position or state, or in virtue of what lies between us, and none of these differing appearances are naturally or reasonably thought of as the object itself. These appearances are what a philosopher such as myself refers to under the heading of sense-data. That there are no precise rules which determine whether in various circumstances we should say that one and the same appearance or sense-datum has changed or that we are now concerned with a numerically different one, does not affect the fact that on any of the usages left open by what we have said and by ordinary language the contrast between a change in the appearance of a certain object with which one is presented and a change in the object itself is absolute.

If it is granted that there is this contrast between the appearance presented and the object perceived, it can hardly be denied that the question as to how these two contrasted elements in perception are related is a proper one for the philosopher. Nor can it be said that objects only present appearances in exceptional cases of perception, for one can always consider contrasts between the appearances it presents one with from where one is now, with that it would present one from another position.

I am not unaware that many philosophers would say that there is a play upon words in moving from the fact that things appear, for instance look and feel, somewhat differently in different perceptual circumstances, to saying that there are looks, feels, or, more generally, appearances, which they present. Other philosophers may even spend a long time refusing to see which among various possible senses of 'appear', 'look', etc, is in question, but I think that the kind of phenomenal differences intended should be clear to someone not being merely captious.

Where one philosopher says that a thing presents a different appearance in different cases and another philosopher says that there is no such thing as the appearance it presents, but that it may certainly appear somewhat differently in different cases, it is not easy to know how the dispute is to be settled. Before pressing more forcefully for my own position there are some preliminary points I have to make.

First, it is by no means the case that the plain man is particularly averse to nouns which, if interpreted as having a reference at all, must presumably refer to such things as I call appearances or sense-data. I am not at all clear what a beautiful *view* is if it is not the joint appearance of a certain set of objects from a certain place. Use of the noun 'appearance' in the sense adopted here is not uncommon either.

Second, the fact that one could 'get by' without a certain noun qualified by such words as 'the' and 'an' and occurring when thus qualified as the subject of sentences, is no good reason for saying that there is nothing such as it seems to designate. One could perhaps have a language geared to absolute idealism in which 'Reality' is the only proper subject of a sentence and in which all the information we provide by talking of material things and persons is conveyed by an enrichment of our adjectives, adverbs, and verbs. I am not in a position to say that this would be possible, but my point is that if it is so, it seems to count not at all against the assertion that there are persons and material things. If I am to be shown that there are no such things as sense-data, I need to be shown positively what is wrong in saying that there are, not just to be shown that I could convey information about them without nouns which refer to them. I would not say that the truth about the world could not be told without that sort of reference to them, only that it can appropriately be told with such reference.

More positively my reason for saying that what changes when I put on my sunglasses is the character of the appearance presented, and that the appearances are real somethings, lies in the fact that if I interest myself in how some change in position, or some change in myself, such as squinting, putting on sunglasses, being very tired, taking too much alcohol, alters the appearance of things for me, I do seem to attend to a real something, my visual field and its various elements, which I seek to characterize or to compare with other somethings of the same status. To attend in this way to that large sense-datum called the visual field and its various parts is quite different from examining a material thing, for in the latter case one must continually peer about one in a way which constantly alters what one endeavours to preserve as the same in the former case, while the predicates one can use to present one's results are different, or different in sense, in each case. Sometimes when I am tired something happens which I am hard put to describe if I do not say that the visual sense-data with which I am presented begin to move up and down. I could perhaps say that things seem to move up and down, but apart from the fact that that suggests perhaps a tendency to make a judgment which I have no tendency to make, this ignores the fact that there really is something I am attending to and characterizing in this way. As for the fact that my language here and elsewhere is largely borrowed from expressions which characterize material situations, that does not mean that when borrowed they do not take on a new sense. The characteristic of my sense-data which I call their moving up and down is indeed a characteristic which my sense-data would have if, without being tired, I looked at things which really were moving up and down, but it is a definite characteristic which would be shared by my sense-data in each case and which can be considered for its own sake.

Let us now turn to another argument which seems to me very compelling, the argument from double imagery. If I look at a candle for a while and then press one of my eyeballs in a certain way, something happens which I find it natural to describe by saying that there come to be two of something of which previously there was only one. If it is said that this phenomenon of the double image does not involve anything which can be properly called the occurrence of two images of the candle, I confess myself baffled. There they are, I can only say, side by side. I can turn my thought to the left one or the right one, and note that one is higher than the other, fainter than the other and so on. I can alter the situation so that the two images get further apart or closer and let them finally coalesce. Perhaps the fact in question can be described without implying that these candle images are countable things in relation to one another, but I confess that such other descriptions seem to me far less appropriate. If there is anything in the world which seems clear to me it is that there really are those two candle images. Can either of these images be supposed to be the candle itself? It would seem absurd to pick out one of them rather than the other for this role. Admittedly one is usually in customary relations to more of the remaining visual field than is the other, but they seem none the less to be too much of a type for one of them to be picked out for such a striking ontological privilege. Can both of them *be* the candle? I do not see how this could really be maintained, for they are different things from one another. I conclude then that we have here two entities which can be called images, neither of which is the candle, yet which may play an important part in my present seeing of the candle, for I suppose no-one will deny that I am seeing the candle.

The next stage in the argument is to point out that, if when I see a candle double, it presents two images to me, then presumably when I see it singly, it presents one image to me. This is not a merely verbal point about what we must say. Doubtless we can avoid saying any such thing if we want to. I am attempting rather to get the reader to dwell on a certain fact, namely that in such a case as this, there is just one of that very sort of thing, which we have called candle images, of which there were previously two. First there were two at a certain distance from one another, then they coalesced into one.

Even if neither of the double images was identical with the candle, could it still be the case that when I see the candle singly, what we have just called the single candle image really is identical with the candle? The idea seems rather absurd. How can the mere fact of a slight push on the eyeball produce such a different situation as it would be doing, if neither of those two images are the candle, while what I just called the single image really *is* the candle? After all, men might have had permanent double vision, as a friend of mine did for some weeks after a motoring accident, and as perhaps some insects have multiple vision. Would such men really be denied some sort of direct access to physical reality open to those of single vision? The idea is rather implausible, surely. No, I do not think we can give such a radically different account of what goes on in double vision from what goes on in single vision. That being so, we must either acknowledge that the images, of which there are two in the one case and one in the other, are all of them to be distinguished from the candle itself, or we must decide somehow that either one or both of the candle images in the double vision case *is* the candle. It cannot be that both of them are, for they are clearly not identical with one another, being at a certain distance, perhaps of different intensities, etc. To choose one of them as actually being the candle is absurdly arbitrary.

I realize that some philosophers will say that one cannot draw consequences about the normal case from the abnormal case of double vision. This is a most peculiar claim. More than one psychologist (e.g., William James and Sigmund Freud) has thought much could be learnt about the normal mind by the study of the abnormal, indeed one might say that taking the so called abnormal seriously and looking for explanatory concepts which will apply equally to it and to the normal is one of the main lines of advance in knowledge. Not that what we are seeking here is scientific knowledge, but I think the same point applies to the pursuit of ontological clarity. Moreover, as I have urged, it would not have been impossible for double vision to have been the normal case.[1] The main thing we insist on, in any case, is that some flaw be found in the specific argument offered.

The step most likely to be challenged is that whereby I move from the assertion that in double vision there are two images, to the assertion that in single vision there is one image. I can only repeat that this is not a question of verbal propriety, but of noting that the sort of thing one is counting when one says that there are two candle images, is still there to be counted in the normal case, only now the count ends at one. (Of course, mere images are not countable – what is counted are images of specific types.)

The reader might do well to be suspicious if he thinks that I am trying to upset some commonsense belief. Double imagery is not such an unusual thing, after all, and people don't seem to find it a challenge to their ordinary opinions. However, I am only emphasizing a distinction which we all tacitly make anyway, and which is to some extent reflected in ordinary language. I do not think that the ordinary man really supposes that his single image of the candle is the candle itself. He is far too familiar with the fact that the images, or sense-data, which things present may change without the thing changing, to have made any such identification. These arguments sound odd only because they really labour

1 It is really rather bizarre that in *Sense and Sensibilia* (p. 91) J. L. Austin speaks of the double image phenomenon as 'a baffling abnormality'. I doubt whether it is baffling to physiologists, and ontologically it is only baffling if one has some deep reluctance to talk of images or sense-data being involved in perception, the number of which may differ from that of the object perceived. If the plain man using his plain language does not find it baffling, as indeed Austin in a somewhat uncharacteristic way, but surely wrongly, seems to think that he does, that is because though he may not articulate it, his ontology is in effect more sophisticated than Austin's. As an after-thought Austin says that the plain man can deal with things by saying 'I see it double' or 'I see it as two', but the fact remains that Austin's direct realist outlook (to characterize him, as it seems to me aptly, with a phrase he might reject as too theoretical) makes him inclined to regard the really quite usual phenomenon of double imagery as 'baffling'. See also my next footnote.

something so obvious, so that one tends to think that they must have some purport more surprising than the one intended. Nonetheless, though in a way the truths in question are obvious, it is easy to become confused about them in philosophizing.[1]

Another 'argument' we may touch on may be called the 'argument from hallucination'. Consider, as many philosophers have done, Macbeth and his hallucination of a dagger before him. Does one not have to be very over-sophisticated, however much one may pose as the champion of the plain man, to fail to recognize that in such a hallucination something is before or in Macbeth's consciousness, just such as would be if he were really perceiving a dagger before him in mid-air, or, if you prefer, were perceiving a dagger before him in mid-air which really existed? That the presence of such a something before or in his consciousness is not enough to constitute its being true that there was a dagger there follows from the fact that there was not a dagger there. That something is a perfectly definite and far from non-existent something and needs to be distinguished from the dagger, which in fact did not exist. We are not suggesting that Macbeth *perceived* this something which we, of course, call a sense-datum. One can say either that he perceived a dagger which did not exist, or that he seemed to

---

[1] On pp. 90–2 of *Sense and Sensibilia* J. L. Austin discusses some use Ayer makes of the phenomenon of double imagery. There is little connection between our discussion and the issue there as to whether there is a sense of 'perceive', and perceptual verbs in general, in which what I perceive need not exist. A. J. Ayer says that 'if I say that I am perceiving two pieces of paper I need not be implying that there really are two pieces of paper there', having the double vision case in mind. Austin objects to what Ayer says on various grounds. So far as our concern goes it is irrelevant whether when I see a candle double I may or may not say that I perceive two candles, though myself I think it would be an inappropriate thing to say. The proper thing to say is 'I am seeing the candle double' or 'I am getting two images of the candle'. Whether I say the former or the latter, the two images are clearly there, two definite individuals in relation to each other and perhaps of contrasting characters, for instance one may be more clearly defined than the other. Austin insists that the fact that one might, in such an exceptional case as this, say 'I see two candles' (or pieces of paper in his discussion) without implying that there are two candles, does not exclude its normally being true that 'I perceive X' implies 'X exists'. I don't see that there can be any comparable objection to my pointing out that a clear recognition of the contrast between the abnormal case of double vision and single vision involves us in acknowledging that in the normal case there is one thing of which in the abnormal case there is two.

himself to be perceiving a dagger, which really he was not doing. I have no special axe to grind on that little question of language.

The sole content of this argument from hallucination lies in its drawing attention to a certain common element present in the situations both of Macbeth's having a hallucination of a dagger, and of a man's really seeing a dagger hanging in mid-air (perhaps on an un-noticed string). To make plainer what this common element is which we have in mind, we must point out that it is not the belief or judgment which might be common to two such cases, the belief that really there is a dagger there. This may become clearer if we point out that Macbeth could decide that there was not a dagger there, and thus make no false judgment, and yet continue to be tormented by this image or sense-datum.

A controversy between two distinguished philosophers[1] once went on as to whether 'this' in 'Is this a dagger that I see before me?' did or did not have reference to a sense-datum. However, neither side took Macbeth to be wondering whether the sense-datum was identical with a dagger, it was rather whether the sense-datum was, in a rather special sense, the ultimate logical subject of the question. We need not go into the niceties of the discussion, but will merely urge that Macbeth was certainly wondering whether the sense-datum was the appearance of a really existing dagger, but that he was not wondering whether it was strictly identical with the dagger.

It is obvious that this element which is common both to the hallucinatory and the genuine seeing of a dagger, and which is not the belief that there is a dagger there (nor, I should add, even the temptation so to believe, though it may produce such a temptation) is not identical with a dagger or with any other physical thing in the hallucinatory case. Does it follow that it is not identical with a dagger in the normal case? May it not be that those two items, though more or less exactly similar,[2] so far as the deluded percipient is concerned, are really quite different, in that the one is a figment of a mind diseased and the other is a real

[1] See *The Philosophy of G. E. Moore* ed. P. A. Schilpp, pp. 677–87, and *Philosophical Essays* by A. J. Ayer, pp. 60–90.
[2] There seems no reason why they should not be *exactly* similar, even if often they are not. I say this in case Chapter V of *Sense and Sensibilia* be quoted against me. It really makes no difference how common or uncommon such exact similarity is (cf. *Sense and Sensibilia*, p. 52).

dagger? Sense-datum philosophers have usually relied on this possibly exact similarity, so far as the percipient is concerned, to rule out the serious possibility of their really being so different as they would be if one were physical and the other not. This sort of reasoning has been challenged by J. L. Austin (op. cit., pp. 50–2). It is worth noting incidentally that Austin's challenge hardly applies to the cases taken in our previous arguments, which did not say that the items in question were so similar, on the face of it, that they could not be so dissimilar in reality, but simply urged that there would be something so absurdly arbitrary in choosing just one of the alternative appearances for the ontological privilege of being the material thing perceived itself, that it seemed to make the idea that one of them was identical (for both could not be) absurd. This defence against Austin's charge does not apply to this case. One may note though, that Austin has some difficulty in formulating the point, since there is no way he can really tolerate of mentioning the thing which can be very or exactly similar in the delusive, especially the hallucinatory, cases and the normal cases. On p. 53 he claims that this difficulty is inherent in the case, but he could hardly have said this if he had been considering a vivid hallucination rather than the stick in water case. I largely agree with him over this latter case, though I would express the point in terms of sense-data. The straight stick in water does not look different from what it is, it simply presents the sense-datum which it is normal for a straight stick in water to present. (We shall take this up again shortly.)

The main thing the hallucination case can do for us is to enable one to fix one's attention on that element in the non-hallucinatory perceptual situation which it shares with the hallucinatory perceptual situation, and which is not a belief or a judgment. We can call this element the sense-datum in each case, but this account leaves open the possibility that in the normal case the sense-datum simply is the physical thing, or at least a part of its surface. G. E. Moore sometimes used 'sense-datum' in a way which left its ontological status open in rather this sort of way.[1]

---

[1] In 'A Defence of Common Sense' (*Philosophical Papers*, Chapter II) and in 'Some Judgments of Perception' (*Philosophical Studies*, Chapter VII) for example. Incidentally, the arguments I give against the identity of sense-data and material things apply also to the identity of sense-data and parts of the surfaces of material things, but I have simplified matters by leaving this to be understood in most cases.

Having offered this additional clue as to just what items it is which we call sense-data, we could then appeal to the other arguments, that from variation, and that from double imagery, to establish that the sense-datum is never identical with the material thing, a point, I must continue to urge, which should be evident to anyone capable of making nice ontological distinctions, and which is tacitly recognized by common sense, without all this argument.

However, I think we can say something more in support of this non-identity, in connection with the hallucinatory case.

How much of the world a concept applies to is implicit in the sort of concept it is. I can best explain this somewhat obscure remark by some examples. I may point in a certain direction and say 'That façade is Georgian', 'That house is Georgian', or 'That college is composed of four buildings, of which that house is the oldest'. In each case I may be confronted, as one might put it, and so may be my interlocutor, with just the same thing, but the concept word which follows 'That' indicates which of various chunks of reality (each related to each by the part-whole relation, and each including some items present to me in a particularly direct way) I am talking about. These different realities have different boundaries, and the boundaries in question are roughly indicated by the concept word. Though the boundaries, here, are spatial, they can be of other sorts. Temporal boundaries, for instance, are also laid down by concepts in this sort of way. But quite different sorts of boundary are also possible, as when reading a philosophically inclined history book I may say that I like the *history* (but not perhaps the philosophy). I mark off thereby a certain part of the reality which is the author's thought, as what I am saying that I like.

Now when I talk of that element in normal perception which it shares with hallucination, and which is not the belief or judgmental component, I mean the boundaries of what I am talking about in the normal case to be no more extensive than those which apply in the hallucinatory case. Even if the element in the normal case is an element in some larger reality than is the element in the hallucinatory case, I am not concerned with that larger reality. If one understands by the sense-datum in the normal case, that which has no wider boundaries than what is obviously in question in the hallucinatory case, I think it will appear that whatever view be taken of the relation between sense-datum and material thing, it cannot be straight identity. There is obviously much more to any material thing (even to part of its surface) than there is to that element in normal perception which could have been present also in hallucination. Thus the closest that one could hope to come to identifying the sense-datum in the normal case and the material thing (or even part of its surface) would lie in claiming that the sense-datum is some sort of component in the latter.

Finally, we may touch on an 'argument' of a rather different sort, which may be called the 'time lag' argument. We all know that, in view of the time it takes light to travel, the stars we see could have gone out of existence quite some time ago without that affecting the fact that we see them now. If an astronomer sees some astral event, it may have taken place a long time before he sees it. We seem compelled to say that we see the stars, not as they are at the time of seeing them, but as they were a long time ago, and that what we see may have gone out of existence by the time we see it. We may not normally speak of seeing temporal phases of things, but simply of seeing things, but to speak in the former way is a convenient way of bringing out that at any moment we can only see an object as it is at some particular moment. In view of the finite speed of light the phase of a thing which we see is always, however minutely, prior in time to the moment at which we see it.

Now when I see a star it seems difficult to deny that there is something which is simultaneous with my seeing it and which can be called the appearance it now presents me with. If one learnt that the star did not exist now, one could attend to the visual appearance that one is presented with in seeing the star, and recognize that that visual appearance can hardly be thought of as having ceased to exist years ago.[1]

[1] In an article called 'Ordinary Language, Common Sense, and the Time-Lag Argument' (*Mind*, January 1964) R. G. Henson argues against Russell's appeal to the finite speed of light to show that we never see stars, nor indeed any nearer physical things outside our skins, since what we *see* must be seen in the state it is in when we see it. Henson claims that an assumption about the proper use of the word 'see' is made here, which at least in the sense Russell puts upon it, is incorrect. It is worth emphasizing, in view of this, that I make no appeal to any principle to the effect that we must see things in the state they are in when we see them, and that my conclusion is not that we never see things outside us. On the contrary, we do see the stars in a state they were in prior to our seeing them. My point is rather that there is an element which is simultaneous with the seeing, and which therefore cannot

I do not point to this time lag consideration so much as a way of showing that there are sense-data, or showing what I mean by the term. Let the argument from hallucination serve to show that. The visual appearance of the star to me now is that element in my seeing of the star, which, without being a belief, could still have been present, without there ever having really been the star which I am perceiving, as in the case of a hallucinatory seeing of a star, or as in a vivid dream for that matter. What is to be derived from the time lag consideration is simply a further reason for recognizing that this element can no more be said, in the case of genuinely seeing a star than in the hallucinatory case, actually to be identical with a star which is being seen.

Some reader may suggest that the thing to which we seem to be drawing attention is simply the perception itself as opposed to the thing perceived. He may then object to our using the word sense-datum for the perception, on the grounds that it is somehow misleading.

Now Hume and other philosophers have sometimes used the word 'perception' to refer to what we call the sense-datum, and there need be nothing wrong in this. However, I think 'perception' is better used not simply to cover the occurrence of the sense-datum in or for my consciousness, but to cover also a judgmental or belief element in the situation. I should take it as more apt if the critic said that what I am calling the sense-datum is simply the sensory experience, visual, auditory, or whatever, and that it is better called an experience than a sense-datum.

Well, what such a philosopher may call the visual experience of seeing a star may be what I call the sense-datum of a star. Certainly, so far as the usage of various traditional philosophers goes, it is not incorrect to call the sense-datum an experience. If what I am talking of is once identified and distinguished from other things it may be called an experience or a sense-datum according to

---

be identical with the phase of the thing seen. One might suppose indeed that the simultaneity arose simply from the fact that it is the date of this element which dates the seeing, but whether this is so or not, makes no difference to the argument. The essential point is simply that a certain bright dot occurs for my consciousness long after the star which is seen may have gone out of existence. That bright dot is what I call the sense-datum. (Note that the date of a physical event cannot be identical with the date of each of the sense-data which belong to or on one view even constitute it.)

preference, for in neither case is it claimed that it is an object of perception, though it may be an object of attention.[1] It seems more natural, however, to talk of my two images of the candle, in the double image case, than of my two experiences of the candle. 'Sense-datum' is to be preferred to 'image', only because there is a narrower sense of 'image' in which images contrast with sense-data.

Moreover, I do not think that those who talked of the experience or awareness of the sense-datum as being one thing, and the sense-datum being another thing, entirely lacked grounds for doing so, since what is in one sense an exactly similar sense-datum may be experienced in different ways, e.g., gladly or sadly, as a clue to action or as something enjoyed for its own sake. We shall say something on this later.

Another reason for not calling the sense-datum an experience is that it seems to me that the visual sense-datum could occur without being related to thoughts and feelings in such a way as to make it a constituent of a mind. It would then be odd to call it an experience. Thus if a sense-datum is an experience, this is in virtue of its relations to other things, and not in virtue of its intrinsic nature.

Furthermore, there are things to be said about sense-data, even when they do occur as elements in a mind (in or before consciousness as we put it previously) which the word 'experience' might misleadingly suggest could not be said. For instance, they may be in spatial relations of a kind to one another, have a shape, be blurred, or moving up and down. In our double image example, one of the candle images or sense-data was to the left of the other. I certainly admit that the use of these predicates and relational words as applied to sense-data is derivative from their use in application to physical things, and that they undergo a certain change in meaning in being applied to sense-data, but still, in this latter meaning, they serve to point out evident facts about sense-data. (That in our use of them the application to sense-data may have come second, does not preclude the possibility that in our application of them to material things we are expressing beliefs the structure of which is brought out more fully by sentences which use them in the sense in which they apply to sense-data.)

Related to this point is the fact that, while one can, for certain

[1]   Cf. Reinhardt Grossman, *The Structure of Mind*, pp. 5ff.

purposes, distinguish that complex visual sense-datum which comprises all the visual appearances involved in my perception of the material world at any one time, up into various different sense-data (for instance, one can distinguish that part of it which is the appearance of a candle to one) it would seem somewhat odd to me to say that one is dividing one experience up into a lot of little lesser experiences.

There may not be very much at issue between me and the person who talks of the sensory experiences involved in perception. Certainly most of the same issues are involved. Granted that when I perceive an apple, I take it that there is more to the case than simply the occurrence of the sense-datum or experience, what more exactly do I take to be the case? In short, in what manner do I conceive the material thing, and how do I suppose it to be related to the visual experience or sense-datum? This is one of many interconnected questions which arise for anyone who thinks in terms either of a sensory experience or of a sense-datum.

That these sensory experiences or sense-data exist should be obvious and the reader may, when he grasps what I mean, claim that all my elaborate arguments have been mere mystery-mongering about something very simple. I can only say that I would quite agree with him, if it were not that this, to us, simple point appears to be denied or ignored by many contemporary philosophers. I suspect that the question as to what exactly a material thing should be taken to be, granted it is something over and above the experience or sense-datum we have of it, is such a difficult one, and has been the source of so much controversy which may seem to get no-where, that these philosophers have tried to avoid having the problem even posed. This is done by refusing to allow reference to sensory experiences or sense-data. It is not, however, some technical terminology which creates these questions, but the real difficulty of getting clear as to just what we do, and just what we should, believe when we are in perceptual situations.

2

Various writers in the last two or three decades have criticized the notion of sense-data, but probably none has been so influential in bringing it into disrepute as J. L. Austin in his posthumously published lectures *Sense and Sensibilia* (1963). It seems appropriate therefore that we should consider some of the grounds of his attack.[1] Austin's book, though short, is very concentrated, and in the short compass we can allow ourselves, we can only consider a small selection of the points he makes. When someone marshalls so many arguments on a point as he does, there is a tendency to think that enough of them must work to do the job, so that answering a few of his contentions may seem ineffective; it is, however, the best we can do here.

As a matter of fact, Austin's book is mainly an attack upon the grounds on which A. J. Ayer introduced sense-data in *The Foundations of Empirical Knowledge* (1940) and is largely irrelevant to our rather different grounds for introducing them, which are perhaps more in the spirit of G. E. Moore and C. D. Broad[2] than of Ayer. Still, as others will doubtless think that Austin's critique is relevant to what we say, some consideration of it is due.[3]

Though I do not want to imply that I think Austin in general the victor in the encounter between himself and Ayer, there are several points in which I do think Austin is right as against Ayer. They are points, however, which could perfectly well have been put within the sense-datum terminology by one sense-datum philosopher as against another. Indeed some of them are in effect developments of points made by C. I. Lewis in *Mind and the World Order* (1929), in which *qualia* function much as do sense-data. Incidentally, Ayer's best treatment of sense-data would seem to be in *Philosophical Essays* (1954) and *The Problem of Knowledge* (1956) rather than in the book discussed by Austin.

The thing to note above all as distinguishing my position from those which Austin attacks, both those attributed to Ayer and others, is that I do not claim either that ordinary people make a

[1] This section may be omitted by the reader unfamiliar with Austin's views or not requiring a critique of them.

[2] It is a rather remarkable fact that the book contains no references to G. E. Moore or C. D. Broad. Had Austin considered Moore and Broad he would have had to revise his views of the usual motives for introducing *sense-data*. For Moore's views on sense-data see especially *Philosophical Studies*, Chapters I and II and V–VII, *Some Main Problems of Philosophy*, Chapters I–VIII, and his article in *British Philosophy Mid-Century* ed. C. A. Mace. For Broad's views see especially *The Mind and Its Place In Nature*, Chapter IV.

[3] Ayer has made his own very effective rejoinder to Austin in 'Has Austin Refuted the Sense-datum Theory?' (*Synthese* 17, 1967, 117–40). It should be fairly clear to the informed reader how far my own comments on Austin coincide with or diverge from Ayer's.

mistake in saying that they perceive material things, for really they perceive sense-data, nor even that it is philosophically helpful to introduce a terminology in which we are said to perceive sense-data rather than material things. Ayer only made the second of these claims. The experiencing of a sense-datum, or simply the sense-datum itself (the question whether these are to be distinguished is taken up later) is distinguished by us as an element in the perception of material things, not as something itself suitably said to be perceived. We are not out to provide some sort of shock to the plain man, as Austin seems to suppose the sense-datum philosopher is always at heart intent to do, whether he admits it or not.

Consider the following:

> The general doctrine, generally stated, goes like this: we never see or otherwise perceive (or 'sense') or anyhow we never *directly* perceive or sense, material objects (or material things), but only sense-data (or our own ideas, impressions, sensa, sense-perceptions, percepts, etc.).
> One might well want to ask how seriously this doctrine is intended, just how strictly and literally the philosophers who propound it mean their words to be taken. . . . It is, as a matter of fact, not at all easy to answer [this question] for, strange though the doctrine looks, we are sometimes told to take it easy – really it's just what we've believed all along. (There's the bit where you say it and the bit where you take it back.) In any case it is clear that the doctrine is thought *worth stating*, and equally there is no doubt that people find it disturbing . . . (*Sense and Sensibilia*, pp. 2–3).

How far these comments are apt with reference to Austin's intended victims I shall not here enquire, but certainly they are quite beside the mark in relation to what we have to say. A sensible sense-datum philosopher does not consider that what he has to say constitutes an attack on common sense. It is precisely his aim to clarify distinctions implicit in ordinary views of the world, in the sense that a plain man who succeeded in giving an explicit statement of his viewpoint would find it useful to make them. Once and for all, then, be it understood, that I do not deny that we perceive material objects; what I say is that the experiencing of sense-data is an element in the perception of material things. The actual words chosen to mark our relation to sense-data, and that to material things, should not be a matter of prime importance, but to draw the contrast by the expressions 'directly perceive' and 'indirectly perceive' is certainly unfortunate. 'Perceive' is the proper word for our relation to material things, not to sense-data.[1]

Thus we are not posing the question Austin considers so simplistic (op. cit., p. 4) as to whether we perceive sense-data or material things, as though these were the only alternatives.

Austin suggests that both sides of the dichotomy, sense-datum/material thing, are equally bogus. Pens, rainbows, after-images, pictures on the cinema screen etc. are said each to be in some ways like their neighbours on the list, in other ways unlike. All are examples of what we perceive. Further examples on a later page (p. 8) include people, people's voices, rivers, mountains, flames, rainbows, shadows, pictures in books or on walls, vapours, and gases.

The one fundamental distinction the sensible sense-datum philosopher insists on is that between what is immediately given, what in a sense can be called the *content* of a perception, and that which is in a broad sense believed in rather than given. Some expressions in ordinary language don't stand for anything of a definite ontological kind, being ambivalent in meaning. On the whole, however, it seems that all the things Austin lists here are perceived (that is, in a sense *believed in*) rather than experienced, except after-images. For all of those other things could be misperceived, could present misleading appearances; also there is no question, so far as ordinary conceptions go, but that they could

[1] Although I think it better to avoid the phrases 'directly perceive' and 'indirectly perceive' for our relations to sense-data and material things respectively, for they seem wrongly to suggest that somehow the ordinary view that we perceive chairs and tables, or even gases and movie films, is mistaken, I do not think the objections Austin mainly raises are very apt. It should have always been obvious that it was not intended to be a contrast akin to that between seeing a thing through a periscope and what, in contrast to this and in ordinary parlance, would be called seeing a thing directly, and there was little risk of any serious thinker being confused here. Once granted that the use is not ordinary, it is no objection to the philosopher's extraordinary use that what is said to be indirectly perceived could not have been directly perceived. There may be two different relations, which one can only stand in to objects of different kinds, and one of these relations may be more direct than the other, in the sense that the less direct relation can only hold in virtue of its terms being each related to some third term by relations one of which is the other relation in question. So far as criticism of the philosophical use of 'directly' and 'indirectly perceived' or 'see' go, the canons for correct usage of 'directly' and 'indirectly see' in ordinary language are quite beside the point (see Austin, op. cit., pp. 14–19).

exist without the presence of percipients. (They can all either be photographed or recorded by machines left to operate when percipients are absent.) On the other hand, although to call an element in the given an after-image is to classify it on grounds other than its given nature, the after-image could hardly be said to present a misleading appearance, and the possibility of this is one of the main things which put something on the material object side of the dichotomy. That all the things on this side are not quite aptly called 'material things' does not affect this fundamental contrast.

Doubtless the heart of Austin's attack on sense-data is his attack on the argument from illusion, as described by Ayer. Though Ayer did not accept it quite in the straight form in which he first describes it, Austin discusses it in this straight form before considering Ayer's special gloss upon it.

The argument from illusion is supposed to have two stages. First it is shown that in various abnormal cases we do not really perceive material things, but something else called sense-data. This is established supposedly because it is said that no material thing exists having the properties we perceive a thing as having. For example, when I look at a straight stick in water what I really see is something bent, but there is no material thing in the situation which is bent. Second, it is shown that it follows from this, that we only perceive sense-data in normal cases. The argument for this second step consists mainly in urging that what we perceive is so similar qualitatively in the two types of case that it is implausible to give such an entirely different interpretation of them as is implied in saying that in one of the cases what we perceive is a real occupant of the material world, while in the other case it is something immaterial.

We need hardly point out that neither our argument from variation nor that from hallucination, though they appeal between them to much the same examples, proceed at all in this way. We do not claim that any so called abnormal cases are cases of perceiving something immaterial. In hallucination the thing perceived does not exist. As for the facts appealed to by the arguments from variation, which remind us that things present varying appearances without themselves varying, it is neither suggested that any of those cases are abnormal nor that they are cases where no material thing is perceived. The latter point goes also for the argument from double vision.

Among Austin's various complaints against Ayer, and others who concern themselves with the argument from illusion, is this. They are said to have confused illusions with delusions, and what is more to have called some phenomena 'illusions' which are neither delusions nor illusions (op. cit., Chapter III).

Austin's own account of the distinction is not as clear as one might have hoped, for the characteristics which he allots to each do not seem necessarily to go together. (It seems a mistake to link the public-private contrast with the degrees of mistaken belief involved.) The main points seem to be that in an illusion nothing totally unreal is conjured up, and there need be no false belief involved (though some of what Austin says suggests that there must be at least a temptation to such false belief), and the phenomenon is public and depends on circumstances external to rather than internal to the percipient. A delusion, apparently, has just these characteristics denied of the illusion.

As in many other cases, Austin attacks his opponents for having failed to make a certain distinction without making out much case for his claim, that, once the distinction is made, it really affects the main line of the original argument.[1] What really matters is the use to which the argument from illusion puts particular cases, not that they are all lumped together as illusions.

However this may be, we cannot be accused of having confused illusions with delusions in our arguments. Our argument from hallucination is concerned only with what Austin seems to call delusions (though it is not quite clear how he would classify an hallucination recognized to be such). Our argument from variation is mainly concerned with facts which Austin is quite right in insisting are neither illusions nor delusions, such as the difference between the appearance of a thing seen from different positions, or seen with or without sunglasses. We have made no appeal to illusions in the proper sense, though on our view they can be described in general as cases where an object or set of objects of a certain character present a sense-datum such as a person of limited experience or attentiveness might rather naturally have expected only to have been presented by an object or set of objects of a different character. This description seems to me to apply fairly well to the old case of the stick half in water, which I think can

---

[1] The attempt on p. 25 (op. cit.) to show how the confusion of illusion and delusion aids the introduction of sense-data seems rather far-fetched.

reasonably be called an illusion, as well as to such cases as the Müller-Lyer diagram and the rotating wheels mentioned by Austin on pp. 14 and 23.

Reference to the stick in water gives us an opportunity to point out a rather sharp contrast between our own approach and that of one who uses the argument from illusion in the form in which Austin attacks it.

As Ayer and Austin see it, the argument from illusion claims that in many cases what we perceive either does have or appears to have qualities which really the material thing (which is the normal candidate for being the object perceived) does not have. The sense-datum is then brought in to be the exemplifier of those qualities. Thus what I perceive when I see a straight stick half in water either is, or appears to be, bent. Another case is seeing a star, where what is perceived either is, or appears to be, a silvery speck.

It is somewhat difficult indeed to get this argument off the ground at all, for, as Austin points out, there does not even seem to be an incompatibility between being straight and looking bent, and one can truly say 'That silvery speck is a star'. Ayer himself does not, in the last resort, think that the argument works, and finally introduces sense-data as the objects of a special but convenient philosophical usage according to which what we perceive must exist with just the qualities it appears to have.

What is mistaken in this approach, and here in a curious way I agree with Austin, is the tendency to suppose that there are cases where an object looks other than it really is, a tendency even more curious when phenomena merely of perspective are taken into account and a penny is said to look other than it really is when seen at an angle. The straight stick half in water looks just as much what a straight stick half in water looks as does the straight stick out of water look what a straight stick out of water looks. Likewise, the star looks just what such an object at that distance does look.

Thus we can side with much of Austin's treatment of the stick half in water. I don't feel that it is entirely inappropriate to call this case an illusion, for the stick does present an appearance which is likely to mislead the inattentive or inexperienced. As Austin himself says, however, what counts as an illusion tends to depend on our familiarity with the phenomenon, so that the cinema might conceivably once have been considered an illusion (see Austin, op. cit., p. 26).

There is no need to look for something which is really bent, just because the stick looks bent. It is also unreasonable to suppose that the quality of what is immediately given in this case fails to conform to the quality of the thing perceived in some way in which it does so in more ordinary cases. The only way I know in which this example is relevant to the introduction of sense-data is that it is one of many cases in which a thing presents an appearance which has some peculiarity requiring explanation. The sense-datum theory does not, of course, itself offer an explanation of this peculiarity, it simply provides a terminology for referring to it. Within the sense-datum terminology one may perhaps say that the sense-datum is bent, but this is to use 'bent' in a sense not applicable to sticks themselves. We need not suppose that the bent sense-datum presents the object less as it really is, than does the straight sense-datum experienced when the stick is out of water. It would only do so as long as we interpreted the latter, but not the former, correctly.

The most plausible case for the argument from illusion, so called, is in fact straight hallucination. That Austin should pay rather little attention to hallucination is understandable, for it is less easily dealt with in his terms than the other cases.

We can take Macbeth again. The argument from illusion would say that since Macbeth sees a dagger, and there is no material dagger there, he must be perceiving an immaterial dagger, that is, a sense-datum.

The next step is to argue that since the hallucinatory dagger is so similar to what is seen when one sees (as it is ordinarily supposed) a real dagger, it must be only a sense-datum that is really seen in the so-called normal cases also.

This argument is to be rejected on the ground that when Macbeth had his hallucinatory vision there was really no such thing as he perceived at all. One can say either that he perceived a dagger which did not exist, or that he only seemed to perceive a dagger, or take one's choice of various other expressions, but there is no reason to think that there is anything either material or immaterial which he perceived. If Macbeth perceived anything it was a dagger, and daggers are sharp ended objects which can stab, not immaterial things.

The point of our argument from hallucination, it will be recalled, was quite different. Hallucinations were merely cited as occasions when a certain something occurs just like what occurs in genuine perception, and which we call a 'sense-datum'.

Austin is concerned to attack not only the claim that in cases of so called illusion we are perceiving sense-data, but also the contention that if this were so, it would follow that what we perceive is always really sense-data.

The main ground that has been given for this latter contention is that what is perceived (or the perception – there tends to be some ambivalence here) is so qualitatively alike in the two cases, that it is implausible to mark them off as so vastly different in ontological status as they would be if one was a real constituent of the material world (or a perception of it) and the other was not. We may call this the argument from gradualism, as it often takes the form of urging that what is perceived (or the perception) in the privileged cases would be members of a very gradually changing series including the less privileged cases.

Let us consider first whether our own approach to sense-data makes use of any such principle. The tone of the argument is closely linked to the view we reject as quite mistaken, that sense-data are to be introduced as things which play a role in perception which plain men wrongly ascribe to material things. On the other hand there is some force for us in one aspect of this argument. The argument from variation establishes that there is something to which we may attend which may change even though the material object has not changed, and which is therefore to be distinguished from the material object itself. Strictly, this argument leaves open the possibility that the material thing is identical with the element in one of the cases and not the other. In rejecting this as a real possibility we are following a somewhat similar train of thought to that of the argument from gradualism. We have mainly urged that, at least in most of the cases, it would be quite arbitrary to choose one rather than the other such element to be the material thing, but we might also emphasize that they are qualitatively so much the same sort of thing (though, of course, *ex hypothesi*, they are not exactly alike) that it is most unlikely that they have such a very different ontological status. I should add, as another consideration, that if criteria were adopted for selecting some as really being material things and others not, the fact that we would find both types juxtaposed in one and the same visual field would make the distinction seem very odd. Surely if I see two pennies at once at

26

different angles, my relation cannot be essentially different to each of them (or to a part of the surface of each of them).

In his critique of Ayer's presentation of this second stage of the argument from illusion, Austin quotes Ayer as saying that there is 'no intrinsic difference in kind between those of our perceptions that are veridical in their presentation of material things and those that are delusive' (Austin, op. cit., p. 44; Ayer, op. cit., pp. 5–9), and objects that Ayer is virtually using 'perception' to mean 'sense-datum', and that thus he is already using a concept he is supposed to be justifying. There is something in this criticism, perhaps, but what it really shows is the extreme difficulty of drawing attention to the rather obvious fact in question without employing some such concept, and this is a point in favour of sense-data. Austin, one may suspect, suffered from some embarrassment himself in having to make the point he was very anxious to make, that really the qualitative similarity is much less than Ayer suggests, without frankly using such a concept. What exactly is it which Austin is saying is not so similar in cases of delusive and veridical perception or experience as Ayer supposes? On p. 49 he uses the word 'seeing' in this connection, and denies that seeing 'pink rats in D.T.s is exactly like really seeing pink rats; or (once again) that seeing a stick refracted in water is exactly like seeing a bent stick.' But, of course, there is no question of anyone's thinking that the whole affair of the drunkard seeing pink rats (or say rather grey rats, which I suppose is possible, so that we have veridical cases for comparison) is exactly like the whole affair of someone's really seeing rats. The absence of rats is sufficient of itself to constitute a big difference. It is only if one concentrates on that particular element in the seeing which we call the sense-datum that there is any question either of exact or rough similarity. (Actually the belief element might also be more or less exactly the same in the two cases, but this is certainly not what is in question, and can be excluded by taking the case where the drunkard begins to realize the true state of affairs without ceasing to be hallucinated sensorily.) I haven't researched the subject myself but I see no reason why there should not be exact similarity here, as certainly there is in some cases of hallucination.[1] In point of fact, Austin

---

[1] I see no reason, also (*pace* Austin, p. 48, who can be met by saying that *dreamlike* is a quality that *most* dreams have, and *pace*, for quite different reasons into which we cannot enter, N. Malcolm, *qua* author of *Dreaming*),

admits (p. 52) that there can be exact similarity, and only urges the rather weak point that this is not 'anything like as *common* as Ayer and Price suppose'.

It is true that Austin does profess to have some difficulty in knowing what it is that is said to be exactly similar (p. 53). In the case of the stick in water, he asks whether the *water* is part of the perception. If so, he says, there is not exact similarity to the straight stick out of water case, while, if not, one is simply making the exact similarity hold vacuously, by ruling out all the features which make a difference (p. 54). It is absurd, however, to raise the question whether the *water* is or is not part of what is more or less exactly similar. What Austin really means to ask, presumably, is whether the look of the water around the lower part of the stick, as well as the look of the stick, is included, though he could not express it thus. The answer to this question need scarcely concern us, for it is not qualitative identity that is required but a difference which is very slight compared with the vast ontological difference which is in question. Incidentally, in our application of this sort of argument to such cases as that of perspectival variation, we are actually aided by recognition of the fact Austin elsewhere so emphasizes that it would be absurd to distinguish perceptions from certain points of view as delusive and others as veridical (cf. Austin, p. 26).

With reference to our own use of the gradualistic argument we may add the following. The causal mechanisms involved in perception are clearly the same whichever of its different visual appearances a thing presents me with, and it would be extraordinary if in one of these cases a quite different sort of confrontation with the physical world took place from that in the other. There is nothing improper in bringing in scientific considerations here, for we are not trying to build up our ontology from some sort of epistemological scratch.

Ayer, in point of fact, did not attach too much faith to the argument from illusion, but Austin argues that his reasons for rejecting it still left standing all that is really objectionable in it.

Ayer holds that the conclusion of the argument from illusion

---

why someone should not have a vivid dream in which his data are exactly similar to those he would get if he were really in the situation he dreamt he was in. I don't dream like that now, but I remember rather well certain childhood nightmares which I think were of this character.

that we directly perceive only sense-data, is really only a linguistic decision, to which there are alternatives. One alternative would be to say such things as that the penny really changes its shape when we look at it from different positions, from some of which it looks circular and from others of which it looks of various different elliptical shapes – things which can be summed up by saying that things are, in Austin's words, 'constantly busy, from moment to moment, in changing their real shapes, colours, temperatures, sizes, and everything else' (Austin, op. cit., p. 58).

Austin attacks Ayer for inattention to the way 'real' is ordinarily used. His interesting discussions of this word in Chapter VII[1] does not, in the end, seem terribly relevant. Ayer could speak of things really changing their shape, etc., as opposed only to appearing differently, and avoid saying that they change their real shape,[2] in which case Austin's comment about such phrases as real shape and colour would not even seem to be relevant. Indeed Ayer often does put it in this way.[3] The philosopher's contrast between appearance and reality is not so far removed from ordinary usage anyway. One could well say that appearance and reality are very different in a certain country, the appearance being that of a liberal democracy, the reality being that of a tight oligarchy. However this may be, we agree with Austin that if the only objection to the argument from illusion were that its conclusion could be escaped in this sort of way, it would be conclusive enough. To allow such things as Ayer mentions as possibilities is to abandon the concept of a material thing, and with it of any particular types of material thing. Someone who adopted this position would not then be disagreeing with the negative part of what the argument from illusion is, so it is said, supposed to establish, namely that we do not perceive material things. Ayer, however, admits this (*Foundations of Empirical Knowledge*, p. 19) and gives another alternative to accepting the argument from illusion. Anyway, the real objection to the argument lies in such things as the lack of even *prima facie* incompatibility between such expressions as 'looks bent' and 'is straight'. In most of these cases there is no contrast between things

[1] The phenomenalist C. I. Lewis, incidentally, said things about 'reality' in *Mind and the World Order* (Scribners, 1929) which fit in quite well with Austin's comments. See, for example, Chapter I, pp. 11 and 16.
[2] This is well argued by J. Bennett in his article 'Real' in *Mind*, October 1966.
[3] See *Foundations of Empirical Knowledge*, p. 16. For use of 'real shape' see p. 14.

as they appear to be and as they are. A penny seen at an angle does not appear *to be* elliptical, though it may in a certain sense appear or look elliptical. There is no incompatibility between this and being circular. We urge, of course, that there is an element in the situation which is different according to the angle of vision.

The introduction of sense-data which Ayer finally approves is based rather on a distinction which he says that there is in ordinary usage between two different senses of 'perceive' and of specific perceptual words, such as 'see'. For instance, in one sense of 'see', 'it is necessary that what is seen should really exist, but not necessary that it should have the qualities it appears to have' (Ayer, p. 23), while in the other sense of 'see', 'it is not possible that anything should seem to have qualities that it does not really have, but also not necessary that what is seen should really exist' (Austin, p. 86). Sense-data are then said to be introduced as the objects of *perception* in a sense of the word which conflates these two senses so that what is perceived must really exist and really have the qualities it appears to have, a usage which is by no means compulsory but for various purposes convenient (Ayer, pp. 24–5, Austin, pp. 86–7).

This, of course, has little relation to our 'arguments' designed to indicate what it is that we call 'sense-data'. However, the question of the two senses of 'perceive' has some interest for us.

At least one of Ayer's contentions on this matter seems correct. 'He perceived X' is sometimes used with the implication that X exists, and sometimes without this implication. One could either say that Macbeth only seemed to see a dagger, or that he did see a dagger which was not really there. Austin may well be right in claiming that there are not two senses of 'see', but only that in different contexts utterances employing it have different implications. It is still of interest that it can sometimes have and sometimes lack this implication, and it is quite proper for a philosopher to seek to avoid confusion by saying that he will use it either definitely with or definitely without such an implication.

The question whether the thing perceived must have the *qualities it appears to have* is rather obscure, for the italicized expression is unclear. On the face of it, Ayer would seem to be right in saying that if the object's existence is implied, its having the character it appears to have is not implied. It would be wrong, however, to infer from this that 'I see an F X' is compatible with the X I perceive not being an F. I can perceive a man who appears to be sleeping, though in fact he is not sleeping. It is doubtful if I succeed in saying the truth about the situation, however, if I say 'I saw a sleeping man'. Similarly, I can see an animal which appears to be a rabbit but is a cat, but the assertion 'I saw a rabbit' would, I think, probably have to count as untrue in this situation.[1] As for the question whether when existence is not implied, it is implied that the thing has the character it appears to have, I suspect that if, in fact, the thing does exist, then the situation may often be just as in the case where its existence is actually implied. For instance, had Macbeth's dagger really been there, but covered with red paint which he thought to be blood, we would not accept our statement 'He saw a bloody dagger', intended as leaving the existence open, but would substitute 'He saw a dagger which seemed to be bloody'. If, on the other hand, the dagger does not exist, it is not so much that it has the qualities which it appears to have, as that there is no room for a contrast between the qualities it has and those which it appears to have.

However, I think the notion of the qualities which a thing appears to have is not a very satisfactory one. To suggest that a penny appears to have different qualities, according to the angle from which it is seen, seems a mistake. The fact that it does, in a certain sense, look elliptical from an oblique angle, does not mean that it appears to have the quality of being elliptical. The shape it appears to have is really a matter of the interpretation I put upon the appearance with which I am presented. Certainly it has the

---

[1] Austin claims (pp. 77–80) that there is unclarity in a distinction which Ayer draws between perceptions which are 'qualitatively delusive' and ones which are 'existentially delusive', or at least that it does not have general application. If a man sees a decoy duck and takes it for a real duck, it is unclear, says Austin, whether I see an existing thing which appears to have qualities which it does not really possess, or whether I see a thing, a decoy duck, which does not really exist. The same point could be as well pressed in the example above. However, Austin is failing to grasp the perfectly good sense and great generality of the distinction. The contrast is between the case where there is a material thing which I have misidentified, and where there really is no material thing which I could possibly be said to have seen. In sense-datum terms it is the contrast between interpreting a sense-datum which does belong to some material object as belonging to a material object of more or less the wrong kind, and interpreting a sense-datum which does not belong to any material object as belonging to a material object (usually of some particular kind).

properties of presenting one kind of appearance from one point of view, and another kind from another point of view, but these are not properties it appears to have from one point of view and not from the other, but properties I may know quite well all the time that it has. I am not denying that its actual shape is a complex property, theoretically definable in terms of the various kinds of appearance it presents, which appearances have shape in a different sense. What I am denying is that one of the shapes of the appearances it presents reproduces or represents the real shape of the object and others fail to do this. Any such appearance presents the shape of the object correctly to one who knows the circumstances of the perception, and can put the right interpretation upon it; for it is just the appearance which an object of that shape does present to a percipient in that situation. The argument from variation, unlike the argument from illusion, does not involve the supposition that certain appearances are illusory and fail to present the object as it really is. We have no need therefore to give an account of the criteria for treating certain appearances as those privileged to present the 'real qualities' of the object in the sort of way Ayer does in the final section of *The Foundations of Empirical Knowledge*. This is not to deny, of course, that there are illusions, i.e., that certain appearances are peculiarly liable to mislead.

In Chapter X of *Sense and Sensibilia* Austin suggests that Ayer's 'real' reason for introducing sense-data lies in his commitment to the idea *that knowledge has foundations*. Ayer, and perhaps Price, are said to be operating on the assumption that the possession of genuine knowledge, apart from knowledge of certain basic propositions, consists in having drawn correct inferences from certain first premisses expressible in what can be called 'basic propositions'. Since all error, on such a view, consists in wrong inference from the foundations, the foundations themselves must somehow be intrinsically free from the possibility of error. Since I can be mistaken in reporting on the material objects which I perceive, it is held that there must be a more radical sort of perception from which we derive our knowledge of the basic propositions. Since the objects of this sort of perception cannot be material objects, about which we can always be mistaken, it is urged that they must be something immaterial, namely sense-data.

In this book I am largely eschewing questions of epistemology. The book is much concerned with what it is to have a belief (in a sense in which one cannot know something to be the case without believing it to be the case), and to some extent with what it is that people tend to believe. It is not much concerned, however, with the grounds on which true beliefs are distinguished from false beliefs, or with what may constitute some beliefs cases of knowledge, though I shall say a word on this latter point shortly. (I do in effect, though, imply a view as to what it is for a belief to be true, as opposed to how this can be assessed.) Since it is so often thought that sense-data are only introduced with such epistemological purposes as those just mentioned, I may as well explicitly disown this motive. I do not think, for instance, that I can arrive at a reasonable view of the world by some process of inference from facts about the sense-data I experience. I can only justify some of my beliefs in terms of other beliefs I hold, and some beliefs must be held without justification, simply because as a matter of fact I find that I cannot honestly doubt them. Among the beliefs I happen to hold in this latter way are beliefs not only in the endurance through time of my own stream of consciousness, together with the sense-data occurring in it, but beliefs in the existence of other streams of consciousness, and also the belief that there must be a material world in some sense of that expression.

Though I do not look on sense-data, or at least on the sense-data experienced by myself, as furnishing the first premisses of all knowledge, I do believe that normal perception consists in being prompted by one's experiencing of a sense-datum, and noticing something about its character,[1] to a belief in the existence of some material object. The question then arises as to what this belief in the existence of a material object usually amounts to, and whether it is subject to variation and improvement. If sense-data are rather basic in the thoughts I shall be developing on this subject, it is not because I have an epistemological outlook such as Austin, correctly I think, attributes to Ayer, but because I find the occurrence of sense-data of various sorts a more readily graspable conception than that of the existence of material things. I feel that I know more clearly what I am thinking about in the former case.

---

[1] What is involved in noticing the character of a sense-datum will become clearer later in the book. It may also be noted, for future reference, that noticing the character of a sense-datum, and forming a material object belief, may be one and the same activity, rather than two activities, the one prompted by the other.

I should perhaps say a word as to whether one has incorrigible knowledge of the character, or rather of the intrinsic character, of one's sense-data.

The case seems to be this. I can notice facts about the sense-data I experience, that is I can notice that they exemplify certain universals. This noticing may take the form of uttering certain words,[1] or of responding in some other distinctive way to the universals which they exemplify. This noticing is not, however, a case of knowledge, for knowledge, I am inclined to say, is true belief, the rightness of which is not a mere flukish accident,[2] whereas this noticing is not a belief at all. If my response is not of a kind commonly correlated in my case with one of the universals exemplified by the sense-datum, there is no case of noticing at all, not a case of erroneous noticing. I might indeed sometimes have a belief that I am noticing something about the sense-datum, and that belief could be wrong, but that is a different matter. A belief about a sense-datum, as opposed to the mere noticing of something about it, is in no way incorrigible, though some such beliefs are ones such that to hold them doubtful would be to cast doubt on one's right to hold anything sure at all.

I am not unaware that there are many questions in this area, and in the whole area of recent attacks on sense-data, especially by Austin, that I may seem to have left unanswered. It is a subject, however, on which discussion tends to be peculiarly endless, and I hope I have said enough to defend my approach against some of the most widely held objections to sense-data.

I shall now return to matters intrinsic to my own enquiry, rather than such as are imposed by the need to meet the attacks of those of an outlook alien to mine.

3

Those who talk of sense-data divide up into those who think that there is a mental act of sensing or experiencing directed onto the

[1] When I notice by responding verbally to the sense-data, my words may also function as expressive of, or even constitutive of, certain beliefs, perhaps about material objects. In this case what I am noticing about the sense-data will *not* be that they have the properties the predicates in the utterance name.
[2] I here adopt J. Watling's account of 'knowledge'. See 'Inference from the Known to the Unknown', *Proceedings of the Aristotelian Society*, 1954–5.

sense-datum, and those who simply think that a sense-datum occurs.

I accept the contention of some act/object accounts of sensing a sense-datum that a sense-datum may be sensed or experienced in different ways, and that this is not a matter of variation in the sense-data themselves. Sensing is not the name of one unique unvarying process. The sensing or experiencing of a sense-datum may be attentive or it may verge towards pure aesthesis. Sometimes sensing has the character of liking or enjoying the sense-datum, at other times it has the character of disliking the sense-datum. None the less I do not think that there are really two things, the act of sensing and the sense-datum, standing in a certain relation.

I hold, rather that the event describable as the sensing or experiencing of a sense-datum involves one particular, not two, but that this single particular falls under two different determinables. The first determinable is *Being of a certain sensible character*, the second is *Being a certain kind of mental activity*. This single particular can equally be regarded as a sense-datum, or as the experience of a sense-datum, but we have to talk about it rather differently according as to which character we are seeing it in.

Suppose we are regarding it as a sense-datum. Then we can say that it must have a certain sensible character. It may for instance have a sensible character partially indicated by 'being a red circular patch'. That is one dimension in which sense-data may vary from one another. But there is also another dimension in which they may vary from one another; that is they also have properties which fall under another determinable. For they have such properties as 'being liked and carefully attended to', 'being barely noticed', and so on. These look like relational properties but in fact they are as much qualities of the sense-datum as are the properties which make up its sensible character.

Suppose that now we regard the particulars in question rather as experiences. Considered this way the particulars also fall under two different determinables: in fact the same two determinables considered from a slightly different point of view. First, the experience has properties which determine the kind of experience it is. An experience may be one of liking or disliking or somewhere in between, it may be attentive to various degrees, and so on. Second, it has such properties as being the experience of a round red blob with a white centre, or being the experience of a low drone. Such properties may look like relational properties but in fact they are as much qualities of the experience as are the properties which make it an experience of a certain kind. They are the same properties as those which when we call the particular a sense-datum we call its sensible properties.

Thus I have some sympathy with those who say that the sense-datum must be distinguished from the experience directed on it. For when we talk of the character of the sense-datum we are normally more concerned with one set of its properties, while when we talk of the character of the experience we are normally more concerned with another set of its properties.

None the less the sensible character of the sense-datum on the one hand and the way in which it is experienced on the other, are simply two distinct determinable properties exemplified by the same objects, in the same sort of way as are colour and shape.

There is something to be said for the view that the real particulars involved are not individual experiences but total states of mind, or total temporal phases of a mind. Thus it may be that we should rather say that at any one time a mind (such as can be described as sensing sense-data) has two sets of properties serving to determine two determinables. The one set of properties are such things as experiencing sense-data of such and such a sensible character related to each other in such and such ways; the other set of properties are such things as attending to this degree to that sense-datum, liking it to this extent and so on. Since individual experience and individual sense-datum would on this view be 'illegitimate abstractions', the problem of what it is for an experience to be *in* a mind would be thereby lightened.

Such a view must make use of a notion of syncategorematic properties, which we shall discuss later. For the mind will not simply have a property like *being very attentive*, it will only have this property *qua* having some property like experiencing a red bulgy sense-datum, while *qua* having the property of experiencing a green blur in the corner of the visual field, it may have the property of being inattentive. A property is syncategorematic if an individual exemplifies it only *qua* exemplifier of some other property. The word 'very', for instance, names a syncategorematic property.

Such a view goes too far, I think, in denying that experiences or sense-data are genuine particulars. All the same we may agree that individual sense-data and experiences are in a certain sense abstractions. Experiences are not bundled together to make up a total mind-state. Rather, they represent the result of thinking of the mind as broken up into parts in one particular way. In so far as talk of the experiences tends to make one forget that the mind is not broken up in this way one may even see the point in calling them illegitimate abstractions.

Could there be unsensed sense-data? If every sense-datum must fall under the two determinables we have talked of (and I think it must do so) then the answer would seem to be negative. For any particular having the sensible qualities appropriate to making it a sense-datum would also have properties of the other kind which makes it a sense-datum experienced in a certain way.

But though a sensible particular must have some characteristics under the same determinable as 'being attentively and appreciatively contemplated', there are various characteristics under this determinable which might be thought in some sense to deserve such an epithet as 'neutral'. Thus at least part of what we might mean by an unsensed sense-datum might be a sense-datum whose determination under this determinable was neutral.

The idea of certain determinations of a given determinable as being neutral is born out when we consider colours, where it seems appropriate to regard *white* and/or *black* as in some sense neutral determinates of *coloured*. But that there are two very different determinates which might be called 'neutral' suggests that there might be disagreement as to what kind of experience of a sense-datum should properly be called neutral. Turning to shape, there might be call to regard the shape of a visual point, such as the sense-datum of a star, as neutral. But I cannot think of any other shape which might be called neutral.

Two contrasting ways of experiencing a sense-datum might be called neutral. First, a condition of pure contemplation where coloured surfaces, in all their suchness, are drunk in with no treatment of them as clues to the activity demand by the situation. Second, a condition where the individual quality of the sense-data is barely noticed but the mind passes straight on to plans of action prompted by the way it has taken the sense-data as clues to something beyond them. These ways of experiencing a sense-datum are very different from each other, but each might perhaps be described as cases of the sense-data just occurring without there being any mental act directed on them. So perhaps if we try to imagine an unsensed sense-datum, part of what we do should be to imagine it as having a character such as one or other of these types of sense-data have.

The remainder of what we have to imagine may be explained as follows. The mind-state of a human being at any typical moment of his life is a total object in which an immense multiplicity of different parts may be distinguished by a semi-illegitimate process of abstraction. We can distinguish various sense-experiences, that is experiences of sense-data, but we can also distinguish beliefs, hopes, fears, thoughts, and what not. It is not altogether impossible to conceive of an impoverished version of this total object, another total object in the same line but much less rich in content, in which only sense-experiences are there to be distinguished. This is indeed compatible with the existence of emotions, for at least some emotions are experiencings of sense-data, which experiences have a certain character, e.g., joyousness. But if we imagine an impoverished mind-state in which only sense experiences are there to be distinguished and that the character of these experiences which determines the mode of apprehension is neutral in one or other of the ways we have indicated, we have something which one might after all prefer not to call a mind-state but a complex of un-sensed sense-fields, e.g. auditory sense-field, visual sense-field and so on. The different sense-fields and the sense-data which are parts of them will still be in some sense illegitimate abstractions from the total object. Let us now suppose a still more impoverished total object in the same line in which only visual experiences are there to be distinguished. For simplicity, let us assume that the sense-data experienced comprise just one visual field. Then granted the quality, *qua* experience, of the experience of these sense-data is 'neutral', we have a totality which might as well be called an un-sensed visual field. It could however, still be described as a very impoverished mind, the sole activity of which was the entirely neutral experiencing of a visual field of a certain character.

We have now given some account of what might be meant by an unsensed visual field. Its parts could be what is meant by un-sensed visual sense-data. But could we have unsensed visual sense-data which do not belong to a visual field?

To answer this we may point out that a visual field can, if we like, itself be regarded as a sense-datum. Then we can say that some sense-data are parts of larger sense-data while others are not. Now in a rather special sense a visual field has shape, and we can perhaps imagine one with a more definite shape if we suppose a visual field which does not differ in character so much in the centre and at the peripheries as does ours. If we now want to think of an unsensed sense-datum of a tomato which does not belong to a visual field, we have to think of it as being itself a total visual field.

I wonder whether philosophers who have talked of unsensed sense-data and have supposed that a physical object is the group of all the sense-data of that object which exist from different possible viewing points may sometimes have forgotten that the visual datum of a given object from point P must either be a visual field itself or be part of a larger visual field. Which do they suppose it is, and if the latter how inclusive a visual field, that is of how wide a stretch of environing objects does it include the sense-data? To suppose that the environmental visual field is of just the 'size' which would be given to a human eye seems arbitrary. Similar questions arise about tactile and other data.

There are, as anyone who sees how these remarks might be elaborated on will realize, all sorts of ways in which unsensed sense-data might exist. We might suppose much, much larger visual fields such as embraced all surfaces from which light reached a given point. Such visual fields would be as though the inner surface of a hollow sphere. Berkeley's God might sense visual fields like this. He would of course sense infinitely many such visual fields and other sense-fields as well. Each visual field would be an 'illegitimate abstraction' from a total object (God's momentary mind-state) which included also other sense-fields and also thoughts, etc. Now a possible way of imagining unsensed sense-data is to think of a momentary mind-state of Berkeley's God. Then consider a reduced version of this total object in which only sense-experiences were there to be distinguished. Then, suppose that these sense experiences are entirely neutral in the qualities which determine the kind of experience it is. We then get something which might be called a total object made up of unsensed sense-fields each made up of unsensed sense-data rather than a mind. But it could be called a mind which did nothing but experience in a quite neutral manner a vast variety of sense-data giving views (visual and otherwise) of the world from every point of view. If this is how the world is, it might be a moot point whether Berkeley was essentially right, though he would have rather over-rated the intelligence of God, or whether the Russell of *Mysticism and Logic* was right in supposing the physical universe to be com-posed of largely unsensed sense-data (or sensibilia). I myself would think a total object like this inappropriately classified as a mind-state, let alone as a divine mind-state. I would also say that if we suppose a world of separate isolated particulars, each a smallish sense-field experienced in a neutral manner, that it would become inappropriate to think of these particulars as experiences. So I do not think it altogether appropriate to say that the person who believes in unsensed sense-data of this sort is believing in *separate* isolated experiences. It is rather that he believes in the existence of particulars comparable in character to elements which can be distinguished in mind-states in that they have determinate natures falling under the same two main determinables, but differing in that they are themselves total objects rather than elements in such, and in that their determinate character in the nonsensible dimen-sion is always neutral.

4

So much for what it is to sense a sense-datum. It is evident that there is more to a man's perception of an apple than his simply sensing a sense-datum belonging to a certain range. Normally he will not only sense a sense-datum of an apple type, but he will take it to be the appearance of an apple, or at least of some material thing. Moreover, in the standard case, the sense-datum actually will be the appearance of an apple.

Whether and when 'Peter saw an apple' should be taken to imply that there really was an apple there, is, as we have seen, a rather doubtful point. It is also a rather doubtful point whether and when 'Peter saw an apple' implies that Peter took himself to be confronted by an apple. If Peter took the sense-datum to be the appearance of a pear, and really it was the appearance of an apple, did he see an apple? If Peter did not even take it to be the appear-ance of a material thing, nor even had an inclination so to do, and really it was the appearance of an apple, did he see an apple? Perhaps people rather seldom do fail thus to take their sense-data, and perhaps there is hardly ever a case where there is no such inclination thus to take presented sense-data, so that the issue scarcely arises. None the less, it seems important to stress that there is to what we ordinarily call perception, a judgmental or belief aspect, as well as the mere sensing of a sense-datum and perhaps noticing its intrinsic qualities. Perception normally involves believing something about the sense-data one is experiencing.

The position is perhaps something like this. Unless Peter took it that the sense-datum was the appearance of some material thing, he would not be *perceiving* in any useful sense at all. If he took it to be the appearance of a pear, but really it was the appearance of an apple, one might still say 'He saw an apple', though one would add 'but mistook it for a pear'. If he took it to be the appearance of a pear, and really it was not the appearance of any material thing at all, one could say either 'He saw a pear (which did not really exist)' or 'He seemed to see a pear'. In short, the real apple cancels the appropriateness of referring to the pear as an object of perception, but if there is no real material thing at all, the thing he thought he was confronted with, *may* figure as an object of perception.

I am not much concerned, however, with these linguistic subtleties. The point I want to emphasize is simply that perception normally or always involves the percipient having a belief to the effect that the sense-datum he is experiencing is the appearance of a material thing, and I now want to enquire just what proposition it is that one believes when one believes this. We must not assume, however, that the propositions people normally believe in perceptual situations, and which can be thus expressed, are the propositions which a reflective person may in reflective moments take to be the best interpretation of the claim that the sense-data we experience really are appearances of material things, though there must doubtless be some sort of equivalence for practical purposes between the propositions.

The truth of the matter seems to be that different people are believing in different kinds of proposition on such occasions as we say that they are perceiving apples. For most purposes it makes no difference which type of proposition is true, provided one of them is, so we do not notice that the same words are expressing quite different ones. Thus when I take a sense-datum in some sense to *be* an apple and when you do so, what we believe about the sense-datum may be quite different and even incompatible. This is not noticed because for all practical purposes it will be the same to each of us whichever of the propositions is true, provided one is, or even provided some further proposition not believed in by either of us is true, where the effects for the purposes we mostly have in hand in truth of this other proposition is the same as that of the truth of either of ours. Thus I believe that the beliefs of someone scarcely touched by modern science, which we might regard as his belief that his sense-data are the appearances of material objects, may be very different from the beliefs equally so describable of a scientist. It may also be that factors quite apart from scientific knowledge have from the earliest times meant that, without its being noticed, people expressed at least partly different propositions by such simple sentences as this. For instance, one's general attitude to the world, whether primarily contemplative or practical, might influence the degree to which one developed a belief in unsensed sense-data. The point is worth repeating that, if the effect of one proposition's being true and that of another's being true on the success of most or all co-operative enterprises is the same, or even seems to be the same, it will not easily be realized that in fact different propositions are assented to.

I shall consider three propositions which might well represent the judgmental aspect of perception of an apple by a plain man. However, many a plain man's mental state in a perceptual situation may be equally classifiable as a belief in any one of them. Prompted to choose one there is no saying which would be chosen. (Philosophers, after all, are originally plain men and they, when forced to be more determinate in their beliefs than plain men, diverge from another.)

Here are three propositions (or rather skeletons of such) about the sense-datum sensed which may constitute a plain man's belief that he is confronted with an apple.

(i) This (sense-datum) is one member of a group of actually existing apple-type sense-data, many of them unsensed, which are related one to another in certain ways.

(ii) This (sense-datum) is the actualization of one of a group of possible apple-type sense-data which are related one to another in certain ways.

(iii) This (sense-datum) is the actualization of one of a group of possible apple-type sense-data which are related one to another in certain ways, and the possibility of these sense-data rests upon the actual existence of some individual of which, the intrinsic nature cannot be known, though it can be known that it satisfies the formal conditions necessary for its being the basis of these possibilities.

It is going to be our eventual task in this work to describe the structure of a mental state or act, which, perhaps somewhat modifying ordinary usage, we shall call 'belief'. It is now to be remarked that there are two great classes of propositions believed (possibly exhaustive of the class of positive propositions believed) and that belief requires different treatment according as to whether it is belief in a proposition belonging to one or other of these classes. What is believed may either be an existential proposition or it may be a possibility proposition. That is, I may believe that a thing or situation of a certain kind exists or I may believe that a thing or situation of a certain kind is possible. Arguably, all positive propositions are of one of these kinds.

It seems natural to expect that it will be easier to explain what it is to believe an existential proposition, than what it is to believe a possibility proposition.

Now if we compare a plain man whose perceptions involve beliefs in propositions of the same type as (i) with one whose perceptions involve rather beliefs in propositions of the same type as (ii), it is clear that the class of existential propositions believed by the first will be far richer than the class of existential propositions believed by the second. There will be something to be said, then, for concentrating attention on plain men of the first type rather than on those of the second type, when we are seeking to clarify the nature of belief in existential propositions. The same contrast does not hold quite so clearly between one who believes propositions of type (i) and one who believes propositions of type (iii). However, the things in the existence of which the man who believes propositions of type (iii) believes are of such a mysterious kind, being things we know not what, that account of belief in them had better wait until we know what belief in things we do know what amounts to, while if we omit consideration of these things in themselves the existential propositions believed in by those who assent to type (iii) propositions appear on the face of it to be just the same as those believed in by those who assent to type (ii) propositions. For this reason I propose to simplify matters by taking it that (i), rather than (ii) or (iii) represents the plain man's view of the world. Apart from this, I am inclined to think that it represents the original unsophisticated outlook we most naturally develop in infancy, and serves us best therefore in considering what belief is at its simplest (which would seem a sensible beginning).

Consider just what existential propositions one who holds the outlook of proposition (ii) is likely to believe.

Such a person will believe in the existence of the sense-data he now senses, and will also believe that various other sense-data 'of his' have existed and will exist. He will also believe in the existence of the present, past, and future sense-data of other people and of the minds which manifest themselves to him by animal-type sense-data. He may believe in the existence of various mental states and mental acts both his own and those of others. But it is unclear that he will believe in the existence of any other contingent things. He whose main belief in a perceptual situation is of character (ii) will probably not actually believe in the negation of a character (i) proposition, but we are taking it that he will certainly not positively believe in it.

Belief in the existence of a physical object will not for such a person really be an existential belief. I am not denying that he really and truly believes in the existence of physical objects. What I am denying is that for one who has this outlook the proposition that physical objects exist is really and truly an existential proposition.

It is here that his difference from the person who assents to character (i) propositions is most striking. For when the latter believes that a physical object exists he believes a genuinely and ultimately existential proposition. For, on this view, the physical object is a group of sense-data all of which 'actually' exist – it is not composed of mere possibilities. Thus for the person for whom propositions of type (i) indicate what he believes when he believes such a thing as *this* is an apple, propositions ascribing existence to physical objects are really and truly existential propositions. This shows how much wider and richer is the class of existential propositions accepted by the believer in character (i) propositions than the believer in character (ii) propositions. So again it seems wise that when we talk of the nature of belief in existential propositions we should, at least in the first place, assume that the

existence of physical objects is interpreted on the lines of proposition (i) rather than proposition (ii) – while proposition (iii)
we ignore for reasons indicated.

We are to assume then that what the plain man believes in
when he believes in the existence of a physical object, is a certain
group of sense-data only a few of which, if any, are sensed. If the
philosopher is forced to conclude that interpreted in this way it is
literally false that physical objects exist, he may palliate his conclusion in various ways. First, it is only in one sense which will
appeal to a plain man as being his sense that physical objects do not
exist. In other senses which may equally appeal to a plain man as
being his sense it may still be true that physical objects exist.
Second, it is only in one sense of 'true' and 'false' that the proposition must be adjudged false. Inasmuch as it may be as good as
true (for most purposes) in this sense it may actually be *true* in
some more pragmatic sense of the word (though the assertion
that it is pragmatically true will itself presumably be true in a non-
pragmatic sense).

It is against this background that our study of believing in
Part III will mainly be conducted. In sections 3 and 7 of Chapter
XII, however, we will consider how the theory of believing which
we shall be discussing can deal with the belief in material objects
when this is construed according to propositions (ii) and (iii) above
rather than according to (i).

5

Before closing this chapter it may be appropriate to say a few
words regarding an aspect of some contemporary philosophical
suspicions of sense-data of a rather different kind from those of
Austin, those which turn on the notion of privacy. It may be
asked whether sense-data are private, and suggested that if they
are, our account of the sort of thing the plain man believes when
he perceives things cannot be right, for surely the plain man's
beliefs are not concerned with anything private.

The question whether things of a certain type are private or
not can mean many things.[1] Perhaps there are two interpretations
of the question of most importance. In asking whether sense-data

[1] See my discussion article 'The Privacy of Experience' in *Mind*, Vol.
LXXVII, n.s. 312, October 1969.

are private or not one might be asking whether the same sense-datum can be experienced by two different people, or one might be asking whether the same sense-datum can be spoken of by two different people. Let us begin by considering the first of these questions.

The fact that people see material things from different points of view and also hear and smell them, and so on, from different points of view, indicates that there will normally be a difference in character between any sense-data of an object sensed by them at once. Since one and the same thing cannot have two opposite characters,[1] it follows that people do not normally sense one and the same sense-datum at once of the material thing. It is to be noted that a difference in the relational properties will also establish non-identity, in particular a difference in the sort of things each sense-datum is related to in its visual or other sensory field. Of course, a thing may have many different relational properties, but to be sensibly adjacent to or compresent with a blue patch and not to be thus sensibly adjacent are incompatible, and the sense-datum I sense of an object in virtue of my position will often differ from the one which you sense of it in this sort of way. But could I somehow experience numerically the same visual field as you? Even if somehow there were complete identity in quality, it would hardly be numerically the same. Each would have temporal relations of the especially direct sort which relate events in one experiential stream, or in an unexperienced unity of the same sort, to qualitatively different objects. Therefore I conclude that one and the same sense-datum cannot be sensed by two people at once. Each unsensed sense-datum also must belong to only one such unity. (I discuss this sort of unity again later in the book, see pp. 249–50, for example.)

Very often, if one asks whether one and the same something can be in two different relations, one means, 'can it be in each of them at a different time?' We must not conclude too readily that one and the same sense-datum cannot be sensed first by you, then by me.

It is, none the less, probably simplest to think of sense-data as momentary entities, in which case you cannot at a later time sense a sense-datum which I sensed earlier. Yet I cannot do so either,

[1] Except where the universals are syncategorematic in the sense of Chapter II, section 6, as is not the case here.

46

that is I cannot – if sense-data are taken as momentary – experience the same sense-datum at different moments. Thus this is not really a further failure in publicity over and above the previous one.

It need not be impossible to consider sense-data as persisting entities. In general, when one asks what it is for one and the same thing – of whatever sort – to be in existence at two different moments, one is asking what relation has to hold between two momentary – or at least briefer – entities for them both to be phases of one and the same persisting entity of the sort in question. This applies to material things just as much as to sense-data.[1] There is no theoretical reason why one should not set up a meaning for talking of the same sense-datum existing at different times, by explaining what conditions two sense-datum-phases, as we may now call what previously we simply called sense-data, have to satisfy in order to be two phases of the same sense-datum. In point of fact philosophers who talk of sense-data have seemed simply to make rather *ad hoc* decisions on the matter, without any great harm being done. It would be possible to lay down a meaning for such persistence which would enable the same sense-datum to be sensed by you and by me, perhaps with an interval of existing unsensed in between. For instance, one might say that two sense-datum phases at adjacent moments and belonging to the same material object, that is, each a member of a certain group, and these two groups related so as to be phases of the same material object, would be phases of the same sense-datum, provided they satisfied the criteria for being *from* the same place (criteria which themselves, in view of the relativity of space, are relative to standards which would have to be decided on) and perhaps also subject to there being a considerable degree of qualitative continuity. There would be little point in trying to formulate some exact meaning along these lines for identity of sense-data across time, and if one is going to talk about such identity at all the convenience of the

---

[1] An attempt to elucidate this point in more detail may be found in my article 'The Common Sense View of Physical Objects' (*Inquiry* IX, 4, Winter 1966). That article contains an account in some ways more detailed of that way of interpreting belief in the existence of material objects which has been mainly stressed in this chapter. I there maintained, however, that it was *the* common-sense view rather than simply *a* common-sense view, as is claimed here.

moment should dictate.[1] There is then no definite answer to the question whether you can sense the same sense-datum as I at a later time.

It might be thought that one could ask about a *momentary* sense-datum sensed by me at a certain time whether it could have been you instead of I who sensed that very one, or whether that very one could have existed unsensed. I think there is something wrong in this question, in the same sort of way as there is something wrong in asking whether this very person which I am could have been born of different persons. Give any *description* you like of me which doesn't actually specify my parents, and it is logically possible that the person of that description should have had parents different from those which in fact I had, but one can't really ask whether one and the same *particular* could have been different from what it is in this way. Similarly, about this very sense-datum which I sense one can't sensibly ask whether someone else could have sensed it instead, though certainly it might have been someone other than myself who sensed a sense-datum of exactly this kind, down to whatever degree of specification you like, provided it is not specified that I sensed it. It would be rather misleading to say that all this implies that the plain man supposes that what he senses is not sensed by anyone else. If one said this without explanation it would probably seem that one was claiming that, according to the plain man at least, two people cannot look at a material thing and see it in just the same way. In fact we neither ascribe to the plain man, nor ourselves hold, any view which would deny that two different people can get qualitatively identical data in seeing, touching, etc. the same object, at least at different times, and extraordinarily close to such qualitatively identical sense-data at the same time. That at the same time they are not numerically identical and that this would be so even if qualitative identity were somehow achieved is something which emerges when the viewpoint which exists in the mind of the plain man in a very inchoate form is spelt out in some detail and decisions on such points have to be reached, but is not, of course, a point the plain man will himself have thought out. I talk here of the plain man, but I must emphasize again my opinion that this is only one of the various alternative views which may in effect be in the mind of plain man (cf. pp. 332–3 and 259).

1 Cf. the footnote on p. 236 of this book.

On this view there is, of course, no question but that two people may see one and the same material thing. Perceiving is largely a matter of believing and the belief which the sense-datum I experience evokes in me may converge on the same material object, the same group of sense-data, which your belief converges on. It should not be thought, however, that these beliefs in the existence of a group of a certain general sort need involve specification of details regarding its every member.

Let us now turn to the quite different question as to whether the language in which sense-data are to be described is in some sense private and whether one can talk about the sense-data sensed by others. Sense-data are certainly not private in any such sense as this. It may be thought that we should enter into some discussion of current debates about so called private languages here. I am afraid that that would take us too far afield.

Perhaps I can usefully say just this much, however. All predicates, and on my view predicates name universals, name something public in the sense that they occur in the experience, or at least can do so, of all of us. All ordinary names, which on my view, in the last resort, and in a rather complicated way, boil down to definite descriptions, also rest upon this public base.[1] The only words which might be said to have a sort of privacy are logically proper names for experiences and sense-data. If I say 'This (ache) is awful', for instance, I use a word ('This') simply to concentrate my attention on an experience, and no one else could use that word to concentrate their attention on that same experience. On the other hand, they can refer to that experience by a definite description, ('his ache', etc.) and what is more they can understand my use of 'This', in the sense that they can know that I am using it to concentrate my attention on a certain experience. It is not the *meaning* of 'This' which is private, for they can use 'This' with the same meaning to concentrate their attention on their experiences, and can know that that is how I am using it. Nor is it the *reference* which is private, for they can refer to that which I refer to as 'This', by a definite description – of course, they also can call the experience itself 'this' or 'that' if they like, but then it isn't for them functioning as a logically proper name. All that the privacy amounts to is that no one else can use 'This' in that sense to refer to the very same thing that I do. All this applies to logically proper names for

1 See Chapter VII.

sense-data. Of course, they are not often used, but various ordinary locutions, on my view, can best be analysed by equating them with longer expressions which do include such logically proper names. The sort of equivalence between analysandum and analysans in question here is what I later call 'subjective equivalence'.[1]

If it is asked how a public language is learnt, one may point out briefly the following. In order that a child be taught the use of language by its parents, the parents must take it that they know on occasion what the child is experiencing, and this is an assumption readily made in practice. I would add that the parents must sometimes also take it that they know what the child is believing, either in a preverbal way, or, at a later stage, in a crude and primitive verbal way. They must then act so that it is conditioned to 'say the right things' granted what it is experiencing or believing. If the parents did in fact know these facts about the child, then the child will be learning to use words with the same meaning as do the parents, in particular, to name the same universals by the same words. (Of course, this is a schematic parody of the learning situation, which is not primarily brought about by the parents in this deliberate way.) If we have no reason to doubt the genuineness of this knowledge, each of us has no reason to doubt that he has been taught to use language as others do. Nor do I imply that language is initially private, and becomes public only by teaching. Surely mankind has developed language socially in a way which depends upon the fact that men were experiencing the same universals, and responding to the same physical facts, and that, in an inchoate way, they were aware of this 'from the beginning'.

A word on the subject of our knowledge of other minds seems appropriate here. As I have already indicated, I do not so much regard material things, however construed, as inferred from the sense-data we sense, as instinctively posited when we experience sense-data. The question then arises as to what sort of thing the ordinary man does instinctively posit, and I answer that in some cases what he posits is the unsensed existence of things of the same sort as he senses, though this does not provide a conception of material things which I think one can be satisfied with on reflection (a point taken up in Chapter XII section 3). Unless some facts are posited in this way, there is no basis for any more advanced and inferential knowledge. We may, on reflection, criticize our

[1] See pp. 148–9.

instinctive posits, but we must even then rely on some beliefs which we just accept because they arise so forcefully in us that it would be hypocrisy to pretend that we did not have them. This is more or less the position both of Peirce and Santayana, and I do not intend to develop the point further here. How does this apply to our knowledge of other minds? Here I think there is an element of instinctive posit, but our belief in other minds, or rather consciousnesses, is also well supported by what may be more basic posits, such as the uniformity of nature, which suggests that it would be very odd that one organism, physically so like all others, should be quite exceptional in having an experiential aspect, or in the sort of experiential aspect it had.

The question of privacy may be raised not only with regard to sense-data, but also with regard to various mental processes much discussed later in this book. How can one take words such as 'believe' as referring to 'private' mental processes when their application must be learnt by attention to what is publicly observable? My answer is implicit in much of the foregoing. Certain assumptions about the similarity of different human minds are involved from the beginning in the learning of language, and must be retained by anyone concerned to communicate with his fellows. It is enough, at least in many cases, that the similarities assumed should be of a very general kind. When, in Part Three of this book, I offer some account of the process I call 'conscious believing' I urge that the very general conditions for its occurrence may be met in very various ways by different people, but that I can hardly think of someone without assuming that something akin to what I identify as conscious believing in my own case goes on in his. Not that this need be all mere assumption, for once granted a modicum of common meanings to our terms there is plenty of room for 'comparing introspective notes'. I may as well remark here, however, that the importance of behavioural senses of words such as 'believe' will also be emphasized.[1]

---

[1] A grasp of what I say later about syncategorematic properties and groups should suggest why I am content in this chapter to interpret the unsensed sense-data view as identifying material things with groups of sense-data, and see no need to talk of logical constructions. On this view, a sense-datum is part of a material thing, but not, of course, a spatial part of it, for the spatial parts of a material thing are all material things.

II

UNIVERSALS

One may best explain what a property (or one-place universal) is by saying that it is a way in which one thing could be like another thing. Two things could be like one another in being red, in being circular, in being heavy.

When I perceive a material object or sense a sense-datum, I can notice various ways in which something else might resemble it. Thus I do not need two things in order to notice a universal. I could notice roundness even if I only saw one round thing in my life, for I could, in looking at the one round thing, become aware of this way in which there might be other things resembling it, even though nothing else does resemble it in this way.

People have been inclined, sometimes, for rather complicated reasons, to confuse sense-data with properties, at any rate with so-called sensible properties. This is quite wrong. A sense-datum which I experience at a certain time is quite particular. But I can notice, while contemplating it, various ways in which there are, or might be, other sense-data resembling it. I may experience two sense-data, either simultaneously, or in succession, and notice that they are like each other in some way. If two things, for example two sense-data, are said to be alike, it is always appropriate to ask what they are alike in being. One sense-datum A may be like B in one way and like C in another. It may be like the first in being red and like the second in being circular.

There is a temptation for people to think that when they experience a red sense-datum, the visual expanse of which they are directly aware is redness itself. But it is not. The visual expanse is the sense-datum, the redness is a way in which it is potentially like other sense-data, and they like it. The temptation to confuse redness with the expanse which is red may be obviated by considering that a uniformly scarlet sense-datum has two properties, redness and scarletness. Since scarlet and red are two different properties, the expanse cannot both be scarletness itself and redness itself. Someone who makes the mistake I am inveighing against will probably say that the expanse is scarletness itself rather than redness itself. Well, that at least establishes that the property redness is something different from the visual expanse. But in fact both scarletness and redness are different from the visual expanse, for they are ways in which this visual expanse could be like other visual expanses, the one a way of being getting on for exactly alike, the other a way of being somewhat alike.

It may seem odd to say that red and scarlet are quite different properties, and in a way it is odd. Indeed the word 'quite' is inept in this context. What one should say is simply that they are different properties. But even this may seem odd. Scarlet, one may say, is a specific way of being red. This is what is meant by saying that they stand in the relation of determinate and determinable. There is, however, a difference between noticing a thing's scarletness and noticing its redness, even granted that the thing is scarlet. One is noting a different resemblance it is fitted to have to other things. So we should allow that scarlet and red are two different properties, and in allowing it we fortify ourselves against any temptation to think of the properties which a thing, a sense-datum for example, has as in any sense parts of it, for it is impossible to find one part of a thing which is scarletness, and another which is redness, yet it may *have* both properties.

I hope I have made it clear what I mean when I say that there are properties, and hence are universals. I mean that there are various different ways in which one thing could resemble another. Is anyone going to deny that this is so? If he admits it, he admits that there are universals in the sense in question.

It has been urged by W. V. O. Quine in his highly influential essay, 'On What There Is' (in his *From a Logical Point of View*), that one shows oneself committed to the existence of beings of a certain sort if and only if the formal statement of one's opinions requires quantification over variables which have such beings for their values. This is only a rough and ready statement of his contention and not altogether precise, yet I do not think the contention, even when more elaborately developed, is as helpful in ontology as it might at first seem. I should like to point out, however, that there are some quite ordinary matters of fact whose statement in the usual logical symbolism seems to involve an unavoidable quantification over beings which, if they are anything, are universals. I may surely come to know, by report, the fact that two ladies, Jane and Mary, wore dresses of the same colour on a certain occasion without knowing what that colour was. Expressed with quantification symbols my information is as follows: (Ef) (f is a colour. Jane's dress was f. Mary's dress was f).[1] I do not see how otherwise the knowledge I would have could be expressed. Admittedly, if I had a fuller knowledge of the situation, I could dispense with this quantification and say something of the pattern: 'Jane's dress was F and Mary's dress was F' in which there is no quantification; but, after all, the use of quantified variables normally does indicate that one is unable to put a definite name to something and is always to that extent a symptom of ignorance. Quine, indeed, would not accept this, but the point is not very essential, for there is no doubt that we have a perfectly definite, though not very full, piece of information here which cannot be expressed without quantification over a variable, the value of which is a colour. A colour such as red, is, of course, a typical example of the sort of thing we call a universal.

Ordinary speech is full of expressions which seem to be informal analogues of quantification over universals. One talks about two things being of the same *shape*, one says that one has seen that same *pattern* before on a different wall, and so on. To treat 'red' and 'round' as referring to entities called properties is not opposed to ordinary speech, as it doubtless would be so to treat 'sake' in the expression 'for his sake', or the expression 'if'. One does not speak of the same, or of a different, *sake* or *if*, as one does of the same, or of a different, colour, shape, or type of animal. To speak of universals is not to speak of some strange entity discovered or invented by philosophers, it is simply to subsume a lot of familiar things, colours, shapes, functions, and types, for instance, under a heading designed to bring out a contrast between them and a lot of other familiar things, such as

[1] I prefer to use 'f', 'g', and 'h' for predicate variables in the proper sense, and reserve 'F', 'G', and 'H' for cases where one pretends to be dealing with a constant.

my pen, my headache of this morning, my doctor, and my cat.

It may be objected that there is no need to use the rather mystical sounding word 'universal' for anything as simple as a way in which one thing could resemble another thing. I cannot see that there is much force to this objection.

The phrase 'way in which one thing could resemble another thing' is a bit of a mouthful, and if one is going to talk briefly about such ways . . . one will welcome some shorter term for them. The word 'universal' does quite well, and I reckon that traditionally such has often been the essential import of the word. 'Property' would do equally well if it were not that 'universal' is intended also to cover relations.

It may be allowed that if 'universal' is to cover relations also we may have to elaborate somewhat on saying that a universal is a way in which one thing could resemble another thing. In point of fact it will turn out that this account can continue to stand after certain explanations are given.

If I am right that essentially what has often been meant by 'universal' is what I have said, and if one admits that there are universals in this sense, then it seems quite wrong to sneer, as do many recent philosophers, especially in Britain, at those who have talked about universals. There is no more appropriate phrase for the items in question, items which there is just as much call to mention on occasion, whether separately or as a class, and to classify, as there is to mention and classify particular things.

Doubtless some who have talked of universals may have tended to think of them as super-particulars of some mysterious sort, and certainly this is altogether inappropriate. This is a temptation to be resisted and (when engaged in historical enquiry) explained, but it is not a particularly sensible way of resisting it to deny that there are such things as universals, in a perfectly good sense of the word. Moreover, such confused thinking seems just as liable to break out, with particular examples, through lack or disuse of such general phrases as 'particular' and 'universal' to remind one of the enormous contrast between things of these two types, as through their use. It would take us too far afield to illustrate this point.

Some philosophers will doubtless continue to insist that universals do not have the degree of reality which I seem to ascribe to them, and will charge me with an illegitimate reification or entification. But is it not absurd to regard either particular things or universals or items of any other ontological kind as the more real, or to argue as to which are and which are not entities? Something is an entity in a perfectly good sense if there is something true to be said about it. A way in which one thing could be like another thing is not *a particular thing*, and in that sense it is not *a thing*, but it is perfectly real as an example of what it is, a way in which one thing could be like another thing.

2. DISCUSSION OF THE RESEMBLANCE THEORY

In saying, as I would, that the word 'red' names a certain universal, redness, I am saying that it names, or serves to bring to mind, a specific way in which one thing could resemble another thing. This applies both to redness as a quality of sense-data and to that more complex property which is redness as a property of material things. (Do not let it be thought, however, that I postulate *redness* in order to explain the meaning of 'red'.) Now a theory about common nouns and adjectives which is often contrasted with the theory of universals is the theory of resemblance. According to the theory of resemblance the same adjective or common noun is applied to various different things not because some mysterious universal named by the adjective or common noun lurks within each of these things, but simply because the things resemble each other. I can imagine its being said of my remarks about universals, that really I am accepting the theory of resemblance and not that of universals as traditionally understood and so frequently disparaged. I may be told, that is, that I am simply dressing up the theory of resemblance in the language of universals. Well, if what I'm saying represents some sort of compromise between the two theories, I'm quite happy. But I would claim that reasons can be given for definitely rejecting the Resemblance theory as usually understood, while I think that what I'm referring to when I talk of universals is essentially what most of those who have talked of them have been getting at.

(*a*) One objection to the Resemblance theory is as follows. One can hardly say that the various things which are called 'red' are so called because they are all similar to each other. For the various green things are all similar to each other, yet they are not called 'red' but 'green'. The resemblance account, put as above, implies that there is no difference in the principle whereby things are called 'red' and the principle whereby they are called 'green'. If the resemblance theorist then says that red things are like each other in a different way from that in which green things are like each other, he will be hard pressed to deny that there are these different ways in which one thing can resemble another. But these different ways of resembling just are what have been meant by 'universals', so that as a denial of universals the Resemblance theory breaks down.

However the Resemblance theorist has an answer to this. He can say that a certain group of particular things is called 'red' quite arbitrarily and that to call other things 'red' is to say that they are like these original things. Likewise another group of particular things is called 'green' quite arbitrarily, and to call other things 'green' is to say that they are like these things. Thus the principle for an object being called 'red' is that it is like the members of one group, while the principle for an object being called 'green' is that it is like the members of another group. For each person the original group of things called 'red' arbitrarily is that of the things to which he heard the word 'red' first applied. Thereafter when he calls a thing 'red' he means that it is like those first things.[1]

(b) One objection to this is as follows. When one is told that the original things are red one cannot be said to notice anything about them in virtue of which one takes it that this word is being applied. To say that other objects are 'red' will mean henceforth that they are like those original objects, but there will be nothing one can call noticing the redness of the original objects.

One can develop this objection thus: On the Resemblance view any assertion of the subject-predicate type, namely 'Object A is F' is the claim that it resembles some other object or objects which are arbitrarily said to answer to that predicate. Thus if the assertion that an object is F is to have any genuine significance there must be another object which is considered quite arbitrarily as a case of the predicate. But I should claim that one might become aware of a property which some object has, and give the name 'F' to this property without knowing whether anything else has this property. Thus one might say 'This is F' of this object and be saying it quite significantly, without there being some other object which answers in an arbitrary way to the predicate 'F'.

[1]   Cf. footnote on p. 60.

All this applies only to predicates which are in some sense simple. A complex predicate such as 'red and round' could of course even on the Resemblance view be applied significantly to one object without there being some other object answering arbitrarily to this predicate, provided there were objects which answered arbitrarily to 'round' and objects which answered arbitrarily to 'red'.

(c) An argument much used against the Resemblance view is that *resemblance* or *being like* is itself a relation and hence a universal, so the Resemblance theory is committed to at least one universal. In that case its general objection to universals cannot be sustained, and it might as well admit the lot.

I agree with H. H. Price that this argument is not so strong as has often been thought.[1] To believe in universals is to believe in a certain class of entities. If one thinks that resemblance is a universal it is because one thinks that it belongs in the same category as certain other entities. If these other entities do not exist and can not even be talked of intelligibly there is no real point in calling resemblance a universal. So if someone who does not believe in universals talks of resemblance he need not be guilty of inconsistency. Since, in his view, resemblance is something quite unique, there is no call to regard it as belonging to the category of universals.

The Resemblance theory holds that fundamentally there is only one kind of fact to be noticed in the world, namely that one bit of the world resembles another bit. Whatever I say about one bit of the world really boils down to saying it is like some other bit. The theory of universals, on the other hand, recognizes a far greater variety of facts. We do not just recognize a resemblance between various situations, we notice the redness of one bit of the world, the roundness of another bit, the horsiness of another bit, and so on.

(d) Let us now consider another argument which has been advanced in favour of the Realist view of Universals and against the Resemblance theory.

An object must always have more than one property. This is

---

1 *Thinking and Experience* by H. H. Price, pp. 23ff. The first chapter of this book is the best thing I know on universals and much of my discussion arises from it. It will be seen, however, that I do not entirely accept his mediation between the Philosophy of Universals and the Philosophy of Resemblances.

not only for such reasons as that, if it is scarlet, it is also red, but also for such reasons as that, if it is scarlet, it must also have some shape-property. Let us suppose then that a certain object serves, as according to the Resemblance theory some object must serve, as a paradigm for the word 'red'. Then, according to the Resemblance theory, calling other objects 'red' is saying that they are like this object. Suppose now that the shape of the object is roundness, as the Realist would put it. In that case it does not appear how it is that various round objects are refused the title 'red', although they are just as like the original object as are the objects called 'red'. It seems, at the least, that the Resemblance theorist will have to admit that there are different types of resemblance, i.e., resemblance in colour, resemblance in shape, resemblance in pitch, and so on. But while one can speak of mere resemblance between objects without admitting that one is thereby talking of a universal, it seems that if one goes on to talk of different types of resemblance, of resemblance in colour, resemblance in shape and so on, one has in effect admitted a realm of universals.

A Resemblance theorist who was persuaded by this argument might allow that there were different types of resemblance, and he might agree that this was to admit universals of a sort. But he might still claim that his modified position was distinct from a theory which admits the 'reality' of such properties as green, round, loud, and so on.

One interest of such a half-way house position is that it reverses the more usual point of view that the more determinate a property is somehow the more real it is, and the more it is a determinable property the less real it is, and treats the latter as derivative from the former. But this half-way house position does not seem very satisfactory. The argument against the original Resemblance theory, that if you have once admitted one universal, namely resemblance, you may as well admit the rest, did not seem very forceful, but a similar argument has more point against the present position. Moreover this view still has the consequence that calling one thing by a colour word informatively presupposes that some other thing has been called by it arbitrarily, whereas it seems on the contrary that one could genuinely be picking out something about an object by applying to it a colour word never applied to anything before.

It is Professor Price (op. cit.) who has put the Resemblance theory in best shape, so far as I know, though he regards the Resemblance theory and the theory of Universals as complementary rather than contradictory. We may now consider a defence of the Resemblance theory which I have derived from him.

In order to get round the difficulty that any given object can act as ostensive definer of many different predicates, falling under various different determinables, the Resemblance theorist may say that it is always several objects, and never just one, which serve to give ostensive definition to a predicate. Suppose that the ostensive definers for 'red' are objects A, B, and C. Then applying 'red' to a new object D is saying that it is as like each of A, B, and C as each of these is to each other. Thus even if A is in the defining group for 'round' as well as 'red', objects which are red but not round will be distinguished as they will not be as like C as C is to both A and B.

Various objections arise to this account of the matter.

(e) It is clear that a born and bred Australian and myself, who have never been to Australia, can give to the word 'red' the same meaning. But in the circumstances described it is impossible that his original defining group can have been the same as mine. Call his defining group S, T, and U, and mine X, Y, and Z. Now when he says 'This is red' he means the same as 'This is as like each of S, T, and U as each of these is to each other', while when I say 'This is red' I mean 'This is as like each of X, Y, and Z as each of these is to each other'. Since these latter assertions have quite different meanings, it follows that we cannot be meaning the same thing by 'red', which is absurd.

This argument challenges the Resemblance theorist to a more careful explanation of just exactly what it is that he is saying, but it is by no means decisive. For there are all sorts of different senses to such phrases as 'meaning the same'.[1]

(f) Another objection is as follows. The Resemblance theory seems to suppose that whenever I believe a proposition to the effect that something is red, I am, in some sense, equally believing

---

[1] A sophisticated Resemblance theorist would not say that 'This is red' was equivalent in anyone's use to one of these long rigmaroles, perhaps not even subjectively equivalent (cf. Chapter VII). He might say that he was explaining how general words *have* meaning, not *giving* their meaning. I don't think that this ultimately removes objections to the Resemblance theory of the sort on which I have laid stress.

a proposition about some other things observed earlier. This seems to me implausible on the face of it, and still more implausible when we reflect on the nature of the reference back to past objects which a mind can make. Since I am not now acquainted with an object I observed in the past and am no longer observing, it seems reasonable to suggest that my reference to it must be of a kind which would find expression in a definite description rather than in a logically proper name. That is, I must refer to it as an object having such and such properties. If this is so it can hardly be that noticing a property in a present object is really noticing its resemblance to a past object, since the past object itself can only be summoned up as the object having certain properties. Admittedly it might be summoned up as the object having other properties than those now in question, but that does not remove the dilemma. For on the Resemblance view the whole stock of properties I can ascribe to objects now are such that ascribing them is really a comparison of them with past objects.

(g) Another point is this. If I consider the class of all red objects which I have observed it seems quite arbitrary which subset I regard as that of the objects now ostensively defining 'red' for me. That seems to count against the Resemblance theory, in a way which is not affected by saying that the class of ostensive definers may change. It remains arbitrary to say of any such class that it is the class of objects serving as definers of 'red' for me at this moment. This arbitrariness is admitted if it is said that alternative classes can be regarded as the class of paradigms – unless the point is that the classes serving this role alter with time, and that is a point we have dealt with. If it is really arbitrary which past objects we say are at present my definers of 'red', it makes it difficult to take seriously the Resemblance theorist's account of the content of what we are believing when we believe that a thing is red.

Actually two forms of the Resemblance theory may be held. The one I think Price intends is that whereby to call A 'red' is to compare it to X, Y and Z as they were when observed in the past. But a verificationist may prefer to take it as a comparison with X, Y, and Z as they are now. (Let us ignore difficulties either theory would have in explicating the phrases 'as they were then' and 'as they are now' without talking of properties.) Such a person may suppose that by calling a thing 'red' I mean that it is like such and such persisting objects which serve as paradigms, on the grounds that final verification of the judgment would be by comparison with these persisting objects. A similar, but not identical difficulty arises here as in the case discussed above, where the judgment is supposed to involve a reference to past objects, namely that it seems plausible to say that we can only recognize the paradigm objects in virtue of their having certain properties.

This is a separate difficulty from any which may be thought to arise from the possibility that the paradigm objects should cease to have the property they are supposed to be defining. This latter difficulty can be met by saying that a certain class of objects which at one stage were suitable definers for a certain predicate may cease to be so, and a different though doubtless overlapping class may have to be chosen. Such difficulty as there is here faces anyone who does not believe in some such implausible property as 'being two feet long' in an absolute sense, when he comes to describe the role of standard-giving objects. Our point is not that no so-called properties should be dealt with on the lines of one or other type of Resemblance theory, only that they cannot deal with properties *en bloc* like this, partly because recognition of or memory of the paradigm objects then becomes unintelligible, partly for reasons indicated earlier.

3 PROPERTIES

It is only honest to remark on the way in which our account threatens to become circular. To say that X is potentially like other things in being F is not indeed to claim that X occurs in a relational fact, but it is, on the face of it, to say that X is capable of occurring in a certain kind of relational fact. Now relations are universals, and later we are going to give a similar account of relations to the one we have been giving of properties. But it seems as though we explain a property as being a potentiality for being in a certain kind of relation. If we go on to explain a relation also as a potentiality on the part of something for being in a certain kind of relation, it will seem that we have explained what universals in general are by reference to a rather special kind of universal, namely a special kind of relation.

Our account of universals probably does break down in the way suggested, if taken as an attempt to define the expression 'universal' in unquestion-begging terms. But if taken as a stimulus to realizing that there are universals, that we really know quite well what they are and that they are not all that mysterious, and as a stimulus to a steady sense of the unutterable difference of a (first-order) universal, a way in which one particular can be like another particular, and the particulars themselves, it seems to me that the assertion 'A universal – or at least a property – is a way in which one thing can be like another thing' is useful and illuminating.

The denial of universals does not always bring with it any explicit commitment to a Resemblance theory. Some philosophers deny universals without feeling the need to supply any alternative theory. They think that all such theories arise from a mistaken attempt to give an answer to the question: Why does a general term, such as 'red' or 'man', apply to many different things?

I suppose that some philosophers see the theory of universals as committing two errors, and the theory of resemblance as committing one. The common error is the belief that a sensible answer can be given to the question: Why do general terms apply to more than one thing? The error peculiar to the theory of universals is that every word is a proper name, or at least that the presumption must be in favour of its being such if it has a certain sort of 'complete' feel about it, as 'man' and perhaps 'red' have, but probably not 'but' or even 'if'.

J. L. Austin pressed the latter charge in an early article in which his scepticism had not yet extended to sensa, but in which universals were under attack. In the course of summarizing what he takes to be the sort of argument used by the Realist about universals he writes:

> It is assumed further, that we make a practice of calling many different sensa by the same name: we say 'This is grey' and 'That is grey', when the sensa denoted by 'this' and 'that' are not identical. And finally it is assumed that this practice is 'justifiable' or indispensable. Then we proceed to ask: How is such a practice possible? And answer:
> a) Since we use the same *name* in each case there must surely be some identical thing 'there' in each case: something of which the name is the name: something, therefore, which is 'common' to all sensa called by that name. Let this entity, whatever it may be, be called a 'universal'.[1]

---

[1] *Philosophical Papers* by J. L. Austin, p. 2. There are many other points made against universals in the same article, most of them beside the point so far as my defence of universals goes.

How far Austin's summary, both the part quoted and the rest, corresponds to any argument historically put forward in favour of universals I shall not discuss. Certainly he has chosen to attack a very feeble line of argument in favour of universals, yet this is the sort of reasoning found in most current attacks on universals.

Let us accept the point that we apply the same word to various different sensa, when we say such things as 'This is grey' and 'That is grey'. Is the question 'How is such a practice possible?' a sensible one?

Certainly it is a rather vague and peculiar question. When people appear to be doing something one does not normally ask how it is possible that they are doing it, unless antecedently one thought one knew of something which would make it impossible. What on earth should make one think it impossible to apply the same *word* to different things (which I think is a less question-begging phrase than calling different things by the same *name*)?

There seems no such antecedent impossibility. If I choose to call two people, or for that matter two sense-data, 'John', what is to stop me? If I choose to greet them both with the sound 'John', that is up to me.

However there is a more pertinent question than: '*How* is it possible to apply the same word to different things?', namely the question: '*Why* do I apply the same word to different things?' and another pertinent question, which is only vaguely to be differentiated from this last one, is: 'What am I doing when I apply the same word to different things?'

The proper answer to both these questions is that the nature of what I am doing is not always the same. There are at the very least two different types of case. One is represented by the fact that I greet two different men by the same word 'John', the other that I greet them both by the same word 'man'.

Surely the proper place to bring in universals is in answering the question: 'What is the nature of such activity in cases where the word "grey" is applied to two different things, and in such other cases as may be like this?' My answer briefly is this: that the mental activity which lies behind the various applications of 'grey' is the noticing a specific way in which the things to which the word is applied are each of them potentially like other things (such as the other things called 'grey') and that the utterance of the word in each case registers this mental activity of noticing. One way of making oneself aware that a mental activity of this sort is going on, is to contrast this kind of application of one word to many things with the kind of application of one word to many things which is made when the word is 'this' or 'John'. For in these latter cases noticing a way of resembling is conspicuous as not being what is expressed. (Certain qualifications would have to be made for 'John', but not for 'this'.)

I cannot see then that the charge made by Austin and by many other philosophers, that a belief in universals arises from an assimilation of all words to proper names (in the simply grammatical sense of that phrase) has any force against the support I have given to the existence of universals. In the first place I have not primarily introduced universals to explain something about language. I have simply drawn attention to the necessary truth that there are various ways in which one thing may resemble another thing. In the second place, in so far as I would make appeal to linguistic matters in supporting the existence of universals, it is not by assimilating adjectives and common nouns to proper names (in the grammatical sense) but by appeal to our sense of the difference between what lies behind our application of a proper name to two different things, and what lies behind our application of a common noun or an adjective to two different things. I have appealed to our sense of the difference between calling two things 'John' and calling two things 'grey'.

I should doubtless remark that I do later urge the fitness of describing adjectives and common nouns as *names* of universals. This is a technical usage which has much to recommend it. It does not in the least affect the point I am making now that the Realist does not in the least assimilate common nouns and adjectives to proper names, in a grammatical sense, and that his theory offers an explanation of the contrast, not an attempt to dismiss it.

What is to be said to the philosopher who objects that one is still asking an improper question when, instead of simply asking how one word can apply to various different things, one asks what distinguishes these two different ways in which one word can apply to various different things? I suspect that the main reason it is thought an improper question is that the available answers are thought improper. In that case I have defended the question in defending my answer. Above all, I would emphasize this. Though I shall talk of universals when I am discussing the meaning of words, I have not introduced universals as hypothetical entities useful for explaining certain features of language. I introduce them because the distinction between particular things and the ways in which one particular thing may be like another particular thing is a basic distinction which anyone who is going to talk carefully about a number of matters must make in one way or another. To contrast particulars and universals is to make the distinction most clearly.

4 FAMILY RESEMBLANCE AND OPEN TEXTURE

It seems to be assumed sometimes that the fact that some words apply to a variety of things linked by family resemblances rather than by a common feature somehow counts against the theory of universals. There seems little justification for this.

A set of objects is said to be connected by a system of family resemblances if each member is similar to various other members in certain respects, but there is no respect in which each member is similar to every other member. If a common predicate applies to them all, then there is no feature such that every object answering to that predicate must have it.

This is interesting, but the statement of it allows that there are things which are alike in a certain respect, or have a certain feature in common. What are these respects and features but the properties some think that talk of family resemblances disposes of? To talk of some of the things falling under a predicate having nothing in common, only makes sense if you allow that there are things in the world which do have something in common with each other.

Besides, in many cases, if we are prepared to talk of disjunctive properties, the difficulty in saying that there is a property named by a certain predicate disappears. While if a disjunctive property cannot be found to fill the bill, this is on account of 'open texture', something to which we shall turn shortly, not to family resemblance.

Actually, when family resemblances are spoken of, it is not usually so much particulars falling under a common predicate which are said to lack a common property, as universals falling under a common predicate.

The most familiar example is 'game'. We are told, perhaps, that there is nothing in common to cricket, ring-a-roses, and poker patience, or at least nothing which they do not share with various activities we would not describe as games. But this is not a list of *particulars*. If instead we take the words which, as I would say, name those universals which, without perhaps all sharing any common feature, all come under the heading 'game', then one will find that the particulars to which those words apply all have something in common in just the way in which the universals are said not to have. For there is, surely, something exclusively in common, quite a lot in fact, to all those particular event-sequences which are games of cricket. In fact, the word 'game' functions in two different ways. In one sense of the word the things which are games are particular event-sequences. Every game of cricket is a game in this sense. In the other sense, the things which are games are universals exemplified by things which are games in the first sense. In this sense cricket, rather than every game of cricket, is a game. The point about family resemblance can be made about 'game' in both senses, but it is clearer to distinguish between them.

The difficulty caused for a realist by the notion of open texture is much more serious. To say that a word has open texture is to say that cases may arise where nothing in our present use of the word determines whether it is applicable to something or not. Words for types of animal supply quite good examples, as does the word 'animal' itself.

Probably the correct way for a Realist to acknowledge the fact that certain words have open texture is to say that they do not name any one definite universal, but that they are in some rather looser relation to every one of a set of alternative but largely overlapping universals.

Could one say that they named indefinite universals? It is not altogether clear why not. There can, after all, in a sense, be indefinite particulars. May not a town have indefinite boundaries? But it is better to say that a thing, whether a particular or a universal, cannot be indefinite, and that indefiniteness belongs to reference, that is the reference of a word can be indefinite, so that it tends to refer to a lot of overlapping things rather than does refer to any one of them. Of an open texture word one may say then that there are in fact a variety of alternative but overlapping universals, of each of which it tends to be the name, rather than one of which it is the name.

So though the concept of open texture is important, it need not make us unhappy with an ontology countenancing universals.

5 RELATIONS

A property, we have said, is a way in which it is possible for one thing to be like another thing. The word 'green' stands for a specific way in which it is possible for one visual expanse to be like another visual expanse. At least that is what 'green' does when it stands for a sense-datum property. The physical-object property it stands for is somewhat different. If we take the view that a physical object is a group of sensed or unsensed sense-data, then 'green' as applied to physical objects still stands for a way in which one thing can resemble another, only the things in question are now groups (of a special kind) of sense-data. The way in which one such group must be capable of resembling another such group in order to be called 'green' lies in its having members which could resemble corresponding members of another group in various such ways as in being green in the sense-datal sense. Those sense-data from different physical object groups correspond which occupy the same position in the system of ideal relations the holding of which makes each group a physical object. It is simpler to concentrate the discussion of universals on sense-datum universals for the most part.

I have just made use of a device which will continue to be useful. Suppose that 'F' refers to some very broad category of individuals, that is, to some property such that we feel that the individuals which have it are a quite different kind of thing from individuals which lack it. Then an F-property is a property which is exemplifiable only by members of that category. We shall also use the expression 'F-relation' for relations which could only hold between Fs. F-properties and F-relations may be described jointly as 'F-universals'.

Let us now turn to relations. For what do 'above' or 'next' stand when they stand for sense-datum universals? Just as we can notice the greenness of a sense-datum A, so, it seems, we can notice the nextness or aboveness of two sense-data A and B.

We might say that nextness is a way in which one pair of sense-data may resemble another pair. We contemplate the pair of A and B and notice its potentiality for resembling other pairs in being a case of nextness.

But what is a pair? Is the pair of A and B to be distinguished from the total sense-datum which has as its exhaustive parts, A and

B, exhaustive in the sense that its every part is either a part of A, or a part of B, or has two parts, one of which is totally within A and the other of which is totally within B? Henceforth we shall call an object of which A and B are exhaustive parts, the aggregate of A and B.

If in noticing the aboveness of C to D I am noticing a property of the aggregate of C and D, then my noticing the aboveness of C to D cannot be distinguished from my noticing the aboveness of D to C, since this also would have been to notice a property, clearly the same property, of the aggregate of C and D – for clearly the aggregate of C and D is not to be distinguished from the aggregate of D and C.

Thus has been born the ordered pair. The aboveness of C and D is said to be a property of the ordered pair C D. The converse ordered pair D C does not have the property of aboveness, but the converse property, belowness.

It may seem pretty obvious, even in the case of nextness, that it is not really a property of the aggregate of the things in contact. For an aggregate object is likely to have many pairs of parts in contact with one another, and noticing the nextness of one pair is distinct from noticing the nextness of another pair. So nextness as well as aboveness must be a property of pairs but not of aggregates.

Yet it is pretty difficult to know what a pair of C and D is, if not the aggregate of C and D. The need for talking of ordered pairs makes things worse rather than better.

My suggestion is as follows: In noticing the aboveness of A to B, I am, after all, simply noticing a way in which the aggregate of A and B can resemble other things. But I am also aware that in order that one thing may resemble other things in this way, it must have two parts, each of which plays a special role in making it potentially like these other things. The role of A is different from that of B, the role of the former is that of the above object, the role of the latter that of the below object.

So a relation between two objects is a matter of their each playing a specific role in making their aggregate resemble other objects (aggregates) in a specific way. In order to express what one notices it is not enough simply to have words which indicate the kind of way in which their aggregate potentially resembles other aggregates. One's words must somehow indicate the role played by each object in producing this resemblance.

Our account has the advantage of not treating 'A is above B' and 'B is below A' as recording two different aspects of the situation noticed which somehow imply each other. What is noticed in either case is that A plays a special role, which may be called the above role, and B plays another special role, which may be called the below role, in making A + B (the aggregate of A and B = A + B) potentially like other things. We could make the order of 'A' and 'B' in the sentence irrelevant, by using a form like 'A + B is a case of *above: below*, with A as above in making it so, and B as below in making it so'. The order does not here have the significance which it does in 'A is above B'. Thus aboveness and belowness are not two distinct relations; they can only be contrasted as two different roles which particulars may play in letting the universal above-below be exemplified by their aggregate.

The remainder of this chapter introduces the reader to three subdivisions in the category of universals, which will be important in what follows. The subdivisions are as follows: (1) Syncategorematic properties, (2) Relational properties, (3) Individual properties.

6 SYNCATEGOREMATIC PROPERTIES

A term is an expression which can be applied to one or more objects by terminating either sentences of the form 'X is . . .' or sentences of the form 'X . . .' and thereby making assertions true or false, presuming 'X' to be a singular term referring to some actual object. Thus 'a man', 'is a man', 'green', 'was green', 'James', 'is James', 'was a windy day', 'going for a walk' 'lived here', 'not strain'd', are all terms, but 'if', 'very', 'slowly' are not. However, 'very' and 'slowly' differ from 'if' in that if placed before or after certain terms, e.g. 'rich', 'digging', 'ran', 'ran down the stairs', they constitute together with that term a new term. On these grounds 'very' and 'slowly' have been called 'syncategorematic terms', while 'if' does not even get that title.

A further restriction on the use of 'term' will bring with it an extension of the use of 'syncategorematic term'. Let us add: In order that an expression be a term it must be the case that if its substitution for the blank in 'X is . . .' or 'X . . .' yields an assertion with a definite truth-value, then it must remain an assertion with that same truth-value, whatever expression be substituted for 'X', provided only that the substituting expression refer to the same actual thing as 'X' did. Thus 'in London' remains a term, but 'brilliant', in one main sense of the word, does not. If 'this novelist' and 'this lecturer' refer to the same person 'this novelist is in London' and 'this lecturer is in London' cannot diverge in truth-value. But 'this novelist is brilliant' and 'this lecturer is brilliant' may so diverge. Expressions such as 'brilliant', which come out as terms on the account given in the first paragraph of this section, but are now excluded, are also to be called 'syncategorematic terms'.

An ontological distinction may be made roughly corresponding to this linguistic distinction.

A syncategorematic property is a property which a thing does not simply have, but which it has *qua* exemplifying some non-syncategorematic property. Slowness is a syncategorematic property. *Qua* changing colour an object may be slow, while *qua* changing positions it may not be slow.

Almostness is an interesting case. One might think that a thing which was almost F would be almost *qua* being F. But this cannot be how it is, since a thing which is almost F is not F. The difficulty can be avoided by saying that a thing which is almost F is almost *qua* having a certain similarity to F things (in virtue of their being F things) without being F. This is not to say that it is almost similar to F things without being F, for that would consist in its being almost *qua* similar to things which are similar to F things without being F. It is to be noted that the relevant sense of 'similar to F things' is one in which something could answer to this predicate though nothing whatever answers to the predicate 'F'. Otherwise one could not say of someone that he was almost a devil, without implying that something actually was a devil.

Syncategorematic properties are often named by adverbs. This may suggest what is true enough, that a syncategorematic property is a way in which a non-syncategorematic property may be exemplified. This may suggest in turn that really the relation between a property and itself syncategorematically qualified is really just that between determinate and determinable. Hence the relation between *moving* and *moving quickly* would be just the same as that between *red* and *pink*.

This appears to be wrong. One can indeed say that pink is a way of being red, but there is no syncategorematic property, S, such that just as a thing which is pink is red in the S way, so an object may be blue in the S way or may have some non-colour property in the S way. A syncategorematic property S must be such that objects may be S or non-S *qua* being F, and S or non-S *qua* H, where F and H are distinct properties.

A syncategorematic property S, might be of either of two types. It might be such that the same object could be S *qua* F and not-S *qua* G. Alternatively it might be such that one object could be S *qua* F and another object S *qua* G, but there could not be a single object with two properties *qua* one of which it was S and *qua* the other of which it was not-S.

Big and small may seem to be two obvious instances of being a syncategorematic property. X may be a small elephant and a big pet. A small F is, roughly, one that is smaller than most Fs. Thus smallness isn't really a way of being an F. 'Big' and 'small' are linguistically speaking syncategorematic terms, but do not really refer to things of the kind we call syncategorematic universals.

7 RELATIONAL PROPERTIES

The fact that an object stands in a certain relation to something, makes it potentially like other objects in certain ways which we may call 'relational properties'. Four types of relational property should be distinguished:

(1) If object A is in relation R to B, it has the property: being R to B. Other things may or may not be in this relation R to B. Being the son of Jeremiah Bentham (1712–92) is a property shared by Jeremy and Samuel Bentham, and not by me or the reader.

(2) If object A is in relation R to B, it has the property: being R to something. Being the son of someone (something) is a property shared by Jeremy and Samuel Bentham, the reader if male, and myself, but not by any girl or any table.

(3) If object A is in relation R to B, and B has property F, then A has the property: being R to something F. Being the son of a lawyer is a property shared by Jeremy Bentham and my cousin Joe, but not by me or perhaps the reader.

(4) By F in the previous paragraph I understood a property which is not essentially individual, that is not a property which at most one thing could possibly have, such as being the highest mountain on earth, or being the only man. Relational properties of

our fourth type consist in being in a certain relation to something with an essentially individual property. *Being R to the one and only F* would be such a property.

Although (4) is liable to confusion with (1) it is really more like (3). Both are a matter of being related to something with such and such a property or properties.

Somewhat artificially, we could treat all cases of (3) and (4) as cases of (2). For a property of the relatum can always be, so to speak, built into the relation. Being a nephew of someone belongs to type (2), being a nephew of a woman belongs to type (3). But if we had the expressions 'nephele' and 'nepheme', so used that a woman's nephews were called 'napheles' and a man's nephews 'nephemes', then we could call being a nephele of someone a type (2) property.

Just as type (4) can be pushed into type (3), type (3) can be pushed into type (2). Thus the real contrast lies between those of type (1) and the rest. We shall distinguish type (1) as 'particular-based relational properties' and types (2) to (4) as 'variable-based relational properties'. Thus Being a son of the present Queen of England is a variable-based relational property, while Being a son of *her* would be particular-based, if 'her' was really a logically proper name (which however it never really is). If one has cause to talk of the relations a thing (whether a particular, universal or fact) has to things other than particulars, type (1) relational properties will need the following subdivisions.

The expression 'R to F' where 'F' names a particular, universal, or fact will itself represent a particular-based, universal-based, or fact-based universal. (The same goes, we may say for future reference, if 'F' *represents* a universal or *completely represents* a fact, as opposed to naming it. The sense of 'represent' in question will be explained in Chapter VII.) If 'F' is only the definite or indefinite description of a particular, universal or fact (and not one which, in the sense to be explained in Chapter VII, *represents* a universal or *completely represents* a fact) then the expression 'R to F' represents a variable-based relational property, either a particular-variable-based, or a universal-variable-based, or a fact-variable-based relational property.

A final point to notice is this: Among the relations which a thing may stand in to various things is the whole-part relation. Those relational properties of a thing which are a matter of its having a certain part or parts, or having a part or parts of a certain kind, or in a certain relation to each other or itself, and which include no element of relation to something outside itself, stand rather apart from what one usually thinks of as a thing's relational properties, and really need to be distinguished from the rest. We may call them intrinsic relational properties, and call other relational properties, extrinsic relational properties. Very often when one talks of a thing's relational properties one means only its extrinsic relational properties. It will be convenient to mark this distinction, which is that often intended when a thing's relational properties are contrasted with its nonrelational properties by the expression 'intrinsic' property and 'extrinsic' property. The intrinsic properties of a thing, then, are its non-relational properties together with its intrinsic relational properties. Its extrinsic properties are its extrinsic relational properties. The intrinsic nature of a thing is the compound of all its intrinsic properties, or to avoid a certain difficulty, we may say that it is an intrinsic property of it sufficiently complex to entail all its other intrinsic properties and no other of its properties.

It follows from these definitions that no two things with parts could have the same intrinsic nature. For they would be bound to have different particular-based intrinsic relational properties. It may be as well then to introduce also the notion of a general intrinsic property. This will be an intrinsic property which is not a *particular*-based relational property. The general intrinsic nature of a thing will be the compound of all its general intrinsic properties, or a general intrinsic property of it sufficiently complex to entail all its other general intrinsic properties.

These uses of the phrases 'intrinsic' and 'extrinsic' have no connections with the notions of contingency and necessity.

8 INDIVIDUAL PROPERTIES

It is necessary to say something more about individual properties.

An essentially individual property is a (logically possible) property such that it is logically impossible that two or more things should have it. A contingently individual property is one which is not essentially individual but which, as a matter of fact, only one individual possesses. Necessarily, a contingently individual property is exemplified. Not so an essentially individual property. Consider, for example, being the only man. We shall constantly use 'individual property' as shorthand for 'essentially individual property'.

Our account of properties as being ways in which one thing can be like another thing may seem to render the notion of essentially individual properties impossible, as also the notion of logically impossible properties.

It is to be noted that logically impossible properties are not such that their existence is impossible but such that their exemplification is impossible. Their existence must be acknowledged. Just as 'Unicorns do not exist' is about unexemplified properties, so 'Round squares cannot exist' is about logically impossible properties. Yet one can hardly say of these latter that they are ways in which one thing could be like another.

Perhaps one may say that they are ways in which one thing could not resemble another. One must distinguish here between not being a way in which one thing can resemble another, and being a way in which one thing cannot resemble another. Particulars and impossible properties answer to the first description, but only impossible properties to the second.

With regard to essentially individual properties, it is perhaps impossible, in the last resort, to recognize most of them as having a proper ontological status, since the utterances which ascribe them implicitly include a negation symbol which in the end we shall have to regard as expressing an attitude of rejection directed towards a certain proposition, or objective as we shall say, rather than as symbolising an element in the objective. To say that X is the highest mountain is to express rejection of there being a mountain higher than it, not acceptance of anything.

The point about negation will be made more clearly later in this book. All that need be said now is that even though individual properties, and hence also type (4) relational properties, are not really genuine entities, it is highly convenient to talk of them, and we shall do so throughout this book. The points we make in terms of them will be translatable into whatever language a proper view of negation will finally indicate as ontologically more proper. (The same applies, indeed, to relational properties in general.)

This doubtfulness about the status of essentially individual properties does not, it should be noted, carry over to negative properties, such as non-F-ness. The non-F-ness of a thing may be a fact. What may perhaps not be a fact is the non-F-ness of all things other than a given thing.

9 COMPLEX AND SIMPLE UNIVERSALS; NATURAL AND ARTIFICIAL UNIVERSALS

Traditionally a distinction has been drawn between simple and complex properties. We shall not make very much use of this distinction, but it is as well to give it some consideration. We shall also formulate a to some extent related distinction between natural and artificial universals.

A distinction needs to be drawn first between compound and complex properties (cf. McTaggart's *The Nature of Existence*, §63).

A compound property is one which consists in the conjunction of two properties (which may themselves be compound). Thus being round and red is a compound property. Any two properties which are coexemplifiable form together a possible compound property. We must also admit the existence of impossible compound properties, such as being F and G, where F and G are incompatible. For how else can one say of such a property that it cannot be exemplified? It is no way of avoiding this difficulty to say that it is the description 'being the compound of F and G' which does not apply, for then one is only shifting the ground to an impossible universal-universal and saying that this is not exemplified in any universal. But an impossible universal-universal is no better than an impossible particular-universal.

Before we go on to discuss complex properties it may be as well to consider negative properties. Is there such a thing not only as roundness or horsiness, but also as non-roundness and non-horsiness?

It is, surely, just as much a feature of the world that some things are not like other things in being horses as that some other things are like other things in being horses. But is this to say that these first things are like each other in not being horses? I find it difficult not to say this. If there are two things which are incapable of resembling other things in a certain way, this very incapacity is a way in which they are like each other. This is what I call a negative property, and negative relations can be explained in a similar way.

It is best to approach complex properties via linguistic considerations. A linguistic predicate is explicitly complex if and only if its meaning is the result of its consisting of meaningful parts put together in some meaningful way. A predicate is implicitly complex if, although not explicitly complex, it is equivalent in meaning to some explicitly complex predicate, and if its meaning is better grasped by someone who realizes that it is equivalent to this explicitly complex predicate than by someone who does not. This last point is a bit vague, but it is intended to serve to stop 'green' being called complex because it is equivalent to 'green in London or green out of London'.

A complex universal is one which can only be specified by a predicate which is complex, explicitly or implicitly. A simple universal is one which is neither compound nor complex.

Compound universals are all complex, but the converse does not hold. Being the highest mountain on earth (if we allow it for the present) is not compound, but it is complex. Negative universals are indeed complex, without being compound. Many familiar universals are doubtless compounds of complex universals, or compounds of complex and compound universals. Probably being a horse is a compound of complex universals.

Does every complex (implicitly or explicitly) predicate specify a genuine complex universal? Or are there cases where although the predicate is meaningful, it does not specify any such universal?

In answering this question I want to put aside considerations arising from the open texture of some predicates. For what happens in such cases, is that there is a range of universals – which perhaps we lack the experience to distinguish between – each of which the predicate could equally be said to specify. For purposes of this question, let us just presume that God has determined that one member of this range is to be the one the predicate is to be considered as specifying.

Considerations arising from the fact that some predicates operate on the basis of family resemblances should not be put aside however. For if open texture is eliminated, a family resemblance predicate will in effect always be nothing more mysterious than a highly complex predicate. It may be equivalent, for instance, to something like 'having at least three of these ten properties A, B, C, D, E, F, G, H, I, J'. If we put 'a few' instead of 'three' then we would have open texture as well, but we are supposing open texture eliminated by act of God.

So does every complex predicate specify a universal?

I shall say that some specify natural universals and some only artificial universals.

The criterion of a natural universal can be formulated in the following recursive fashion.

Definitions:

Simple properties and negations of simple properties are called elementary properties.

Simple relations and negations of simple relations are called elementary relations.

Compounds of elementary properties are called element-compound properties.

Compounds of elementary relations are called element-compound relations.

Conditions of natural universalhood:

(1) An elementary property is a natural universal and property.

(2) A compound of natural properties is a natural property.

(3) An elementary relation is a natural universal, and a natural relation.

(4) A compound of natural relations is a natural universal, and a natural relation.

(5) Being in a natural relation to something is a natural universal. (Relational property type (2)).

(6) Being in a natural relation to something which has a natural property is a natural universal. (Relational properties type (3)).

(7) Being in a natural relation to a definite (named) particular is a natural universal. (Type (1) relational property.)

Later we shall be discussing the distinction between real and ideal relations. It is as well to note here that many ideal relations which are not disjunctive in character may be classed as simple relations for purposes of this definition. A syncategorematic relation, whether ideal or not, may be simple. The same goes indeed for some syncategorematic properties.

The intention of the distinction is to point a contrast between groupings of particulars which rest on real resemblances between them, and groupings which bring quite dissimilar things together for some special purpose. It is hard to deny that whereas there is a real resemblance between any two green things and between any two horses (which does not hold between any green and any non-green thing, or between any horse and any non-horse) there is not a real resemblance between any two red-or-green things or between any two horse-or-trees (which does not hold between a red-or-green thing and a neither-red-nor-green thing or between any horse-or-tree and any neither-horse-nor-tree).

It may be said that the real question is: What are the simple universals? or, What are the marks of a simple universal? But though this question is important, I think what I have already said makes a worth while point. It tells us that granted F is a real respect in which two things may resemble, and that G is also, then Being F and G is to be regarded as a real respect of resemblance, while F or G will not be so regardable, and tells us further things of the same sort. This seems to me to be good sense.

It may be as well to say the following about simple universals.

When noticing that two things are similar in a certain way, one may not realize that this way in which they are alike could be distinguished, if someone taught you how to do it, into two or more different ways in which they are alike. Or one may be sure that it is thus distinguishable, but not be able to specify the separate ingredients. One would perhaps be rash ever to assume that a way of resembling one notices is not breakable down in this way, but if one cannot break it down one may treat it as an un-analysable basic way of resembling.

It does not matter much that one does not know whether a way of resembling can be broken down in this way or not, for one can decide to treat it as simple and unanalysable until such time as one has reason to do otherwise. A certain relativity in one's notion of simplicity is quite in order. Thus one can treat the way in which one horse is similar to another as simple, even though it is really analysable – apart from the matter of open texture. By treating it as simple, I mean that one can take it on trust as a natural universal, without showing that it is analysable into simple universals in the approved manner. However, in treating a universal as simple, without really claiming it to be so, one must at least have a hunch that if it is analysable into more basic universals, it will be an analysis of the approved type, and will not involve such dis-junctive aspects as would make it an artificial universal. Can this claim safely be made for such universals as Being a horse? I am inclined to think that it can be made for the universal Being a whole and undeformed horse in present constitution, but not perhaps for Being a horse.

If this is so, then it must be allowed that 'horse' does not specify a natural universal in quite as simple a way as one might suppose. All the same there is a natural universal to which it is closely related, a compound of a whole lot of natural properties, each of which what we call a horse usually has, and such that anything describable as a horse will have 'most of'.

I say 'in present constitution' in case anyone thinks that ancestry has something to do with whether an object is actually a horse.

It must be remembered that the point of open texture is being allowed for independently of this discussion. It must also be realized that in denying that a natural property can have disjunctive properties among its components, or be disjunctive, I am not saying that it cannot have determinable properties among its components, or be determinable. Both it and its components normally will be determinable. But a determinable such as *red* is not a *disjunctive* property.

Having allowed that it is over simple to say that there is a natural property which we recognize in every horse, we can still insist that when I identify something as answering to the word 'horse' it is still always because I notice a compound natural property which the thing has. Where it is a whole and undeformed horse the natural property I notice is likely to contain more elements than where it is maimed or deformed, or where indeed it is seen at a distance. So there are a series of different though overlapping compound properties which evoke the word 'horse' in me.

A word should perhaps be added on a distinction which I might be thought to have been making with the phrases 'artificial' and 'natural' universals. To avoid confusion I shall talk about artificial and natural *concepts* in discussing this latter distinction.

It might be said that the concept of a tree or a horse or an atom is a natural concept, and the concept of a table or a Prime Minister is an artificial one. The distinction here is not so much the very simple one that things falling under the latter concepts are made (or elected) by men, or at least only satisfy the concept as a result of human activity, while those which fall under the previous concepts are neither made by men nor made to fall under the concepts by men. For if man learns to make trees the concept of tree would remain a natural concept in the sense I have in mind.

The distinction is rather this. In applying one type of concept, one is saying something about what the thing is like in itself, or what relations it is in to other things, exclusive of purposes.

This is a different distinction from ours. On the face of it, it could be an entirely natural property of a thing that it was designed for such and such a purpose. It would, of course, be a relational property, doubtless a highly complex one, but it need not contain disjunctive elements, nor perhaps anything else making it artificial in our sense. That two things were designed for sitting on may be a matter of a specific kind of natural resemblance between two world-chunks and of the corresponding roles played by each of them in making the world-chunks of which each is a part fitted to resemble another such world-chunk in the relevant way.

III

FACTS

When I notice the redness of your tie and also notice the redness of my tie, I am noticing the same property. Redness is the way in which the ties resemble each other, not two things, one in each tie, which are more or less alike. Since the redness of my tie is the same individual as the redness of your tie, it would seem to follow that if I notice the redness of your tie I at the same time notice the redness of my tie.

This we can accept as true, if the expression 'the redness of your tie' is understood in a particular way. But it is clear that the expression can also be understood in such a way that 'I notice the redness of your tie' does not entail 'I notice the redness of my tie', nor does it even entail it in conjunction with 'My tie is red'. It seems that we must distinguish between the property of redness which your tie has, which is identical with the property redness which my tie has, and redness-as-a-property-of-your-tie which is not identical with redness-as-a-property-of-my-tie.

Should someone say that the redness of your tie is not a different thing from the redness of my tie, and that what we are confusedly saying is that the fact that your tie is red is a different fact from the fact that my tie is red, I should agree, provided the charge of confusion is dropped. We have the property redness, and we have the particulars A and B, but we also have, or may have, the distinct individuals, the redness of A and the redness of B. These two latter individuals may with equal appropriateness be called 'particularized universals' or 'facts'.

An objector might suggest that the redness of this and the redness of that are the same individual, the divergence being simply in the connotation of the expressions denoting it. The phrases are connected as are the phrases 'A's father' and 'B's father', where A and B are brothers. But if he insists that no other way of interpreting the expressions is required, he ignores the fact that it makes sense to say that the redness of this and the redness of that diverge in properties, as for instance they will do if one has political significance and the other does not, or even if one has been noticed by someone and the other has not.

If one takes particulars and universals seriously, but does not so take facts, it seems that one puts particulars and universals apart in two different realms and provides no way for them to meet.[1] I experience particular A and I experience particular B; I also notice properties F and G. If we talk only of particulars and universals, we cannot distinguish between noticing the F-ness of A and the G-ness of B and noticing the G-ness of A and the F-ness of B. But clearly these must be distinguished.

Two things are to be noted concerning facts thus understood. First, a fact cannot be identified with a truth, if the latter is something quite on a level with a falsehood. That a fact is not a true sentence or assertion should be obvious. But it needs to be said also that a fact is not a true proposition. Propositions are supposed to form a class of entities, some of which are true and others of which are false, and the false ones are supposed to have quite as good an ontological status as the true ones. One cannot say that truth and falsehood are comparable to existence and nonexistence, being and nonbeing. With facts it is otherwise. If there is such a fact as the greenness of *this*, then there is no such fact as the redness of *this*. It isn't that the greenness of this has a certain property (e.g., enters into certain relations with other things) and that the redness of this has a certain contrary property. It is simply that there is such a fact as the greenness of this, and that there is no such fact as the redness of this. If one wishes to say that 'the redness of this' does refer to a fact, one must recognize that this can only be so in the sense in which 'My pet unicorn' refers to an animal.

It is sometimes supposed that the only reason why facts are not to be called 'true' or 'false', is that the notion of fact incorporates

[1] Cf. R. Grossmann, *The Structure of Mind*, pp. 66–82. It may be noted that our facts and particularized universals are not at all things of the sort Grossmann calls perfect particulars, though these also are referred to by such phrases as 'the redness of this'.

that of truth already. This is not the reason why what I call facts cannot be classified as true or false. There is not something, which if it is true is a fact, and if it is false is something else on the same level.

The key to our use of the word 'fact' is that a fact, in our sense, is the exemplification of a property by a particular, or of a two-place relation by two particulars, or of an n-place relation by n particulars, and that this is to say the same as that it is a property of something, or a relation between things, in a sense wherein a property of one thing cannot be a property of another thing, and a relation between certain things cannot be the same thing as a relation between certain other things.

There is a certain misunderstanding to which some of what I have said is perhaps liable. I talked of the redness of your tie being different from the redness of my tie. Now what might be meant by saying this is that the determinate version of redness exemplified by your tie was not the same determinate version of redness as that exemplified by my tie. Yours might be scarlet, mine pink. This is not what I have in mind, however. For even if both ties exemplified exactly the same completely determinate version of redness, I would want to point out that in a sense the redness of one is not the redness of the other, the being red of the one is not the being red of the other. Moreover, let 'red$_1$' be the name for the completely determinate version of redness in question. Then not only is the being red of the one not the being red of the other, but the being red$_1$ of the one is not the being red$_1$ of the other. This has nothing to do with any claim that no two things are of exactly the same colour.

It may be admitted that it would be a further quite natural use of the phrase 'the redness of this' to mean 'that completely determinate version of redness which this exemplifies'. But such a use of phrases of this form is one we shall avoid in this book.

In the previous chapter we talked of noticing properties 'in' particulars, and said that this consists in noticing a way in which the particulars in question could be like other particulars. In this chapter we have pointed out that noticing the redness of this does not entail noticing the redness of that (another red thing) and have suggested that noticing the redness of this is noticing a fact, or a particularized universal, rather than a universal. Thus it seems that we have to substitute noticing facts for noticing properties.

Does this mean that we cannot properly talk of noticing universals after all?

I think one must admit that there are not two mental acts, noticing a property and noticing a fact. To notice a property is to notice a fact and vice versa.[1] The difficulty is that a property has to play two roles. It is something which is common to *this* and to other things. But it, or something closely related to it, is also the peculiar possession of *this*.

To notice that this is green, to notice the greenness of this, is to notice a potentiality in this for resembling other things in a certain way. One might say that the property is this way of resembling, while the fact is the potentiality of *this* for resembling in that kind of way, and that the one mental act which is the noticing of the greenness of this involves both being aware of this way of resembling in its own right, and being aware of it as something which this particular object has the potentiality for.

A last point requires to be made about such phrases as 'particularized property' and 'particularized quality'. Some philosophers seem to use the phrase 'particularized quality' to refer to particulars of a special type. This seems to be true at least of Professor Strawson in the footnote on p. 169 of *Individuals*, where he takes the subjects of 'His anger cooled rapidly', 'His cold is more severe than hers', and 'The wisdom of Socrates is preserved for us by Plato' as referring to particularized universals. I do not mean that I think it obvious that these phrases refer to particulars, but that Professor Strawson makes it plain that he thinks so. If they are particulars, they cannot, of course, be particularized universals in our sense.

There is no doubt that a phrase such as 'His smile' can refer to a fact, in my sense of this last word. It will do so wherever it is replaceable by 'His smiling'. For instance, 'His smile caused

1 Perhaps the Platonic doctrine of *universalia ante rem* amounts in part to the claim that universals can be noticed other than in particulars. I am not clear what sense can be attached to such a claim. On the other hand I would support the doctrine of *universalia ante rem* as against the doctrine of *universalia in rebus* in the claim that to say that there is a universal of a certain kind does not imply that that universal is exemplified. My reasons for doing so should be clear if I point out that there is a property named by 'Being a king of France in 1960' and even 'Being a round square' and that if there were not 'There is no king of France in 1960' and 'There are no round squares' would both lack meaning.

surprise' and 'His smiling caused surprise' are interchangeable, and the subject expressions both refer to the same fact. But if one says 'His smile was broad' one cannot replace 'His smile' by 'His smiling'. In this case 'His smile' would seem to refer to a particular of some kind, and hence not to what I call a particularized universal.

But what sort of particular is a smile in this sense?

Strawson seems to think that smiles as particulars arise in a certain manner from a certain universal being exemplified by people or animals, as opposed to by smiles. For this reason they can be regarded as dependent upon those particulars known as people or animals. That this man smiled gives rise to a certain particular which can be called his smile.

It is not quite clear to me that smiles are dependent upon people or animals in this way. Couldn't the smile have come before the Cheshire cat? But even if they are dependent, it may be that they are simply dependent in the way in which full backs are dependent upon soccer teams, which does not seem as fundamental as what Strawson requires, for though a particular's being a full back is dependent upon something else's being a soccer team, it is inappropriate to say that the particular which is a full back is dependent on the soccer team. Full-backs are particulars, but being a full-back is a complicated relational property which therefore a particular cannot have unless it is appropriately disposed towards other particulars. Similarly, perhaps, a pair of lips, which is a particular, is a smile as long as it has a certain shape and stands in a certain relation to the rest of a face. Or rather, the pair of lips will not be the smile, for that is something which will endure when the smile is gone, but a brief temporal phase of the pair of lips will be the smile, and this phase itself is a particular – a particular of a kind the word 'event' is sometimes used for.

In general, I would say that such expressions as 'John's smile', 'John's death', 'John's anger', 'John's wedding' may refer to things of two different kinds. Sometimes they refer to facts, that is to particularized universals in my sense, but not in Strawson's for they do not refer to particulars. Sometimes, however, they refer rather to events, where by an event I mean either a temporal phase of some standard enduring particular (or of a part of it) or an aggregate of simultaneous and spatially contiguous such phases. Events thus understood are genuine particulars, for the parts and temporal phases of a particular must themselves be particulars.

2 THE EXEMPLIFICATION REGRESS

In a discussion of Facts it seems appropriate to say something on the problem as to whether Exemplification, which seems in some way to be an element in facts, is to count as a relation. If it does, a vicious regress seems to arise, but if it does not, its status appears problematic. This problem is related both to Bradley's argument against the reality of relations, and to Frege's distinction between saturated and unsaturated entities.

One is inclined to say that Exemplification is a relation which a particular may stand in to a property, and that Exemplification of . . . with respect to – is a three-place relation which a particular may stand in to a relation and a particular. The fact that A is red, thus becomes the fact that A exemplifies redness, and this becomes the fact that A exemplifies exemplification with respect to redness, and so on. This is felt to be vicious.

We deal with this as follows. Every fact has a certain structure. This structure is given to us when we consider that different elements in the fact play different roles in that fact. In the fact which is the redness of A, the particular A plays the role of thing exemplifying, and the universal redness plays the role of thing exemplified. There are just these two roles in the fact and it has two elements, one playing each role. In the fact of A's aboveness to B, there are three roles. Aboveness plays the role of thing exemplified. Being the relation it is, any fact in which it occurs in the role of thing exemplified will have two other roles to be played, the role of thing above and the role of thing below. A plays the above role, B plays the below role. The fact has three roles and three elements, one to play each role. In general, connected with each n-place non-symmetrical relation there will be n distinctive roles to be played by other elements in any fact in which that relation plays the role of thing exemplified. The nature of these roles may be said to be determined by the relation.

A possible addendum to this account is as follows. To talk of exemplification as a relation is not incorrect, though it is not a relation which occurs in such facts as that of A's redness and A's being above B. Parasitic on the fact in which A plays the exemplifying role and redness plays the exemplified role is another fact in which exemplification plays the role of relation exemplified, and the two other roles determined by this relation are played, one of them by A and the other by redness. The regress here would not be vicious. The basic fact would be the fact with just two roles and just two elements, A and redness. The fact with three roles and all the further facts would arise from this original fact, would be based on it, rather than it on them. So there would be nothing vicious in this regress. One could then say that A does stand in the relation of exemplification to redness, but that this relational fact is not the one which 'A is red' represents, but simply a fact the existence of which is implied by it. Thus there really is a relation of exemplification which can be discussed (cf. McTaggart, *The Nature of Existence*. Chapter IX, section 88).

There is, however, another way of putting the whole matter which is for a number of reasons more satisfactory. A fact such as A's redness is in a certain relation to A and in a certain relation to redness. The first relation is that of fact to the thing playing the exemplifying role in it. We may call it the fact-subject relation, though it must not be thought of as a grammatical relation between linguistic items. The second relation is that of fact to the thing playing the exemplified role in it. We may call this the fact-predicate relation. When one talks about A and redness being in the exemplifying relation one to another one is adverting to the fact that A's redness is in the fact-subject relation to one and the fact-predicate relation to the other. This is a higher order fact than A's redness, a fact in which A's redness plays one of the subject roles, and in which A and redness play the other two subject roles. There are a whole series of such higher order facts but none of them contains a relation called exemplification as an element. Similar, but more complicated remarks apply with regard to relational facts. The fact of A's being above B is related to aboveness as fact to predicate, to A as fact to *above* subject and to B as fact to *below* subject. These latter two relations, of course, only hold between facts and particulars if the facts are in the subject-predicate relation to aboveness — but the same *sort* of thing will be true of all relational facts.

3. PROPERTIES OF UNIVERSALS AND OF FACTS

Do universals have properties? It seems difficult to deny that they do. Surely there are various different ways in which one universal can be like another universal. For example, redness and roundness are alike each other in being one-place universals, and nextness differs from them both in not being so. A property may have the property of being a visual property or of being a tactile property. One could not indeed say anything about properties if they did not have properties. Moreover if properties did not have properties there could be no meaning in asserting that *there are* properties or are properties of certain kinds, if we take the view (deriving from Russell) that to say 'There are Fs' is to say that F-ness is exemplified and that to say that a certain single thing exists is to say that a certain individual property is exemplified.

We may note in passing as an implication of this view about existential propositions (which we accept) that the sentence 'Blueness exists' is meaningless unless 'Blueness' is equivalent to some definite description. Now certainly 'Blueness' and 'blue' are not in most such occurrences so equivalent. One might suggest that if 'Blueness exists' is used meaningfully it probably means 'The property named by "Blue" exists' and hence means 'The property of being named by "Blue" is exemplified'. But certainly 'Blueness' and 'Blue' are not normally equivalent to 'The property named by "Blue" '.

But if 'Blueness exists' is, in the most typical sense of 'Blueness', meaningless, there certainly are sentences to the effect that there are universals of certain kinds which appear to be meaningful and true.[1] Examples are many, but let us consider 'There are nonsymmetrical relations'. To what sentence of the form 'F-ness is exemplified' could this be equivalent? Presumably to 'Being a non-symmetrical relation is exemplified'. But if there are exemplifiers of Being a nonsymmetrical relation then clearly these exemplifiers are universals with this property, which establishes the point that universals may have properties.

An attempt might be made to deny this conclusion by saying that a sentence of the type 'There are f-type universals' means '(Some) f-type universals are exemplified'. However this would be to give 'There is' statements a completely different logic when it is universals which there are said to be, and when it is particulars which there are said to be, and there seems little justification for this. Moreover, it leads into self-contradiction if

[1] There are also false ones, of course. 'There is a colour which is shared by your tie and by mine' may be false. This example also brings out the point that statements concerning the existence of universals may be contingent.

one continues to say (as one must, for if one asks whether there are any universals satisfying a certain condition one does not necessarily mean 'any exemplified universal'), 'There are universals which are not exemplified'. On this theory one would have to take this as meaning '(Some) universals which are not exemplified are exemplified'.

So we must grant that there are universal-universals, that is universals exemplifiable, if at all, only by universals. Similar reasons should make us grant that there are universal-universal-universals, and so on; also that there are fact-universals.

This much granted, it can hardly be denied that among, say, the properties of redness is that of being exemplified by this pillar box. After all, here is a way in which redness may resemble certain other properties. There is a certain shape-property, for instance, which it resembles in this way. Following the suggestion of the last section we may say that the property possessed by redness of being exemplified by A is really to be identified with the relational property of being related to the fact of A's redness by the predicate-fact relation.

4 CONTINGENT, ESSENTIAL, AND QUINTESSENTIAL PROPERTIES

Once granted that properties have properties it is important to emphasize the distinction between the essential and the contingent properties of a property. Redness has the property of being a colour and the relational property of being more like brownness than blueness is, and it could not have been without these properties without, as one quite absurdly puts it, having failed to be itself. It also has such properties as that of being referred to by the word 'red', being exemplified by something, being exemplified by something round, being exemplified by A. These properties it might easily have been without, and they are called its 'contingent properties'.

No such distinction can be made between the properties of a particular. It is not that all the properties of a particular belong to one of these types; it is simply that no such distinction is to be made at all. It would be quite wrong, for instance, to take this as implying that all the properties of a particular belong to it only contingently. One can, of course, take a subclass of its total properties, which one chooses to call for some purpose or other its essential properties, dividing the remainder of its properties into essential and contingent according as they are or are not entailed by these. But since calling the original properties essential is relative to some such specific purpose, such a distinction is altogether different from that with regard to the properties of properties.

A further distinction of some interest needs to be made within the properties of a property, that between its quintessential property and its essential but not quintessential properties. The quintessential property of a property serves to specify utterly and completely what it is. Consider the property of being red and round. It is the quintessential property of this property that it is the conjunct of redness and roundness.

Unanalysable properties do not have a quintessential property. Being red is not a matter of being this and that, or either this or that, or anything of that sort. It is not to be equated merely with the disjunction of all its absolute determinates. For in saying of one of these determinates of red that it is such a determinate one is not just saying that it is one of the disjuncts of the disjunction of itself together with certain other properties. Such a disjunction would have a unity based on the fact that all its disjuncts were determinates of red, so that their being such determinates could not be a matter of their being disjuncts in the disjunction. Even if I am wrong in thinking red unanalysable the lack of a quintessential property will characterize any unanalysable properties which there are.

The essential properties of a complex property, i.e., one with a quintessential property, are that quintessential property and all those properties which are entailed by it. Clearly the essential properties of an unanalysable property cannot be thus explained.

The properties of relations can be distinguished into quintessential, essential and contingent, in just the same way, and unanalysable relations will not have quintessential properties.

It can readily be seen that every *fact* has a quintessential property, and essential properties following therefrom. Also, of course, it has contingent properties. The quintessential property of the fact of A's redness is the property of containing A in the exemplifying role and redness in the exemplified role. A contingent property of it might be that it was the ultimate ground of the truth of an utterance made at a particular time.

We have said that the properties of a particular do not divide into the essential and the contingent. This does not mean, however, that the distinction between internal and external relations has no point. It is a genuine distinction if interpreted thus: Suppose it is a fact that A is R to B. Then R is internal to its terms if and only if A's being R to B follows logically from two facts of the types A's being F and B's being G, where F and G are completely non-relational properties. Otherwise it is external. A better term for 'internal' here is 'ideal', and for 'external', 'real'. (These terms are derived from Meinong, but not perhaps given quite the same definition.) Similarity can be an ideal relation, while nextness will always be real. This distinction is one we shall have cause to consider in some detail later.

IV

THE EXPERIENCE OF
NOTICING A UNIVERSAL

I may notice the exemplification of a universal by a material thing, or I may notice the exemplification of a universal by a sense-datum. The former is a more complex affair than the latter, though in fact the latter normally only occurs as an element in the former. Noticing the exemplification of a universal by a material thing involves noticing some character of a given sense-datum and having a belief that a material thing of a certain character is present. Believing is the subject of Part Three of this book. In this chapter, therefore, we shall confine ourselves to the more elementary phenomenon of noticing some characteristic of a sense-datum, or of some other immediately experienced object, or of an experience, and the phrase 'noticing a universal' will refer to this phenomenon alone. Without some such discussion of at least this most elementary sort of noticing of universals our discussion of universals would be left disconnected too long from any discussion of our mental relation to them. This chapter also supplements our discussion of the sensing of sense-data in Chapter II, section 3.

If I experience a scarlet sense-datum, I may or may not notice its redness, I may or may not notice its scarletness. These two alternatives are independent of each other. Thus noticing a property in a sense-datum is something quite different from experiencing a sense-datum with that property. So we may put the question: Granted I am experiencing a red datum what more is required in order that I notice its redness?

It is difficult to see what answer can be given other than

something along the following lines. My noticing the property F in a datum of mine consists in my having another experience with some property G, where this property G is such that I tend to have an experience of kind G when I have an experience of kind F, and never have G experiences at other times (apart from certain special cases to be mentioned later).[1]

Some philosophers would be inclined to say that noticing a property in a sense-datum can only be a matter of directing the right word at it.

Our account can allow this as a special case. The kind of experience G which goes along with the kind of experience F and constitutes my recognition of it may be that kind of experience which one has in uttering to oneself a token of the word 'green'.

But our account allows also for non-verbal noticing or recognizing. If feeling states of a certain kind are evoked by red sense-data and not by others, the occurrence of a feeling state of that kind may constitute one's recognition of redness. It seems to me that I notice many facts about my sense-data on which I offer no *verbal* comment.

It may be suggested that the noticing a certain kind of sense-datum may consist in a distinctive type of behaviour regularly evoked by data of that kind.

In considering this suggestion one must distinguish between physical activity and the experience of physical activity. An action, typically, has the following elements: a set of physical events of a certain character, the occurrence in the agent's experience of sense-data belonging to these events, a realization on the part of the agent that physical events of this character are going on (involving his body) and perhaps some sort of acquiescence in these goings on. The effects of these physical events which are to follow may be the main character of them which serves to determine what action is being done. The physical events themselves I call the physical performance. The sense-data (together perhaps with certain emotional feelings) are what we call the experience of the act, and must not be confused with the belief or knowledge states which constitute the agent's awareness of what is going on, though they will of course be important prompters to this awareness.

[1] See p. 233.

It may be remarked in passing that it is obviously circular to make my consciousness of what I am doing one of the determinants of what I am doing. If what I am doing is not just a matter of my physical movements, but of my consciousness of something, the relevant consciousness must be my consciousness of certain characteristics of my physical movements, and my expectations regarding their effects. My hanging up of a picture on the wall is a matter of my body's movements having certain effects and of my acquiescent realization that my body's movements are having these effects.

The account we have given of noticing a property in my sense-data allows that my experience of acting in a certain way may constitute such an act of noticing. Whenever I experience a bull-type sense-datum I may experience the execution of a particular type of precipitate flight. It will be unusual for me to have this experience when my body is not actually in such flight, though this may happen in a dream, and even more unusual for it to happen without my believing that my body is in such flight.

But should one not allow that the physical movements themselves may constitute an act of noticing? Well, not being an experience, they cannot constitute the *experience* of noticing a universal. It was this that we wanted to analyse. We need not deny that they can be regarded as acts of noticing in some non-experiential sense.

What about the belief or knowledge states which also figure in a typical action? Can they also constitute experiences of noticing universals in sense-data? We shall make a good deal of use later of the notion of noticing universals in sense-data, when we discuss believing. So even if beliefs, say about material things, can in some way function also as experiences of noticing universals in sense-data, it will be best for the present to seek our examples of experiences of noticing universals in sense-data among such experiences as are not beliefs, or at least among experiences which, even if they *are* beliefs in virtue of facts about them of a type we have yet to investigate, are also simply experiences with certain intrinsic characteristics of a 'non-intentional' type, and which we need only consider in this latter way when asking how they function as acts of noticing universals in sense-data.

Our account requires a qualification. The property of the experience which does the noticing, and which constitutes it an act of noticing, must be a *natural* property, in the sense previously explained.[1] The property noticed may possibly be artificial but the property in question of the act of noticing must be natural. Otherwise one could claim that a property had been noticed by a person X showing some highly artificial property of a disjunctive kind which was possessed, often and only, by experience which occur together with experience of data of the kind said to be noticed.

It is impossible that I should notice all the properties, even all the natural ones, of all my experiences; there must be experiences which are acts of noticing properties of other experiences, or of things experienced, and are so in virtue of having certain properties, which they are not themselves noticed as having. Not that there is any particular stage at which a hierarchy of noticings must stop. Where an experience is an act of noticing the fact that some other experience or thing has a certain property F, and is such an act of noticing in virtue of having the property G, the fact that it is G is always the sort of thing which can be noticed. It is only that there must be some last term in such a hierarchy, not that any such fact is the last term in virtue of its own intrinsic nature.

I have talked mainly of noticing the properties of sense-data, but, as my last remark suggests, one may notice the properties of anything which is experienced, and of any experience. The relation between the properties of a sense-datum, and for that matter the properties of an image, and the properties of one's experience of them, was something I tried to explain in Chapter I and does not require further remark here. In view of those earlier explanations, it may not seem improper if, for the sake of brevity, I let the phrase 'F experience' cover not only those experiences which are F but those which are *of* an F particular, and similarly with all replacements for F. Similarly, an experience A's being described as R to an experience B will cover A's being *of* something which is R to that to which B is *of*, and likewise with all replacements for R.

Properties of all sorts which an experience or a thing experienced (which we may call jointly 'things within experience'

[1] See p. 78.

or 'experiential particulars') may have are noticeable, with the important exception of such relational properties as consist in the way in which things within one's experience relate to things outside one's experience.

2

There are however puzzles in our account, especially these two.

(1) It is surely not enough for recognition of property F that the mind contain at that time an experience with property G, which property occurs often with, and only with, property F. It must also be true that the G experience is somehow in response to the F thing. What is this relation of being in response to?

(2) Suppose that F experiences and G experiences always come together. It seems on our account that we would have to say both that each G experience would be the noticing of the accompanying F experience and vice versa. Is this really acceptable?

It may seem obvious that the experience which does the noticing should start after the experience the property of which is noticed. But if one took this point seriously one would presumably have to say that what one notices at a given time is always strictly that something had a certain property a moment ago, not that it has it now. This seems a very dubious claim. Moreover though problem (2) could be solved in this way, it would not remove problem (1). For mere succession in one mind seems no more adequate an account of the relation in question than mere co-occurrence.

It seems to me that I can notice in my experience relational facts representable as follows: This experience is in response to that experience. Thus when I experience a red patch, I may have another experience, for instance the experience of uttering 'This is red', and there just is between them a relation we may call 'Being in response to'. There is no need to give any other account of my noticing of this relational fact than is to be given of the noticing of relational facts in general. However, we need not suppose that the relation which links a noticing experience with a fact noticed is very often itself noticed. It should be remarked, perhaps, that it is not a causal, nomic, or universalizable relation that is in question.

One important case, but by no means the only important case, where I claim to notice this relation is between the experiences which constitute utterance on my part of remarks about things within my present experience and the things on which these remarks are made. Thus if I say 'This is a bad headache' it seems to me that this relation holds between my experience of saying this and the headache I have, holding most strongly between utterance of 'this' and the ache. It is found even more strikingly between an utterance of 'Ow' and a pain. It often holds between my remarks about physical objects in my environment and the sense-data of those objects which I experience. The phrase 'Being directed at' might be more suitable in some ways than 'Being in response to'; but we shall require the former phrase for a quite different purpose later. One phrase makes one experience sound the more passive, the other the other.

If anything it is the experience which is in response which is the more active. It may even be that 'A is in response to B' is susceptible of being analysed as equivalent to 'A is active at a time when B is passive, and A's moment of maximal *activeness* coincides with B's moment of maximum *attentiveness*[1] (not to that to which it is in response, but to that of which it is the experience) and no simultaneous experience is as active as A or as attentive as B'. It would follow that only one pair of experiences could exemplify the relation *Being in response to* at a time. This does not seem an unacceptable implication.

I do indeed find, or notice, this relation of *Being in response to* holding between certain of my experiences. But am I not giving rather too special a place to this relation in the analysis of noticing? Could not some other relation play the same role? Does it not perhaps do so with other people? Surely what is important in order that G experiences should serve for the noticing of F-ness is that there should be some relation such that G experiences occur often when, and only when, they are in this relation to an F experience, not necessarily this very relation which I call 'Being in response to'.

Is there any limitation upon the type of the relations which might play such a role? Evidently they must be natural relations, else the notion of there being such a relation in the case will be altogether too loose. It seems clear also that the relation must be manifested entirely within some tract of experience (though

[1] Cf. Chapter I, pp. 35ff.

whether this need be a specious present is doubtful). If it were not manifested in some tract of experience, that is, if its holding or not was a matter in part of a relation of the situation to something quite outside experience, noticing would hardly be something which took place within experience, and hence could not be described as an *experience* of noticing. It must also be a relation which makes it impossible for the act of noticing to occur before the experience whose property is said to be noticed.

It is arguable, then, that we should say that though the relation *Being in response to* is a good example of a relation which may play this role, other relations may do so as well.

Does this revive the paradox that if F experiences and G experiences always occur simultaneously and in a certain relation, one can say both that an F experience is an act of noticing the G-ness of the corresponding G experience and that the G experience is an act of noticing the F-ness of the corresponding F experience? I am not quite clear how it is to be avoided. However if G experiences sometimes occur without F experiences that is enough to establish that the noticing is not two way and that the latter are the acts of noticing. In what follows, at any rate, I shall take it that noticing a universal in an experiential particular is normally a matter of the occurrence in response to that particular of an experience of a sort, instances of which often and only occur in response to particulars, if the particulars exemplify that universal.

Let us now turn to some further points about the relation of noticing. First a point to do with the noticing of determinates and determinables.

Suppose I experience a scarlet (hence also red) datum, and I have experience B in response to it. Suppose B has property G, and that G is such that an experience in response to another experience is only G when the other experience is of a red datum. Thus I recognize the redness of the datum. Suppose now that G is a determinable, and that G_1 is one of its determinates, and that B is G_1. Suppose also that an experience in response to the experience of a datum is only G_1 if that datum is scarlet. The B experience will constitute recognition both of the redness and of the scarletness of the datum. It may, then, be true that where property G serves in the recognition of property F, various determinates of G serve in the noticing of various determinates of F. If, however, the determinates of G, which experiences in response to red data have, do not have any correspondence to the determinate of red in question in each case, then B may be a recognition of redness, but not of scarletness. It is, of course, possible that recognition of scarlet and recognition of red, both take place, but that the properties which 'correspond' to them in the recognizing experience, or experiences, are not related as determinate and determinable. Thus I may recognize the redness of a datum by responding to it with an experience with the property (call it property J) of *being an experience of uttering 'red'*, and recognize its scarletness by responding to it with an experience with the property (call it property K) of *being an experience of uttering 'scarlet'*. Clearly, K is not a determinate of J. They are not even exemplified by the same experience. Another possible case, at least theoretically, is one where the properties playing these roles are properties of the same experience, but not related as determinate and determinable.

3

To experience a particular which has a certain property, or to experience particulars which stand in certain relations, is distinct, on our account, from noticing that property or that relation. But is there not another distinction, which we have so far ignored, between those of the universals, exemplified by particulars which one experiences, which are themselves experienced, or, to put it another way, the exemplification of which by the particulars is experienced, without necessarily being noticed, and those which are not experienced?

Suppose one feels a red object. Does one not experience an object which is in fact red, but of which one does not experience the redness? Contrast this with seeing such an object. Suppose again that one sees two objects at a distance, one of which is in fact nearer to the tree one is standing just behind than is the other. Cannot one distinguish the case where one experiences the greater nearness to the tree of the one than the other, and the case where one does not, even where neither is a case where the relational property in question is actually noticed? One might say that in the one case the universal is there for one to notice, even if it is not noticed, while in the other it is not. The distinction is most obvious when only one of the cases includes a sight of the tree, but it could be made even when both did so.

As the reader will doubtless have realized, there is really no call to make the distinction in these cases. The red object one feels is a physical object. What one experiences is a sense-datum which is merely part of a red object. The sense-datum given to touch cannot itself be red, though it can belong to a group of sense-data, giveable to different senses, which together constitute a red object. Similarly, the distinction in the relational cases may be put like this. In each case the two sense-data belong, one to a certain physical object A, the other to a certain physical object B. One's sense-datum of the tree also belongs to a certain physical object, namely the tree (call it C). Each physical object consists of many different sense-data. There are sense-fields which contain a datum belonging to A, and a datum belonging to B, and a datum belonging to C. If in an appropriate number of these cases the datum belonging to A is nearer to the datum belonging to C than is the datum belonging to B, then the physical object A is nearer to C than is B. This does not mean that in every sense-field including data of any one of these objects, or even in every one including data of all three objects, there is an included A datum which is nearer to an included C datum than is some included B datum. The difference we were inclined to describe as that between experiencing objects which in fact exemplify the relation, and experiencing their exemplification of the relation, boils down to the difference between experiencing data which do not exemplify a certain relation and experiencing data which do exemplify it.

However, the distinction between experiencing data which exemplify certain universals, and experiencing their exemplification of certain universals, is not one to be brushed aside altogether. The data I experience certainly do have properties the exemplification of which I could not be said to experience. For instance, if the tactile datum which I experience has the property of belonging to a red object, I could not be said to experience its possession of this property, as I could be said to experience (say) its possession of hardness.

It seems that one does need some sort of distinction between the manifest properties of a datum and its non-manifest properties. I propose to say that a certain universal is manifested or manifest within a certain stretch of experience if and only if some thing or things within that stretch exemplify the universal, and if its or their exemplification of the universal is not in whole or in part a matter of its or their standing in certain relations to anything outside that stretch of experience. Normally when I talk of the manifest properties of a datum I shall be thinking of such of its properties as are manifest within a specious present to which it belongs. Similar remarks apply to relations. The relata must both fall within the stretch in question, and the relation must not include any relation to things outside the stretch in which it is said to be manifest.

It is convenient to say that one experiences those properties of one's data and of one's experiences which are manifested within a specious present. If I experience a red datum attentively, I experience both redness and attentiveness, though I may well not notice or be aware of them. Equally I may be said to experience those facts which contain only experienced particulars and their manifest universals.

But suppose that A and B are both experienced particulars, and that a certain relation between them is manifest in a certain area of experience, which is extended further in the temporal dimension than anything which can be recognized as a specious present. Is it impossible to say that this relation has been experienced? The difficulty lies in part in the unclarity of the notion of the specious present. Whatever the right answer is, one should probably insist that the longest stretch of experience such that universals manifest within that stretch may be described as experienced, should coincide with the longest stretch within which one is prepared to talk of noticing universals.

4

It might appear that our account of noticing implies that a universal cannot be noticed the first time that it is experienced, for it cannot then be true that some experience, which occurs in response to that which exemplifies it, occurs often in response to such experiences or data. It is to be understood, however, that an experience which occurs in response to some experience or datum which is F is a noticing of its F-ness, provided that it is going to be true henceforth that some property which it has occurs often and only in response to F experiences or data. It need not matter that previously it occurred in response to things of a different sort, provided that henceforth it is going to occur only in response to F data or experiences. Still less need it matter that experiences of this kind may have occurred previously without being in response to anything, nor need a few subsequent occurrences which are not in response to anything affect their status, when they are in response to F data or experiences, as acts of noticing their F-ness.

Just as there must be a first time in which a G experience occurs as the noticing of the F-ness of something, so there must be a last time, and this need not be because G experiences never occur again (for that person), in response to anything, but because they change their function. In short, what is required in order that G experiences serve during a given period as acts of noticing F-ness is not a lifelong correlation of the sort we have described, but one throughout that period, which must however be of a certain length, long enough, at least, to contain many distinct and separated G experiences.

It may be that an adequate account of the conditions under which an experience, which occurs in response to an experience which has a certain property, qualifies as an act of noticing that the latter experience has this property, can only be given by introducing a counterfactual conditional element. Thus 'I notice that experience A is F' may be equivalent in meaning to 'I have an experience in response to the F experience A which has some property G such that even if I had not been having both a G experience and an F experience at this time it would still have been true of me, that if I had had an F experience I would have been likely to have a G response to it, while there is no other kind of experience, such that I might have had an experience of that kind, in response to one of which I would have had a G experience'. If I have any doubts regarding the preferability of this account to the one given so far, they represent qualms about counterfactual conditionals in general.

It will be convenient to have some word for the property which plays the role of G in the above. Let us call it 'the specifying property'. The property which plays the role of F is, of course, called 'the noticed property', it may also sometimes be called 'the specified property'.

It is not impossible that there should be more than one specifying property for a certain property, with respect to one mind. There is, of course, no reason why one and the same property should not have different specifying properties in different minds.

5

It is now time to consider in what the noticing of relations, as opposed to properties, consists. I shall confine the discussion to two-place relations, since relations with more places than this can be dealt with along the same lines, as should be obvious.

What is required in order that I notice such a fact as that sense-datum A is above sense-datum B? It seems that I must have two experiences, one, which we may call C, in response to A, the other, which we may call D, in response to B, and that C must be in a relation R to D, such that the mind has a tendency to have two experiences each in response to certain experiential particulars, and in relation R to one another, only when the thing to which the first experience is in response is above the thing to which the second is in response.

We may express the matter slightly differently in order to conform to our earlier discussion of relations. Suppose that S is a relation and associated with it are the two roles S_1 and S_2. Suppose now that this relation is manifested in my experience by two particulars A and B, A playing the S_1 role and B playing the S_2 role. That is, I experience the fact $S(S_1A,S_2B)$. In order that I notice this fact, I must have two experiences C and D, such that C is in response to A, and D is in response to B, and C and D manifest a (natural) relation R, which has two roles R_1 and R_2 of which C plays role R_2 and D plays role R_1; it must further be the case that the mind has a tendency to have two experiences in relation R to each other often when and only when the experience playing the R_1 role is in response to one experience, and the experience playing the R_2 role is in response to another experience, and these other two experiences are manifestly in relation S to each other, with the one to which the R_1 one is in response playing the S_2 role, and the one to which the R_2 one is in response playing the S_1 role. (I have deliberately confused the numerical order in order to show its irrelevance.)

A point to be borne in mind here is that two experiences may well be parts of one experience. For instance, if I experience visual datum A and experience visual datum B these experiences may be, one might almost say, illegitimately abstracted parts of an experience of the visual expanse covered partly by A, partly by B. Suppose that A is above B. The relation in question can equally be regarded as between two experiences, or as between two things experienced. Equally the noticing of the aboveness of A to B, which on our account involves two experiences, one related to A, the other to B, can be regarded as one experience involving items in relation.

If an analysis of the relation Being in response to—which we mentioned earlier[1] is correct, it might seem to follow that the two experiences which occur in relation as noticings of the presence of a certain relation cannot be simultaneous one with another, so that even if the relation which is noticed is atemporal the specifying relation must be one which is only realized across time. I think that this is likely often to be the case, but it does not follow, for the two experiences which do the noticing may be stretched across time, with non-simultaneous moments of maximum activity, while the specifying relation between them may be one manifested in each moment of their occurrence.

Let us now give two examples of what noticing that A is above B might consist in. It might consist in the experience of saying 'This is above that'. If it does, this is because (i) the experience of uttering 'This' occurs in response to A, and the experience of uttering 'That' occurs in response to B; (ii) these two experiences are related by the one preceding and the other following an experience of uttering 'is above' (it is of course equally correct to regard the uttering of all three phrases as one experience); and (iii) experiences of uttering 'This' in response to one object and of uttering 'That' in response to another object tend to occur in the relation *Coming before and after an utterance of 'is above'* often when and only when the first object is above the second object.

Another way in which I might notice that A is above B would be as follows. I have a feeling of a peculiar kind F in response to A, and I have a feeling of a peculiar kind G in response to B, and I tend to have an F feeling in response to one thing and at the same time a G feeling in response to another thing often

[1] See p. 98.

when and only when the thing related to the F feeling is above the thing related to the G thing.

An interesting possibility is this. Suppose that A is above B, and suppose that I have in response to the totality of A and B an F experience, and suppose that I have F experiences often in response to, and only in response to, totalities containing one item above another. It would seem that this would be noticing the presence of the above relation, without noticing what was above and what was below. Is this a sensible way of so describing such a situation?

A certain objection might be taken to the intelligibility of what we have described. Since every visual datum except a point includes two items one above the other, what we have described is a case where an F experience occurs in response to every visual datum which is not a point. As such, it is hardly a distinctive response to a specific kind of visual situation, and we will be having numerous F experiences all our seeing life. But surely some distinction can be made between striking and unstriking instances of aboveness? This distinction seems an objective one, that is, it is one which holds independently of questions of what we tend to notice. One might then regard F-ness as specifying aboveness if it is more likely to occur in response to a visual datum the more striking an instance of aboveness it is.

Let us alter the case slightly. Suppose that I tend to direct F feelings in pairs, so that I tend to direct one F feeling at one object, and one F feeling at another object, often when and only when, the two objects stand in the relation of aboveness (= below-ness). Such a kind of noticing seems to make no distinction between the thing above and the thing below, though it answers to the required description for noticing aboveness. Do we want to say that in such a case we notice that a pair exemplifies aboveness, but do not notice which is above and which is below? On the whole it would seem simplest to count such a case as a case of noticing (say) that A is above B, if A is in fact the above one, and B in fact the below one. For one has certainly noticed that they together exemplify aboveness, and one has not positively made a mistake as to which is above which. Noticing indeed is not the sort of thing which can be mistaken, so that if one did develop differential responses to the thing above, and the thing below, there is no way in which one could get it wrong.

6

Having concluded our discussion of the noticing of relations in general, let us now turn to a very difficult question, which is not without some importance: Can one notice that the relation *Being an act of noticing that* holds between a certain experience and a fact? Is such a fact as that one has noticed the F-ness of A itself susceptible of being noticed?

The first thing to point out is that *Being an act of noticing the fact that* is a relation which links, not a particular and a particular, but a particular and a fact. However we may see our problem as concerning rather the nature of the relation between particulars: *Being a noticing of a fact about* – and of all the more determinate forms of this relation which are given when the fact in question is specified.

The fact that one has noticed the fact that this is F is the fact that one has experienced a particular which is (manifestly) F and that one had an experience in response to this particular which had some property g such that one has g experiences often and only in response to F particulars. It is difficult to see how one could notice this fact without noticing the fully determinate fact in which a definite (though not necessarily especially determinate) property occurs as the specifying property. In short, suppose that the following (in which we are to imagine that the capital letters and demonstratives are constants, not as they really are variables) is a fact: This is an H experience and it is in response to that which is an F experience, and I have H experiences often in response to and only in response to F experiences. This fact entails the less determinate fact: This is a noticing of the F-ness of that. What I am suggesting is that one could not in any sense notice the latter fact without having noticed *some* determinate fact of the character of the first.

There is a certain fact which is a *part* of the first fact which is quite easily noticed. I can notice that *this* (which is in fact the noticing experience) is in response to that. I can notice that the particular experience which is in fact my uttering of 'This is red', is in response to that, which is in fact, and manifestly, a scarlet datum. Or I can notice that this (a feeling of a certain kind) is in response to that (the scarlet datum again).

However, in noticing that an experience, say the experience of uttering 'This is red', is in response to that datum (which is in fact scarlet) I have not *ipso facto* noticed that it is an experience of noticing the scarletness of that. So far as what I have noticed goes, it might be a noticing rather of the scarletness of that, or not an act of noticing at all. In order to know that the experience is a noticing of redness, I must somehow know that a certain specific property it has (and it will have other properties besides that of being an experience of uttering 'This is red') characterizes experiences in response to other experiences often if and only if those other experiences are of something red, rather than, say, often if and only if, those other experiences are of something scarlet. What form can this knowledge take? Can it take the form of noticing?

Is there any special difficulty about the noticing of individual facts of the form: 'b is an experience of uttering "This is red" and b is in response to a and a is red'? What we have here is a compound fact with three conjuncts, each of which is of a kind the noticing of which seems quite straightforward. Probably no distinction needs to be drawn between noticing three facts at more or less the same time, and noticing their conjunction. If there is any difference it is perhaps that where the conjunction of them is said to be noticed the experiences of noticing each conjunct must somehow inter-penetrate each other. Presumably this could happen in the present case.

Suppose now that I notice a succession of compound facts of this form, differing only in the particulars which play the roles of a and b. Can I be said to have noticed the conjunction of all these facts? One now faces the question whether when one has noticed over a certain period of time each of a set of facts, one can be said to have noticed the conjunction of these facts. There is no *moment* at which one could be said to be noticing the conjunction, but may not the noticing of some facts be itself an experience spread over time, especially when the fact noticed is itself one spread over time?

Consider the noticing of such a time-extended fact as this, which is not even a compound fact. *A was a trumpet blast followed by B which was a long drum roll followed by C which was another trumpet blast.* The fact that such a fact is noticed would consist in the fact that there are experiences in response to each of A and B and C and these experiences are of a kind related to each other in such a way that only experiences in response to particulars in this relation are experiences of this kind in this relation. Noticing of this kind would be bound to be spread across the same time as is the fact noticed.

But surely something needs to be added which it is very difficult to be clear about. Although the act of noticing, like the fact noticed, may be spread across time in this way, it must surely have a certain sort of unity. The unity in question seems to be that which is implied when one says of two experiences which occur at different times that they belong to the same specious present. A specious present is presumably some tract of experience which has a special sort of unity, so that, although some of its elements occur before others, they go (in some rather obscure way) into the making up of one moment in one's life. It seems to me that one would not very happily talk of a time-extended fact as having been noticed, unless the act of noticing it, and hence the fact itself, all belonged within one specious present. On the other hand, once it is allowed that the specious present is a tract of experience genuinely extended in time, there seems no ground for laying down some *a priori* limit to the length of this time. It also seems a possibility that whether a certain tract of experience has the kind of unity which would make of it a specious present is a matter of degree, so that such a tract can be more or less of a specious present. For rare persons the hearing of a whole long symphony may constitute something approaching a specious present.

I think we may say, then, that two acts of noticing which belong to the same specious present constitute an act of noticing the conjunction of their respective facts. Granted what we have said about the specious present, it is a matter of degree how far successive acts of noticing constitute an act of noticing the conjunction of their respective facts.

We are approaching our goal of showing how there could be a noticing of a fact, which fact entailed that an experience B was the noticing of the F-ness of an experience A. But in order to reach our goal we need at least to be able to include in the compound fact noticed the fact that there were no experiences, during the tract of experience in question, of uttering 'This is red' which were in response to experiences not of something red, or of some fact which entails this.

How then can I notice not only that B is an utterance of 'This is red' and is in response to A which is red, and that D is an utterance of 'This is red' and is in response to C which is red . . . and that

N is an utterance of 'This is red' and is in response to M which is red, but also notice all this in conjunction with either the fact that besides B and D and . . . and N there are no utterances of 'This is red' within this tract of experience or alternatively that there are no experiences of uttering 'This is red' which are not in response to something which is red? Something else which would do as a similar addition would be noticing that B and D and . . . and N and P and R are the only utterings of 'This is red' within this tract of experience and that P and R are not in response to anything.

We shall go a little into the problem of negation elsewhere, but for the present it may be enough to dwell on the fact that to say that there are no Fs within a certain portion of experience apart from A and B and C and . . . and N is to say that A and B and C and . . . and N are the complete group of Fs within that tract. Surely this is the sort of thing which can be noticed? It may be that there is a certain characteristic relation which links a set of acts of noticing some one universal and a certain portion of experience often when and only when they are the noticings of all the instances of that universal manifested within that portion of experience.

There seems no reason in principle why one should not equally notice that A and B and C are the only Fs in a longish specious present. If such noticing took a linguistic form it might occur in the following way: I say over this longish period of time 'This is F . . . and this is F . . . and this is F, and those were the only Fs there were', where there is a 'this' is response to each of A and B and C. This would be an act of noticing that A and B and C are the only Fs throughout a certain period provided that utterance of 'This is F' is a specifying property for F-ness, and that a specious present often and only contains such instances of noticing F-ness, followed by 'and those were the only Fs there were' if that specious present contains no instances of F-ness not thus noticed. Linguistic ways of noticing are, of course, always the easiest to specify publicly, since one can do so by stimulating an icon of the experience in question, but it need not be the case that such noticing is linguistic.

Thus, the brevity of our specious present being an empirical fact, there is no *a priori* impossibility in a mind noticing the compound fact that during a certain period, however long, B and C and . . . and N were the only experiences of saying 'this is red' and B was in response to A which is red, D in response to C which is red, and . . . N in response to M which is red.

This fact which a mind might theoretically notice logically implies the following so-called fact (though strictly speaking it is not a fact, as we shall see): N is in response to M and has a natural property such that experiences with that property occur often and only in response to things which are red. This 'fact' is one we have been inclined to identify with the 'fact' that N is an act of noticing M's redness. Let us for the moment take it that such identification is correct.

The relation between the *fact* we are concerned with and the 'fact' is much the same as that between such a fact as that *A* is red and the 'fact' that something is red. I shall now introduce the convention, the rationale of which may become clearer later, that if one has noticed a certain fact one may also be said to have noticed any 'fact' the appropriate designation of which is identical apart from the replacement of one or more constants of some kind by variables, to the appropriate designation of the *fact* noticed, and apart from any decrease in definiteness as to the number of particulars in question. Following this convention we may say that we have described a situation in which someone has noticed that N is an act of noticing the redness of M.

It seems then that one could notice the 'fact' that N is a noticing of the redness of M, if our original analysis of noticing is correct. The possibility exists in principle if not in practice. However if the 'fact' in question contains a counterfactual element, the position is more obscure, as one might expect. Nothing very useful can be said on it without a full analysis of counterfactuals.

V

GROUPS

One of the most common relations which may link one particular to another is the part-whole relation.

The most obvious instances of the part-whole relation are public space ones. That a certain brick is part of a certain house is a fact about their public space relations. But the public space part-whole relation is only a species of a more general relation. That one visual datum is part of another visual datum is not a fact about their public space relations but about their private space relations. However, the part-whole relation is still more general than this. It need not always be a spatial relation in any but a rather stretched sense of 'spatial', though I do not deny the utility of such a stretched sense of 'spatial'. A headache of mine at the moment, for instance, is part of that totality which makes up my present state of mind. Moreover, a headache may itself have parts, a duller part and a more acute part. I am likely to localize these in different parts of my head, that is, to think of them as being at different parts of my head. But logically prior to any such localization as this, the exact interpretation of which we may pass over, is the existence of different parts of the headache thus to be localized.

A thing is not, of course, shown to have parts simply by the fact that it has different properties. The properties of a thing are not its parts. But sometimes one may only notice that a thing has parts by noticing that it has different properties which are in a certain sense incompatible, and realizing then that the different properties are exemplified by different parts of it.

I cannot offer any analysis of the part-whole relation, and doubt whether it is illuminatingly analysable. One can only go round in circles. One can say, for instance, that where B is a part of A, A consists of B and of something or things else as well.

Closely related to the part-whole relation is the relation of Being an aggregate of. This is a relation which may link any number of particulars greater than two. That is, facts containing the relation Being the aggregate of, as the thing exemplified, differ from one another in the number of things playing exemplifying roles. We have such facts as A being the aggregate of B and C, D being the aggregate of E and F and G, H being the aggregate of I and K and L and M, and so on. It is generally thought that we do not have the same relation where the number of places varies. But this seems to be a case, and not the only case, where we should recognize a single relation capable of being exemplified with a varying number of places. There is one role which might be called the master role, that of being the aggregate, and there is another role which may be filled by a varying number of aggregata.

A is the aggregate of B and C and . . . and J, if A is as much of the world as consists in all of B and C and . . . and J taken together. One might put it thus. The aggregate of B and C and . . . and J is all of B and C and . . . and J considered as jointly forming one particular. But this is slightly misleading. For it suggests that they have somehow to be considered together in order to be one particular. However, there is a particular which is the aggregate of B and C and . . . and J, provided each of these is a genuine particular, whether any one chooses to think of it as one particular or not. For every particular is simply a certain chunk of reality, and every chunk of reality is a particular.

One may offer the following as something approaching an analysis of Being the aggregate of. An object x is the aggregate of objects y, z, and . . . and w if and only if y is part of x and z is a part of x and . . . and w is a part of x, and every other part of x either has a part which is or is itself related either as whole to part or as part to whole either to y or to z or to . . . or to w. (N.B. The alternation is non-exclusive.) This is undoubtedly a necessary truth, but I do not think it provides an analysis of the relation.

Let us consider some examples of the aggregate relation. If we take the expressions 'trunk', 'leg', 'head', etc. in a sufficiently broad way (so that, for instance, my hand is part of my arm) every normal human body is the aggregate of a trunk, a neck, a head, two arms, and two legs. Let us take a particular human body, A, and let B be the trunk, C be the neck, D be the head, E the left arm, F the right arm, G the left leg, H the right leg. Then A is the aggregate of B and C and D and E and F and G and H. Now it is very likely that someone will complain that A is not simply the aggregate of these seven particulars. A , it may be said, is not just an aggregate of these seven particulars, it is these seven particulars in certain relations.

This objection rests upon a confusion between particulars and universals. The property Being a human body is not the same property as Being the aggregate of a head, neck, trunk, two arms and two legs. The first property entails the latter, but not vice versa. Or rather the first entails the latter, if the latter is taken as meaning 'complete and undeformed human body' as I shall understand it to mean henceforth.

There are three properties of A which it is important to distinguish.

(i) Being a human body.

(ii) Being the aggregate of a head, a neck, a trunk, two arms, and two legs.

(iii) Being the aggregate of B and C and D and E and F and G and H. There are various relations between these properties of A, but they are definitely distinct properties.

It is quite true that every (complete undeformed) human body is the aggregate of a head, a neck, a trunk, two arms, two legs. But it is not simply in virtue of this latter property that a human body is a human body.

Provided B and C and . . . and J are genuine particulars, there must be such a particular as the aggregate of B and C and . . . and J.

This point is easy enough to make in the case of physical objects. When I refer to a certain physical object that which I refer to is as much of the world as falls within certain spatio-temporal boundaries. I need not exactly refer to it as such; my point is simply that this, among other things, is what every physical object is. The boundaries of those physical objects of which we most often talk are normally such that a chain of spatio-temporally continuous parts of the object join any two non-adjacent parts of it. But there is no difficulty in the concept of a physical object where the boundaries are comparable to those of Pakistan rather than of England. Such a self-separated area of land as Pakistan has reasons for specially interesting us, for political reasons, and so we treat it as one particular. But it is no more, and no less, one particular than any other self-separated area of land. Every portion of space-time, whether self-separated or not, is a particular.

There seems no reason for not extending this point to non-physical particulars. Every particular is a certain chunk or portion of the Universe. Self-separated chunks are just as much there, just as much have properties and stand in relations to one another, as self-connected such chunks. Nor need we draw the line at a particular which is the aggregate of a physical and a non-physical particular. I am not inventing strange entities here, just saying that since, as shall be seen better later, a chunk of reality cannot itself be called one or many, but only one or many *qua* some other property, any chunk of reality you choose to think of is as much one chunk as many chunks. As there is no real distinction between chunk and chunks of reality, there cannot be chunks of reality such that one cannot, quite correctly, talk of that particular which is their aggregate. This is not to say that some such particulars, as for instance 'the table at which I am now writing, the oldest rabbit in Australia, and the last medicine taken by Lewis XV'[1] are not fantastic, in the sense that it would be fantastic to interest oneself in them, except as illustrating a philosophical point.

It may now be remarked that a particular which figures as the aggregate in a fact containing *Being the aggregate of* as thing exemplified, will normally figure also in other such facts. The human body A is not only the aggregate of B and C and D and E and F and G and H. It is also the aggregate of M and N and O and . . . where we must imagine every cell of the body enumerated. Moreover it is also the aggregate of the aggregate of B and C, and the aggregate of D and E, and the aggregate of F and G and H. There are any number of different facts about it of this kind.

Again, Great Britain is the aggregate of England, Scotland, Northern Ireland, and Wales, and also the aggregate of all the counties in Great Britain.[2]

It should now be pointed out that Great Britain is also the aggregate of England, Scotland, Northern Ireland, and Wales and all the counties in Great Britain; the aggregate of Great Britain

[1] Borrowed from McTaggart, *The Nature of Existence*, p. 133. The reference, but not the meaning, has of course, changed in my borrowing.
[2] Again an example borrowed from McTaggart. But the concepts we are explicating should not too readily be identified with any explained by McTaggart.

and Wales; the aggregate of Sussex, England, Northern Ireland, Scotland, and Wales, and so on. If A is the aggregate of B and C and D etc., B and C and D etc., must make it up, but it does not matter if – to use McTaggart's phrase – they *more than make it up*.

The following diagrams may illustrate some points in this connection.

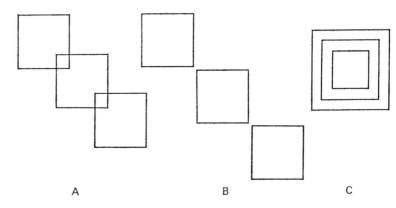

Each of A, B, and C is the aggregate of three squares (i.e. delineated square areas). But one of the three squares of which C is an aggregate is C itself. C is the aggregate of C and D and E (giving these last two the appropriate references). It is also the aggregate of C and D, and the aggregate of C and E. A is also interesting. It is the aggregate of three squares, but it is also the aggregate of five squares. This does not mean simply that it contains five squares, it means, or rather is equivalent to the truth that there are five squares such that every part of it is at least partly a part of one of these squares. There are both five squares and three squares which fulfil this condition.

To remove any final ambiguities on these points consider the two following diagrams, G and H.

G contains two triangles, but it is not an aggregate of triangles. H, on the other hand, is both an aggregate of two triangles, and an aggregate of three triangles. It is also a triangle. To say that it is an aggregate of three triangles, is to say: '(Ex) (Ey) (Ez) (H is an aggregate of x and y and z and x is a triangle and y is a triangle and z is a triangle)'. That is, it does not refer to the actual triangles

n question (apart from the fact that the expression H happens to
lo so). Clearly one could also assert of H simply that it was the
aggregate of some triangles, without specifying how many. In
act, it has this latter property twice over, so to speak. Its being
he aggregate of three triangles, and its being the aggregate of
ome triangles, are both variable-based relational properties of it.

In admitting that there are such things as aggregates, we have
not enlarged our ontology by adding any further category on a
evel with that of particulars, universals, and facts. For every
aggregate is a particular. It is even possible that every particular
s an aggregate.

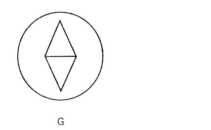

G

H

If, however, we went on to talk about classes, it would seem
that we would be enlarging our ontology, for a class as normally
conceived seems to be something of a quite different order from
anything we have so far recognized as a particular.

What grounds are there for distinguishing classes from
aggregates?

The reason for distinguishing them usually given is that there
are many predicates which are ascribable to members of one of
these categories, and not to any members of the other. In particular, numerical predicates are said to be applicable to classes but
not to aggregates. The aggregate of twelve human bodies cannot
be said to be twelvefold. It is just as much N-fold, for instance,
where N may be taken as the number of cells in such an aggregate.
Equally it can be regarded as one great mass of flesh, and could be
ascribed various other numbers. The truth is, it is said, that
numerical predicates are not applicable to it. That which is twelvefold is the class having those twelve men as its members. On the
other hand, the aggregate of the men will have such a predicate as
Being 144 stone in weight, which will not apply to the class.

I do not know of any very good argument for saying that th class does not have a weight. It would seem to be a deductio from the claim that the class is not a particular, and is in some sens or other abstract, rather than a reason in support of this claim. Th same reason, that it is an abstract object, would make one say tha it cannot be in a place. Thus one could say of the aggregate c twelve men that it was in a certain room but not of the class o twelve men. Since one can surely say 'The jury is in that room' i suggests that such a phrase as 'the jury' refers to the aggregate o the twelve jurors rather than to the class of the twelve jurors. Ye if this is so, one cannot say that the jury is twelvefold, which seem a difficulty.

On the whole, it seems that the main argument for distinguishin classes and aggregates, at least classes of particulars from aggregates is that numerical predicates apply to one and not to the other.

To make the point quite clear, let us introduce the expressio 'hunk' to mean 'head, or neck, or trunk, or leg, or arm'. Then on cannot say that the aggregate of twelve men is twelvefold, for it i no more twelvefold than it is eighty-four-fold or N-fold. Similarl predicates such as 'numerous' are inapplicable to an aggregate.

However this argumentation does not really seem very effective for surely anyone who said that a certain aggregate of men wa twelvefold, would be prepared to allow that it was only considere as an aggregate of men that it was twelvefold. He would admi that considered as an aggregate of hunks it was eighty-four-fold

That is, numerical properties can indeed be ascribed to aggre gates, but they are syncategorematic properties. *Qua* being a aggregate of one kind a particular may have one numerica property, *qua* being an aggregate of another kind it may hav another numerical property. It must be remembered that thoug one may use such a phrase as 'Considered as' there is nothin subjective about syncategorematic properties. It is a quite objectiv fact that *qua* being such and such a particular is so and so, whil *qua* being such and such else it is not so and so.

Something needs to be said about the sort of properties or which these number properties are syncategorematic. They are of two main types. A particular which is the aggregate of B, C, an D will be threefold *qua* being the aggregate of B, C, and D. Suppos now that B, C, and D are all Fs. Then it will also be three-fold *qu* being an aggregate of Fs.

An important point to remember is that it is possible for a particular both to be an aggregate of three Fs and to be an aggregate of four Fs. Then it will be true that *qua* being an aggregate of Fs it is both three-fold and four-fold.

There is, however, a third kind of property on which a numerical property may be syncategorematic. A particular may be the aggregate of all the Fs. Here it is impossible that a situation like that just mentioned should arise. Being a certain definite number-fold *qua* being the aggregate of all the Fs excludes being a certain definite other number-fold.

The number properties which particulars may have *qua* being aggregates of various kinds may be regarded as numbers of a certain kind, not necessarily the natural numbers of arithmetic. The most I claim is that some simple numerical statements of every day ascribe these numerical properties to particulars.

As we have explained the term 'aggregate' there is no such thing as a particular being one-fold *qua* being an aggregate of a certain kind. Is there then no such property as one-fold-ness of the same general character as two-fold-ness, three-fold-ness, and so on, of the sort we are concerned with?

There are various conventions which might be adopted, but it is probably best to enlarge our concept of the relation *Being an aggregate of*, and allow that each thing is an aggregate of itself. It is, after all, true that each particular is as much of the world as consists in itself. It is also true that every part of a particular is related either as part to whole or as whole to part to that particular. One cannot however have a formula quite corresponding to the one we had before, as a particular is not a part of itself.

If one allows that a particular is the aggregate of itself, then as such it will be one-fold. If it is an F, then it will be one-fold as an aggregate of Fs.

There is no such thing as a none-fold aggregate. To talk of an aggregate as being none-fold is to say that there is no such aggregate.

It is now time to introduce the word 'group' as I think this may be suitably understood. My claim is that the meaning of 'group', thus explained, is the meaning which such words as 'group', 'class', 'collection' and so on have in ordinary language wherever they are used, as they often are, to refer to things which are not essentially different in character from that of which they are groups. That is, when they are so used that a group of physical things is physical, a group of visible things is visible, a group of mental things is mental. I do not mean that in this usage every predicate applicable to members of the group is applicable to the group, but that the most basic predicates applicable to members are predicates of the same general kind as some applicable to the group. Thus if I can buy a tomato, I can buy a collection of tomatoes. A pair of shoes (a pair being a dual group) is made of leather just as much as is each individual shoe. Groups of this sort are not the recondite abstract entities of the mathematician and the logician; but that some of the latter are prepared to countenance groups, while being sceptical about such other 'abstract' entities as properties, may be because the terms 'class', 'set', 'group', and so forth retain some of the comforting feel and concreteness which they rightly have in the ordinary usages we have indicated. I am not claiming, by the way, that *groups* could replace *classes* or *sets* in logic or mathematics. What we have there, I should imagine, is a special way of talking about universals.

My suggestion is this: When I talk of the group of B, C, and D, or of the group of Fs, I am talking of that particular which is the aggregate of B, C, and D, or of all the Fs, but I am giving warning that whenever I ascribe properties to it of a character syncategorematic on being an aggregate of a certain kind I am ascribing them *qua* being the aggregate of B, C, and D, or *qua* being the aggregate of the Fs, and not *qua* being an aggregate of some other kind. I am also giving warning that certain other predicative expressions are being used in a special way.

Thus when I refer to the group of the Apostles I am indeed referring to the aggregate of the Apostles. However, there is a difference in role between the expressions 'The aggregate of the Apostles' and the expression 'The group of the Apostles'. Many sentences of the form 'The group of the Apostles is F' are to be understood not as equivalent to 'The aggregate of the Apostles is F', but as 'The aggregate of the Apostles, *qua* being the aggregate of the Apostles, is F'.

Various consequences follow from this. 'The aggregate of the Apostles is two-fold' is as true as 'The aggregate of the Apostles is twelve-fold'. Both can only mean 'The aggregate of the Apostles is two-fold (or twelve-fold) *qua* being something' and, as such, they are both true. The aggregate of the Apostles is two-fold, for instance, *qua* being the aggregate of a treacherous apostle and an aggregate of faithful apostles. On the other hand, 'The group of the Apostles is twelve' is true and 'The group of the Apostles is two' is false. Similar points go for words like 'numerous', 'few' and so on.

Roughly speaking, for 'The group of . . .' one may always read 'The aggregate of . . . *qua* being the aggregate of . . .'. One may take it that where 'F' is non-syncategorematic 'A, *qua* being G, is F' is true if and only if A is both F and G.

Something should be said about such expressions as 'is a member of', and 'contains'. These are syncategorematic predicates, the predicates on which they are syncategorematic being ones which name properties which are matters of being an aggregate of a certain kind, 'x is a member of y, *qua* being an aggregate of . . .' means 'x plays the role of an aggregatum in the fact that y is an aggregate of . . . or in the basic fact which underlies this fact'.

Clearly John plays the role of an aggregatum in the fact that the Jones family is the aggregate of Father, Mother, John, and Jane. Thus 'John is a member of the Jones family, *qua* the latter being the aggregate of Father, Mother, John, and Jane' is true, if rather trivially so. But it is necessary to explain what is meant by the phrase 'the basic fact which underlies this fact'.

Wherever it is a fact that something has a relational property of types 2, 3, or 4, this must rest upon the fact that it has a relational property of type 1. In such cases the fact of its having a specified relational property of type 1 may be described as the basic fact underlying the fact that it has a specified relational property of one of the other types. In some cases there may be more than one such underlying fact, rather than anything which can be called the underlying fact. Various different basic facts underlie the fact that I am the owner of a book. In that case, in our present formula, 'the fact which underlies this fact' must be taken as meaning 'one of the basic facts which underlie this fact'.

It should be noticed that the basic underlying fact will often be the conjunction of two facts, one a purely relational fact, or a conjunction of purely relational facts, the other a non-relational fact, or a conjunction of non-relational facts. That X has the relational property of being father to some fools will, for instance, depend upon the conjunction of some such facts as that (1) X is father of Y and X is father of Z and X is father of W and (2) Y is a fool and Z is a fool and W is a fool. In such a case we may call the purely relational fact or conjunction of facts the purely relational part of the basic fact which underlies the fact that X is the father of some fools.

Hence the sentence 'He is a member of the aggregate of fools, *qua* its being the aggregate of fools' is equivalent to 'He plays an aggregated role in a basic fact underlying the fact that the aggregate of fools is the aggregate of fools'.

It follows from our remarks about the word 'group' that this sentence can be re-expressed as 'He is a member of the group of fools'.

It should now be clear that if John is a fool, 'John is a member of the group of fools' is true, and so is 'John is a part of the group of fools'. That is, presuming that there are other fools; otherwise he would *be* the group of fools. The following is also true 'John's nose is a part of the group of fools'. But 'John's nose is a member of the group of fools' is false.

It may be remarked that although 'is a member of' functions as a syncategorematic relational predicate, syncategorematic on a predicate applicable to the 'second' relatum, it is not quite the name of what we previously regarded as a syncategorematic universal. It is more correct to say that though it seems to specify a relation between two particulars, it really specifies a relation between a particular and a fact, a fact about the particular which seems to be the 'second' relatum.

Some comment needs to be made about the use of 'is identical with' and related expressions as placed between expressions one or two of which is of the form 'The group of . . .'.

As has already been made clear, the aggregate of the British counties is identical with the aggregate of England, Scotland, Wales, and Northern Ireland. The particular which is the one aggregate is the other aggregate. It is equally true that each aggregate is identical with Great Britain. Great Britain is also both identical with the group of England, Scotland and Wales and Northern Ireland, and identical with the group of the British counties. But are we to say that the group of England, Scotland, Wales and Northern Ireland is identical with the group of the British counties? If the expression 'is identical with' is regarded as non-syncategorematic, then one must say that they are identical. I do not want to go into the question of the exact meaning of 'is identical with' but it does seem clear that A and B simply either are identical, or are not identical. They are not identical *qua* the one being such and such and the other being so and so, and perhaps non-identical *qua* something else. Thus the group of the British counties is identical with the group of England, Wales, Scotland, and Northern Ireland.

On the other hand, there is need of some such predicate as 'is the same group as' to be interpreted as equivalent to 'has the same members as'. Spelling it out more completely 'The group of Fs is the same group as the group of Gs' means the same as 'The purely relational part of the basic facts which underlie the fact that the aggregate of Fs is the aggregate of Fs and that the aggregate of Gs is the aggregate of Gs is the same fact'. One can express this more briefly either by saying 'The aggregate of Fs *qua* being the aggregate of Fs has the same members as the aggregate of Gs' or as 'The group of Fs has the same members as the group of Gs'. For 'has the same members as' we can always write 'is the same group as'. If one puts 'is the same group as' between two expressions not of the form 'The group of . . .', or without adding something of the form '*qua* being an aggregate of . . .' to each expression, one's remark will either be incomplete, or will be as though terminating with '*qua* something or other in regard to the first, and *qua* something or other in regard to the second'. In the latter case the assertion will amount simply to the assertion that they are the same compound particular.

It should be noted that 'is the same group as' is not related to 'is identical with' as is such an expression as 'is the same apple as'.

In general 'X is the same F as Y' means 'X is an F, and Y is an F, and X is identical with Y'. It is not correct to say that a thing can be the same such and such, but a different such and such else. When one is tempted to say this it is because one has not realized that where 'X is the same F as Y' and 'X is a different G from Y' are both true, it is because 'X' or 'Y' or both have a different reference in each case, even if a closely connected one. Thus 'X is a different F from Y' entails 'X is not identical with Y'. This is a quite general point and our remarks about groups are no exception to it, for 'F' here stands in only for genuine predicates, and 'group' is not a genuine predicate. It is a quite special word having the function I have tried to describe. Thus 'X is the same group as Y' does not mean the same as 'X is a group, and Y is a group, and X is identical with Y' and is not entailed by it.

Can a group have groups as members? Certainly it can. But there is no distinction between the group of certain groups and the group of those aggregates, those particulars, which those groups are. These groups are the same groups, not simply identical aggregates. Let us try to make this point clear with our usual example. The United Kingdom is the group of England, Scotland, Wales, and Northern Ireland. It is also the group of the English counties, Scotland, Wales and Northern Ireland. It is also the group of the English counties and the group of Scottish counties and the group of Welsh counties and the group of Northern Irish counties. For England is identical with the group of English counties, Scotland with the group of Scottish counties, and so on. Now if group A has the same members as group B it is the same group. The properties of a group are the properties of the corresponding aggregate *qua* being an aggregate of the things spoken of as members of the group. But these syncategorematic properties are syncategorematic on the property of being an aggregate of certain particulars, they are not syncategorematic over again on certain properties of those particulars. 'The group of X, Y, and Z is G' means the same as 'The aggregate of X, Y and Z, *qua* being the aggregate of X, Y, and Z is G'. It does not mean something of the character 'The aggregate of X, Y, and Z, *qua* being the aggregate of X *qua* H, Y *qua* J, Z *qua* K, is G'. Hence if X is the group of Ds, Y the group of Es, Z the group of Fs, everything which can be truly said of the group of X, Y, and Z, can be truly said of the group of the group of Ds and the group of Es and the group of Fs. Thus every group of groups is a group of particulars.

This means that there is no class paradox with reference to groups.

One can indeed say of some groups that they are members of themselves. If a square is divided into four squares, and it is, as it may be, the group of squares on a certain page, the group of squares on that page will be a member of itself. On the other hand, the group of the four smaller squares will not be a member of itself. Although it is identical with the first group it is not the same group as it is.

On the face of it, then, we can talk about the group of all groups which are not members of themselves, and meet the familiar paradox that if it is a member of itself it is not a member of itself, and that if it is not a member of itself then it is a member of itself.

If there is a group of which every member is a self-excluding group, that same group will also be a group of which every member is a self-belonging group. The converse only holds if all particulars have parts. As a member of another group a group is not to be distinguished from the aggregate with which it is identical. It is possible for groups A, B, C, and D each to be a different group, and yet for the group of A and B and the group of C and D to be the same group. This will be so (for instance) if A and C are identical, and B and D. Every particular which has parts is both a self-belonging group and a self-excluding group. Thus the group of all groups which are not members of themselves is also a group of groups all of which are members of themselves. It does contain itself as a member, and as a member it both is and isn't a self-belonging group. For the group of all self-excluding groups is the group of all particulars which are identical with self-excluding groups, and hence also a group of particulars each of which is identical with a self-belonging group. It is in fact the group of all compound particulars and as such is the aggregate of all particularistic reality.

While on this subject it is worth remarking that there certainly is a paradox about the property of not exemplifying oneself. On the face of it, some properties do and some don't exemplify themselves. The property of being red isn't red, but the property of being a property does exemplify itself. Then one asks: 'Does the property of not exemplifying oneself exemplify itself or not?' and runs into paradox.

The most straightforward way of dealing with this is to agree that there is a hierarchy of universals. There are particular-universals, that is universals of which instances must be particulars. Then there are particular-universal-universals, that is universals of which instances must be particular-universals, and so on. Then the property of being a particular-universal will not exemplify it-self, and the property of being a particular-universal which does not exemplify itself will be identical with the property of being a particular-universal. This property will itself be a particular-universal-universal, hence only exemplifiable by particular-universals, hence not exemplifiable by itself.

A difficulty about this doctrine is that the properties of Being a particular and Being a universal will be properties on different levels, whereas one is inclined to think of them as being on the same level. The answer to this difficulty is that the sense in which they are on the same level is different from the sense in which they are not on the same level.

It seems then that one should not strictly speak of universals. One should speak of particular-universals, of fact-universals, of particular-universal-universals, of fact-universal-universals, and so on. Normally by 'universal' will be meant a particular-universal. Note that 'This particular is not a particular-universal' can be treated as false rather than as meaningless.

In coming to these views about the nature of groups I have been a good deal influenced by Chapters XV-XVIII of Mc-Taggart's *The Nature of Existence*. However there are several ways in which my account diverges from that of McTaggart.

Groups as described both by McTaggart and myself can only have particulars for members. Is there then no such thing as a group of properties, a group of relations, or a group of facts?

I do not think one could reasonably suppose that there could be individuals known as groups of properties in quite the same sense of group as that in which there are groups of particulars. For it does not seem that one property can be the aggregate of other properties, in quite the same sense of 'aggregate', as that in which a particular can be an aggregate of particulars. One might suppose that a conjunction of properties was an aggregate of properties. But in that case an aggregate of the colours would be an impossible property, Being red and green and . . . . If F and G are incompatible, we are indeed bound to allow that there is such a property as the conjunction of them, though an un-exemplifiable one, but it seems hard to believe that, if we talk of the group of the colours, we are talking about this rather recondite entity.

In this respect the disjunction of two properties will do better as their aggregate than will a conjunction of them. For every two possible properties there is a possible property which is their disjunction.

This suggests another point. The particulars A and B can only go together to make up one compound particular. But one might wish to say that there may be at least two 'compound' properties made up of the properties F and G, namely their disjunction and their conjunction. One might reasonably say that both *Being F and G* and *Being F or G* have the same parts, put together in different ways. There can be no parallel to this in the case of particulars.

My suggestion is that by 'The group of F and G' one might mean either 'The disjunction of F and G, *qua* being the disjunction of F and G' or 'The conjunction of F and G, *qua* being the conjunction of F and G', and that for most purposes it does not matter which one chooses. If I say 'The group of F properties is fivefold' I could often equally mean either 'The disjunction of all F properties *qua* being the disjunction of all F properties is fivefold' or 'The conjunction of all F properties *qua* being the conjunction of all F properties is fivefold'. But since the conjunction is often that rather recondite thing, an impossible property, it is convenient to take 'The group of F properties' as meaning 'The disjunction of all F properties *qua* being the disjunction of all F properties'.

The same goes for relations. Talk of the group of certain relations, as far as ordinary language goes, could be talk either of the disjunction or of the conjunction of these relations, as such. But we may regularize matters by making it always the disjunction which is in question.

When, on the other hand, we come to facts, it is evident that talk of a group of facts can be identified with talk of the conjunction of these facts. It may even be more illuminating to say that a conjunction of facts is a group of facts. For of every two facts there is a conjunction, while it is difficult to make any sense of talk of disjunctive facts.

Thus talk of a group of certain properties, or of a group of certain relations, has the relation to talk of the disjunction of those properties, or of the disjunction of those relations, which talk of a group of certain particulars has to talk of the aggregate of those particulars. And talk of the group of certain facts is related to talk of the conjunction of those facts in this same way.

Thus, unlike McTaggart, we are prepared to extend the notion of groups so that there can be groups of universals and of facts, as well as groups of particulars.

Part Two

SEMIOTIC BACKGROUND

VI

PRAGMATIC AND
SEMANTIC MEANING

The purpose of this chapter is to distinguish between pragmatic and semantic meaning.[1] This is a distinction which can only be made, however, within the meaning of a sentence which expresses a propositional attitude.

A sentence-utterance is propositional to the degree to which it is appropriate to ask such questions as: 'Do you agree with him?' 'Did he really mean what he said?' 'Have I properly grasped what he was saying?'[2] It is ceremonial to the extent to which such questions are inappropriate, and the nearest one can get to them is something like 'Was that a proper thing, or the proper thing, to say at that point?' or 'What are the social implications of that remark?' I am not saying, by the way, that the latter question cannot be asked about propositional sentences.

A sentence-utterance is the saying of a sentence by someone on a particular occasion. Such saying may be public or solitary. It may be that one says the sentence to oneself in the essential privacy of inner speech. No-one else has much opportunity to ask whether such an utterance is sincere, but one may ask it of oneself.

When one asks whether a propositional sentence-utterance is sincere, one asks whether the speaker really has the propositional attitude which the utterance purportedly expresses. If I say 'There is only one God' this question can normally be asked. If I say 'The Queen! God bless her' it cannot properly be asked.

[1] Many authors have made the same or a related distinction in these or other words. C. Morris originated something like this use of these words.
[2] Cf. Austin, *How to do things with Words*, p. 79.

The difference between a propositional utterance and a ceremonial utterance is one of degree. Moreover, while there are completely propositional sentence-utterances, being purely ceremonial is rather something to which utterances get closer and closer, without there being many, or even any, which are completely ceremonial, that is entirely non-propositional.

Propositional sentence-utterances, and propositional sentence-utterances only, have pragmatic meaning, and this is a matter, we shall claim, of the propositional attitudes they express.

What is a propositional attitude? A propositional attitude, one might begin by saying, is an attitude directed at a proposition. But what is a proposition? A proposition in the relevant sense must be something which one may believe to be the case, wish to be the case, intend to be the case, and so on. One may believe it to be the case that Britain is governed by men who think ahead, one may wish it were the case that Britain is governed by men who think ahead, or one may (if suitably situated) intend it to be the case that Britain is governed by men who think ahead.

It is tempting to say that a propositional attitude is that which is described by some sentence of the form: 'x v'd that p'. But this will not do. On that account 'He asserted that it was raining' describes a propositional attitude. But assertion is not what an utterance can express. Rather the expression of a belief is an assertion. Thus one must at least introduce the restriction that a sentence describing a propositional attitude must not imply the occurrence of any public linguistic activity.

The word 'proposition' is too much associated in most people's minds with declarative sentences and assertions, as opposed, say, to imperative or optative sentences. Moreover, the ontological status of what is referred to by the expression 'proposition' is perplexing. I shall therefore replace *proposition* by *objective*, explaining the latter's ontological status as follows.

In our chapter on facts we pointed out that every fact has a quintessential property and various essential properties implied by it. Thus the fact of A's redness has the quintessential property of containing A in the exemplifying role, and redness in the exemplified role, and has among other essential properties, the property of having redness in the exemplified role. Suppose now that we wonder if B is red. We have before our minds the fact-property, *containing B in the exemplifying role and redness in the exemplified role,* which property is the sort of property fitted to be the quintessential property of a fact, and our wondering whether B is red is our taking up a certain attitude to this fact-property. Equally, if I wonder whether, believe that, or disbelieve that there is anything at all which is a unicorn, I am taking up a certain attitude to the fact-property, *being a fact with being a unicorn in the exemplified role.* Note that I am not wondering whether, believing that, or disbelieving that, there is such a fact. I am wondering whether, believing that, or disbelieving that, there is a unicorn, but this is to take up certain attitudes to the fact-property mentioned. Fact-properties of this kind are what I call 'objectives'.

We shall stick to the phrase 'propositional attitude', even though we talk of them now as directed onto objectives rather than propositions. The phrase is familiar to most readers, and is not liable to suggest a special connection with cognition rather than volition, as is the phrase 'proposition' itself.

To know the pragmatic meaning of a sentence-utterance, then, is to know what propositional attitude it expresses, or purports to express. To know the semantic meaning of a sentence-utterance is to know what objective it is which (or to know some characterization of the objective which)[1] is the object of the propositional attitude which it expresses or purports to express. The only sense in which a sentence-utterance specifies a certain objective is that it picks it out as that objective which is the object of whatever propositional attitude it expresses.

---

[1] As will be seen in the next chapter, in some cases one may know the pragmatic and semantic meaning (in a given language) of some utterance in virtue of being able to infer from it that the speaker has a belief, or a wish, or whatever, which concerns a certain particular, without knowing precisely the individual property in the objective which applies to that particular. In other cases where the objective believed, wished, or otherwise entertained by the speaker concerns a particular not simply as the one which has a certain individual property but in a fashion more direct, the hearer may know only that it concerns *some* definite particular of a certain sort. Thus 'inferring the propositional attitude expressed by an utterance' will often not be inferring that a certain objective is believed, wished, or whatever, but that some objective of a certain sort is believed, wished, or whatever. The indefiniteness of most objectives (the non-quintessential ones) believed, wished, or whatever as regards the actual facts which may exemplify them should not be confused with the indefiniteness here in question as to the objective believed, wished, or whatever.

A certain ambiguity may be found in our account of pragmatic meaning. Does the pragmatic meaning just tell us the type of propositional attitude expressed, that is, whether it is a belief, a wish, or what? Or does it also tell us at what objective (or at an objective of what sort) it is directed? Indeed a similar ambiguity belongs to the expression propositional attitude itself. On the whole it seems more convenient to say that identity of pragmatic meaning includes identity of the objective (or sort of objective) in question. Thus pragmatic meaning determines semantic meaning, but not vice versa.

A word about the expression 'sentence-utterance', which should usually be understood henceforth as an abbreviation for 'propositional sentence utterance', is called for. It would be convenient if we could understand this latter phrase as equivalent to 'an utterance with pragmatic meaning', or perhaps rather as 'an utterance with pragmatic meaning, having no parts which have pragmatic meaning'. That is, its parts would not have pragmatic meaning in the sense of that phrase so far developed. However these parts which do not have pragmatic meaning might be instances of a word sequence of which other utterances do have pragmatic meaning, as for instance in the case of the antecedent and consequent in a conditional sentence utterance.

I suggest that the utterance of a certain sentence in a certain situation be described as calculated to express a certain propositional attitude if on the basis of the usual linguistic habits of the speaker it can be inferred with very high probability that he has that propositional attitude. And I suggest that it be said actually to express that state, if not only is this condition satisfied, but it is also true that he has that propositional attitude.

To know the pragmatic meaning of a *sentence* in the linguistic habits of a certain speaker is to know (in practice or as a matter of theory) what highly probable inferences can be made, from its utterance by him in any normal situation, about the propositional attitudes he has.

To know the pragmatic meaning of a sentence in the linguistic habits of a certain community is to know the same thing about members of the community in general.

The meaning which a sentence has in English may not be quite the same as that which it has in Mr Smith's English. For instance, 'slightly' may mean in his English what is usually meant by 'very', if he is given to irony. On the other hand, it is more likely that 'slightly' with a certain (somewhat unusual) intonation means in English what 'very' means in its most usual intonation, and that Mr Smith is just peculiarly given to using 'slightly' with that special intonation.

The most likely sort of divergence in the meaning, which a sentence has for Mr Smith and the meaning which it has in English, is that it has certain more specific meanings in Mr Smith's English. That is, knowing it is Mr Smith speaking, one can make an additional inference one could not make if one merely knew that it was an Englishman speaking.

There is, of course, the English of various sub-classes of Englishmen. There is also correct English. But what is correct English may be to some extent a matter of preference rather than of fact.

2

What bearing does the pragmatic meaning of a sentence have upon its use in communication?

One way of elucidating the bearing might proceed as follows: One might point out that as well as there being such a thing as uttering a sentence, there is such a thing as acquiescing in the utterance of a sentence.

In the linguistic repertoire of an individual there are always (I presume) certain acts such that when they occur in a certain relation to the utterance of a sentence by someone else (or even the speaker?) the same inferences to the states of that individual can be made as if he had uttered that sentence himself. Among such acts of acquiescence which exist in English are the saying of 'I agree' or 'I know' after an utterance by someone else. But there are many other acts of acquiescence which do not consist in uttering anything commonly recognized as a word, and which are therefore more difficult to specify, though in fact we constantly rely upon them. Certain sorts of silence, certain expressions of face, belong to this category. The fact that they do allow such inferences, and that they are systematically related to what are admittedly linguistic acts, makes it permissible to call them also linguistic acts.

To the same general category as acts of acquiescence, belong acts of rejection. There are also acts of modified acquiescence, such as are tantamount to making the utterance in some modified form. Saying 'yes' in response to a question obviously belongs to this category.

I have already indicated that the 'inner' utterance of a sentence to oneself may just as well have pragmatic meaning as may an 'outer' utterance. Such inner utterance may consist in the passing of images of words through one's mind, or in incipient speaking movements. Certainly no one else can infer from such an utterance that I have a certain propositional attitude. None the less a connection between those words and a certain propositional attitude may exist, such that from the fact – were it known – that those words had run 'through my head', together with knowledge about my linguistic habits – including my habits of inner speech – it could be inferred with high reliability that I had that propositional attitude. Thus the 'utterance' may have pragmatic meaning.

Suppose that I am reading, and that as I read an inner speaking of the words read occurs. In this case my production of the words is in response to a visual stimulus which is in a certain specially close relation to the inner speech, in that every individual sound-image, or whatever, is in response to a discrete part of the visual stimulus, according to a fixed association. (This is a rough indication of the way in which such visual stimulus differs from the visual stimulus from the environment when I describe it.) In this special case, the usual inferences cannot be drawn. For it should not be inferred that I have the beliefs, the wishes, the hopes and so forth which, if I was producing the sentence other than in a reading context, it could be inferred that I have. However, if I perform certain other acts, besides the reading, or perhaps even if I refrain from performing certain acts, then the fact that I am doing so allows the usual inferences – were there anyone to draw them – from my production of these words to be drawn after all. Thus these various performances, or even non-performances, serve in effect as acts of acquiescence directed at the words I am producing in the reading situation. Doubtless that which serves as an act of acquiescence in the reading situation differs from person to person.

Suppose now we consider someone listening to somebody else speaking, without joining in the talk much. Let us take the extreme case of someone listening to a radio talk. Here he simply hears the words of the talk; he probably does not produce them himself at all. Can anything be inferred from the fact that he hears those words about his propositional attitudes? Presumably not. But what I suggest is that here again, there are certain things he may do, normally purely private things, such that if he does them we may make the same inference as we would make if it was he who was talking. Again, it may even be that it is the absence of certain things which allows this inference.

One might hope to make use of the notion of acquiescence for an expansion of the notion of pragmatic meaning. What one would try to do is claim that the pragmatic meaning of a sentence for a given speaker or group of speakers is given by all the inferences which can be drawn about their propositional attitudes not only from utterances of it in various circumstances, but also by acquiescence in it in various circumstances. Such a definition has the advantage that inferences derivable from one's reactions to hearing a sentence belong to its pragmatic meaning for one.

But suppose I am reading a book in which the author says 'I was born in London'. According to our account, if I respond to my reading of this with an act of acquiescence, the same inference is drawable about me as would be drawable if I had said – in a non-reading context – 'I was born in London'. It is tempting to say that such an inference would be mistaken, and that from an act of acquiescence to this sentence the inference which can be drawn is the same as if I said in a non-reading context 'The author of this book was born in London', while looking at that book. But as 'act of acquiescence' has so far been described this would only show that the act in question was not, when directed at this sentence, an act of acquiescence, but an act of modified acquiescence. Surely this shows a need to revise the definition of act of acquiescence.

To do this, we should take it, from the start, that when I read or listen to someone speaking, I am making my own in-ferences about the propositional attitudes of the speaker or writer, basing myself on my knowledge of *his* linguistic habits, and that the acts of mine which should be called acts of acquiescence, are those acts which are a reliable sign that I either have or am in the process of falling into those propositional attitudes which I have inferred that the speaker or writer has. If I want you to know that I thus acquiesce, I will choose acts of acquiescence in my reper-toire, which I know you will recognize as such. But acts of acquiescence need not be produced for purposes of communication like this.

This may, anyway, seem a better account of what goes on when I read or listen than that implicit in what I said before. For that account suggested that from reading or hearing your words I fell straight into propositional attitudes directed on to the things you talked of, while this account suggests that I do this via forming beliefs about what your propositional attitudes, directed onto those things, are; and this may seem a better account.

On the whole, it does not (after all) seem that there is much point in regarding it as part of the pragmatic meaning of a sentence that one who acquiesces in it has a certain propositional attitude. One may, indeed, say that linguistic acts often are determined in their pragmatic meaning largely by what the speaker has just been hearing, but it does not seem fruitful to regard the pragmatic meaning of these reaction utterances as part of the pragmatic meaning of the utterance reacted to.

3

So let us return to the question of communication after this false but not unrevealing start.

I suggest that the essence of communication is the making clear to other people that one has various propositional attitudes. This may be a mere platitude, but some philosophers might say that it was misleading.

Suppose, looking outside, I see snow falling, and I say 'It's snowing'. It sounds a bit absurd to say that I am making clear to you that I believe or know that it is snowing. Isn't it rather that I am simply drawing your attention to the snow? If an analysis of such drawing of attention is asked for, one may say that it consists simply in saying something which I know will direct your attention to the snow. Letting you know something about my state of mind has nothing to do with it, it may be said.

But is it not true that you have understood my utterance if and only if you take it as a sign that I believe (or know) that it is snowing? Certainly if on looking out you decide that the 'snow' is the feathers of doves falling from a ledge where they sit above, and are therefore not prompted to the belief that it is snowing, it does not follow that you do not understand me. What you do or do not believe about snow has nothing to do with whether you have understood me. So long as you take it as a sign that I believe that it is snowing, you have understood me, and not otherwise. Is it really unreasonable to say that the reason you look out of the window is that you have heard me make noises which you take as a sign that I believe it is snowing? It is only unreasonable, I suggest, if one thinks that one can only take something to be the case, if one describes the something to oneself in an elaborate inner monologue.

But if I say something of a less immediately checkable nature, that this is what is involved in understanding becomes still more obvious. If I say 'The Conservatives will win the next election', you don't immediately fall into the belief that the Conservatives will win the next election. Rather you fall into the belief that I believe this, and then wonder whether I am right in believing this or not.

On such subjects as you take me to be an authority on – be it only my doings this morning – you do indeed almost immediately fall into believing that which my words express my belief in. But it is fair to say that your belief in this objective is an inference from your belief in the objective that I believe in this objective.

It must be remembered that language is not only used in communication. I run through inner monologues. The sentences I then utter are symptomatic, in virtue of my linguistic habits, of my having various propositional attitudes. But I am not speaking in order to let my propositional attitudes be known.

What gives the sentence 'It is snowing' its meaning is that its utterance by an English speaker is a generally reliable sign that he believes that it is snowing. This fact can be made use of by those who wish to reveal their belief states in communication. But it cannot be said that it is a reliable sign that the speaker is trying to get someone else to believe that it is snowing.

It may be said that the saying aloud in the presence of another of 'It is snowing' is a reliable sign that the speaker wants it to be thought that be believes that it is snowing, and that this is part of the pragmatic meaning of 'It is snowing' in general, and of this utterance of it in particular. I would agree to this. But I would still point out that the simplest way of giving the maximum information about the pragmatic, indeed generally about the meaning, of the sentence 'It is snowing', is to say that its utterance, public or private, is a generally reliable sign that the speaker believes it is snowing. This is true of it under a much wider range of circumstances, than those under which it is true of it that it is a reliable sign that the speaker wishes it to be thought that he believes that it is snowing.

But there is more to it than this. When I say 'The Conservatives will win the next election' it may be that that is symptomatic not just of my belief that they will, but also of my wish to let you know that I have this belief. But the relation between this wish and the utterance is rather different from that between the belief and the utterance. To get an utterance related to this wish as this utterance is to the belief we need the utterance 'I wish you believed that I believe that the Conservatives will win the next election', or 'Oh that you believed that I believed that the Conservatives will win the next election'.

There is a sense in which I am deliberately expressing my belief about the Conservatives by saying 'The Conservatives will win the next election' and not deliberately expressing it when I say 'I wish that you believed that I believe that the Conservatives will win the next election'. One deliberately expresses a certain propositional state when one deliberately emits a sign that one is in that state. Thus when I deliberately express my belief that p I pick on a sentence which I know you will take as a sign that I have this belief. The sentence 'S' deliberately expresses a propositional attitude A if and only if 'S' has been produced in order to produce a correct belief that the speaker has propositional attitude A.

If one may infer that a person is deliberately expressing his belief that the King is dead by saying 'The King is dead', one may infer that he wishes us to believe that he believes that the King is dead. This inference will be based upon a knowledge of the speaker's linguistic habits. It seems then that one can say that his sentence expresses his wish for us to believe that he has the belief. It will however be a useful restriction upon our use of the word 'express' if we say that where a sentence deliberately expresses a propositional attitude, it cannot also be said to *express* the wish that the speaker be believed to have that propositional attitude. This will save us from having to say that in communication every utterance expresses a wish.

4

Do imperative sentences express wishes? That is, can one always infer with high probability from the utterance of an imperative to the existence of a wish? I believe that this is indeed so, and that it is the distinctive feature of the imperative form to express wishes, usually deliberately but sometimes, at any rate in first person forms, undeliberately. I suspect that people may still say to themselves in moments of stress such things as 'Let me only have courage'.

Anyway I would claim that 'Shut the door' or 'Please, shut the door' is calculated to express, probably deliberately, a wish that the door be shut.

Are there any serious reasons against the view that such imperatives are calculated to express wishes, and that this is the characteristic function of this grammatical form? It may strike some people as rather trite to say this. That's not a reason for rejecting it. But maybe some philosophers think that what it is to have a wish is analysable in terms of a readiness to utter imperatives. This is no more and no less plausible than the claim that what it is to have a belief is analysable in terms of a readiness to utter declarative sentences. Neither claim, anyway, need conflict with anything we have said. We need not deny that in some sense or other the utterance of a declarative (or an imperative) may actually in some part embody the belief (or wish) it is said to express. In a later chapter there will be some discussion of what such embodiment might amount to.[1] But to believe or wish can't just be to make the noises, and that the making of the noises embodies a belief or a wish will be something that has to be inferred from the linguistic habits of the speaker.

5

It is to be noted that a speaker cannot, on our definition, express a propositional attitude he does not have. What then shall we say of the case where he deliberately speaks in a way which would usually express a certain propositional attitude in order that others shall believe that he has that propositional attitude? One can simply say that he is pretending to express that propositional attitude, or that the utterance purports to express that propositional attitude.

[1] See p. 325.

But now a certain complication needs to be introduced. When I infer one of X's propositional attitudes from what he says, in virtue of his linguistic habits, it may be that the habits in question are ones peculiar, at least in part, to himself, or it may be that all the relevant linguistic habits are those of each member of a certain group to which he belongs. In short my inference to his having that propositional attitude may be reliable in virtue of the habits of each member of a certain group, or it may be that it is reliable in virtue of habits peculiar to himself.

Presuming that the inference is successful in a given case, we may say that he expresses the propositional attitude in the language of the group or only in his own language, according as to whether it is the linguistic habits of each member of the group or those peculiar to himself to which appeal must be made. Similarly, he pretends to express it in the language of his group, or in his own language, according to whether he is trading on people's knowledge of group habits or of his own peculiar habits, in order to carry out his deception. What a sentence-utterance expresses in the language of a group must be included in what it expresses in the language of the individual, but the converse does not hold.

We may sum things up as follows: To ask the pragmatic meaning of a sentence-utterance is to ask what it expresses, deliberately or otherwise, or what it pretends to express. The answer may of course be that it has no pragmatic meaning; but assuming it has, one must distinguish the pragmatic meaning it has, taken as a sentence in the language of some group, from the pragmatic meaning it has, taken in the individual language of the speaker.

To know the pragmatic meaning of a sentence in the language of a certain group is to know all that can be inferred regarding the speaker's propositional attitudes from its utterance in all possible different situations, in virtue of the linguistic habits of each member of the group. To know the pragmatic meaning of a sentence in the individual or peculiar language of an individual is to know all that can be inferred regarding his propositional attitudes from its utterance in all possible situations by that individual in virtue of his linguistic habits. If all that can be known is that no such reliable inferences can be made then the sentence has no pragmatic meaning in the language in question.

To ask the semantic meaning of a sentence-utterance, is to

ask simply on to what objective or on to an objective of what sort that propositional attitude is directed, which needs to be specified in giving its pragmatic meaning. So to ask the semantic meaning of a sentence in the language of a certain group is to ask what can be inferred in all possible circumstances from its utterance regarding the objectives towards which the speaker has a propositional attitude. The relativity of pragmatic meaning to the group according to whose language the question is asked carries over to semantic meaning, of course.

To ask the pragmatic or semantic meaning of a word or phrase can only be to ask how it contributes to determining the pragmatic or semantic meaning of sentences in which it occurs. To ask the pragmatic or semantic meaning of a word-utterance is to ask how it contributes to determining the pragmatic or semantic meaning of the sentence-utterance in which it occurs.

6

Brief mention should be made of a third type of meaning which a sentence must possess. I shall call this type of meaning 'syntactic meaning', though its elucidation requires a reference to pragmatic meaning which would not be allowed in such studies as many philosophers and linguists would alone want to call 'syntactical'.

The syntactic meaning of a sentence, as I understand it, is a matter of the contribution made by utterance of it to the pragmatic, and hence also the semantic, meaning of other utterances which stand in certain relations to utterance of it.

It could, for instance, be said to be part of the syntactic meaning of 'John is ill' that a sentence which immediately follows in the same conversation and in which the first singular term is 'he' is one in which 'he' refers to the same person as did 'John'. Thus 'John is ill' helps to specify the semantic meaning contributed by 'he' in such an utterance. This is a very general aspect of the syntactic meaning of any sentence containing an ordinary proper name.

Consider the two sentences 'Tom kicked Jim' and 'Jim was kicked by Tom'. These have the same pragmatic meaning, but different syntactic meanings. For if one says afterwards 'After that he burst into tears' this utterance has a different pragmatic meaning in either case.

The syntactic meaning of an utterance is the influence which it has on the pragmatic meaning of surrounding utterances. Clearly this depends to a great extent on the grammatical structure of the original utterance in question. It might then seem that we should regard the way in which the pragmatic meaning of a sentence-utterance is built up from the arrangement of its elements as included in its syntactic meaning. To have the same syntactic meaning two sentences would, at the least, have to be intensionally isomorphic. However, although the structure of an utterance is the main determinant of its syntactical meaning I would rather stick to the definition of syntactical meaning given.

Two sentences could doubtless only have identical syntactical meanings by being the same sentence. It is best to regard syntactical synonymy as a matter of degree.

From a philosophical point of view syntactical divergence between pragmatically synonymous sentences is interesting primarily where it does not consist in one sentence being a standard grammatical transformation of the other. It is arguable, for instance, that 'Dropping bombs on cities is wrong' and 'I disapprove of dropping bombs on cities' come close to being pragmatically synonymous, and that the divergence between them is mainly syntactic. This latter divergence is exemplified if utterance of each is followed by 'I can't accept that' or 'Nonsense' uttered by someone else, which will have a different pragmatic meaning according to which it follows.

There is much to be said for the view that 'Dropping bombs on cities is wrong' expresses a special sort of wish directed on the objective that people do not drop bombs on cities (or a *negative wish* directed on the objective that people do drop bombs on cities). Whether 'Dropping bombs on cities is wrong' and 'I disapprove of people dropping bombs on cities' have the same pragmatic meaning or not would (in that case) seem to depend on whether the latter expresses this same wish, or whether it expresses awareness of the existence of this wish on one's part. But on either view they would have a radically different syntactic meaning, which would serve to explain why they tend to introduce different sorts of conversation. Since a whole range of standard conversational responses, verbal and otherwise, are given a different pragmatic meaning, a different sort of conversation follows most easily and naturally on each remark.

VII

TYPES OF REFERENCE

A discussion which aims to give precise meanings to various terms usually needs, to begin with, some rather vague terms to indicate the general area within which distinctions are being made. For this reason, I shall deliberately use a certain term in a vague way. The term in question is 'refer', also its cognates, 'reference', 'referent' (meaning 'thing referred to'), etc.

I shall now endeavour to give to the terms 'denote' and 'connote' an exact sense, one derived from, but not entirely in conformity with, traditional usage as encapsulated in J. S. Mill's *A System of Logic*. The first thing will be to describe a meaning for these terms wherein it is only singular terms which *denote* and *connote*.

In using the expression singular term, I wish for the present to refer to such terms as refer, or in W. V. O. Quine's convenient phrase, purport to refer, to one *particular*. 'Singular term', as I use it for the moment, refers to the same terms as does 'Concrete singular term' for J. S. Mill.

The singular term 'The present President of France', as used by anyone talking ordinary English, at the period I am writing,[1] refers to Charles de Gaulle. It refers to him, on any occasion, in virtue of the fact that he has a certain *individual* property, namely being the President of France at the time of that occasion. This fact may be expressed by saying that the expression *denotes* the man, De Gaulle, and *connotes* the essentially individual property of being the present President of France.

The noun 'denotation' may refer either to the relation between

[1] 1965.

a singular term and what it denotes, or to the thing denoted by a singular term. I shall adopt the latter use. The relation may be called 'the denoting relation' or merely 'denoting'.

I shall also adopt the corresponding use of 'connotation'. The connotation of a singular term will be the essentially individual property which it connotes. The relation between them will be called 'connoting'.

It has long been debated whether a proper name such as 'Charles de Gaulle' has denotation and connotation. My view will be given shortly.

I am using such phrases as 'denote' and 'connote', as also 'refer', and all other expressions for modes of reference which I may introduce, primarily for a relation which an expression stands in to something only when considered in its occurrence in a particular utterance by a particular person at a particular time. In this primary use, 'The present President of France' will denote De Gaulle as it occurs in the utterance I made this morning, when I said 'The present President of France certainly likes to keep people guessing'. It does not, considered merely as a noise or a mark (strictly as a property which particular noises or marks may have), denote at all. However, talk of an expression denoting something may mean that in any typical utterance in which it occurs (within perhaps some fairly obvious context of space and time) it will denote the thing in question. Precisely similar remarks go for all other semantic terms I am using. I should remark perhaps that I count my assent to an utterance of *yours*, which I *understand* in a certain way, as a different utterance on my part of the same sentence as you uttered. I also count inner private utterances of sentences as utterances.

Obviously one can say of 'The present President of France' and of 'De Gaulle' that they refer to De Gaulle without specifying the occurrence of the expressions in question, because the referent is the same for every typical occurrence. One cannot in the same way talk of the referent of 'This'. But one can say that 'This' typically does have a referent, and just one referent, and one can discuss the nature of the semantic relation it has to its referent. 'This' counts as a singular term, for in every typical occurrence it refers to just one particular. The same goes for a word such as 'I', but here one can say that it always refers to something in a certain easily statable relation to its utterance (that of utterer to utterance).

The expression 'The present President of France', occurring in any utterance, connotes a certain property, the property, to put it rather roughly, of being the President of France at the time of this utterance. Anyone who sees that this expression consists in certain shorter expressions which are arranged in a certain way, and who knows the meaning of these shorter expressions, can tell thereby that this is the property it connotes. One may say that the expression *explicitly* connotes that property. If the expression 'De Gaulle' connotes an individual property, one must allow that its connoting is implicit rather than explicit.

Suppose one man says to another 'The man you were so angry with yesterday lives over there'. The singular term in the subject position here may connote not the property of being the only man you were so angry with yesterday but the property of being the only man you were so angry with yesterday in my (the speaker's) presence. That is, it may be this latter property which a man must possess in order to be the referent of the singular term, not the former property. Examples of this kind could be multiplied. In such a case one may say that the definite description is not completely explicit.

It should be noted that on occasion a definite description may be not so much incompletely explicit, as explicit to the wrong effect. That is, the compound meaning which one might take the expression as having on the basis of its component expressions may be such as would supply a connotation for the expression different from what it has. I might for instance say 'The President of India has arrived in England' when I have heard that Mr Shastri has arrived here.[1] Now Mr Shastri is not the President but the Prime Minister of India. One may want to say, not that I uttered a falsehood but that I said something true about Mr Shastri, though I used the wrong description by which to refer to him. If one is justified in saying this, it is because the connotation attached to the expression 'The President of India' by me on that occasion is an individual property which Mr Shastri in fact has, although that property would more correctly have been connoted by 'The Prime Minister of India'. A more extreme but still possible case would be one where a man is generally thought to be the author of a book, say *The Wisdom of the North*, but is not in fact the author. If I then say 'The Author of *The Wisdom of the*

[1] Written in 1965.

North is ill' when I hear news about the reputed author of the book, my utterance may rightly count as true even though the real author of the book is in fine health. For my expression may connote the property of being generally considered the author of this book (which is compatible with either being the real author or not). This holds whether I did or didn't suspect at the time of the utterance that the reputed author was not the real author. Thus in many cases 'The F' connotes the property of being the reputed F, rather than the actual F. This is so even in many cases where there is no reason for anyone to suspect that the reputed F is not the real F, and where indeed he is the real F. For in many such cases if it should have turned out that the reputed F was not the real F it would be to the reputed F rather than the real F that the speaker should be taken as referring. Thus successful reference can be made to something by a wrong description.

The question 'To whom or what was I referring?' may be distinguished from any question as to whom or to what a listener could properly be expected to take me as referring. Doubtless I normally want my listener to know to whom I am referring. But in some cases my listener can only know that I believe some objective of a certain sort, without knowing what that objective is. If that is so, it may often be that the answer to the question 'To whom was I referring?' turns on what the actual objective of that sort is which I believe, rather than on anything known to the listener. If I say 'A is G', the listener may know that I believe an objective of the form 'Something is uniquely f and is G' without knowing the value of 'f'. If the value of 'f' is in fact 'F' then, unknown to the listener, it is to that particular which is uniquely F that I am referring. The most common situation of this sort, however, is that the listener, though he does not know the value of 'f' knows that it is such as to make the speaker be referring to object X (known to the listener perhaps as being the J). One may say here that the listener knows what 'A' denotes in that utterance, but does not know the private connotation in virtue of which, so far as the speaker is concerned, it does denote it.

Wherever a definite description is incompletely or wrongly explicit (so far as a certain language goes) there will be a definite description (in the language) which explicitly connotes the connotation which the original definite description had implicitly.

In some sense of the word 'equivalent' the original incomplete or misleading definite description is equivalent to the completely explicit definite description which gives its real connotation. The question whether an ordinary proper name has a connotation or not must, if it is a question for serious debate, be logically equivalent to the question whether a proper name is, on each occasion of its use, equivalent (in the sense indicated above) to a completely explicit definite description. For there is, of course, no question of a proper name having an explicit connotation, that is one determined by the meaning of its constituents. If an ordinary proper name is equivalent (in the relevant sense) to a completely explicit description we may call the latter its descriptive equivalent. Thus if 'John Smith' has a connotation when it occurs in such an utterance as 'I met John Smith yesterday' there will be some descriptive equivalent of it. It might for example be 'the man with freckles whom I first met on a C.N.D. march'. I shall call this kind of equivalence 'subjective equivalence'. That it holds is something not determinable by public language rules, but only by knowing the actual objective of a certain general sort believed by the speaker. It is not, of course, a relation of synonymy in any ordinary sense.

When the expression 'De Gaulle' occurs on one's lips there is always a property which it connotes, and a definite description which would explicitly connote this property. But 'De Gaulle' (neither in this occurrence nor any other) is in no wise synonymous with this its descriptive equivalent. In order that you shall be said to have *understood* me, in the ordinary sense of the term, it is not required that you know to what the name in my utterance of it was subjectively equivalent. Rather, the connotation the name has for you must be such as to give it the same denotation.

Not every singular term has connotation. There are uses of words such as 'This' and 'That' where these expressions do not connote at all. The word 'This' may apply to a certain object I am now attending to, without doing so because that object has a certain individual property. It does not in such a use even connote *being the object I am now attending to*. For one thing I may be attending to two objects at once, to only one of which 'This' refers. It would obviously be absurd to say that 'This' connotes *being referred to by 'This'*.

This use of 'This' is not a common one. Only philosophers

(too few of them!) say such things as 'This is red' where 'This' refers to a sense-datum attended to. Still, if such a mode of reference is intelligible, it is a legitimate object of study and instrument of clarification, however seldom such utterances are normally made. 'This' is, however, sometimes used by ordinary people in this way. Consider, 'This is awful' where 'This' refers to a pain now experienced.

One must refer to logically proper names to explain ordinary demonstratives properly. When 'This' or 'That' is used in ordinary demonstrative fashion they are connotative, and denote physical objects. But if one wishes to give a descriptive equivalent of 'This' in such a usage one will require an expression which contains a nonconnotative 'This'. Thus in 'This is a house' the word 'this' may be subjectively equivalent to 'The physical object of which *this* is a sense-datum'. The 'This' here italicized is nonconnotative.

I shall say that singular terms such as 'This' (in this special use) which refer to particulars but lack connotation are logically proper names and that they alone name particulars. Allegiance to this technical Russellian usage does not indicate that I believe names in the ordinary sense fail to *name* in any way in which they might have been expected to do so. 'Denote' and 'connote' are best kept as complementary, and of a term which does not connote I shall say that it does not denote. The denoting and naming relations are very different.

2

Let us now turn to certain expressions of the type which Mill and Quine call 'singular abstract terms'.

Consider the expression 'My favourite colour'. As uttered by me this expression refers, as it happens, to redness. It does so in virtue of the fact that the property redness has the individual property of being the colour I like most.

Clearly there is every reason to say that this expression connotes the individual property *being the colour I like most* and denotes the property redness. Just about everything said so far about connoting and denoting applies here. So one may allow that it belongs to a class of expressions which denote one single property and connote a certain individual property, such as is exemplifiable by a property.

Now consider the sentence 'Red is a vivid colour'. Here 'Red' evidently refers to Redness. It does not refer to this property because this property has some other property which one could regard as its connotation. It refers to it in something like the same direct way as 'This', when it is nonconnotative, refers to something.

Should one say that 'Red' denotes redness but does not connote anything? I have already urged that 'denote' and 'connote' should be considered as complements. In accordance with what was said above about 'This' it seems appropriate to say that 'Red' occurs in this sentence as a logically proper name for redness.

Consider now the word 'red' as it occurs in 'My car is red'. Here it occurs as the predicate, not as the subject, as in 'Red is my favourite colour'. Occurrence as a predicate is its more typical occurrence. Should one say that it connotes, or that it denotes, or that it names, redness? Or should one introduce some new term for its relation to redness?

Saying that it denotes redness may be ruled out. For if it denotes redness there must also be something which it connotes. and clearly there is nothing for it to connote. Anything which may incline one to say that it denotes redness, will be equally catered for by saying that it names redness. Just as 'This' in the right contexts, and 'Red' in 'Red is a vivid colour', manage somehow to focus attention directly on a particular and on a property respectively and do not apply to them in virtue of the fact that they possess a certain individual property, so it would seem does 'red' in 'My car is red' somehow manage to focus attention on redness.

The choice lies between 'names' and 'connotes', unless a third expression is to be introduced.

The fact that 'red' (as a predicate) focuses attention directly on the property redness does not of itself show that 'naming' rather than 'connoting' is the required expression, for one might well say that where an expression denotes and connotes, it is on the connotation that it focuses attention directly. The expression, 'My car', is connected with a particular physical object, because that object includes among its properties the essentially individual property, *being the only car I possess*. It is connected with the property of being the one car I possess directly, that is, not in virtue of the possession by this property of some higher order property. But if connotation and denotation are to remain complementaries, one should not say that 'red' connotes the property redness unless one has something else for it to denote.

It is not, indeed, required that every expression which connotes should actually succeed in denoting. The expression 'Jeremy Bentham's elder brother' connotes without denoting. However, an expression which connotes must be such that it is appropriate for us to look for something which it denotes.

In the connoting-denoting type expressions so far considered the expression denotes whatever has the property which it connotes. The properties in question were individual properties, which meant that such an expression could denote only one thing. Following the same principle one would have to say that if 'red' connotes redness, then it denotes everything which has the property redness. Put a bit more precisely, one would have to say that 'red' denotes each red thing. Thus it would stand in the denoting relation to many individual things. Denoting would, in these cases, be a one (or many) to one relation.

Such is the traditional view expounded by J. S. Mill in his *Logic*. It may be remarked, however, that, traditionally, the noun 'denotation' is supposed to refer in the case of a predicate type word to the class of things denoted by that word. In the case of 'round' the denotation will be the class of round things. Since the class, as logicians usually conceive it, and likewise the group, of round things is not itself round, it follows that a predicate type word does not normally denote its denotation.

There would then be a contrast between subject-type expressions and predicate-type expressions. For in the former case it does seem sensible to use 'denotation' to refer to the thing denoted by the expression, just as 'connotation' refers to what it connotes. It seems a pity to have to say that the denotation of a so-called general term is not what it denotes. To avoid this one might say that a so-called general term has many denotations, or one might say that a so-called general term denotes the class of objects of which it can be predicated, and does not, after all, denote each individual such object. On the latter view, denoting is a one (or many) to one relation in the case of so-called general terms as well as in the case of so-called singular terms. But one can no longer say that whatever has the property connoted by an expression is denoted by it.

So if redness is said to be the connotation of 'red' (occurring as a predicate) one must say either that it denotes each individual red thing, or one must say that it denotes the class of red things. I think that there are such disadvantages to either way of speaking that one should give up talk of denotation and connotation here.

In the sentence 'My car is red' the expression 'My car' connotes a certain property and denotes the object, namely my car which has the property. Now surely the point, so to speak, of the connotation is to bring me into a relation, which can be called 'talking about' to my car. I may only get to the car, the denoted object, through the connotation, but get to it, in some sense, I do. The denoted object is specified in order that my knowledge of it shall be increased.

All this seems to be lacking if each red thing or the class of red things is taken as denoted by 'red' (as a predicate).

Consider first the view that 'red' denotes each red thing, in the sentence 'My car is red'. Now there is a tomato lying on a plate in Australia which is denoted by 'red', as it occurs in this sentence, according to the view in question. But surely this tomato has nothing to do with what I am saying when I say 'My car is red'. And so on with all the other things denoted by 'red' except my car itself. To talk of 'red' (in this sentence) as denoting each of those things suggests a closeness of connection between each of those things and this sentence which simply does not hold. Much the same objection applies to the idea that 'red' denotes the group of red things.

If the only choice were between saying that 'red' connoted the property redness, and saying that it denoted it, one might be thrown back again on saying that it denoted it. Certainly it seems that the property redness is connected with the sentence 'My car is red' in more the same sort of way in which my car is, than the sort of way in which that tomato in Australia is, or than a group which contains such things as that tomato is.

However, there is no need to make this choice. For it is rather by saying that 'red' (as a predicate) is a logically proper name for redness, that one will bring out just the right analogies.

Just as 'This' in 'This is red' and 'Red' in 'Red is a vivid colour' draw attention to a certain particular and a certain property, respectively, in a quite unmediated manner, so does 'red' in 'My car is red' draw attention to a certain property (redness again in fact) in a quite unmediated manner. Just as the relation between 'this' and a particular and 'red' (in 'Red is vivid') and redness is not complementary to some other equally important relation, so 'red' is not thus complementary in 'My car is red'.

But what of Mill's and Quine's distinction[1] between an abstract singular term for a universal and a concrete general term for concrete things, the contrast between 'Redness' and 'red'?

All that really needs preserving in it may be preserved by saying that the name of a universal may occur either as subject or as predicate of a sentence. There is no question of minimizing *this* distinction.

A true sentence stands in a certain relation to a fact. There will be more on this relation later. Let us agree for the present to call it 'representing' or 'representation'. Every fact, as we have seen, has a structure, that is to say, its elements play different roles in it. When a sentence represents a fact, it must have, for each element of the fact, an expression which refers to it. There must also be some indication of the role played in the fact by each element referred to by an expression in the sentence. Now a universal can occur in a fact either as thing exemplified or as thing exemplifying. So when a sentence contains a name for a universal it must indicate whether the object named plays an exemplifying role or the exemplified role. One way of doing this is to put the name for the universal in a certain position in the sentence. Another way is to modify the name itself. If one or other of these devices shows that the universal named by an expression plays the exemplified role in the fact represented, then that name is said to be the predicate of the sentence. If one or other of these devices shows that the universal named by an expression plays an exemplifying role in the fact represented, then that name is said to be a subject of the sentence.

One device for making a name for a universal into the predicate of a sentence is to precede it by the so-called copula 'is'. It is convenient to regard the copula as actually part of the name for the universal, when that name is modified in such a manner as to make or help to make it the predicate of the sentence. Thus in 'My car is red' one can take 'is red' as a name of redness, a name modified so as to make clear that it is the predicate. Similarly, in 'Redness is vivid', 'Redness' is a name of redness, so modified as to emphasize that it is the subject of the sentence.

1   J. S. Mill, *A System of Logic*, Book I, Chapter II. W. V. O. Quine, *Word and Object*, Chapter III.

I have rather over-simplified the role of the copula here. For one thing I have ignored its part in determining the time at which the universal is supposed to be exemplified. But this does not matter for the present purpose.

Just as in 'This is red' the expression 'is red' is a name for the property redness, but a name modified so as to make clear that it is the predicate, so in the sentence 'De Gaulle is a man', 'is a man' is a name for the property, being a man. The same reasoning holds here as in the case of adjectives. If one chose to say that 'is' was not part of the predicate, but simply a bit of machinery for indicating where the predicate is to be found (which is just as legitimate a way of putting it) one would say that just as 'red' names redness so 'man', *in this sentence* names *being a man*. There will be some discussion of common nouns as *subjects* later. It would be a mistake to think that if 'man' names *being a man* in 'De Gaulle is a man' it does so when it occurs as a subject. A predicate which names a universal normally requires modification if it is to become a subject which names it. I can say 'De Gaulle is tall', but I must say 'Tallness is an advantage', not 'Tall is an advantage'. I cannot indeed say 'Manness is an advantage', but must say rather 'Being a man is an advantage'. If I did say the former, however, it would probably be taken as equivalent to the latter. Colour words such as 'red' are exceptional in that they can function as names for universals either in the subject or in the predicate position.

One can always transform a name for a universal of the predicate type into one of the subject type by making use of the expressions 'Being' or 'Being a' as in the example above. It does not matter whether the predicate is a common noun and a copula, or an adjective and a copula. The copula with a common noun, of course, differs from that with an adjective in including the indefinite article.

If one regards the copula as part of the predicate, rather than as a device pointing to the predicate, one may say this. A predicate is always a verb. A subject is always a noun. A logically proper name for a universal always has two forms: a verb form and a noun form. Which form it has determines whether it is subject or predicate in the sentence in which it occurs.

Naming may at first look more like denoting than like connoting. However, in an important way it is really more like connoting. Naming and connoting are direct reference relations, denoting is an indirect reference relation. That an expression denotes an object arises from the holding of two other 'relations', that of connoting between the expression and a certain individual property and that of exemplification between the object and that individual property. Neither naming nor connoting depends upon any such intermediary as is the connoted individual property in denoting.

3

So far I have distinguished three reference relations which may connect an expression and a property: connoting (this only applies to individual properties), denoting, and naming. I now turn to a fourth one.

If one considers the expression 'red or blue' one may be inclined, at first, to say that, just as 'red' names *being red*, so 'red or blue' names the complex property *being red or blue*. But there is a reason against saying this. If 'red or blue' were simply the name of the property being red or blue, there should be no property of this property in virtue of which it referred to it. But does not 'red or blue' refer to being red or blue in virtue of the fact that being red or blue is the disjunction of red and blue, i.e. has the property being the disjunction of red and blue?

Should one say then that it connotes being the disjunction of redness and blueness and denotes being red or blue?

I am against saying this for the following two reasons:

(1) Traditionally the denotation of the predicate has been the class of things to which it applies, and its connotation has been the property in virtue of which it applies to things. I have rejected this terminology. But so far, being concerned with grammatically simple predicates, I have not introduced a *conflicting* style of talk about the denotation and connotation of the predicate. I have simply said that the predicate names a property, and does not denote and connote at all. To say, however, that in 'this is red or blue' the expression 'is red or blue' connotes being the disjunction of redness and blueness and denotes being red or blue would be in positive conflict with that traditional usage, which identifies its connotation with being red or blue and its denotation with the class of things which are red or blue.

(2) The expression 'my favourite colour' denotes redness. There is an obvious indirectness about its relation to redness as compared

with that of 'red' to redness. Suppose now the property red or blue was the one requirement for the ties to be worn at a certain dinner. Then 'the property required of all ties to be worn at this dinner' would denote red-or-blueness. Obviously its relation with the property it denotes would have the same kind of indirectness as does the relation between 'My favourite colour' and redness. It seems fairly obvious that in terms of this contrast between a direct and an indirect kind of reference the relation between 'red or blue' and red-or-blue-ness belongs with the relation between 'red' and redness, not with the others. Saying the relation was that of denoting would seem to put it on the wrong side. In short, granted that 'red or blue' can't be called a logically proper name, it must also be said that it is really much more like a logically proper name than it is like a denoting expression.

It seems necessary to distinguish two new semantic relations. When an expression refers to a property in virtue of the fact that that property has a certain essentially individual property as one of its essential properties, it will be said to represent the property to which it refers and to signify the property in virtue of which it refers. An expression denotes a property via an essentially individual property which is one of that property's contingent properties. An expression represents a property via an essentially individual property which is one of its essential properties. Thus 'red or blue' *represents* the complex property being red or blue, and signifies the individual property, being the disjunction of red and blue. An expression which represents a property may either be a noun or a verb expression, that is, fitted either to be subject or predicate of a sentence. 'Being red or blue' and 'is red or blue' are respectively one and the other.

Clearly 'signify' and 'represent' contrast in just the same way as do 'connote' and 'denote'. But the intimacy and directness of the representing relation makes it more like the naming relation than the denoting relation. Another similarity is that an expression cannot purport to represent or name a property and fail to do so, in the way in which it can purport to denote and fail to do so, and that a predicate can name or represent a property but cannot denote one.

In 'My car is red' the expression 'is red' is a name of redness, put into verb form to show that it plays the exemplified role in the fact represented. *Mutatis mutandis*, the same can be said of 'is red or blue' in 'My car is red or blue'. On the other hand, if I say 'My car *is of my favourite colour*' the italicized expression represents not the property of redness, but the property *Being of my favourite colour*. This property is in a sense a relational property.

4

Consider the sentence 'A man came to mend the window.' Does the expression 'A man' refer to anything? If so, what and in what mode?

It is, surely, a particular variable, with a range of reference limited to men. Clearly it can't be said to denote any particular individual man. To say that it refers to the group of men, and to say that it refers to the property *being a man*, would each mislead in different ways. The best brief way of putting it is to say that 'a man' in this context ranges over men, and has its range determined by the property, being a man. One need not think that strictly speaking there is anything which is its range. It is simply that there are things which have the property which we may call its range-determining property.

Contemporary philosophers who see language from the vantage point of Russellian symbolism tend to give short shrift to plurals, as they are not needed in the canonical form suggested by this symbolism.

Yet it is desirable to have a way of talking about the reference of 'All men' and 'Dogs' (or 'Dogs in these parts'). These expressions belonging to ordinary language cannot just be left out of account, because an ideal language could do without them.

Only a brief hint as to how the reference of plurals should be described will be given here. There are many uses of the plural I shall leave quite undiscussed.

Most sentences with a plural subject fall into one or other of the following two categories. First there are sentences such that there is some one definite group of things which has to satisfy a certain condition if the sentence is to be true. Second, there are sentences such that some group or other has to satisfy a certain condition if the sentence is to be true.

In the first group fall the following. '*My hands* are swollen', '*The Joneses* are coming to tea', '*All God's children* go to heaven', '*All men* are mortal', '*These* are red circles'.

One may say that each of these italicized plural subjects, except the last, denotes a certain group and does so in virtue of that group having a certain property which the subject expression connotes. Equally it seems appropriate to say of the last, if the use of 'These' is comparable to the use of 'This' where 'This' is a logically proper name, that it is a logically proper name naming a group. The predicate in each case names the property of being a group of a certain sort.

Now consider 'Some men are happy', 'Some of my friends are rich', 'Some of my friends are not rich'. There may be various different groups of men, such that their being groups of happy men, is enough to make the first sentence true. This is so whether one treats the predicate as requiring that the group contains happy men or that it be composed of happy men. Just as 'All men' may be considered a denoting expression which connotes *being the group of all men*, so 'Some men' may be considered as a variable with a range of reference limited to groups of men, with the range-determining property *being a group of men*.

More common perhaps in ordinary language than uses of plural phrases where they mean either 'All . . . s' or 'Some . . . s', are uses where they mean either 'Most . . . s' or 'Typical . . . s'. If these latter plurals are taken as referring to groups, it must be presumably as denoting expressions and not as variables. 'Bulls are fierce' presumably means 'Most bulls are fierce'. It may be best to say that 'Bulls' here denotes the group of all bulls, and connotes being the group of all bulls, and that 'most' qualifies the predicate rather than the subject, so that the predicate is in effect equivalent to 'is largely composed of fierce beings'.

It would be more accurate to say: 'All men' connotes *being the aggregate of all men* and denotes that chunk of reality, namely a certain mass of flesh, which has this property, but that it also serves to tell one that, if the predicate which follows it names or represents a property syncategorematic on being an aggregate of some specifiable kind, then this chunk of reality is being said to exemplify that universal specifically *qua being the aggregate of all men*. This is loosely summed up by saying that the subject expression denotes a group rather than an aggregate.

Some of the predicates which are applied to plural expressions are not of the kind which are syncategorematic on being an aggregate of certain things. Consider, for example, 'My books *take up a lot of space*' or 'The Smiths *are here*'. In these cases one could as well say that the subject denotes the aggregate as denotes the group.

There may sometimes even be a possibility of ambiguity as to whether the predicate names a property syncategorematic on being an aggregate of the things in question (or as we might put it ascribes a property to the group), or whether it ascribes a non-syncategorematic property to the aggregate. For instance, 'My books are very heavy' or 'My cases are very heavy' could be taken either way, that is the predicate may have the force of 'is an aggregate of heavy things' or may have the force of 'is a heavy particular'.

Does *denoting* continue to be a one (or many) to one relation in the case of these plural subjects? Certainly each expression denotes one single group. Does this show the same prejudice against plurality as seems to be implicit in a Russellian canonical language? No. What 'Cats' really denotes is the aggregate of cats, that is the chunk of reality made up of all the cats. To say that this chunk of reality is one or that it is many are both equally inept. This chunk of reality is many-fold *qua* being composed of cats. It is one-fold *qua* being a particular in its own right. One does not readily consider it in the latter way of course, but it is a particular in its own right, whether we consider it this way or not.

None the less, there is an important sense in which denoting remains a one (or many) to one relation, though this is quite compatible with its denoting many things (not each of many things).

One may define a one (or many) to one relation as a relation R for which the following law holds: '$aRb.aRc. \supset b=c$'. On this definition, denoting as here described, is a one (or many) to one relation. True, the expression 'Cats' denotes many cats. It also denotes many catparts. But then the following is true. 'The cat-parts denoted by "cats"=the cats denoted by "cats".'[1]

A group of particulars is a particular. We agreed to regard a group of properties as the disjunction of those properties. In 'Cows lie down before it rains' the expression 'Cows' denotes an aggregate which is a particular in its own right. In 'Chromatic colours are vivid' the expression 'Chromatic colours' represents (rather than denotes) the disjunction of all those colours. Of this

[1] See pp. 122–3.

disjunction one may say that, considered as a property in its own right, it is one-fold, while considered as the disjunction of those colours it is many-fold. What has been said above about plurals will apply, except that representing and signifying replace denoting and connoting. 'Chromatic colours' signifies the property of being the disjunction of each property which has the property of being a chromatic colour. It represents the disjunctive property in question, but it also indicates that predicates ascribed to it are normally to be taken as syncategorematic on its being the disjunction in question.

5

It seems reasonable to take it that since in 'A is F' 'A' refers to A and 'is F' refers to F-ness, that 'A is F' as a whole refers to a fact having A and F-ness as its elements.

There are at least two good reasons for refusing to say that the sentence names the fact. (1) A logically proper name owes its significant utterability to there being something which it names. But 'A is F' may be false, in which case there will be no fact for it to name. (2) A logically proper name does not refer to that to which it refers because it has a certain meaning determined by the meaning and arrangement of its parts.

It has sometimes been held that a sentence refers to an entity called a possible fact. Some possible facts are actual, some are not. A sentence is true if and only if the possible fact to which it refers is actual. Such a view would remove the first objection above. However, there seems no more reason to accept such beings as possible facts, than to accept possible particulars. If talk about possible particulars boils down to talk about may-be-unexemplified particular-properties (i.e. as on the theory of descriptions), it seems reasonable to take it that talk of possible facts will boil down to talk about may-be-unexemplified fact-properties.

On this basis one might propose that, instead of saying a sentence refers to a fact which may or may not be actual (cf. singular nouns refer to things which may or may not exist), one should say that it connotes a fact-property, and, if this is exemplified by a fact, denotes that fact.

But consider what the fact-property connoted by 'A is F' would be. It must be the property of containing A in the exemplifying role, and F-ness in the exemplified role. If a fact has this property, it is an essential, indeed a quintessential, property of that fact. Thus it is better to talk of this property as signified rather than as connoted, and the fact as represented rather than as denoted. Be it noted, however, that an expression may purport to represent a fact and fail to do so in a way in which an expression cannot purport to represent a property and fail to do so.

An expression may either signify a quintessential fact-property, or merely an essential fact-property. I shall say that an expression completely represents a fact if it signifies its quintessential property. I shall say that it incompletely represents a fact if it signifies one of its essential properties, but not its quintessential property. These signified fact-properties are what we have called objectives.

Only a sentence in which all the terms are names or representations will completely represent a fact. 'A is F', where 'A' and 'is F' are names, will completely represent A's being F, if it is true. The objective it signifies may conveniently be *represented* thus: 'Being of the form *A is F*'.

A true sentence represents a fact; a false one does not. In either case understanding the sentence involves knowing the kind of fact it is fitted to represent, that is knowing a certain property which a fact must have if the sentence is to represent it. At least this is so in simple cases.

In those cases where the public pragmatic meaning of a sentence allows one to infer only that some objective of a certain sort is believed, there is no objective which it publicly signifies. One may say that privately it signifies whatever the actual objective of that sort is which is believed, and that if true it privately represents the fact or facts exemplifying that objective. This is not quite the same thing as saying that it signifies this objective in the private language of the speaker, which is only true if the fact that he believes just this objective could theoretically be inferred from regular, though peculiar, speech habits on his part. In the cases I have in mind, the hearer will normally be able to know that the objective signified is one such that any fact exemplifying it contains the same particulars, and one or more of the same universals, as any fact exemplifying a certain other objective known to him and that the two objectives are materially equivalent. The same goes, of course, for propositional attitudes other than beliefs. When one adopts a superficial analysis, as is often convenient, and treats an ordinary denoting proper name, for instance, as though it were a logically proper name, these difficulties are hidden.

When a sentence is composed of names and indications of the role the named objects play in the fact in question (leaving aside the factors which show what sort of propositional attitude is expressed) it is clear enough what the property or objective in question is. The sentence 'A is F' signifies being a fact with A as thing exemplifying, F as thing exemplified. Sentences thus composed of names and role indications may be called basic subject-predicate sentences. 'aRb' is, of course, subject-predicate, with two subjects, 'a' and 'b'.

6

With some sentences which are not of this character, it may not be quite so obvious from a theoretical point of view, what their objectives are. I must content myself with a few hints on the matter.

Consider the sentence 'My left thumb is blistered', and suppose that 'A' is a logically proper name for my thumb. Then the fact which would be completely representable by 'A is blistered' or, (de-sentence-izing it by removing pragmatic meaning) 'The being blisteredness of A' is a crucial part of what the original sentence represents. But it is not the whole. The whole fact in question is the one which would be representable thus: 'A is my left thumb and A is blistered'.

What does 'My left thumb is blistered' signify? It does not signify being a fact consisting in the conjunction of one fact with A as subject-thing and being my thumb as predicate-thing, and another fact with A as subject-thing and being blistered as predicate-thing. It does not signify this, for when I say 'My left thumb is blistered' I do not have to be thinking of a certain particular to which I am attending with the thought 'This is my left thumb and this is blistered' (where 'This' like 'A' names my left thumb). What it signifies rather is being a conjunction of two facts which both contain the same subject-thing but the first of which has *being my left thumb* as predicate, the second of which has *being blistered* as predicate. In short, it signifies; being of the form 'x is my left thumb and x is blistered'. The peculiarity of this kind of objective is that it features an essentially individual property.

Just as 'The President of France is tall', granted that it is true, incompletely represents a fact which would be completely represented by a sentence like this: 'This is uniquely a president of France and is tall', so will 'All lions are fierce', supposing it true, incompletely represent a fact which would be completely represented by a sentence like this: 'This is the aggregate of all lions, and *qua* being the aggregate of all lions, it is an aggregate of fierce beings', or more briefly by, 'This is the group of all lions, and, as such, is a group of fierce beings'. The objective in question here features the essentially individual property *being the aggregate of all lions*. This property could be further explicated as *being the only group of lions which is not part of a group of lions*.

In offering this interpretation of 'All lions are fierce' I am not denying that there are alternative uses of the sentence in which it could not be treated along these lines. There is, for instance, the use in which it could be true because there were no lions.

We may deal with 'No lions are gentle' quite simply, by regarding it as equivalent to 'All lions are non-gentle'.

As for 'Some lions are fierce' and 'Some lions are not fierce' these will require the same treatment as 'Some man is wise' and 'Some man is unwise'. These sentences signify objectives which might be exemplified by each of many facts, and if they are exemplified by several facts they will incompletely represent each of these facts. The facts in question will be ones which might be completely represented by such sentences as 'This is a man and is also wise', 'This is a group of lions and, as such, is a group of fierce beings', 'This is a man and is also non-wise', 'This is a group of lions and as such is a group of non-fierce beings', or alternatively, but not equivalently, 'This is a group of lions, and, as such, is not a group of fierce beings'.

Suppose I see some lions and notice a fact representable thus: 'These are lions'. (I ignore the fact that what would, strictly speaking, be *noticed* would be that certain appearances were lion appearances.) The existence of this fact is enough to establish truth of 'Lions exist'. (I am assuming that the sentence claims that more than one lion exists.) It seems appropriate, therefore, to say that 'Lions exist' represents every fact of the character 'x is a group of lions', and signifies *being a fact with being a group of lions in the exemplified role*.

Let us now turn to 'Unicorns do not exist'.

It is not easy to see how there *could be* a fact represented by 'Unicorns do not exist'. That is, it cannot be the exemplifying of a universal by certain particulars which makes this sentence true, not even if these universals be negative. No amount of things not being unicorns makes it true that unicorns do not exist.

Among various possibilities the most hopeful seems to be this: The only objective signified by 'Unicorns do not exist' is that signified by 'Unicorns exist'. Their semantic meaning is the same. The difference is in pragmatic meaning. The former expresses disbelief, the latter belief. Thus 'Unicorns do not exist' is true if and only if it does represent a fact. If one said 'Would that unicorns did not exist' one would presumably on this view be expressing a negative wish, that is a propositional attitude related to wishing as is disbelieving to believing. One might call this attitude 'a *dis*wish'. In general, one taking this view will presumably claim that all or some propositional attitudes come in pairs, a positive and a negative version.

Yet there are objections to saying that the negation belongs to the pragmatic meaning. It is useful to be able to say such things as that 'Ghosts do not exist' and 'Would that ghosts did not exist' have the same semantic meaning but different pragmatic meaning, while 'Ghosts do not exist' and 'Would that ghosts existed' differ in both types of meaning.

This objection can be avoided by introducing a distinction between positive and negative semantic meaning. The normal kind of semantic meaning will be positive. But a sentence which is calculated to express a negative propositional attitude of one kind or another (disbelief, diswishing, diswilling, etc.) to an objective may be said to signify that objective negatively, and if the objective is exemplified to represent the fact or facts in question negatively, while a sentence which expresses a positive propositional attitude to an objective may be said to signify it positively. Saying that two sentences have the same semantic meaning will normally mean that they signify the same objective and either both do so positively or both do so negatively.

Still, though one might introduce this notion of negative semantic meaning, there is a clear sense in which the negation here in question belongs to the pragmatic meaning. It is a matter of the propositional attitude expressed, not a matter of the objective signified. Of course, not all negation is pragmatic in this way.

Negative universals may figure in objectives which are positively signified.

It seems impossible, however, to count *Being the only F* as a genuine universal. For to say of a thing that it is the only F is surely to say that it is F and that no other F exists, which is hardly simply ascribing a property, even a relational property, to the thing in question.

In the last resort, perhaps, it should be admitted that so called individual properties are not genuine properties. Perhaps in the deepest analysis one ought to say that 'The F is G' positively signifies *Being of the form 'x is F' and 'x is G'* and negatively signifies *Being of the form 'x is a pair of Fs'*. But I do not think that this affects the utility for most purposes of saying that it signifies *Being of the form 'x is uniquely F and x is G'*, and talking of *Being uniquely F* as the connotation of 'The F'. Equally one might have to say that 'All Fs are G' really signifies positively *Being of the form 'x is an aggregate of Fs, and qua being an aggregate of Fs, is an aggregate of Gs'*, and negatively signifies *Being of the form 'x is an F and a G'*. It is still useful to say that 'All Fs' denotes the group of Fs and connotes *Being the group of all Fs*. The same sort of thing applies to some expressions which it is convenient to describe as representing type four relational properties.

I have said that a sentence, or more accurately, a sentence-utterance[1] signifies an objective, and if true represents a fact or facts.

Strictly I ought to modify this by saying that a sentence always signifies an objective, but that this signifying may be positive or negative, and that where the signifying is negative 'false' must be substituted for 'true' in the above. Yet it is usually more convenient to treat a sentence, which from the most fundamental point of view signifies an objective negatively, as positively signifying a negative objective, and to understand by 'signify' 'positively signify'.

7

It seems that the objective *signified* by a given sentence may normally be *represented* by a 'that' clause derived from that sentence. The objective of 'My dog bites' can be represented by the expression 'That my dog bites'. 'That my dog bites' (in a suitable context) is a

[1] See p. 146.

singular term which represents the fact-property signified by 'My dog bites'.

To represent at length the significatum of the expression 'That my dog bites' is an elaborate thing, obvious enough, however, which it is to be hoped one will not often have to do. Here goes, however: 'Being (not having) the property being a conjunction of two facts in the first of which being my dog is in the exemplified role, and the second of which being a biter is in the exemplified role and in each of which the same thing is in the exemplifying role'. Note that this long expression contains no reference to the sentence 'My dog bites'. I shall leave it to the reader to consider what the significatum of the long expression may be.

I suggest that 'that' clauses sometimes represent objectives and sometimes represent, or purport to represent, facts. If I say 'He believes that Hitler invaded Russia' the 'that' clause represents an objective. If I say 'That Hitler invaded Russia is amazing' it is probable that the 'that' clause represents the fact of Hitler's invading Russia. One would say then 'Hitler invaded Russia' and 'That Hitler invaded Russia' (in the sentence in question) both represent the same fact, but the former also serves to show that it is supposed to be in the exemplifying role in a higher order fact represented by the whole sentence: 'That Hitler invaded Russia is amazing'.

I have only discussed sentences of a certain logical simplicity, and have not dealt, for instance, with sentences which are built up truth-functionally or otherwise out of simpler sentences. Probably some congruous extension of what I have been saying could be made to sentences of other types, but I shall not here elaborate any such extension.[1]

---

[1] The question whether 'The F is G' entails or presupposes 'The F exists' is ignored in this chapter. In either case, the F must exist for it to be true, and this must be believed by one who asserts it seriously. In either case, there are two distinct ways in which such an utterance may fail. Whether both types of failure are described as cases of falsehood makes no difference to the essential facts. The same goes, of course, for 'The F is not G'. Whether this is treated as the contrary or the contradictory of 'The F is G' is of consequence to systems of formal logic but not to the understanding of ordinary utterances of this type.

Part Three

IMAGING AND BELIEVING

VIII

ACTS OF BELIEF AND THE INTENDING RELATION

It is commonly acknowledged that 'believe' is usually a dispositional word. The difference between a behaviourist and a mentalist over such statements as ascribe beliefs to people is not usually as to whether they refer to a disposition or an occurrence. More probably the difference is this, that while the behaviourist takes it that such statements claim that certain physical events, e.g., certain movements of the man's body, would occur or be likely to occur in certain more or less determinately specifiable situations, the extreme mentalist thinks that the claim is rather that certain private mental events would occur, or are likely to occur, in certain more or less determinately specifiable situations. A moderate mentalist[1] might claim that what was in question was the likelihood of certain mental and certain physical events occurring.

There is an important distinction between two ways in which an interpretation of a statement of the form 'He believes that p'

---

[1] Since 'behaviourism' usually refers to a doctrine which denies private mental events altogether, or at least gives them an absolutely minimal place in the analysis of statements 'about the mind', anyone who gives them any place of importance at all is, in contrast at least a moderate mentalist. If he gives them a place (in the analysis of such statements) far more important than he gives physical events, then he can be called an extreme mentalist. It seems worth remarking that a theory which asserts a synthetic identity between private mental events and brain states, while acknowledging that the statement that a certain mental event occurred is never logically equivalent to the statement that a certain brain event occurred, will be, from the present point of view, tantamount to mentalism, provided that the statements that certain mental events occur, are treated as crucial elements in typical statements 'about the mind'.

can be taken as dispositional. Some of those who acknowledge that 'belief' often or always refers to a disposition would hold that it was a disposition to perform certain mental acts, which are propositional in the sense in which 'mental' verbs appropriately followed by 'that'-clauses are propositional. Others would hold that it refers to a disposition to do things which are not propositional.

Let us consider the first view a moment and distinguish three more specific forms of it. First comes the simplest view. According to this there are two senses of 'believe'. In one of these it refers to a certain kind of mental act, instances of which occur in the life of each of us at certain definite moments. At a particular moment, for instance I may perform a mental act of believing that a man called 'Johnson'[1] is President of the USA. In the other sense of the word 'believe' it refers to a disposition to perform mental acts of this kind on certain types of occasion. In short, the disposition called 'believing that P' is a disposition to believe that P in the non-dispositional occurrent sense.

Second comes a view not really much different from this. According to this view the disposition called 'believing that P' is a disposition to perform mental acts of a specific kind which are also *that* P, only this kind of mental act is not called believing. An example of a specific form of this view would be one which said that believing that P is being disposed to *judge* that P under certain circumstances which, presumably, the view would go on to specify. The difference between this and the former view is really only as to the word which is most suitably used for the kind of occurrent mental act in question.

Third comes a view according to which believing that P is a disposition to do various different things under various different circumstances but either all or many of these different things are propositional. Examples of the things in question might be acts of hoping, acts of expecting, acts of willing, and so on. Obviously such a third view could take many different forms. In particular the question arises as to what extent the mental acts in question would be *that* P and to what extent *that* other things.

The view that belief as a disposition is a disposition to perform mental acts which are propositional in character, whichever of the three forms indicated it may take, may seem an essentially mental-

[1] 1965.

istic view. Occurrent propositional mental acts can hardly have a place in behaviourist philosophy. Yet could not a behaviourist hold a very similar view and say that believing that P is a disposition to hope that, to wish that, to expect that, certain things under certain circumstances? He would have to add, however, that hoping that, wishing that, and expecting that are not occurrent propositional mental acts, but dispositions. These dispositions would have to be dispositions for doing things of a non-propositional character. Thus in the last analysis believing would be a disposition to do things non-propositional. One who holds that though the word 'believe' often refers to a disposition it is not (even in the last analysis) a disposition, or at least not entirely a disposition, to do things non-propositional, would seem to have a difficult task if he is to avoid mentalism of some kind. For an occurrence, as opposed to a disposition, a tendency, or anything of that sort, which is propositional in character, certainly sounds as though it is something irreducibly mental. Yet it is to be noted that one might hold that there were occurrences, as opposed to dispositions, which were propositional, without holding that these occurrences were propositional considered apart from their relations to other particulars (their relations to facts or propositions is, of course, a different matter). On the face of it, then, a physical occurrence might be propositional in virtue of its physical relation to other physical particulars.

Still, on the whole, the view that belief as a disposition cannot be a disposition to do solely non-propositional things is likely to be a mentalist one. The converse, however, by no means holds. A mentalist may hold that a belief is always a disposition, and a disposition for doing things of a non-propositional character, for instance, for having certain feelings, or certain images, under certain circumstances.

It seems to me clear enough that in fact there are experiences which must be regarded as propositional in character, and that when we talk of someone's beliefs in a dispositional sense, at least part of what we are saying concerns his disposition to have such propositional experiences. Thus I side with the first of the two main views I distinguished. Moreover, I think that there is one specific kind of propositional experience, a tendency to have which is *a crucial part* of having a belief in the dispositional sense. But although I claim that there are experiences which are propositional,

I leave it open whether to any extent their being so is a matter of the relations they stand in to other particulars.

Is the kind of experience to which I give such a prominent place to be called 'believing', 'judging', or what?

Let me indicate in a rough way the kind of experience I have in mind. You, the reader, doubtless believe as I do that the sun is larger than the earth. We are not for ever contemplating this fact of the sun being the larger. On the other hand, I think that there is a state of mind in which one directs one's thoughts upon this fact. One puts oneself into this state if one sets out to make it clear to oneself just what it is that one is accepting when one accepts that the sun is larger than the earth, and to renew one's acceptance of it if one still sees fit. But one's contemplation of this fact need not come about in this way. It occurs whenever one can be said to be having, at a particular moment, the thought that the sun is larger than the earth.

Shall we call mental acts or experiences such as these beliefs (or perhaps rather believings) judgments (or perhaps rather judgings) or what?

'Judgment' suggests a restriction which I do not want suggested. To talk of the act of judging that P suggests an act of arriving at the acceptance of P for the first time, or at least of arriving at it again after a period when it was called into question. It suggests likewise a present weighing of evidence or careful sensory scrutiny. We need a term which covers equally cases where one is clearly conceiving a certain situation, and taking it as a really existing situation, without this being the terminus of an *immediately prior* process of finding out, estimating, or what not. I might direct a mental act of the kind I have in mind on the proposition that my wife is pregnant, without my present mental state being one of judging that she is pregnant from her appearance or from thinking about certain facts serving as evidence for this conclusion.

One might say 'At that moment I was thinking that my wife was pregnant' or 'I was having the thought that my wife was pregnant'. One might also well say 'I was reflecting on the fact that my wife was pregnant'. However, one can be described as *thinking* during a period when one is not accepting any of the propositions one is entertaining; also the word tends to be used especially for processes of problem solving, while the word 'reflect' is restricted in a way the converse to that of 'judge'.

On the whole the best word for our purpose seems to be 'believe'. Our use of it may sometimes seem a bit unnatural, but this may actually be less misleading than would use of some of the other words whose very naturalness may suggest a more limited type of mental act or experience as being the subject of our enquiry than the one we intend. Thus we shall use 'believe' not only to refer to a disposition, but also to refer to a certain kind of occurrence, that is, a certain kind of experience or mental act. To contrast this kind of occurrence more clearly with the disposition we shall sometimes also call it 'the experience of believing that . . . ', 'a belief experience to the effect that . . . ', or 'the mental act of believing that . . . '. We shall also tend to refer to the occurrence of such experiences by saying things like 'He is believing that . . . ', 'He was believing that . . . ', and so on. When, on the other hand, we wish to emphasize that our reference is to a disposition we shall say rather things like: 'He has the belief that . . . ', 'He had the belief that . . . ' and so on. We shall usually be referring to the disposition, moreover, when we say 'He believes that . . . ', or 'He believed that . . . '.

We ordinarily think of a belief as something which lasts over a period and which at different times is conscious to different degrees, is sometimes more in the forefront and sometimes more in the background of our consciousness. When the belief is conscious the degree to which its content is realized may vary a great deal. The time when the belief may be said to be more in the forefront of the mind, and its content be said to be being envisaged with a fair degree of clarity, are the times when the person is having what I call a belief experience. This suggests that different experiences may be belief experiences to a varying degree, and that there may be borderline cases.

If I have a belief in a proposition of a very generalized sort, such as that South Africa is a police state, it is likely to break down, when brought fully into consciousness, into the having of various more specific beliefs, such as that there are people in prison there without trial, that public demonstrations are reacted to by the police in an excessively violent manner, that many publications are banned, and so on. One cannot say that the conjunction of these propositions, belief in which is experienced, is logically equivalent to the proposition that South Africa is a police state. It could have been a police state in different ways. Yet it may be that the coming into full consciousness of such a generalized belief must consist in the experiencing of some more specific beliefs of this sort.

We often distinguish so called intellectual assent to a proposition from assent to it in the realization of what it really amounts to. Thus I may assent in an intellectual way to the proposition that there are old age pensioners who cannot afford fuel for heating purposes, without, as one says, really bringing it home to myself what this amounts to. Assent to propositions of this type is, of course, usually associated with a disposition to utter certain sentences. However the difference between the person who merely assents intellectually to the proposition, and one who brings home to himself what it really amounts to, is not a difference between understanding the sentence and not understanding it. I may assent to such a sentence, knowing quite well what the sentence means, and yet not bring its meaning home to myself.

The belief which is in a mind over a long period is presumably a disposition, that is a dispositional property of persons, a universal of some (certainly problematic) kind. The propositional attitudes of Chapters VI and VII were all of this category. There is no need to interpret an enduring belief as something which exists over long periods as an unconscious continuant (consisting in a continuous series of unconscious occurrents) and which sometimes emerges into consciousness.

Thus there is no particular which is one's belief that such and such over a longish period. On the other hand, when one's belief is conscious there is a particular which is one's present believing, namely the belief experience. It might be suggested that the only particular in question is oneself or one's mind, which has the property at this moment of consciously believing that such and such. However, it is evident that when one has this property, it is not all the contents of one's mind which contribute to giving one this property. There is one particular part of one's present mind phase the characteristics of which are such that one is said to be having this conscious belief. That characteristic of it, which makes it the case that one is consciously believing that such and such, is what I call the property of being a belief experience, or being a believing or act of believing, to a certain effect. The part of one's present mind phase which has this characteristic is a belief experience or act of believing.

If we never really have moments when we envisage the situations in which we are said to believe, then, in some ultimate sense, we are not really possessed of any conception of the world we live in. Thus my interest in belief experiences arises partly from a value judgment. It is because men are not merely complicated parts of the world, but are capable of experiencing a sense (sometimes correct, sometimes incorrect) of how things are, that their cognitive operations have a value which, say, the operations of computers, as long as computers do not have experiences, will never have.

The question with which the remainder of this book is concerned is: How can an experience, a fleeting event in someone's mind, be propositional, in the way in which it must be to be a belief experience, and granted that it is propositional, that it is *that* something, what can make it a believing that, rather than a wondering whether it is the case that an imagining that or any other such thing?

2 FORMULATION OF OUR MAIN PROBLEM ABOUT BELIEVING: WHAT IS THE INTENDING RELATION?

An act of believing, a belief experience, is an event which in some way refers or points beyond itself. If I, sitting in my room at home, am believing that my wife is drinking coffee with the Simpsons, then in some peculiar way the experience I am having is connected with the situation of my wife and the Simpsons sitting drinking coffee in their sitting-room. That is so, at least, if my believing is true.

There is something very extraordinary about this relation between a true believing and the fact in virtue of which it is true. There is no sort of relevant physical connection, it would seem, between my experience of believing that my wife is at the Simpsons, and the situation of my wife being at the Simpsons, or my experience of believing that the Governor of Rhodesia is a sick man and the situation in which his sickness consists, if there is such a situation, yet undoubtedly these situations are in some sense referred to by my experience of believing.

I have said rather vaguely that the experience of believing refers to a *situation*. Strictly, the relation I am interested in is that which holds between a believing and the fact, where there is one, to which it refers. I am asking about the relation between my believing that the Governor of Rhodesia is sick and the fact which is his being sick.

Although we shall approach the problem as concerning a relation between a mental act and a *fact*, we shall not really be dealing with a problem very different from that dealt with by writers who discussed rather the relation between such mental acts or experiences, and the particulars they are in some way about. William James (whose 'The Function of Cognition' and 'The Tigers in India'[1] seem superior to most other work on the topic) seems, on the whole, to have posed the problem in these terms, though doubtless he was never very precise in regard to such ontological distinctions.

Henceforth, we shall substitute for the word 'refer' here, the more specific word 'intend', a not uncommon philosophical usage. A mental act (e.g., an occurrent belief or wish) which can be described as *that* something or other, will be said to *intend* the fact which is represented by the sentence which follows 'that', supposing that there is such a fact.

A mental act of believing is an event in its own right, so to speak, with properties other than the property of pointing beyond itself in some obscure way. An experience which is an act of believing would seem often either to be, or to include, the experiencing of certain images or sense-data. Whether it always does so, and must do so, is a point we shall discuss later.

If I believe that my wife is having coffee at the Simpsons, I may have a series of visual images of my wife and the Simpsons having coffee together. That series of images or the experience of them, is the mental act of believing, or is at least part of it. Moreover, if it is not the whole of it, it is difficult to know what else the act of believing can consist in except further images, including perhaps imaged words, possibly some sense-data, and together with these certain emotional or conative feelings.

In saying that the imagery in which the belief experience at least partly consists was imagery of my wife at coffee with the Simpsons, we have ascribed to the images a relational property, derived from a relation to the fact of my wife being at coffee with the Simpsons, or perhaps rather from some complicated set of relations in which the images stand to such particulars as my wife, the Simpsons, certain coffee things, and so on. But these

1 William James, *The Meaning of Truth* (1909), pp. 1–50.

images are themselves, considered in their own right and apart from any relations they may have to anything other than themselves, particulars of certain shapes and of certain colours, standing in spatial relations of a peculiar sort one to another. The intrinsic properties of images have been the subject of much dispute, but it seems sheer confusion to deny that they are particulars having their intrinsic character, and that the fact that they have the intrinsic properties which make up this character can be distinguished from the fact that they are in some sense *of* an external situation.

If we suppose that the belief experience also includes certain emotional feelings, these also will have their intrinsic properties. Perhaps one of these feelings will have that property which makes it describable as a sinking feeling, or it may be joyous, or it may be a feeling of irritation, or what not. That there are such intrinsic emotional properties of feelings is a point which should not be denied on the ground that the only words available for naming them function normally not simply as names for such pure qualities of feeling, but at the same time as names for the role they play in the total life of the organism.

If the mental act of believing also includes the imaging of certain word-sounds, then there will be another set of intrinsic properties exemplified, namely the intrinsic auditory properties of those word-sounds. Similarly with regard to other sorts of word-images.

The problem of intentionality, or of the intending relation, is the problem of how it is that this portion of experience, with its own intrinsic properties, in some sense points beyond itself so that if the world external to it is propitious, there are certain particulars, distant in space, and in other examples in time also, such that the exemplification of certain universals by those particulars is intended by this portion of experience. It is the problem also of the relation between the intrinsic properties of acts of believing, and also of such other 'propositional' acts as there may be, and their property of pointing beyond themselves.

Let us imagine that 'F', 'G' and 'H' each names an intrinsic property of a certain belief experience, and let us take it that 'F and G and H and . . .' represents a compound property which supplies a very full description of its intrinsic character. What is meant by saying that this experience which is F and G and H and . . . is an act of believing that my wife is at coffee with the Simpsons?

It seems adequate to reply that to say this is to say that the experience in question is such that if there were a fact of a certain sort (exemplifying a certain objective), a fact in which being my wife, being the Simpsons, and having coffee together occur as things exemplified, then that experience would intend it. In short, the property of being an act of believing that such and such, is always the property of being fitted to intend a fact of such and such a sort, a fittingness which can only fail to be fulfilled by there not being any fact of the appropriate sort.

We see, then, that once we call an experience an act of believing that my wife is having coffee with the Simpsons, we have said something from which, in conjunction with the assertion that there is such a fact as my wife having coffee with the Simpsons, it follows that it is an experience intending that fact. This accounts for a certain oddness in asking what it is for an act of believing that P to intend the fact that P. One is inclined to ask somewhat irritably: 'What else, granted that there is such a fact as that P, could such an act of believing do?' But if we ask rather how it is that an experience which is F and G and H and . . . manages to intend, or what it is for it to intend, the fact that P, the oddity has been removed. Certainly this experience is an act of believing that P, and this is a matter of its being fitted to intend a fact of a certain kind. We want to know what it is for an experience to intend, or be fitted to intend, a fact of a certain kind.

3 IDEAL, QUASI-IDEAL, AND REAL RELATIONS: THE INTENDING RELATION

My true act of believing that my wife is at the Simpsons having coffee is a certain experience, having certain intrinsic properties, which stands in the intending relation (whatever that may be) to the fact which consists in certain particulars exemplifying, according to a certain pattern, Being my wife, Being the Simpsons, and Having coffee together. Yet it is obvious that there could have been just such an experience which was my belief that my wife is having coffee at the Simpsons without there being any fact of the kind in question. Thus Being a belief that my wife is having coffee at the Simpsons cannot be identified with Being in that intending relation to a fact of that kind. It has to be identified, rather, with Being such as will stand in the intending relation to a fact of that kind, if there is such a fact. This cannot, strictly speaking, be called a relational property. It is a property of a kind to which we should now give some attention. It is a property which is a potentiality for being in a specified relation.

Consider the property Being taller than the five-foot postman who delivered the letters this morning. This is a relational property of type four.[1] Clearly I cannot have this relational property unless someone is the five-foot postman who delivered the letters this morning. On the other hand even if there is no such five-foot postman, it is clear that I can be fitted to have this relational property, in the sense that I do actually have a certain property (Being over five foot, or Being five foot ten), such that my having this property and there being such a five-foot postman would together logically imply that I have this relational property.

Every key is fitted to fit any lock that conforms to certain conditions, but possibly there may be no such lock. If there is a lock of that character the key stands in the relation *fits* to it. If there is no such lock, it is still true that it is fitted to stand in the *fitting* relation to objects of a certain kind.

A division of relations to which we must now appeal is that into real relations and ideal relations. As I shall understand the distinction it may be defined as follows. Notice that ideal relations are not really supposed to be unreal.

'R' names (or represents) an ideal relation if and only if 'xRy' logically implies that there are corresponding truths of the form 'Fx' and 'Gy' which logically imply 'xRy', in which 'F' and 'G' name general intrinsic properties.[2] Other relations are real relations.

Let us consider some examples of ideal relations. Being similar to, Being of the same height as, Being taller than, Being richer than, are ideal relations; Being above, Containing as a part,[3] Being eaten by, Being son of, are all real relations. The attempt to classify various 'mental' relations on this scheme raises interesting questions. *Loves*, I fear, is an ideal relation.

Suppose that there are two general intrinsic properties (as complex as you like) F and G, and a relation R, such that 'Fx' and

---

[1] See p. 72.
[2] See p. 74.
[3] Note that *containing a G* would be an intrinsic general property, but even if B is the G in R, *containing B* would not be a general intrinsic property of R. Note also that *being the G* and *containing the G* are not intrinsic properties.

'Gx' jointly imply 'xRy'. In that case R is an ideal relation. Suppose now that there is a particular, A, which is F. Whether or not there is any particular which is G it seems apt to say that A is fitted to be R to a G or the G. For A has an intrinsic property such that if we ever learn that there is an, or a one and only, G, we can deduce from these two facts together that A is R to this thing which is an or the F.

One might then define the sentential function 'a is fitted to be r to a g' as equivalent to 'Among the general intrinsic properties of a is a property, f, such that if one thing is f and another thing is g it follows that the first thing is r to the second thing'.

This definition does not specify that the possible arguments for 'g' name general intrinsic properties. There is however one restriction upon the arguments available for 'g' which seems advisable. Let us say that where 'G' is such an argument, it must not follow from a thing's being G that that thing is R to something, where 'R' is supplied as an argument for 'r'. This will avoid our having to say such vacuous things as that a man is always fitted to be the father of his son. Actually rather than put restrictions upon the possible arguments for 'g' it will be simpler to redefine 'a is fitted to be r to a g' as equivalent to 'Among the general intrinsic properties of a is a property f such that if one thing is f and another thing is g, then it follows that the first thing is r to the second thing, while it does not follow simply from a thing's being g that there is something which is r to it.'

At this point it may be asked whether there is any need to include the proviso that the property in the role of 'f' should be one of a's general intrinsic properties. That we did so was because we were initially interested in making certain points about ideal relations. But in fact it seems quite appropriate to amend the definition in the following broadening way, and make 'a is fitted to be r to a g' equivalent to 'Among the properties of a is a property f such that if one thing is f and another thing is g, then it follows that the first thing is r to the second thing, while it does not follow simply from a thing's being f that there is something to which it is r, and it does not follow simply from a thing's being g that there is something which is r to it'. To this we may add that if one conjoined with the definiens here 'and f is a general intrinsic property of a' one may regard it as defining 'a is intrinsically fitted to be r to a g' and if one conjoined to it instead 'and f is not a general intrinsic property of a' one may regard it as defining 'a is extrinsically fitted to be r to a g'.

It seems that 'a is intrinsically fitted to be r to a g' logically implies 'r is an ideal relation'. Moreover, it is only certain real relations which allow of something being extrinsically fitted to be in them to things of a certain kind. These real relations I propose to call quasi-ideal relations.

There are various other but related senses of 'fitted' which one might have introduced. One might, for example, have introduced a sense of 'a is fitted to be r to a g' equivalent simply to 'a has a property f, such that if one thing is f and another thing is g, then it follows that the first thing is r to the second thing, while it does not follow simply from a thing's being f that there is some g thing to which it is r, and it does not follow simply from a thing's being g that there is some f thing which is r to it'. A thing which is *above* B would thereby be fitted to be above an object which was *below* B in this sense, but not in our other sense. Here the relational fact arises out of two independent facts, so to speak, but the independent facts have the same relation in the exemplified role. However we shall stick to the sense of 'Being fitted to be R to a G' indicated above, and dividing into extrinsic and intrinsic being fitted to be.

Let us now consider not so much sentences of the form 'a is fitted to be r to a g thing' as sentences of the form 'a is fitted to be r to the g'. It is to be noticed, first, that every sentence of the latter form is equivalent to a sentence of the former form. For instance, 'B is fitted to be S to the H' is equivalent to a sentence of the former form with 'uniquely H' as argument for 'g'. Thus in defining 'a is r to a g' we have also defined 'a is r to the g'. We are simply making use here of the general equivalence of 'the g thing' to 'a uniquely g thing'.

In the sentence 'A is fitted to be R to the G', the expression 'the G' occurs in a peculiar way, for it implies no sort of existential claim. I may say truly of a man that he is fitted to be less evil than the devil, without implying that there is such a thing as the devil. In ordinary language there is liable to be a confusion between relational properties and such properties as that of being fitted to have a certain relational property.[1] Thus it is not unlikely that

[1] I have introduced 'fitted' as a technical term designed for avoiding this confusion. I have not been elucidating some ordinary use of the word.

someone who says 'He is less evil than the devil' means what we express as 'He is fitted to be less evil than the devil'. Again, someone who says 'He loves God', and does not mean to imply the existence of God, must mean what we express by 'He is fitted to love God'.

We have implied that being fitted to be R to the G is not a relational property. This point has to be qualified however. Certainly it is distinct from the relational property resting on the relation R. It can however be seen as a relational property consisting in being in a certain relation (not the relation R) to the property *Being uniquely* G. Thus being fitted to love God does not consist in being in a certain relation to God. It could however be said to consist in being in a certain relation to the property *Being God*.

Let us say that two properties are *basis* properties for an ideal or quasi-ideal relation, where if one thing has the first property, and another thing the second property, then it follows that the first thing is in that relation to the second thing, while it does not follow from the fact that a thing has the first property that there is something to which it is in that relation, and it does not follow from the fact that a thing has the second property that there is something in that relation to it. For any given ideal or quasi-ideal relation there may be an indefinite number of pairs of basis properties. Where two things have basis properties for a certain relation to hold between them, these two facts may be said to be the underlying basis facts upon which the holding of that relation between them rests. The properties may also be said to be the basis properties which underlie this exemplification of the relation. It is convenient to say *the* basis facts upon which a relation rests, but in fact there will normally be alternative pairs of basis facts upon which the holding of the relation between two particulars rests. In *most* cases this is simply because one may select more or less determinate properties as the *basis* properties possession of which by the relata underlies the holding of the relation between them. That my tie is brighter than yours rests equally upon my tie being red and yours grey, and upon mine being scarlet and yours dark grey.

Suppose now that we have the R-ness of A to B as a fact of the initial kind, and that the F-ness of A and G-ness of B are the two underlying basis facts. What one may also say is that the fact of the R-ness of A to B being a consequence of the F-ness of A conjoined with the G-ness of B, derives from the fact of F-ness being in a certain relation to G-ness. Let us say that this relation is T. In these circumstances we shall say that R is an ideal, or quasi-ideal, relation holding between the particulars A and B, and that T is a *Platonic* relation holding between the universals F and G.

We can also say the following. The F-ness of A has as an essential consequence the fittedness of A for being R to a G thing. And we can say that the fact of the fittedness of A for being R to a G thing being an essential consequence of the F-ness of A derives from the fact of the T-ness of F to G.

Can we not now add this? The fittedness for being R to a G on the part of A is an essential consequence of the having by A of the property of having some property which is T to G. The possession of this latter property by A is a matter of its being in a certain relation to Being G, the relation of *Having some property which is T to . . .* Let us use 'S' as an abbreviation for 'Having some property which is T to'. Then we can say that not only does the fittedness of A for being R to a G follow from the F-ness of A, it also follows from this less determinate fact about A, the S-ness of A to Being G. Let us call S here a sub-Platonic relation. A sub-Platonic relation is one which can only hold between a particular and a universal, and the holding of which between a particular and a universal is a matter of the particular having some specified or unspecified property which is in a specified Platonic relation to the universal.

A Platonic relation may be defined as an essential relation between universals. It is clear that in the case of every ideal relation and every quasi-ideal relation, there must be a certain Platonic relation such that every pair of basis properties for the ideal or quasi-ideal relation exemplifies that Platonic relation. I shall talk of the Platonic relation in question as *sustaining* the ideal or quasi-ideal relation.

One might ask whether a Platonic relation is not itself an ideal relation. Is it not sustained by a higher order Platonic relation between higher order universals?

This is excluded by our definition. If A is in the ideal relation R to B, that is in virtue of a property being exemplified by A and a property being exemplified by B, such that from a thing's exemplifying either of these properties it does not follow that it is in the relation R to anything. But if A and B are universals and R a Platonic relation between them any properties of A and B which could plausibly be singled out as basis properties will be properties such as could not but have been exemplified. This being so, a thing which exemplified one of them could not have failed to be in the relation R to a thing exemplifying the other. The whole point of talking about ideal and quasi-ideal relations was to explain the notion of fittedness, and this has no place in regard to the essential properties of universals. A universal can, however, in virtue of one of its contingent properties be fitted to be in a certain relation. Such a relation will be an ideal or quasi-ideal relation.

Our definition does however allow contingent *facts* to be in ideal or quasi-ideal relations to each other or to particulars, even on the basis of their essential or quintessential properties. For the essential and quintessential properties of contingent facts need not have been exemplified.

Let us now turn back to the question of what it is for an experience to be an act of believing that something or other. It is clear that the property *Being a belief that my wife is at the Simpsons* does not consist in being in a certain relation, that of intending, to the fact that my wife is at the Simpsons but in being fitted to be in the intending relation to the fact that my wife is at the Simpsons. In 'being fitted to be in the intending relation to *the fact that my wife is at the Simpsons*' the italicized words form a definite description[1] of a type which does not involve any assertion of existence.

Thus where 'intending' holds between an experience and a fact there must be underlying basis facts about the experience and about the fact, and the basis properties in question must stand in a Platonic relation from which the fact that they can function as basis properties for the relation can be said to derive. We have a word already for properties of the sort which presumably function as basis properties of the fact, namely 'objectives'. But of what sort are the things which can function as basis properties in the experience? We shall call them 'contents'. A content is a property of an experience such that there is some objective such that if an experience has that property and a fact exemplifies that

---

[1] A definite description which *represents* rather than *denotes*.

objective, then it follows that that experience intends that fact. Let us label the Platonic relation between content and objective the relation of reflecting.

At this stage certain diagrams will be useful.

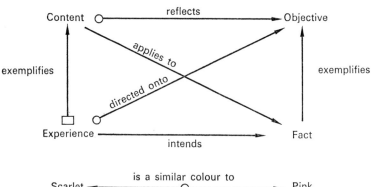

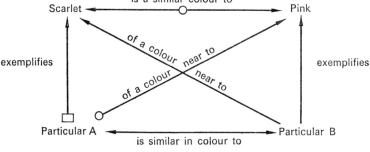

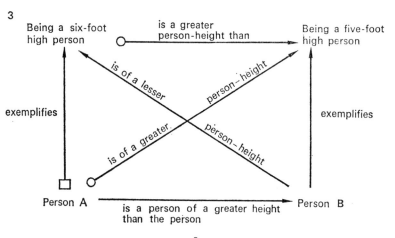

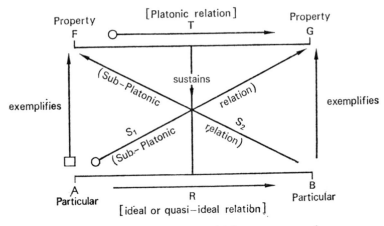

Figure 1 charts the relations which are our main concern. Figure 4 exhibits a general pattern of relations which will hold whenever an ideal, or a quasi-ideal, relation holds. Figures 2 and 3 are examples of ideal and quasi-ideal relations respectively. They also contrast in that Figure 2 gives us an example where the ideal or quasi-ideal relation is symmetrical. For Figure 3 I have chosen Being a person of a greater height than, rather than Being of a greater height than, as it is more straightforward to find basis properties which do not imply being in the relation in question to something in the former than in the latter case. One would probably have to distinguish various different senses of being of a greater height than before one could decide whether it was ideal, quasi-ideal, or what. Being a person of a greater height than does reasonably well as a rather absurd example of a quasi-ideal relation.

Figure 1 serves to introduce the expressions 'directed on to' and 'applies to' in a technical sense which may occasionally be useful. In Figure 1, as in the other diagrams, lines ending in a circle, or with a circle in the middle, represent relational facts of a kind which there are bound to be, granted only that the line ending in a square represents a fact. There may or may not be facts of the other kind.

To every ideal or quasi-ideal relation there must correspond a Platonic relation and vice versa. Investigation of the one is really equivalent to investigation of the other. On the whole it seems more appropriate to phrase one's questions as questions about the ideal or quasi-ideal relations between particulars rather than the Platonic relation between universals.

In illustration of this consider how one might best approach the question: 'What is the analysis of the relation Being a picture of?'

Being a picture of, in at least one sense in which these words may be taken, is an ideal or a quasi-ideal relation. One can have a picture of the such and such, or more correctly, a something fitted to be a picture of the such and such, without there being any such and such. (There is a contrast here, perhaps, with the relation Being a portrait of.) It must equally be true, of course, that there might have been such a thing as the such and such without there being any picture of one. If this is correct, then when X is a picture of Y, that must be because a certain property of X stands in a certain Platonic relation to a certain property of Y. But if one wanted to explain the relation *Being a picture of* one would find it less than helpful to rephrase one's question as concerning the Platonic relation.

Our main question, henceforth, then, concerns the character of the content of a belief-experience, and the nature of the intending relation. The formal characteristics we have ascribed to the content of a belief experience and to the intending relation are more or less the same as those ascribed to them by other philosophers who have used these terms, above all by philosophers of the mental act school, whose views the English reader will gather most readily from J. N. Findlay's *Meinong's Theory of Objects and Values* and R. Grossmann's *The Structure of Mind.*

IX

SIMPLE IMAGISM

What is the content of a belief experience, What is the intending relation? It does seem that the answer to these questions, which springs most naturally to the human mind, is that a belief experience is an experience of imagery, that the content is the intrinsic sensible character of the imagery, and that the intending relation is resemblance of a certain kind. British empiricists of the past usually seem to have tended to some such view as this, while those philosophers who have rejected such a view have treated it as a widespread and natural mistake which it must be their first task to correct. Philosophers of the Brentano mental act tradition felt the need to make it plain that their *contents* were not images or image-properties, while Twardowski, who introduced the notion of *content*, started by thinking of contents in just these terms.[1] Bertrand Russell espoused a largely image view of belief in *The Analysis of Mind*. Moreover, there is not exactly a wealth of alternative views which do more than present a tidy terminology. Let us see then whether anything can be done with an imagist theory of believing.

It seems probable that there is such a thing as image believing and that some imagist theory correctly analyses it, but that there are also equally important acts of believing of other kinds. But if we find an imagist theory which really shows what it is for image believings to be fitted to intend facts, it is *prima facie* likely that it will help us to understand how non-image believings are fitted to intend facts.

1 See J. N. Findlay, *Meinong's Theory of Objects and Values.*

2 SIMPLE IMAGISM EXPOUNDED

A simple imagist might propound the following thesis. When I experience the belief that my wife is at the Simpsons having coffee, I am experiencing certain images. These images are very like the sense-data in the existence of which ultimately consists the fact (if such fact there be) of my wife being at the Simpsons. Believing in the existence of a thing of a certain kind is simply a matter of experiencing imagery fitted to resemble a thing of that kind. Equally if I experience an image which is like a certain group of things, then my experience is a belief experience intending the fact that that group has a certain character, namely the character which makes it like the image. This character may, of course, be a matter of its members being in certain relations. There is no special problem here about relational facts.

This only amounts to a view about the nature of such acts of believing as are expressible in positive existential sentences. The imagist will have to enlarge on his theory in some way to cover other cases. It will conveniently simplify our present task, however, if we confine ourselves to the question how imagism can cope with acts of believing which are thus expressible. If it breaks down here, there is no need to look further, while if it does not, one can consider the question of other sorts of believing later.

If we do not accept that ordinary sentences about the existence of certain physical objects are genuinely existential the sort of belief to which this theory is going to be applicable will be very limited. Thus I must reiterate the point I made in Chapter I to the effect that in our discussion of believing it will be simpler, for the present, to take it, for the most part, that when a person believes in the existence of a physical object he is believing in the existence of a group of actual sense-data, many or all of which are not experienced by anyone. This also allows us to take it that there is a straightforward sense in which images may be fitted to resemble physical objects, or at least be fitted to resemble parts of physical objects.

On this view, the fact that my wife is having coffee at the Simpsons, is the fact that various sense-fields exist (whether sensed or not) containing sense-data of certain kinds and related to each other in ways such as make them views of the same scene. The most obvious sense-fields in question are the various visual views of the scene, but tactile and other sense-fields are important. Perhaps one should add that there must also exist certain minds related to these sense-fields in such a way as to make them animators of those human bodies the present phases of which are constituted by certain groups of sense-data from various of these sense-fields. The most likely form for this relation to take is that each mind as well as containing various thoughts and feelings going on at this moment also includes some of these sense-fields.

Let us suppose that there is such a fact as that of my wife having coffee at the Simpsons. Such a fact will be the conjunction of various lesser facts, such as the fact that a certain sense-field is of this kind, and that a certain other sense-field is of that other kind, and the fact that this sense-field is in this relation to that experience, and so on. It is fairly clear what the imagist will say is required for an experience to be a belief experience intending any one of these component facts. It must be the experience of images which resemble the particulars, the sense-data or the experiences, in that fact, with respect to their possessing the properties the fact ascribes to them. But what experience is going to be a belief experience intending that compound fact itself?

It seems plausible to say that a belief experience intending part of a compound fact may be a part of a belief experience intending the whole of that compound fact. Thus the belief experience which intends the fact that my wife is having coffee with the Simpsons may simply be a group of belief experiences each intending a component of that compound fact, such that each component is intended by one member of the group. Presuming the members of this group occur in succession rather than simultaneously the total belief experience will be an experience spread out in time. Doubtless the imagist would have to insist that the group has that special sort of unity which successive experiences sometimes have, and which we describe as their belonging to the same specious present.

So to believe that my wife is having coffee with the Simpsons is, at the least, to experience any number of image fields each resembling either a visual appearance of the scene, or a set of noises from the scene, or a set of tangible qualities or appearances belonging to the scene, or something of the sort.

Clearly if this is really what is required for me to experience belief in such a simple situation as that of my wife having coffee at the Simpsons, I am seldom if ever going to experience beliefs which intend, or are fitted to intend, facts of this kind. My occurrent believings will intend much more minute sensory facts, and my belief in facts of the more usual kind, will at most consist in my disposition to believe occurrently in the various components of this fact.

The imagist might propose the following modification of his view. To experience belief in a compound fact which contains many components is to experience belief in some selection (perhaps it must be, in some sense, a representative selection) of the compound facts, and to be in a state of specially strong readiness for experiencing belief in each of the remaining facts.

It will be as well to clear up certain points about the logic of resemblance which will allow a more exact statement of this simple imagist position.

Resemblance, in the most general sense of the word, may either be an ideal or a quasi-ideal relation. For two things may be said to resemble in virtue of their extrinsic rather than their intrinsic character. Intrinsic resemblance, on the other hand, that is resemblance resting upon intrinsic character, is, it is virtually tautological to say, an ideal relation.

When two things resemble, the basis properties one might pick out could be in either of two Platonic relations to each other. They might be properties identical one with another. The basis property might be the same in each case. Or they might be rather in a relation we may call 'Being a similar property to'.

If A is pink and B is scarlet one might say that A and B resemble each other exactly in being red, but resemble each other inexactly in that one is scarlet and the other pink. Exact and inexact resemblance may be either intrinsic or extrinsic.

Suppose A and B exactly resemble each other intrinsically *in being F*. One can only say that they exactly resemble each other intrinsically *tout court* if they have all general intrinsic properties in common. On the other hand if A and B inexactly resemble each other intrinsically in that one is G and the other H, one may say that they inexactly resemble each other intrinsically *tout court*.

Being intrinsically exactly similar to is (surely) an ideal relation. But the basis properties here must be general intrinsic natures and the Platonic relation between them is identity (not similarity). Is this a genuine relation? If not, we are departing from our original account of an ideal relation. It seems harmless to call it a relation for present purposes.

Let us now consider two facts, the F-ness of A and the F-ness of B. These two facts give rise to a further fact, the resemblance of A to B. This is a case of an ideal relation holding and the sustaining Platonic relation is identity as between universals. It is convenient to say not only that the particulars resemble but also that the facts resemble. Now consider two other facts, the G-ness of A and the H-ness of B, and let us suppose that G and H are similar universals. These two facts also give rise to the resemblance of A and B, as well as the more specific fact of their inexact resemblance. Here again it is convenient to say that the two facts resemble each other.

Consider the three facts C's J-ness, C's K-ness, and D's J-ness. Each of these facts resembles one or both of the others. But there is a difference in the character of the resemblance. Fact one resembles fact two by containing the same particular in corresponding roles; fact one resembles fact three by containing the same universal in corresponding roles. Where one fact resembles another in virtue of containing the same particular in corresponding roles I shall say that it resembles it particularistically. A fact's containing a certain particular is one of its intrinsic properties, but not one of its general intrinsic properties, so that a particularistic resemblance is not an intrinsic resemblance. For the general intrinsic properties of a thing are those of its intrinsic properties which are not particular-based relational properties. On the other hand its containing certain universals is among its general intrinsic properties, and can underlie its intrinsic resemblance to another fact. Such intrinsic resemblance between facts, the resemblance which rests on their containing the same or similar universals, I shall call conceptual resemblance.

Two facts will exactly resemble each other intrinsically or conceptually if and only if they have the same universal or universals playing corresponding roles. They may be said to resemble each other inexactly intrinsically, or conceptually, if they contain similar universals playing corresponding roles, or some similar and some identical universals, playing corresponding roles. Particularistic resemblance cannot be divided into exact and inexact resemblance.

Our talk of resemblance between facts should always be taken to concern conceptual resemblance unless otherwise stated. But of course facts may resemble in all sorts of extrinsic properties, quite apart from their intrinsic properties, whether general or particular-based.

It should be noted that if A is F and B is F these two facts resemble each other exactly, but it does not follow that A and B resemble each other exactly.

We can now reformulate the imagist view already described in a rather more precise way. To have a belief experience which intends a certain fact is to experience an image fact which has a conceptual resemblance to that fact, or at least to be thus related to some parts of the fact and especially ready to be thus related to each of the other parts.

Will the image fact resemble the intended fact exactly or inexactly? Presuming that the intended fact is not about images, the particulars involved will resemble each other inexactly, for on the one hand they will be imagy in character, and on the other hand they will not. It does not follow that the relevant facts about the images will only resemble inexactly. If we say that an image is red in the same sense as a sense-datum is red, then the fact that a certain image is red will resemble the fact that a certain datum is red exactly. On the other hand there will also be a related pair of facts which resemble each other inexactly, namely the fact that the one is a red image, and the fact that the other is a red datum. Let us take it for the moment that a resemblance of either kind will do. In the case of inexact resemblance, however, we must take it that some pretty close sort of inexact resemblance is required.

There are any number of objections which can be raised to an imagist view as simple as this. None the less let us examine it patiently and learn from it.

One might object that such an imagist theory cannot account for the indeterminateness of most of our believings. It cannot let us believe that there is a cat in the garden, without making us believe regarding some definite kind of cat, that there is a cat of that kind in the garden.

Consider an experience which is an act of believing that a red sense-datum exists. Such a believing is, from the point of view we have adopted, often an element in an act of believing something about the physical word, though it will not be the whole of such a believing.

According to the imagist, to experience this belief is simply to experience the redness of an image. Likewise to experience belief that a scarlet sense-datum exists is simply to experience the scarletness of an image.

If we are to believe Berkeley, a red image must be of some determinate shade of red. It follows that if a man experiences belief in the existence of a red sense-datum, there must be some specific shade of red such that he experiences belief in the existence of a sense-datum of that specific shade.

Perhaps the imagist might say: 'In point of fact the beliefs we experience about a given situation always are far more determinate than are the words we use to express them. Our public claims only give a little of the way we are actually taking it that things are in the bit of the world they concern.' It does seem odd (however) to say that I must either experience a belief that my wife is to the left or a belief that she is to the right of Mrs Simpson, when I believe that they are together.

Perhaps the imagist will say that a belief is indeterminate to the extent that there is equal readiness for having imagery of any one determinate of a given determinable as any other. Alternatively he may challenge the Berkeleyan assumption about the determinate character of imagery. We shall have something to say on this point later.

Another difficulty for the imagist looks rather the opposite of that just considered. It arises from the undoubted vagueness and fragmentariness of much imagery. Yet even though my image of a situation may be fragmentary and vague, I am surely not believing that the actual situation is composed of fragmentary and vague sense-data.

This difficulty appears simply to be a part of a larger difficulty. Even if the imagist is right in claiming that an act of believing in the existence of an F is an experience of an F-like image, he can hardly be right if he goes on to claim that for every property that an image of mine has, or even that for every natural[1] and intrinsic property, I am believing in the existence of something resembling my image in this respect. Otherwise I would never be believing in the existence of anything so much as in the existence of an exact duplicate of the imagery I am experiencing.

What is meant by calling images fragmentary? There is an

[1] See p. 78.

inclination to think of the visual field as follows. All the visual data I experience at any one time, apart from the visual field itself, are parts of the visual field, and parts in a definite position within it. Moreover the visual field always, or at least mostly, remains of the same shape, and every position in it is always occupied by something, so that a main part of its character at any moment could theoretically be given by saying how each such position is occupied. The fields in which visual images occur are not very like this.

Actually, visual sense-data are by no means always parts of some neatly ordered visual field. Nonetheless visual data come much nearer to that description than do images, and that is what is meant by saying that they are less fragmentary. A fairly similar account in terms of fields can be given of what is meant by calling images of other kinds fragmentary.

But what is meant by saying that images are vague? One thing which is often meant is that they fall under certain determinables without falling under specific determinates of those determinables. What sense can be made of such a notion? One attempt to answer this question might run as follows.

It is absurd to think that a particular can fall under a determinable without falling under a determinate of that determinable. On the other hand the class of determinates such that *a sense-datum* falling under a specified determinable must exemplify one of them may not exhaust the class of determinates of that determinable. Conceivably there may be different determinates of that determinable which an image may exemplify. Possibly one determinate of the determinable exemplifiable only by an image may be equally alike various different determinates of that determinable exemplifiable by a sense-datum. This might lead one to say: It doesn't exemplify any of these determinates (exemplifiable by a sense-datum) exactly, but exemplifies each of them vaguely. Thus the determinable red might have determinates red_1, red_2, red_3, . . . red_n, exemplifiable by sense-data (and perhaps by images as well), and determinates red_a, red_b, red_c, . . . red_p, exemplifiable only by images. A red_a image might be equally like red_1, red_2, red_3 sense-data, a red_b image equally like red_4, red_5, and red_6 sense-data, and so on. One might then say that a red_a image was vaguely red_1 and vaguely red_2 and red_3 as well.

Suppose now I have a red_a image. The imagist will say that I am believing that a datum falling within the range red_1-red_3 exists. This seems all right, but it remains something of a mystery why I am not believing in the existence of another red_a image.

To meet this, the imagist might refine his view thus: There are certain properties exemplifiable only by images. Some of these are properties in respect of which an image could resemble an image exactly or inexactly, but in respect of which it could not resemble a non-image at all. Others of them are properties in respect of which an image could resemble another image exactly or inexactly, or a non-image inexactly. Besides these, there are properties which an image can share with a non-image such as a sense-datum, in respect of which therefore it could resemble a non-image exactly or inexactly. Now when I have an image I am believing in the existence of something of a kind as like to this image as something which is not an image can be. That is, for each of the properties of an image which a non-image can have, I am believing that there is a non-image having all those properties. That is, I am believing in the existence of something having all those properties of the image which a non-image could have, and all those properties which are the minimum necessary for making it inexactly resemble the image in respect of those properties of the image which on its side can be the basis of such inexact, but not exact, resemblance. As for those properties which could not be the basis of a resemblance, either exact or inexact, to a non-image, they play no part in determining the character of that which is believed to exist.

One consequence of this view is that one could not have beliefs about the existence of images. Conceivably the imagist could offer some alternative accounts of such believings.

The intending relation is now rather over-shadowed by one which, on the imagist view, holds between an image fact and a non-image fact when experience of the image fact intends the non-image fact. Let us say that the image fact, which may also be called the symbolizing fact, *symbolizes* the non-image fact, which may also be called the symbolized fact. To say that an image fact symbolizes a non-image fact appears to be to say simply that the non-image fact is as like the image fact as a non-image fact can be.

The resemblance between the two facts is intrinsic or conceptual resemblance. Is it exact or inexact resemblance, or sometimes the one and sometimes the other? This question cannot be answered until we make it quite clear what sort of fact the image fact is. Is it merely a fact about an image, or is it in part the fact that something is an image? It seems best to say that it is the latter, and insist that the symbolizing fact is an image fact in the strong sense that it ascribes to its particulars universals only exemplifiable by images. At the same time we may add that the symbolized fact is a non-image fact in the strong sense that it ascribes to its particulars universals only exemplifiable by non-images. Such a stipulation ensures that the symbolizing relation is asymmetrical.

Let us suppose now that I experience an image fact, the image-redness of A. By image-redness I mean the property of being red in the way in which only an image can be red, or simply the property of being a red image. Suppose also that a certain object B, not experienced by me, is datally red, that is, is a red datum. Then A's image-redness symbolizes B's datal redness. Obviously if C is datally red A's image-redness symbolizes C's datal redness also.

The symbolizing relation is clearly an ideal relation. A diagram here will serve to give names to the different relations involved.[1]

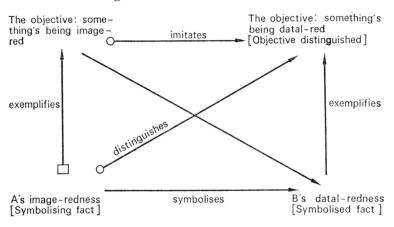

---

[1] The word 'imitates' will sometimes have its meaning extended so that universals figuring in the imitating objective are said (in this occurrence) to imitate the corresponding universals in the imitated objective. I should also warn the reader that on occasion I may use all these terms in somewhat looser ways, which should not however be misleading. For example, I shall sometimes write as though the terms of certain of these relations were images or data, where strictly they are facts about them.

(One relation is left unnamed.) The square and circle at the ends of a line have the same significance as on pp. 187-8.

Symbolizing and distinguishing are somewhat analogous to representing and signifying, and to a lesser extent denoting and connoting. Whether there is anything more here than an analogy is not a point for present exploration. The following point may be noted, however. The appropriate verbal expression for a believing would always seem to be a sentence which signifies an essential rather than a quintessential objective, and hence is only capable of representing a fact incompletely. For a sentence completely representing a fact, say 'A is F' or 'A is R to B' would seem bound to express a noticing rather than a believing. Thus one might be tempted to say that the symbolizing involved in believing is always incomplete.

Let us call an image fact which distinguishes an objective a symbolizing fact even when there is no fact which it symbolizes.

Let us now return to our experience of the fact that A is image-red, and let us suppose that A as well as being red, is pink and round. In that case the same experience which is an experience of A's redness will also be an experience of A's pink-ness and roundness. For an experience of a fact ascribing an intrinsic character to a particular is simply an experience of that particular. It follows from the imagist view as so far outlined that this experience will be an act of believing quite a number of different things. In being an experience of the fact that A is red it will be an experience of a fact fitted to symbolize any fact to the effect that something is a red datum. In being an experience of A's pinkness it will be an experience of a fact fitted to symbolize any fact to the effect that something is a pink datum. In being an experience of A's roundness . . . and so on.

Suppose now that there is a certain object which is a red datum. Let us call this B. The fact that A is a red image will symbolize this fact. But this does not mean, of course, that our experience is the belief that B is red, it is simply the belief that something is red. If C is another red sense-datum it will equally intend the fact of C's datal redness. But it will not be a belief that C is red. What we normally do when we say that a belief is that something, is indicate the objective onto which it is directed. According to our simple imagist view this is a matter of the objective distinguished by the symbolizing fact. This objective will be signified by a sentence containing existentially bound particular variables rather than logically proper names for particulars. Perhaps it could contain both, but it must contain the former.

3 DIFFERENCE BETWEEN BELIEVING AND MERE IMAGINING

There is an obvious and on the face of it devastating objection to simple imagism. It consists simply in the patent fact that we can experience images without believing that something similar to the images exists in the outside world. One can imagine situations without believing in their existence. Moreover imagery may play a part in such propositional attitudes as desire, as well as in belief. Thus the imagist must give some account of the difference between believing and other propositional attitudes, perhaps especially imagining.

Among thinkers of a more or less imagist persuasion (in some of their phases, at least) who have discussed this question, we have Hume and his talk of vivacity, William James and his talk of the sense of reality, Russell and his talk of a belief feeling. Indeed this often seems to be regarded as *the* problem about belief.

Much the same alternatives arise for the imagist here as for the non-imagist. An imagist might say that to experience an image fact fitted to resemble a non-image fact of a certain kind is, other things being equal, to believe in a fact of that kind. It can however cease to be a case of believing if it enters into certain relations with other experiences. A non-imagist who held likewise that presence of an idea together with absence of anything serving to negate it is belief in the existence of an object answering to the idea was Spinoza. On such a view mere entertaining of an idea or proposition is believing plus something, rather than believing being a matter of mere entertaining plus something. Other propositional attitudes, besides mere entertaining, may be seen likewise as believing plus something which stops it being believing and makes it into willing, pretending, or whatever. On the other hand the imagist may say that experiencing an image fact fitted to resemble a fact of a certain kind, becomes believing only when accompanied by certain other elements, while accompanied by alternative elements it may become willing, pretending, or whatever. This view could again have a non-imagist equivalent.

A certain ambiguity liable to be present in views of the first of these two kinds should be noted. Suppose an imagist who claims to support the first view and says that merely to have an F-like image is in itself to believe that an F exists, unless certain belief-cancelling features are present. It is possible that in putting forward this rather unplausible sounding view what he really has in mind in this. Believing that an F exists is having an F-like image and being affected by this image in certain ways (say certain behavioural ways). However a person who has an F-like image always is affected in these ways unless certain special features are present which check the development of these effects. Thus such a thinker is not really identifying the believing merely with the occurrence of the image, but saying that the situation where an image has the effects necessary to make it a belief is the normal situation, and that it can only fail to have these effects when inhibited in some positive way. Such a view is really very different from one which takes the potential likeness of an image to some external event as the complete essence of belief in such an event.

Let us now consider some of the main ways in which thinkers of an imagist outlook have sought to distinguish believing from mere imagining or, what they usually fail to distinguish from this, the mere experience of imagery.

It will be proper to begin with the greatest of all imagists, David Hume.

4 HUME'S THEORY OF BELIEVING

An opinion, therefore, or belief may be most accurately defin'd, A LIVELY IDEA RELATED TO OR ASSOCIATED WITH A PRESENT IMPRESSION (*Treatise*, p. 96, Selby-Bigge edition).

I take it that Hume's analysis of what it is to experience an act of believing in a fact of a certain kind would be, or is, this. I experience an image fact fitted to resemble a fact of that kind, my experience of this image fact has a special sort and degree of liveliness or vivacity, and it has this vivacity as a consequence of having been evoked, according to laws governing the association of experiences, by an experience of some sensory fact. This is some little way from Hume's actual language, as it uses language marking ontological distinctions somewhat foreign to Hume, but I don't think it misrepresents his view. By a sensory fact I mean a fact about what Hume would call impressions.

Hume believed that ideas or experiences with liveliness of the kind in question did not occur except when evoked by a present impression. But how would he answer us if we asked him whether if a lively idea did happen to occur not evoked by a *present* impression it would be a belief? For instance, if I suddenly now form a lively idea of a friend of mine jumping into a river, and if there is no impression which can be said to have evoked it, would Hume say that this would be a belief that my friend was jumping into a river? Perhaps he would say that a lively idea could not occur just like this, but that is rather unplausible, and on the whole seems a very unHumean piece of *a priori*-ising. Actually it seems absurd to suppose that every such lively idea is evoked by a present impression. Surely the immediate cause of some lively ideas lies entirely in unconscious brain activity. I suspect that though Hume was firmly convinced that all lively ideas owed their liveliness to their association with present impressions, he would have allowed that *if* there had occurred a lively idea not thus evoked it would have been a belief.

It is very difficult to know what such an analysis of believing amounts to for it is not at all clear what sort of vivacity is in question. According to Hume, the difference between an impression and an idea is a matter of degree of force and liveliness. Is a belief an idea which is nearer an impression in this respect than are other ideas? But surely the imagery with which I may think of unicorns may be as lively in this sense as the imagery with which I think about horses? Surely such imagery as accompanies my reading of what I take as fiction can be as lively as the imagery which accompanies my reading of what I take as history? Hume notices this difficulty in the Appendix to the *Treatise*, when he discussed the effect of poetry (p. 630).[1] In the Appendix he admits the impossibility of really explaining how believing differs from imagining by talking of vivacity, and insists only that believing is a special manner of conceiving our ideas. But it is hard to identify any single unstructured quality (whether vivacity be the apt word or not) in one's experience, of which one would be prepared to say

[1] David Hume, *A Treatise of Human Nature* ed. L. A. Selby-Bigge.

that a man whose experiences all lacked that quality could have no beliefs at all. I have nothing against unanalysable qualities, nor against the assumption that the experiences of others exemplify the same such qualities as do mine, but there is no such quality which I must assume to be present in the experiences of anyone whom I regard like myself as a cognitive being. Thus if this is Hume's position it must be rejected.

5 BERTRAND RUSSELL'S VERSION OF IMAGISM

> The content of a belief may consist of words only, or of images only, or of a mixture of the two, or of either or both together with one or more sensations. It must contain at least one constituent which is a word or an image, and it may or may not contain one or more sensations as constituents (*The Analysis of Mind* by Bertrand Russell, p. 236).

Russell then is not a pure imagist, for he thinks that believing (he is using 'belief' to mean what we call 'an act of believing') may be a purely verbal affair. However it is his account of image believing which concerns us here. It should be noted that the word 'content' in the above corresponds rather to our *symbolizing fact* than to our *content*.

Russell holds, then, that for an act of believing to occur there must occur a certain content, and in the case of image believing this content consists in images. What this comes to in our terminology is that for an act of believing to occur there must be experience of a certain image fact which we call the symbolizing fact rather than the content. But if we are to have belief rather than some other propositional attitude something else must occur, according to Russell, and this something else he calls a belief feeling. Actually he thinks that there are three different kinds of belief feeling, memory feeling, expectation feeling, and bare assent feeling.[1] His idea that the time element in the case of memory and expectation is supplied solely by the belief feeling and does not belong either to what he calls the content or to what he calls the objective reference does not seem to me a happy one. However we shall have to leave this point on one side. In what follows I shall be thinking simply of what he calls *bare assent*.

Russell seems to take the simple imagist view which identifies

[1] Bertrand Russell, *The Analysis of Mind*, p. 250.

the symbolizing relation with resemblance. His view is admittedly complicated by his holding that just as there is a fact to which a true belief points, there is a fact from which a false belief points away, but it seems that the relevant relation between the 'content' of a true image belief and the fact it intends or points to is supposed to be resemblance.

Suppose I experience an image belief that fire-dwelling salamanders exist. Then, according to Russell, I would experience an image fitted to be sensibly like a little lizard-like creature moving about in the flames of a fire, and together with it and in a specific relation to it a belief feeling.

If we now imagine a Russellian pressed as to just what character this feeling has, it is hard to see what else he can say but something of the following sort: 'The difference between mere imagining and believing is this. In mere imagining one has images which, if there were salamanders, would be like the salamanders. In believing, one not only has the images, but one has a feeling that something like these images really exists, where "really" presumably means "among the non-images".'

Russell does not actually give this description of the feeling or sensation of bare assent, but he says something of very much the same sort in describing the memory-feeling. He says: 'We might be tempted to put the memory-belief into the words: "Something like this image occurred"' (p. 179). If this is a temptation to some extent to be resisted one gathers that this is not because the feeling is not the sort of thing to be expressed in a structured sentence, but simply because the structure here indicated is a bit too subtle, making a distinction between 'This' and 'Something like this' alien to the simple state of mind in question.

If then the memory feeling is to be described as something expressible by the sentence 'This occurred', or 'Something like this occurred', it is evidently equally suitable to describe the feeling of bare assent as something expressible by 'This occurs (or exists)' or 'Something like this occurs (or exists)' – where the present tense is timeless. However if we make the feeling propositional like this, if we make it the feeling *that* something, as opposed merely to a feeling of a certain distinctive kind, the Russellian is in obvious difficulties. For this feeling is in effect itself turning out to be a belief, and not merely as it was supposed to be one element present in every belief. Yet what can the feeling that something like these (images) exists be but the belief that something like these (images) exists? It is hard to avoid letting the so-called belief feeling become itself a belief in this way. Granted this, it is clear that the Russellian is explaining belief in terms of belief. Or at least, he is explaining belief in common or garden propositions in terms of belief in propositions of a special type about images.

This does not show that the view is necessarily useless, but it shows that it is a very much less comprehensive account of the nature of belief than might have been hoped for.

Perhaps the Russellian might hope to move on to some account of what it is to experience belief in propositions of this special type. Presumably such an account would exemplify the following very abstract form. To believe that something like a certain image one is experiencing exists, is to react to this image in manner X, or to react to its having such and such a property in manner X.

If such an account of these fundamental believings became available doubtless our problems about believing, or at any rate about image believing, would be over. But I suspect that after such an account had been given, one would no longer find it very suitable to refer to the situation of someone reacting to an image in manner X, as having a belief about it, or even as having a feeling that *such and such* about it.

What all image theories are in need of is some account of the difference between merely having images, and having images and treating them as representatives of 'external' realities. To say that treating these images in this way is feeling that something like them really exists helps us very little, even if it does not actually hinder us. The problem of what it is to treat an image as the representative of an outside reality remains.

6 FAREWELL TO SIMPLE IMAGISM

This concludes our discussion of simple imagism and of views which represent only slight qualifications of it. Such views can hardly be accepted as satisfactory and that for a variety of reasons. For one thing they do not offer any satisfactory account of the difference between mere imagining and believing. The addition of the quality of vivacity or a belief feeling does not really help here. Moreover, it should be clear that they do not really offer a satisfactory account even of what it is to be thinking of a situation, let alone be thinking of it in a believing manner. The mere fact that certain images flitting before my consciousness resemble, or are fitted to resemble, a certain situation, cannot constitute my thinking of that situation. As has been pointed out by H. H. Price,[1] the image with which I think of dogs may in itself be as like a fox as a dog. It cannot be merely its resemblance to a dog, then, which makes it the thinking of a dog. Admittedly, some lessening of this difficulty occurs if one takes into account not only the actual imagery, but the imagery which this will develop into if given its head, for the further possible images might be definitely more dog-like than fox-like. All the same, mere resemblance between image and thing thought of hardly seems to give the essence of the intending relation. For then it isn't at all clear why, when I experience a sense-datum, I am not said to be thinking of a similar image, or of another similar datum.

Simple imagism has one great charm. It makes intending an ideal relation (as opposed simply to a quasi-ideal relation), as other theories, whether of an imagist character or otherwise, always fail to do, whenever they do more than merely salute intentionality as a thing *sui generis*.

It is very difficult, surely, to get away from the idea that the fact that one's state of mind at any given time is one of thought or belief about certain things is an absolutely intrinsic feature of that state of mind, so that there could not be an exactly similar state of consciousness which was not a thinking of those same things. To accept this idea simply is to accept the idea that intending is an ideal relation. For it is to say that what makes it the case that a present state of consciousness is fitted to intend what it is fitted to intend is its intrinsic character, and not any of its extrinsic relations. If one's account of what it is to experience a belief or a thought to a certain effect appeals to something beyond the intrinsic character of the present state of consciousness, say its effects on or connections with, the activities of one's physical organism, then it must be admitted that the same state of consciousness might not have been a belief or thought to that same effect at all. This goes against the grain.

[1] See *Thinking and Experience*, pp. 269ff.

X

IMAGIST-ACTIVISM

There are four main traditional forms of imagism known to me. A classic account of three of them is to be found in Russell's *Analysis of Mind*, Chapter XII. The following propositions present the chief tenet of each form.

(1) Imaging and believing are the same thing, except perhaps that imaging ceases to be believing if certain further eventualities, say further images, somehow cancel its usual status.

(2) Believing is vivacious imaging. (This is the one ignored by Russell.)

(3) Believing is imaging plus a Belief Feeling. (This is Russell's view.)

(4) Believing is imaging which leads to action or a readiness for action.

The first three have been discussed. The present chapter is devoted to the study of the last, which I shall call imagist-activism.

On this view 'X believes that P' is equivalent to 'X experiences an image fact which distinguishes the objective P, and this experience produces a readiness for action in him'. For the notion of distinguishing the reader should refer to the diagram on p. 199 of the last chapter.

The proponent of this view is under no obligation to explain why experience of one image fact produces a readiness for action, and another does not. Russell's reasoning on this point on p. 247 of *The Analysis of Mind* is not very happy. No one concerned to analyse the concept of believing is obliged to say what circumstances actually produce belief, unless being caused in a certain way actually enters into the analysis of believing, which on the present theory it does not. So although there must, doubtless, be some explanation of the fact that one image experience produces effects on action, or readiness to act, and another does not, it is not for the imagist-activist to provide this explanation. Least of all does he proffer as the causal explanation of the readiness to act, the fact that the imaging was a case of believing. The fact that the imaging[1] took place might perhaps be a causal factor. That's a quite different matter.

A question now to be asked is this. Is an image experience a case of believing merely because it produces readiness for some action or other, or must it not rather be because it produces a readiness for appropriate action?

Presumably the latter, for mere imagining might surely have some sort of effects on one's readiness for action.

The imagist-activist, we may take it to begin with, lets the account of distinguishing and symbolizing given by simple imagism stand.

My experience of the fact that a certain image is F will, if F is sufficiently similar to G, be a case of thinking of the existence of Gs. But in order that this experience should be an act of believing that something is G, or that Gs exist, it is required, according to imagist-activism, that this experience should produce in me a readiness for appropriate action. Thus although it is part of its *intrinsic* nature to be a case of thinking of the existence of Gs, it is only part of its *extrinsic* nature to be a case of believing in the existence of Gs.

To what is the action supposed to be appropriate or relevant? Presumably to the existence of Gs.

We may now point out that the imagist-activist might do well to bring in the kind of behaviour caused by the image experience not only as making the experience into a belief in something, rather than a mere thought of something, but also as a determinant of the objective distinguished by the image-fact.

Suppose, for instance, that I experience the fact that an image exemplifies the image-universal F, and that the datal universals, G, H, and I are all equally and very similar to F. Then on the

---

[1] 'Imaging' means having an image, experiencing an imagy particular. It does not mean imagining, i.e., imagining what it would be like for something to be the case. This usage stems from H. H. Price. See *Thinking and Experience*, p. 246. Cf. note on p. 225 of the present book.

theory so far elaborated, I will be thinking as much of the existence of Hs as of Gs. I will presumably be thinking of the existence of something which is G or H or I. If appropriate behaviour is caused I will *believe* in this. But let us now take it that the behaviour caused is appropriate to the existence of Gs, but not to the existence of Hs or Is. Will not the imagist-activist say that it is the existence of Gs, and not the existence of Hs or of Is, which is believed in?

At this point the imagist-activist might entirely throw out the idea that the F-ness of an image, when it does not cause behaviour appropriate to the existence of Gs, can in any sense be said to distinguish G-ness. He may say that it is only through the combination of the two features – the fittedness of the F-ness of the image to resemble the G-ness of certain objects, and its causing behaviour appropriate to the existence of G objects, that it can be said to distinguish the existence of G objects. Without the second point, no distinguishing is achieved at all, and one cannot say that the existence of Gs is even being thought of.

There is much in favour of this repudiation of the idea that mere fittedness of an image of mine to resemble objects of a certain kind can make it true that I am thinking of the existence of objects of that kind. But if the imagist-activist does this, he must at some stage explain what merely thinking of a situation as opposed to believing in it is, and this appears a little difficult if that which makes of an experience a belief in something, i.e., the causing of appropriate activity, is identified with what makes it even a thought of that something. Still the difficulty may be surmountable. He might say that in mere thinking of a situation a behavioural readiness was caused, and at the same time frustrated. Thus merely thinking of a possible state of affairs would be an inhibited version of believing in that possible state of affairs, and that is by no means an unplausible contention.

On the other hand, if the imagist-activist does take this step, he has abandoned for ever the notion that what I am thinking about at any moment depends entirely upon the intrinsic nature of my present state of consciousness. Not only whether I believe in the existence of Gs, but even whether I am thinking of the existence of Gs, will turn on the modification made by my experience to my readiness for certain behaviour.

We need not pin a decision on him regarding this point for the present.

We must ask next what it is that constitutes behaviour appropriate or relevant to a certain objective.

One view is that behaviour is appropriate to a certain objective if and only if it is a kind of behaviour which would arise in the agent on occasion when he had direct awareness of a fact answering to that objective. Thus behaviour is fitted to the existence of pouring rain if and only if it is such as occurs when one is aware of a fact of the character 'This is pouring rain'. Another view is that behaviour is appropriate to a certain objective if and only if it is behaviour the success of which depends upon the actualization of that objective. The trouble about this second view, is that it makes the statement that certain behaviour is appropriate to a certain objective, and hence eventually the statement that the agent believes in this objective, require for its support the ascription to him of certain purposes – for success is relative to purpose. But having a purpose, on the face of it, as much involves the performance of mental acts directed upon an objective as does believing. Thus we would merely substitute for the question how a belief is directed at an objective, the question how (say) an intention is, and it is not obvious that the latter is the easier question. It seems, therefore, more hopeful to consider the first account of what it is for behaviour to be appropriate to an objective.

It is to be noted that it is demanded of an act of imaging which is to be an act of believing that it affects one's behavioural dispositions, not that it affects one's actual behaviour. If someone says that an act of believing is an act of imaging which produces appropriate behaviour it is a fairly obvious objection to him to say that some of my beliefs apparently have no effects on my behaviour. Thus, to use an example borrowed from Russell, my believing on various occasions that Charles I was executed has no apparent effect on my behaviour. It is likely indeed to have an effect on my linguistic behaviour. But it should be obvious that items of linguistic behaviour will not do for that appropriate behaviour which can make a belief out of an image experience. Not all linguistic behaviour caused by imagery is assertion, yet it is only if it is assertion that it can be held to transform the image-experience into a belief experience. But what distinguishes assertion from other types of utterance? Whatever it is which marks this distinction is probably the very same thing as marks the distinction between mere imaging and believing, and if we knew what this was, we would not need to bring in the linguistic behaviour.

2

There are two main reasons why we must reject the view now described. First, it will not allow us to draw any distinction between the mere imaginings and the believings of a mind which is for some reason unable to produce effects in the physical world. Perhaps it will not even be able to ascribe imaginings with a definite objective to him. Second, it seems paradoxical to assert that the fact that I am now believing something depends upon the remote effects of my present state of mind, rather than on something close to its intrinsic nature. Let us take these reasons for rejecting the view in turn.

(1) Consider the case of a completely paralysed man who believes that his wife is planning to murder him. It is doubtless true that if he had such a belief, and were not paralysed, he would have a disposition to avoid his wife and the food she prepared. Can we say of the paralysed man that he has any such disposition? One is certainly inclined to say of him: 'If he were not paralysed, then in certain kinds of circumstance, he would move away from his wife.' But is not what one really means simply this: 'In certain kinds of circumstance, he would wish that he was moving away from his wife, though these wishes would not be actualized as wishes normally are'? To be paralysed is to be such that wishes of a certain kind which ordinarily come true cease to do so. If a paralysed man has a wish for X (and X is the sort of thing which normally results from a wish for X) then we say that if he were not paralysed he would produce the event X. But it is analytic that a man who wishes for X will bring about X unless he is paralysed, not because wishing for X is to be defined in a certain way, but because paralysis is. It is analytic that wishes of a certain kind normally come true, because it is part of what we mean by there being a *normal* (i.e., unparalysed, among other things) man in the room, that there be a body and a mind such that the body brings about events of a certain kind if the mind has certain wishes, and the body is in the room.

If this view is correct, we see that when I say of the paralysed man who believes that his wife is murdering him, 'If he were not paralysed, then he would move away when his wife approached' I am not ascribing to him a genuine dispositional property. I am simply deducing from 'He wishes to be at a distance from his wife' the trivial consequence 'If his wish to be at a distance from his wife tended to become true, he would tend to be at a distance from his wife'. This does not say anything more than that he wishes he were at a distance from his wife.

Admittedly when a man is paralysed there is a physical explanation for his wishes not tending to come true. This does not alter the fact that essentially what we mean by calling a man paralysed is that his wishes do not have their normal effects, and not that his body is in a certain state.

It may be urged that if we call the physical basis of his paralysis state S, then we can ascribe to him the truly dispositional property 'would move away from his wife, if not in state S'. That is so, though the statement is essentially a deduction from 'He wishes to move away from his wife', and 'His wishes of that sort would be realized if he was not in State S'. Moreover, it is complicated by the fact that if he were not paralysed, he might well not have such a wish, which springs, perhaps, from a morbid belief caused by his paralysed state. So one should add 'as long as he retains his wish to do so', which makes the statement simply equivalent to the statement that elimination of state S would eliminate the paralysis.

Waiving aside this last difficulty, one may still insist that it cannot be involved in the meaning of statements ascribing a belief that a man would behave in certain ways if he were not in state S, where 'S' gives the physical basis of paralysis. For clearly one can know about believing without knowing anything about S states. One must claim, rather, that it is sometimes involved in ascribing experience of certain beliefs to someone that, if his wishes for events of a certain kind F tend to come true, then under certain circumstances events of type F would occur. But if some such thing is involved in the ascription to him of experience of certain beliefs, it seems obvious that it is because the ascription to him of certain wishes is involved in it, and the trivial deduction is added that if his wishes of that type come true, then the wished for events would occur.

I think one may reasonably suggest on this basis that the plausible view is not that believing is imaging which produces a disposition to certain bodily behaviour, but that believing is imaging which produces a disposition to a certain type of wishing.

These points will appear still more evident to anyone who is prepared to countenance the logical possibility of a disembodied mind. To me it appears quite evident that there could be a mind which observed the physical world from a certain point of view but which could not produce any effects on the physical world, and could not be described as animating a body. To ensure this last point, we can assume that the point of view alters without the mind's having any choice, and does not alter concomitantly with the movement of some physical object along the path of the changing point of view.

To imagine this situation, we have simply to imagine visual and auditory experience such as we have now, with the complete absence of any visual or auditory datum belonging to a body which changes position concurrently with change in the point of view. We do not even have to exclude somatic sense-data and tactile data, though the former must have no basis in a body, and the latter must not relate to the contact of other things with any *one* physical object.

The question then is: Could such a mind have any beliefs? To me it seems clear that such a mind could conduct intellectual operations and have beliefs. I would say also that it could have wishes, though since its wishes would be ineffective, these wishes, at least in so far as about the physical world, would never be volitions (which are simply wishes of a type which usually come true).

If we allow that believing would be possible to such a mind, we must allow that believing is not to be defined in terms of the effects of imagery on dispositions to overt action, action on the public scene. Such a mind would not have any dispositions to produce public events. It might wish for certain public events, and one could, of course, say of it: 'If its wishes caused their own fulfilment, then such and such would happen'. This would not, however, be to ascribe any genuine behavioural disposition.

I am not saying that such a mind could do nothing. I am not denying it all control over its private mental states. What I am arguing is that such a mind, incapable of public action, could still believe, and that therefore believing cannot involve a disposition to public action. Whether it involves a disposition to private action is a separate question.

What emerges from this discussion is that the concept of believing does not contain the concept of a disposition to overt behaviour, but that it may contain the concept of a disposition to purely mental behaviour. There seems some indication that it may involve the concept of a disposition to wish in a certain way.

(2) Our second objection is less definite, and by no means unconnected with the first objection.

The starting point for our investigation has always been the belief that there are moments in our life when we really grasp what it would be like for something to be the case, and hold that it really is the case. The nature of such moments must surely be sought more in their own inner character than is allowed for by imagist-activism. It cannot lie in some remote causal effects they have. That at a given moment I assented to the idea that things are thus and thus, cannot depend upon what happened after the moment of that experience, still less on what would have happened if things had been other than they were.

This objection should not be pressed too far. Once simple imagism is abandoned it will be difficult to find any view which makes the objective on to which a belief experience is directed depend entirely on the intrinsic character of the experience. Still, there may be greater or lesser departures from this ideal. It seems that imagist-activism constitutes too great a departure from that ideal.

We reject imagist-activism, then, though we shall eventually look with some favour upon a theory in many respects similar.

3

Three difficult questions will now be considered which might be put to the imagist-activist. It is important for us to see how he might answer them, as similar questions will arise for the theory we shall later propose in its place.

First difficult question for the imagist-activist:
Must there be innate behavioural responses to each distinct kind of sense-datum about which we may have beliefs?

According to the imagist-activist, to believe in an objective is to experience an image fact which serves as a substitute for a non-image fact answering to that objective. It does this if and only if it evokes just such behaviour as experience of such a non-image fact would do.

This might almost seem to suggest that the imagist-activist postulates that for each sort of sense-datum, such that one can believe in the existence of such a sense-datum, there is a behavioural response innately linked to that sort of sense-datum. Such a postulate seems unplausible. However the imagist-activist may develop his position without any such postulate, as follows. There are certain types of behaviour innately associated with the sensing of certain types of sense-data. Thus there may be a certain response innately associated with experiencing the phenomenon of extreme heat, such as a movement effecting withdrawal from the heat source. The simplest kind of belief consists in an image occurring which is like a certain phenomenon, and which produces the behavioural response innately associated with experience of that phenomenon. However, it would be a mistake to suppose that the behavioural response, the carrying over of which from a certain kind of datum to a certain kind of image, is one's believing in the existence of a datum of that kind, has to be an unconditioned response to such data. The imagist-activist may appeal here to any plausible account of response conditioning.

He may postulate that the human infant has a tendency to emit quite randomly responses of quite a wide range. (The word 'response' is here used in a stretched sense to refer to any identifiable kind of behaviour, irrespective of whether it is really in response to anything or not.[1]) He also postulates that certain kinds of sense-datum are rewarding and others punishing. This really means no more than that certain kinds of sense-datum are such that if such a sense-datum occurs after a certain response has been emitted, and if that response occurred contemporaneously with the sensing of a sense-datum of a certain kind, then when a sense-datum of that kind is sensed again the probability is increased that the original response will either be repeated (if it had been followed previously by a so-called reward), or that it will not be repeated (if it had been followed by a so-called punishment).

The situation is complicated by the fact that at an early stage one's responses to the data sensed probably will come to be determined in part by events which the imagist-activist would regard as early forms of believing. One consequence of the course of my experience may be that when I sense certain sense-data I tend to

[1] Cf. B. F. Skinner, *Science and Human Behaviour*.

have images resembling certain other sense-data usually associated with the sense-data now sensed. Having these images may produce in me a tendency to responses associated with those other sense-data. This will be the belief in the existence of those other sense-data, according to imagist-activism. Moreover, mere readiness for such imagery will be a sort of believing. It is obviously virtually impossible to say whether the fact that my reaction to one kind of sense-data is of a sort originally proper rather to data of another kind frequently associated with the first kind, has come about with or without the aid of any tendency for imagery resembling data of the second kind. Yet in the latter case belief will be involved, while in the former it will not.

What it seems best to say is that belief in the existence of sense-data of a certain kind is a matter of reacting to imagery similar to those data with a response usual for those data, and this response may either be an unconditioned or a conditioned response to those data. When it is a conditioned response, it may have become conditioned through a process involving belief or through one which did not. A vicious regress would occur if such conditioning always involved belief: but there seems no reason to say that it always or even normally does so.

Second difficult question for the imagist-activist:
Would it not be very odd to respond to an image with the same behaviour as to a datum?

Imagist-activism describes believing as the reacting to images as though they were data. But would it not, in many cases, be very odd to react to the images involved in one's believings as one would to such data as they most resemble? If I did, wouldn't it show that I had mistaken the image for a datum? It seems odd to identify believing with the making of a mistake.

It may anyway have struck the sophisticated reader that some of the previous discussion has combined different conceptual levels in what is often said to be an illegitimate way. I have talked of reactions to sense-data as consisting in physical actions or movements. But if the stimulus is described in sense-datum terms, should not the reaction be so described also?

But however we analyse the relation between sense-data and physical objects we can hardly object to saying that when I experience sense-data of a certain kind I normally react by a certain physical movement, if this happens to be the truth. It might be different if we were trying to give a causal explanation of the physical movement, but that is not in question. Actually, on the theory that for a sense-datum to be the appearance of a physical object is for it to be a member of an appropriate group of sensed and unsensed data the physical movement itself is ultimately a matter of an indefinite number of sense-fields changing their character in corresponding ways. These sense-fields will all be views, not necessarily visual ones, of my body in its immediate environment, or possibly in some cases simply views of some part of my body. If the movement is an experienced action of mine, then some of these views will belong to my stream of consciousness. It may well be claimed that for it to be properly speaking an *action*, I must be *aware of*, in the sense of *have correct beliefs about*, certain characteristics of the physical movement, in particular have certain beliefs about its consequences likely or actual. Perhaps other conditions must be satisfied as well. But however this may be, certainly if the action is an experienced action there must occur in my stream of consciousness sense-datal events which are *views* of the physical reaction. These sense-datal events may be called the sensory reaction. They must not be thought of as existing in some problematic ethereal spiritual realm. They are the views I experience of the physical reaction of my organism.

According to imagist-activism the standard response to data of a certain kind which in believing is carried over to images is a certain physical movement. It may or may not insist that this movement should satisfy whatever conditions to do with consciousness are required in order to make it an action. Anyway, when it talks of a certain physical movement it refers to a universal, and the question is 'To what universal?' It may seem obvious that in most cases it will be a matter of a certain characteristic transformation of the relations between the organism, that is, a certain physical object, and such physical objects in its environment as stand in certain determinate spatial relations to that physical object of which the datum is an appearance. How could this reaction be carried over to the image, since there is no physical object of which the image is an appearance? The most plausible solution would seem to be to say that although the image is not in quite the same way as is a datum the appearance of a physical object, it is fitted to be what we might call the virtual appearance of a certain physical object, and that what is carried over is a certain characteristic transformation of the relations either which the organism has to such physical objects as stand in certain determinate relations to the physical object of which the image is a virtual appearance, or which it has to such a place as would be occupied by that physical object if it existed.

There seem to be two main ways in which an image can be fitted to be the virtual appearance of a certain physical object at a certain place from a certain point of view.

Firstly, it may be simply very like the view which would be experienced of that thing from a certain place. Thus suppose that there is a cat up a certain tree in my garden. There exist any number of views (experienced or otherwise) of the cat up that tree. That these views are all views of the same place turns largely, it should be borne in mind, on their ideal relations. Such spatial relations as are real relations can only hold within a view, not between views. (Thus 'real' space is mainly a matter of ideal, not of real, relations.) Now if I experience a certain image view, it may have a sufficiently detailed nature to give it a place among the set of fields which in their totality make up that scene. It will in fact be the 'same' place as is also occupied by one of the datal views.

What makes it only a virtual view of that region and not an actual view of it is that its occurrence does not belong to the same causal system as do the actual views. A change in one of the actual views, e.g. a movement of the cat-datum down the tree-datum, is always accompanied by a corresponding change in all the other actual views, but need not be accompanied by any change in the image view, which is therefore called *virtual*.

Suppose now that when I see a tiger the result is always an increase in the distance between my body and the place (i.e. the objects we call unmoving) where the tiger was sighted. That is, I respond to the tiger datum by activity which increases the distance between my body and the place where the object of which the datum is a view is situated.

If this is carried over to an image fitted to be the virtual appearance of a tiger at a certain place, what would happen would be something such as follows. I have an image of a tiger which is fitted to be a virtual appearance of a tiger at place P, and I respond by an increase in the distance between my body and P.

But there is an obvious point to be made here. If I am not in fact experiencing any data belonging to place P, I will only distance myself from P if I'm familiar with the look of P and have a present sense of my spatial relations to P.

The imagist-activist might say that to have this sense of one's spatial relations to place P just is to react to image fields fitted to be virtual views of place P with movements affecting one's relations to the objects at P in the way in which movements in response to similar views of place P would affect one's relations to those objects. The conditions under which one gains a sense of one's spatial relations to a place characterized in a certain way would be a matter for the psychologist to investigate.

The second way in which an image can be fitted to be the virtual appearance of a certain physical object at a certain place from a certain point of view turns upon real relations between the elements in one's consciousness, rather than on ideal relations between different fields. Images may either be in spatial relations to data just such as data have to each other, or may be in a relation to data which has come to act analogously on us to the way in which spatial relations between data work.

The cases which most concern us are visual images, since it is these which one who takes an imagist view of belief is most likely to have in mind, at least when the beliefs concern the physical environment rather than the mental states of others. It should not be supposed, however, that the theory insists that the images in question must be visual. Completely presented it would strive to make analogous points about images belonging to the other senses.

An image may be more or less eidetic, that is it may actually be in a certain part of the visual field, in a more or less straightforward way. I do not think that this is very common. But if we suppose an image in a particular part of the visual field, imagy enough not to be a hallucinatory datum, the imagist-activist would say that it constituted belief in the existence of a datum there of a corresponding kind, if it effected a movement of the organism in relation to the part of the physical world of which that part of the field is an appearance, such as would experience of a datum of that kind there. But, of course, there is something very curious about this case, for such a belief is, *ex hypothesi*, false. There is no such datum there. This really may seem a case of what we said the imagist-activist must avoid making all believing seem, the mistaking of an image for a datum. The puzzles of such a case need not concern us much, however, since it is not this type of imagery which is normally thought of as figuring in believing. Such imagery comes near to hallucination. However, hallucination might in a curious way sometimes be veridical, if it suggested the presence of something actually there, but not affecting our senses.

More important is the case where an image has a sort of spatial relation to data, without being a constituent, properly speaking, of a datal field. Suppose I experience a datum of a bush. I may also have an image of a tiger. This image (if not eidetic) can't be in a straightforward sense *behind* the tree datum, but I suggest that there is a relation it may be in to that datum which is a sort of way of *being behind*.

One visual datum may have a datal property of being further forward than another datum. How exactly this relation is to be analysed is a difficult phenomenological question. In part it is a function of the amount of the visual field occupied, and of the intrinsic character of the datum, but apart from visual characteristics we may take it as an experiential character of the datum that a certain sort of bodily feeling goes with it. This bodily feeling is a sign of varying readinesses on the part of the organism to reach out for, avoid, or move towards the object of which the datum is an appearance. Now I suggest that the bodily feelings thus associated with sense-data determine a set of relations which can be called spatial between the data such as echo to some extent (are partly isomorphic with) the visual relations of the data but which in certain respects go beyond them. In terms then of the bodily feelings with which it is associated, an image, say a tiger image, which is not properly speaking in any visual relation of being further back than a visual tree datum, may be related to it in terms of the bodily feelings associated with each of them in a manner which can be called *being behind the tree datum*. In terms of bodily feeling it is related to the tree datum as is one visual datum which is behind another.

It may be said that one visual datum cannot be behind another, so that bodily feeling cannot connect an image to a datum in the way in which it connects one visual datum which is behind another. To this there are two replies. First, in virtue of *gestalt* effects it may seem that it can be, as where a tiger datum is behind the datum making up the bars of its cage. But secondly, if this be disallowed, *being behind* may be construed as a function of degree of visual distantness and identity of position in the visual field regarded as a plane. Now perhaps one datum cannot be behind another in this sense. But they can have more or less close plane relations and they can be related as being more or less distant in visual terms. There may be law-like relations between the spatial system set up by the bodily feelings, and the relations determined jointly by plane relations and relations of visual forwardness and backwardness, which allow us to talk of the bodily feeling determined by identity of plane position and difference of a determinate amount in visual forwardness, even though this is not a combination actually realizable in the relations between data.

At any rate all that the imagist requires is that an image may, in terms of the spatial system of associated bodily feelings, be said to be behind a certain sense-datum. But I would add that relations more visual in character probably enter into situations such as the imagist-activist appeals to as well.

The essential thing here is really the following rather general point. An F-like image, which is in a high degree of a certain relation R to the data in the visual field, may be said to be being treated as would an F datum in that same degree of R to the other data in the visual field, even if there could not be such an F datum, under the following condition. The F image has evoked a reaction which can be recognized as a reaction of a type which regularly occurs in response to F data which are in relation R to certain other data, but modified (further than it ever can be where only data are in question) in a way which goes with an increase in the degree of R between the data.

We may indicate this roughly by our tiger example. It may be true of me that, when a tiger datum is farther back in the visual field than a certain tree datum, I respond with movements which distance me from both tree and tiger (i.e. from the objects of which these data are appearances) and that this movement slows down the further distant these data become from all other data in the visual field. So if I experience a tiger image which is to a certain degree behind a certain tree datum, then I react to it, so far as is possible, as though it were a tiger datum, if I make myself distant from the tree of which that tree datum is an appearance. I cannot, of course, distance myself from the tiger of which the tiger image is an appearance, since there is no such tiger, not even if, harking back to the previous case, there is one of which on the basis of similarity it might be called the virtual appearance.

Putting the point very roughly, we may say that if an image has to data many of the relations, perhaps to degrees impossible in the case solely of data, which hold between data, and which constitute part of what might be meant by their spatial relations one to another, I may react to these data as I would if there were a datum like that image in those relations to them, and that this constitutes my believing that there is such a datum in those relations to such data. The image may then be said to be the virtual appearance, in a different sense from the previous one, of such a physical object as would actually present such a datum.

The same difficulty might seem to arise here as was mentioned with regard to believing depending upon taking an eidetic image as a symbol for a datum. There is no such datum in these real relations to the data to which the symbolizing image is thus related. So that to believe in the existence of such a datum is to believe falsely.

But this can be answered as follows. There may be some sort of unexperienced field which contains just such data as those in just such real relations to just such a datum as that. My combined datal and visual field thus acts as a substitute for such a datal field, and my reaction to it as though to such a field constitutes belief in its existence. This belief in unexperienced sensory fields of various kinds is precisely what we have distinguished as being our belief in an external world.

The whole subject has become most complicated, but I hope in a rough manner to have indicated that the idea, on the part of the imagist-activist, that we may react to images as though they were data of various kinds, is not an absurd one, however difficult it may be to describe just what the reaction is which is carried over from data to images.

Third difficult question for the imagist-activist:
Does the imagist-activist explain adequately why *symbolizing* and *intending* are asymmetrical relations?

Does imagist-activism adequately explain the asymmetrical or at least non-symmetrical character of the relations of symbolizing, imitating, and intending? For if I react to images of certain kinds as I do to data of certain kinds, it will be equally true that I react to data of those kinds as I do to images of those kinds. Why not say that my experience of the data is a belief in the existence of such images, as well as the converse?

The imagist-activist can deal with this as follows: An image objective imitates a datal objective not only because it is similar in itself and similar in its results, but also because the habits of the organism in virtue of which those results are evoked were in the first place habits of reaction to data and only subsequently became habits in reaction to images. This ensures the required asymmetry in a way not open to the simple imagist. Incidentally, we have here committed the imagist-activist to one rather than the other of the alternatives mentioned on p. 210 of this chapter. We have made him introduce the behavioural reponses into the definitions of such expressions as 'symbolize' and 'imitate'.

Both simple imagism and imagist-activism as so far developed seem to make it impossible to believe in the existence of images of a certain kind. Yet surely I must be able to believe not only in the existence of unexperienced data, or of data experienced by you (and of feelings of yours, which are data in a sense), but also in images experienced by you?

What I have in mind here is belief in experiential particulars which are imagy in quality, rather than belief in experiential particulars which play a certain symbolic role in experience. (This is a distinction we shall take up shortly.) Not that I deny that one can believe in the existence of the latter. Obviously one can. But our problem at the moment is as to how one can experience a belief of the former and logically simpler kind.

To believe in the existence of an image of a certain kind would presumably be to experience an image of a similar kind and react to it as though it were of the first kind. But this seems rather silly. What better symbol could I have for one of your images than an image of just the same kind? To insist that the symbol must be only of a similar kind and not of the same kind in a case like this where it could be of the same kind seems odd. But on the other hand, if I have an image of the same kind and react to it as I normally do to images of that kind, it will not be clear how any element of substitution or symbolism can come in.

The answer, briefly, would seem to be this. If I believe in the occurrence of an image in another's mind, in order for it to be the mind of another which is envisaged, a *sensory context* must be envisaged for such an image different from that actually figuring in my own experience. In the simplest case, that is, I imagine the image occurring in a consciousness containing a view of the world from the position you occupy, rather than simply take it as it comes in the context of a consciousness containing my view of the world. Thus I experience an image complex which is fitted to resemble a state of consciousness in which an image of a certain kind occurs together with sense-data of a certain kind. I react to this image complex *as though* it were such a state of consciousness which, of course, it is not. The fact that one of its elements is more or less exactly like one of the elements in a state of mind such as it is fitted to resemble, does not affect the point that the complex as a whole differs from the one it is fitted to resemble by being entirely imagy instead of partly datal. Moreover the habits with which I now respond to it are habits belonging in the first place to the realm of my reactions to mental states of mine which are largely datal.

The subject of belief in Other Minds will receive some further attention in Chapter XII.

6

Before we leave the subject of imagist-activism I want to consider the possibility that just as imagist-activism seemed an improvement on simple imagism, so a form of activism which is not imagist at all, might seem an improvement on imagist-activism.

It might be urged that what has really emerged as important in analysing a man's belief in a state of affairs of the kind 'There is a tiger at place P' or 'There are tiger data at place P' is that he acts as he would do if he were directly aware of a state of affairs of this kind. The imagy[1] state of affairs of which he is aware is seen simply as a stimulus to such behaviour or as producing a tendency thus to behave. It may then be urged that if the behaviour, or the behavioural tendency, could be produced without the imagy state of affairs, all that was essential for the existence of a belief would be there. Thus one might identify someone's believing in a certain state of affairs with his being inclined to

[1] This expression, borrowed from H. H. Price (in *Thinking and Experience*), names the property of being an image or pertaining to *images* in the quality sense. It is by no means synonymous with 'imaginary'.

act as though he were directly aware of it, while admitting that awareness of an imagy state of affairs involving similar universals may on some occasions serve to produce or reinforce this inclination.

This is a fair enough comment, but it would be likely to show that the nature of the problem to which we have looked for imagism of various kinds for a solution has been forgotten. We distinguished in Chapter IX between belief as a disposition and believing as an experiential occurrence. We claimed that there was such a thing as this latter, that there are moments when one is consciously aware of what it would be like for something to be the case, and consciously supposes that it is the case. One can hardly equate these moments with a mere tendency on the part of the organism to move about in certain ways, or even with its actually moving about. If we abandon imagist-activism and talk of the behaviour, or the behavioural tendency alone, and drop all talk of the imagery, then we have given up any attempt to concentrate attention on the *experience* of believing.

Let us now consider another way in which one might move on from imagist-activism to an activist position which was not imagist. This theory may be called substitute-activism and developed as follows.

What is essential in the imagist-activist view is that to say of an image state of affairs that it acts as a substitute for a certain sensory state of affairs is not saying that it resembles it, but saying that consciousness of it produces the same behaviour as would consciousness of the latter. The similarity of the two may explain why the one is able to act as a substitute for the other, but it is not what one's being a substitute for the other consists in. May we not say then that to believe in the existence of something is to experience something else which acts as a substitute for it? This obviously points the way to the claim that the experience of *words* may be just as fundamental a form of belief experience as is the experience of images. This may be led up to by pointing out that we can suppose the resemblance of an image to the thing imaged being steadily reduced without the important thing, the ability of one to evoke the same behaviour as the other, being at any time lost. Such a reduction will be like the shift from iconic language to non-iconic ones.

Thinkers in the imagist tradition have tended to regard verbal thinking as a substitute for image thinking, and image thinking as a substitute for direct experience. They have acknowledged that one can think in words without having any images (other than the words themselves), but they have supposed that this was only thinking because the verbal processes were associated with an ability to produce images of the situation thought about.

One way in which the unwilling imagist-activist might be coerced in this direction, would be by pointing out that on his own showing words are direct substitutes for something quite unlike themselves, namely images, so that it is hard to see why they should not be regarded as direct substitutes rather for things.

It is as well to note here that there is a liability to confusion in discussions of the relation between word thinking and image thinking, until it is made clear in what sense the running of *words* 'through one's head' may sometimes be classifiable as image thinking.

Our use of the word 'image' requires some clarification in this connection. There seems to be a qualitative difference between the experiential particulars we call images and those which we call data. One possible use of the expressions 'is an image' and 'is a datum' is simply to name the two qualities which underlie this difference. But there are other possible uses of these words, not clearly distinguished, because as a matter of contingent fact, when used in these other ways the expressions will be predicable of almost just the same things. Thus 'is an image' may name some symbolizing function – presumably not definable along *simple* imagist lines – which as a matter of fact is performed only, and usually, by things which are images in the quality sense, or, more probably, it may name the conjunction of the quality and the performing of that function. On the other hand 'is a datum' may name, not the quality, but that relational property (only possessed, according to common belief, but not always possessed, by particulars with that quality) of belonging to a group of actually existing (but largely unexperienced) data such as make up all the views of one physical object. 'An image' may then be used to mean an experiential particular which is not a datum in this sense, though in its quality it may be a datum. There are other possibilities as well.

Our use of 'is an image' and 'is a datum' has been in the solely qualitative sense. In the case of 'image' this is appropriate. We are considering various views as to how images, in the quality sense, may symbolize. Thus if the word 'image' is to be used as an instrument rather than as an object of clarification, we must not include the symbolizing function in its meaning.

Verbal thinking may be divided into two types, that which consists in the production of publicly perceptible events and that which does not. If I am thinking to myself (and not soliloquizing or writing) then it seems plausible to urge that in many cases the words (in the sense in which a word is the particular event I produce on a particular occasion) are images, in the quality sense. They may either be auditory images or throat-movement images, or perhaps sometimes visual images (resembling written words). Sometimes indeed they may be less imagy in quality than datal, and in such cases they are doubtless usually datal in the sense that they are appearances of physical throat movements. But in some cases they seem to be imagy in quality, and non-datal in their relations to the physical world. Let us say in this case that they are image words.

Is thinking in image words to be regarded as image thinking or not? Obviously there is a sense in which it is image thinking. When people discuss the possibility of imageless thinking, they are regarding thinking in image words, and presumably indeed, thinking in datal words as well, as image thinking. However, for our purposes the sense in which thinking in image words is not image thinking is more important. Surely there is such a sense, but how is it to be explained? How can it be classified other than as image thinking if its 'stuff' is imagy?

A brief answer is this. Image thinking in the sense of our concern is not simply thought conducted in images, but thought conducted in images which are images of that which is being thought of. When an instance of the word 'cat' runs through my mind it may be an image, but if I am using it to think of a cat, my thinking is not image thinking in the relevant sense since an image instance of the word 'cat' is not an image of a cat. But what is the sense of 'of' here in question? Presumably this. An image (in the quality sense) is an image of an F if it is F-like and experience of it acts as a substitute for experience of an F.

It should be noted that in this sense of 'of' an image instance of the word 'cat' is not to be regarded as an image of an auditory instance of that word. If an image instance of the sentence 'The cat is still out in the garden' runs through my mind I react as I would to an experience of the fact that the cat is out in the garden still (or rather to a fact about sense-data which goes partly to make up this fact), not as I would to experience of the fact that auditory data instancing that sentence had occurred. My experiencing the former fact might lead me to open the door to the cat, while my experience of the latter might lead me, rather, to say 'Well go and let it in then'. In the sense we explained in the last paragraph an image instance of the word 'cat' is normally not an image *of* anything, for there is nothing which it both resembles and acts as a substitute for. The sense in which it is an instance of the word 'cat' is a different one, and consists in its being an imagy instance of the universal *Being an occurrence of the word 'cat'*.

Should the imagist-activist regard substitute-activism as an improvement on his theory?

Perhaps he should move some way towards substitute-activism by allowing that not all belief experiences are of the imagist kind. Yet he might still claim a special importance for those which are. Merely to react to one state of affairs as though it is another state of affairs which it does not at all resemble is vastly inferior (he may say) as a way in which the absent may become virtually present to the case where the same reactions are in response to almost the same universals as are, or would be, exemplified by the absent state of affairs. Someone with no capacity to envisage in this latter way the existence of things not objects of his present experience could not be said in any very full sense to have beliefs at all. Such envisagement of the absent is what all real believing aspires to.

XI

IMAGIST-MENTALISM

The difficulties we have found in the various imagist theories so far discussed have not been difficulties in imagism as such, but difficulties in particular versions of it. On the whole we have felt able to defend imagism as such against various attacks. Let us now see whether an imagist theory can be constructed which avoids the difficulties of the previous theories, and which does not have special difficulties of its own. If objections to this theory seem such as will apply, so far as well founded, equally to any form of imagism, it will provide us with an opportunity for a final assessment of imagism.

We may call the theory now to be presented imagist-mentalism, to contrast it with imagist-activism. For it is a mentalistic counterpart of that semi-behaviourist theory.

Imagist-activism claims that a belief experience of the most fully realized kind is an experience of the exemplification by certain images of universals akin to those which would occur in a fact of the kind believed in, but that experience of such an image fact only constitutes belief in the relevant kind of fact when we react to the experienced fact with behaviour or with the acquisition of behavioural dispositions of the same kind as we would have reacted to a fact of the kind believed in with, and when the habits of reaction from which this springs were originally directed only at data, and were later transferred to images.

My reason for rejecting imagist-activism lies in its insistence that the relevant reaction to the experienced fact is a matter of bodily behaviour, or of a tendency to such being acquired. It seems to me evident that I can indulge playful scepticism about the material world without at the same time indulging in a scepticism as to whether I have had belief experiences, whether true or false, directed on the objectives, which I take myself to have had belief experiences directed on.

I do not (indeed) take a scepticism which would lead me to believe in nothing but the stream of my own experiences seriously. 'Animal faith' is enough to keep me (like Santayana) believing in an external world of some sort. But surely such scepticism is logically coherent, that is, the occurrence of my series of experiences is logically compatible with the existence of nothing else, and surely the course of my experiences considered in itself, and quite apart from anything outside it, determines that I have experienced certain beliefs. This is not to deny that in the more usual dispositional sense of 'believe' I may also believe many things my belief in which cannot be simply deduced from an account of the experiences I have actually lived through.

To meet these objections and to retain much of imagist-activism it is only required that we replace behaviour, and the likelihood of behaviour, as the relevant responses to imagery which derive from responses to data, by certain purely experiential responses.

If we do this we arrive at the following theory. A fully realized belief experience in a certain kind of fact will be an experience of images which exemplify universals similar to those which would occur in a fact of that kind, together with an experience in response to this experience which would have been a standard response to an experience of a fact of the kind said to be believed in. For example, if I experience the exemplification by an image of the property of being cat-like and near me, and I react to it with an experience of kind F, and if an F experience is a standard and specific reaction to the exemplification of cat-ness by a datum which I experience, then my experience of the image's being cat-like and near me will constitute belief in the kind of fact in which cathood and nearness to me is exemplified, in short in the existence of a cat near me.

The most important question which arises for such a theory may seem to concern the kind of experiential reaction in question. But in point of fact the theory says that any kind of experience will do, provided being of that kind is a natural and intrinsic property of an experience. Roughly, it is saying that to believe in the existence of a cat near me is to experience the cat-like-ness and nearness of an image, and to feel about its cat-likeness and nearness as one would to a cat's being near one if one experienced such a fact. Or more strictly it is saying that to believe in the actual existence of an appearance of a cat near me, is to feel about some image like such an appearance, as one would about such an appearance if one experienced it. Fully to experience belief in the existence of a cat near me would involve experiencing such belief in the existence of an indefinite number of such ideally cohering appearances, but belief in the existence of one such appearance may be supposed normally to do duty for the rest.

2 RELATION BETWEEN BELIEVING IN THE EXISTENCE OF AN F AND NOTICING THAT SOMETHING IS F

A certain connection exists between the theory now under consideration, imagist-mentalism, and what was said in Chapter IV on 'The experience of noticing a universal'. It was claimed there that to notice that a particular now experienced exemplifies a certain universal is to have an experience in response to that particular, which experience exemplifies a universal which only such experiences exemplify as are in response to a particular exemplifying that certain universal. We called the universal in question exemplified by the original particular the specified universal, and the universal in question exemplified by the experience directed on to it the specifying universal. Now our imagist-mentalist theory is saying something like this. To believe in the existence of an F object is to experience an F-like image on to which is directed another experience with a property which is a specifying property for F-ness.

This cannot however be quite right as it stands. For the property of the image which we call F-like-ness[1] must either be

[1] A terminological point which should be made clear is this. Very often in this book a phrase such as 'F-like' is to be taken as though it were the *name*, not a representation in virtue of its similarity to F-ness, of a certain universal, which universal it is, of course, assumed is in fact similar to F-ness. That is, when we talk of the fact of the F-like-ness of an image, we are *not* talking of the fact that the image is fitted to resemble things which are F, but of that fact which ascribes to it the property in virtue of which it is fitted to resemble things which are like F. It would be more accurate if we did not talk about its

F-ness itself, or a property which is similar to F-ness. In either case, that of its being F-ness itself, and that of its being a property similar to F-ness, a problem, a different one in each case, arises.

Let us first make the supposition that F-like-ness is not F-ness, and that the image is F-like without being F. This is the position adopted by the simple imagist and the imagist-activist. (See Chapter IX, pp. 198-9.) In that case it is logically impossible that an experience directed on to it should have the specifying property for F-ness, granted the definition of specifying property previously given. According to that definition G-ness is a specifying property for F-ness if and only if G experiences are often directed on F data and never on anything else.

We shall have to weaken our account of what it is for G to be a specifying property for F (and hence of what it is to notice F-ness), if we are to make use of some such notion here. Let us say that G is a specifying property for F if and only if G experiences are often directed on to F particulars, and if any occurrence of G experiences directed on to non-F particulars is *an effect* of a previously existing connection between G experiences and F particulars. In that case we can allow that a G experience may occur in response to a non-F but F-like image.

It is a pity that causal notions have to be introduced here, but it seems virtually unavoidable.

Let us now make the supposition that F-like-ness is F-ness itself. In that case my believing that there is an F object will consist in the experiencing of an image which is actually F, and the directing on to this image of an experience with a specifying property for F-ness.

The difficulty in this case is that we seem to have described the situation in which one notices that the image is F. But clearly noticing that one's image is F cannot be equated with believing that there is an F datum.

This difficulty suggests that the imagist-mentalist, like the imagists previously discussed, should say that the universals occurring in the symbolizing fact are essentially image-universals. An image may be F, but it cannot be an F datum. What is in

---

F-like-ness but talked about its G-ness and then explained that G is similar to F. However, it is usually simpler to use the phrase F-like, and it is hoped that the reader will bear the present explanation in mind where it seems appropriate.

question here, of course, is the qualitative sense of 'image' and 'datum'. Thus, if what is believed is that there is an F datum it is required that the experience directed on to the F image have a property which specifies Being an F datum – not merely Being F. When such an experience is directed on to the F image it cannot provide us merely with a case of noticing that the image is F.

Thus according to imagist-mentalism, to experience the belief that there is an F is to experience an image which is F-like but not F, and to react to it with an experience with an F-specifying property. It will be convenient to introduce the phrase 'obliquely specifies' to name the relation in such a case between the F-specifying property and F-like-ness.

3 BELIEVING IN RELATIONAL OBJECTIVES

We have explained what it is, according to the imagist-mentalist, in which believing that there is an F consists. But what is it to believe that there is an F which is in relation R to a G? Following along lines laid down by our previous discussion of noticing a universal, it would seem that the imagist-mentalist should answer thus. It is to have two images, call them A and B, such that A is F-like, B is G-like, and A and B are in an R-like relation, and to direct on to A an F-specifying experience, on to B a G-specifying experience, and for the experience directed on to A to be related to the experience directed on to B by an R-specifying relation.

More generally we can say this: To believe in a certain kind of fact is to have images which manifestly occur as the subjects of a fact of a certain kind which is similar, as involving similar universals at corresponding places, to the kind of fact believed in, and to react to the images with experiences of a kind such as have together the specifying properties for the kind of fact believed in, i.e., such as would constitute noticing of such a fact if it were present instead of one merely containing similar universals.

4 ILLUSTRATIONS OF BELIEVING AS CONCEIVED BY THE IMAGIST-MENTALIST

Properties which act as specifying properties when a universal is noticed may be of many different types, but two stand out as of special importance: first, emotional qualities; second, the qualities which constitute an experience a private or public uttering or hearing of a certain word-sequence.

In our discussion of imagist-activism we took as an example a case where someone believes that there is a tiger at a place P. What sort of account can the imagist-mentalist give of such a believing? We distinguished two main forms which the symbolizing image fact may take. It may be that an image field is experienced which is similar to place P and which includes a tiger image. Alternatively, it may be that a tiger image is experienced, and is in at least a partial sense in certain spatial relations to an experienced datum. For instance, it may be behind the appearance I am experiencing of a bush. Let us take this second case first. What specifying kind of experience for a tiger behind a bush may I have in response to a tiger image behind a bush?

It might consist in a certain kind of feeling of fear directed to the tiger and the place it occupies, which in the believing case would be directed to the tiger image and the place it 'occupies'. There might be a special kind of terror evoked by experience of a tiger appearance in a certain position in the visual field, and not evoked by data of other kinds.

Alternatively, it might simply consist in uttering the words 'There is a tiger *there*', where the noise 'there' is in response to the place occupied by the tiger datum.

It is to be noted that we are not taking it that the words 'There is a tiger there' strictly speaking express the belief that there is a tiger there. For when directed at a tiger datum and the place it occupies they constitute my noticing the character of the datum, the character possessed by the appearance of a tiger at a certain place, not strictly speaking my noticing that there really is a tiger there. The latter is something which can only be believed, not noticed. In point of fact such words are likely not only to constitute the noticing that a certain sense-datum has this character, but also to be at the same time a sign of the existence of a belief that other sense-data exist, such as are required to make it the appearance of an actual tiger at an actual place. This belief will typically have only a dispositional existence and not actually be realized in a belief experience. There is no reason why the very same verbal occurrence should not both constitute my noticing the present character of my sense-data, and at the same time be a sign of the dispositional existence of certain beliefs. From our present point of view, then, *Being the utterance of the sentence 'There is a tiger there'* is being considered solely as a specifying property for the intrinsic character of such data as are fitted to be appearances of a tiger at a certain place. When an experience with this property occurs in response to a tiger image at a certain place in the visual field, it constitutes belief that there is a tiger datum at such a place in just such a visual field. Thus we have actually experienced belief in one part of that total state of affairs which would constitute there being a tiger at such a place. Belief in the remaining elements of such a fact will normally only exist dispositionally.

A third alternative form the specifying property might take is that of being a conjunction of a feeling of fear directed at a particular place in the visual field, together with the experience of murmuring 'tiger'.

There are further possible forms the specifying property may take, which are of especial interest.

The imagist-activist took the standard reaction as being the moving of one's body in such a way as to distance it from the place of which that part of the visual field is an appearance. Now although the imagist-mentalist will not wish to have the movement of the body as the specifying property, there is not apparently any reason why he should not have the kind of experience represented by 'having that part of the visual field where the tiger datum is located, getting more and more distant' as constituting the relevant specifying property. Where an experience with this specifying property is directed at a tiger image in certain spatial relations to the visual field, instead of to a tiger datum, what will happen will be that the experienced visual field will change in such a way that the data to which the tiger image is as it were nearest will get more and more distant.[1] Being distant is here

---

1 In discussions of the present kind it is all but impossible to use words in a rigidly constant meaning. There are some senses in which a given place in a visual field cannot get more distant. But what is regarded at the next moment as the same visual field as one existing at a previous moment depends upon the context. Often successive views from the same place, whether experienced by the same minds or not at all, are regarded as the same visual field, though even here 'from the same place' clearly can change its meaning with altering contexts. *Here* someone's successive visual fields from changing points of view are talked of as the 'same' visual field, and to talk of a place in it getting

taken as a visual property possessed to a varying degree by different data in the visual field. Together with these purely visual properties of experience may go the various non-visual properties of the experience of flight, and these may belong as well to the specifying property for there being a tiger datum at a certain place in the visual field.

If this is allowed as a possible specifying property, and there seems no reason why it should not be, then the imagist-mentalist can take over the purely experiential aspect, wherever there is one of a distinctive kind, of all those standard responses which might figure in the imagist-activist account.

What of the paralysed man, and the disembodied mind, of whom we made so much in our discussion of imagist-activism?

The first two kinds of possible specifying properties for approaching tiger data which we mentioned provide forms which this belief might assume in the case of paralysed and disembodied persons. Where the specifying property is a peculiar kind of terror, or where it is an experience as of uttering certain words, there seems no reason why such a person should not have an experience of one of these kinds in response to a tiger image which is getting nearer and nearer in his image field, and that constitutes his belief that a tiger datum is getting nearer and nearer. There is, of course, no reason why there should not be for a given universal two different specifying properties from the point of view of a single person, and sometimes one of these and sometimes the other of these might figure in his belief that the universal was exemplified. When there are two different specifying properties for a universal it must be true of each specifying property separately that, apart from derivative cases, experiences with that property never occur in response to things not exemplifying the universal said to be specified.

Disjunctive properties being artificial cannot, but some other complex properties may, be specifying properties. Consider an experience with elements exemplifying the two properties *Being an experience of terror* and *Being an experience of flight from the place occupied at any moment by a persistent something*, such that the terror

---

more distant is to talk of the successors in virtue of qualitative continuity of various data in the original field (and of the place which they define) being more distant in the later visual field than were those original data in their original field.

increases in inverse relation and decreases in direct relation to the degree to which the experience is of successful flight, that is to the degree to which the place of the certain something becomes distant. Being an experience of this character might be a specifying property for *Being a tiger datum at a succession of different places*, a property exemplifiable by a persisting sense-datum.

It is clear enough how such a specifying property might be exemplified by the experience of someone actually in flight from a tiger. But consider rather a paralysed man left seated in the open who experiences a tiger datum at a distance. It is likely that he will have the incipient experiences of one in flight, a frustrated version of its earlier stages. But if the distance of the tiger datum increases rather than decreases, his terror will increase proportionately (that is in inverse relation to the greatness of the distance), while if it decreases the terror will lessen. Thus this tract of experience will have specifying property for the datum being a tiger at a succession of different places.

It should be clear from this how the experience of belief in a tiger datum altering its place might occur. For a paralysed man who for some reason has an image of a tiger constantly changing its spatial relations to the objects in his visual field, his treating the image as though it actually were a tiger datum will be a matter of incipient flight experiences taking place, and of his terror increasing or decreasing according as to whether the places in the visual field to which the image is 'nearest' are more or less distant.

It is clear that a number of variations could be woven on this theme, but the general line of thought should be clear enough. In general, we may say that for many kinds of data the specifying property will consist in the more or less complete experience of certain achievements and an increase or decrease in some unpleasurable experience, and/or decrease or increase in some pleasurable experience, according to the degree to which the achievement experience is complete. This suggests that the belief experiences about the material world (as of course also the corresponding noticing experiences) of the paralysed and of disembodied spirits is or would be somewhat unpleasant, which is perhaps not surprising. But it should be noted that there is no reason why over a period the specifying properties for a given kind of datum should not change, and thus the nature of the believing experience change also. Distinctive feelings of a more contemplative and less active sort might replace experiences of certain types of action.

An interesting and rather special case of the replacement of one sort of specifying property by another is that where an image version of an action experience replaces the datal version.

An old man may react to a ball flying through the air with an image of the action of running and catching it, rather than with the experience of such an action. Anyone may react to a flowing river on a warm day with an image of stripping and jumping in, when there are factors which inhibit the actual doing so. A man may respond to some types of behaviour with imagery of hitting the agent, as perhaps he would have done in childhood. These imaged actions then serve as noticings of various characteristics of the data we experience. They may also get carried over to imagery resembling those data and serve to make the imagery symbolize such data.

It would also seem likely that sometimes imaged actions would replace actual action, or rather the experience of actual action, with reference to images, though in the case of data actually experienced action rather than imaged action is evoked. Could these imaged actions serve to make the images symbols of the data, in spite of the fact that data of that kind are greeted by actual experienced action rather than imaged action? This raises certain complications, but presumably the imagist-mentalist would allow that it might do so, provided it was true that if data of a kind *and in a context* such as are said to be believed in had been experienced then imaged action rather than experience of action would have been evoked.

So far we have discussed the imagist-mentalist's account of believing that there is a tiger datum at P, where the image being as it were at P is a matter of its being in a certain sort of spatial relation to presently experienced data. What of the case where the image is like a datum at P simply in the sense that it is in a context similar to the data of a certain place, as, for instance, a tiger image in a certain sort of image field would be like a tiger in Trafalgar Square, if its image field resembled a view of that square?

Where the specifying property does not consist in being an experience of action directed at a place in a certain spatial relation (which might be identity) to the place of the datum or substituting image, no special problem arises. If I had certain special feelings about a certain place, say the place where my house is, so that a view of that place filled with flames, would cause a particular type of anxiety, then an image of that place filled with flames which caused that same anxiety would serve to symbolize that place, i.e., in fact my house, in flames. But suppose the specifying property is rather a matter of being an experience of rushing with cans of water to the place of the flames, then it is unclear how an image of that place in flames could evoke an experience with this property unless it were in some sort of quasi-spatial relations to presently experienced data.

What would have to be allowed here by the imagist-mentalist, as in effect it was by the imagist-activist, is that in some cases the spatial relation of the datum believed in to presently experienced data is not in any way imitated by the images experienced, but is simply determined by the action experienced in response to it. So that in this sort of case the fact that the image scene symbolizes a fire in certain spatial relations to me now does not turn on anything to be found in the images, but on the behavioural experiences evoked.

It is to be noted, however, that it may be true in some sense that there is a readiness to produce imagery which does reproduce the spatial relations which one treats as holding between the imaged scene and presently experienced data. There may be a readiness to have imaged fields, perhaps of a map or aerial view type – but there are other possibilities also – of an all embracing kind, part of which corresponds to the original imaged scene, and another part of which corresponds to the present visual field, the totality of which image field exhibits the spatial relations between the two. Or the relations may be exhibited by a series of 'overlapping' views.

Indeed such an illustration of the spatial relations between an imaged scene and the present visual field may quite often be experienced in a sketchy form. There is then a real resemblance between the imagery I experience and the set of aerial views or 'overlapping' views in which I believe. This sort of way in which the place of an image may be specified may shade into the case previously discussed where the image actually is in a sort of spatial relation to experienced data.

We should perhaps point out that a detailed account of the belief experiences people actually live through is not being offered by imagist-mentalism as here presented. That would be the task of an introspective psychology such as has now been more or less abandoned, but which will surely one day be revived. What is offered is simply an account of certain formal conditions which must be satisfied if an experience is to be a belief experience to the effect that there are sense-data of a certain kind. To make these abstract conditions a bit clearer and to show in a very rough way how actual experience might meet them a few crude illustrations have been given. But the way in which actual experience may meet the conditions is certainly much richer and more complicated than these illustrations indicate.

Our final assessment of imagist-mentalism must wait until we have considered in the next chapter, how the imagist-mentalist might account for the possibility of believing various different more or less problematic kinds of thing.

XII

DIFFICULTIES AND APPLICATIONS OF IMAGIST - MENTALISM

I BELIEF IN LOGICAL NECESSITY

In this book we have been concerned and will be concerned almost exclusively with believing in contingent propositions, but a word must be said at some stage about believing in logical necessity. In this section, then, we shall consider what an imagist-mentalist might say on the topic.

Belief in logical necessity is the taking in of Platonic relations which hold between universals. There is no such thing as believing in logical falsehoods, though there may be states of mind in which one thinks oneself to be taking in the Platonic relations between universals usually given certain names, but in which one has not really focused on the right universals.

The simplest case of believing in a logical necessity is a development from noticing an ideal relation which links two experienced particulars.

If while experiencing a square image and a triangle image I *notice* that the former has more angles than the latter, I notice an ideal relation which holds between two particulars. But I may not in any way bring home to myself the fact that it is an *ideal* relation.

How may I do this? I do it if I set myself to change the relation *having more angles* without changing the intrinsic character of the terms between which the relations hold. Let us suppose that I have noticed that A is a closed figure made up of four straight lines, and that B is a closed figure made up of three straight lines. I have also noticed that A contains more angles than B.

I may now set myself to remove the latter relation while letting the figures each retain the properties mentioned. I will, of course, fail. A peculiar feeling of confusion will come over me if I continue setting myself to achieve the first change, while keeping the first two factors unchanged.

I suggest that the basic experience of logical necessities consists in finding that such efforts lead to bafflement.

But what happens when one sets oneself to produce such a change? The answer may be something like as follows.

When a universal is a specifying universal for a certain other universal, it often becomes the case that not only does the specified property evoke the specifying property but the specifying property evokes the specified property. There may be some special feeling which accompanies the specifying property whenever it is going to have this effect. This may be at least part of what is involved in setting oneself to do something. A universal is *as it were* specified and then appears in order *actually* to be specified. There may or may not intervene bodily movements, according as to whether the universal needs to be exemplified by an image or by a datum.

The system of specifying universals has a structure which *to some extent* reflects the system of specified universals. Thus where a certain complex specifying property occurs it may tend to be followed by a corresponding complex specified property. In some cases, however, the specifying properties may be combined so that there is no possible complex universal specified, only an impossible one. An impossible universal cannot, by definition, be exemplified, though it can in the way here roughly indicated be specified. One comes across such a logical impossibility when a specifying property for it, occuring in a manner such that specifying properties occurring in that manner are normally followed by what they specify, leads only to a feeling of bafflement, after which experience of the specifying property ceases.

In the case we have regarded as the clearest, an ideal relation is realized to be the necessary result of certain intrinsic properties of the terms between which it holds, when a specification of a change in that relation without a change in the intrinsic properties, breaks down in the manner indicated. Logical necessity is brought home to one by bafflement.

The actual intrinsic quality of bafflement is not so important, however. The point is that for one who can take in a logical necessity there is a certain way in which he reacts when an impossible universal is as it were specified. Being a feeling of bafflement is in a certain sense the specifying property for logical impossibility, only it does not come in response to an instance of the impossible, which is impossible, but to a specification of the impossible, which is not impossible.

We may sum things up so far by saying that one takes in the necessary dependence of one universal's now being exemplified upon another's now being exemplified, if one feels bafflement when one sets oneself to let the one continue being exemplified without the other.

Let us now ask whether, when one *believes* that two universals are exemplified by particulars in a certain relation one can cognize the logical dependence of the holding of that relation on the exemplification by the two particulars of those universals.

In believing in the existence of particulars exemplifying those universals and in that relation, one will (according to imagist-mentalism) be experiencing a pair of particulars exemplifying similar universals and in a similar relation, and reacting to them as though they exemplified rather the believed in universals and relation.

It would be in conformity with the general spirit of imagist-mentalism to claim that the resemblance between the imitating image universals (not the specifying universals) and the imitated believed in universals must be such that, during what can reasonably be called one stretch of thinking, the Platonic relations between any two imitated universals are echoed by the holding of the *same* Platonic relations between the imitated universals. Thus what is impossible will be unbelievable. Unless this were so, there would not really be the sort of resemblance between image fact and symbolized fact which the theory supposes.

The next stage in our argument demands some attention to mental acts not much considered by us as yet.

The imagist-mentalist must give some account of thinking of situations without believing in them. His view is that to do this is to believe in them in a muffled way, that is only a muffled version of the specifying properties occurs. It is a feature of human consciousness that faced (by one's beliefs or experience) with the actual one thinks a lot, that is has a suppressed or muffled belief in, situations which are not actual. Also one has hopes and fears for the future, that is (as the imagist-mentalist would describe them – a point we shall come to later) a special type of half belief about the future.

Just as a universal is sometimes evoked by its specifying universal rather than the other way round, so an image universal may sometimes be evoked by a property which obliquely specifies it (that is, specifies that for which it is a substitute,)[1] rather than the other way round. We may say that experiencing the belief that there are two particulars of certain kinds and that a certain relation between them depends upon their being of these kinds, is experiencing bafflement if one tries to think of (without believing in) the relation being absent though they remain of these two kinds.

But one can generalize further and say that to experience *belief* that exemplification of one group of universals implies exemplification of another, consists in feeling baffled when specifying properties, such as might normally have been followed by the imagining of exemplification of the one without the other, are followed instead by bafflement. That is, to have beliefs about the Platonic relations between universals not now being experienced will be to find that when all seems set for imaging a situation (in which those universals would figure contrariwise to what their Platonic relations would allow), no such imaging follows, but only bafflement. At this point the experience of specifying universals will be dropped. There is a special interest here where the specifying properties are emotional. Certain emotions *as it were* specify impossible situations, and it is only when all the conditions for experiencing the image symbols of that which they specify are favourable, and bafflement follows, that the emotions can be got out of the system. Thus an attempt to envisage death or free will, as certain emotions specify them, leads to bafflement and a cessation of the emotions.

Granted the Platonic relations between the image universals are the same as those between the imitated universals, one cannot experience a fully realized belief in a logical impossibility. It will only be of inferior and undeveloped sorts of belief experience that it could ever be said that they intended an impossible situation.

[1] See p. 234.

A rather curious sort of belief, which deserves mention, and which we shall have cause to refer to later, is one to the effect that there is a universal (not necessarily an exemplified one) in a certain Platonic relation to some conceived universal[1] (which one does not necessarily believe to be exemplified) which former universal one does not experience or conceive. One who looks for the solution to a logical problem is often implicitly believing this, and trying to conceive or experience the universal in question.

Here what may be taken to happen, at least in fully developed cases, is that one experiences an F-like image and treats it as an F, in a muffled way which constitutes it a case of thinking of an F rather than believing in one. One then sets oneself to conceive of something which is in a certain ideal relation to such an F, that is which has a property Platonically related in a certain way to F-ness. One will do this (perhaps) by directing on to the F image and to some other very vague image a specifying universal for this Platonic relation in a spirit which amounts to an anticipation that the vague image will develop so as to satisfy this response. If bafflement is produced and a dropping of this specifying universal we have the belief that something is an impossibility, as indicated. But if we do not have bafflement, but the specification experience remains without finding its object, we may say that we have belief in the existence (not exemplification) of such a universal without any ability to conceive it. If in truth there is no such universal, then we do have something which might be called belief in a logical falsehood.

2 IMAGIST-MENTALISM AND TIME

(i) To recognize a tune or a sentence, that is to notice the time-extended character of a series of sounds, is to notice the temporal order of a group of distinctive elements. In such cases one has an experience in response to the series of data, or in response to the time-extended datum, of a kind which one would not have had in response to a series or time-extended datum of another kind. The noticing experience will contain elements in response to each of the elements of the time-extended datum of which the individual character can be said to be noticed, but the specifying

---

[1] A universal may be said to be conceived, as opposed to noticed, when some image-universal is being experienced as imitating it.

property (for a series of that kind) which the noticing experience exemplifies may be mainly a matter of the character which the noticing experience has acquired by its termination, and this termination may be subsequent to termination of the time-extended datum which has to be noticed, though they must both belong to the same specious present.

My noticing the character of a certain sequence of sounds might consist in an experience which terminates in saying 'That was "D'ye ken John Peel?"' and which contained only rather an indistinct feel which we might call a feel of growing familiarity as the tune proceeded. A mere so-called feel of familiarity cannot constitute my noticing the character of anything, for it is not a distinctive specifier for any specific property – but it may constitute the character of the earlier stages of a whole number of specifying properties.

Equally, I may notice a tune by the emotional feelings of a distinct kind which it evokes. Likewise with a sentence. (Or I may notice the character of the sentence by having imagery which imitates the objective the sentence signifies. That is, the image-properties will both specify the character of the sentence and their exemplification by the images will distinguish an objective, belief in which the sentence expresses.)

Granted that I may develop a distinctive set of habits for responding to increasingly elaborate time-extended data, there is no reason why these habits should not be transferred to time-extended images, and serve to convert the experience of such images into belief in the existence of time-extended data of the relevant kinds. Moreover, if my habits of reacting to time-extended data are sufficiently definite for it to make sense to talk of how I would react if I experienced even more complex time-extended data than I do experience, then a response of this kind to an elaborate time-extended image might constitute belief in the existence of a time-extended datum of a kind more complex than any I have ever experienced.

But where do *past* and *future* come in? We shall assume that the past is adequately analysed as the aggregate of events earlier than the events experienced by the speaker at the time of speaking, and the future as the aggregate of events later than the events experienced by the speaker at the time of speaking.

Experience of the belief that some event I experience was

preceded by an event of some kind might consist in experiencing an image resembling the other event and coming just before this experienced event. Thus if we allow capital letters to represent certain kinds of data (i.e., certain datal properties) and the corresponding small letters to represent similar kinds of images (i.e., certain image-properties), we may say that if we experience A followed by B, and react as though to A followed by B, we are believing in the existence of a time-extended event A followed by B.

Suppose one watches some event with an interesting history. One sees pigeons being released from cages in a French village on July 14th. A dim vision of the sort of history one supposes this proceeding to have may rush through one's mind. An image view of the storming of the Bastille and of prisoners being released, then a vague rush of indistinct images such as an all but momentary vision of a path through space-time from that event to this might be like, followed by the present view of pigeons being released – an experience of a series of impressions of this sort might constitute something approaching an experience of the belief that there was previous to this event by many years such an event as the storming of the Bastille, and a release of prisoners therefrom now commemorated in this fashion.

Again, to take a different sort of example, suppose I come in and see my books strewn over the floor. Then I have a series of images of my children throwing them about and departing, the series concluding with another view of the books strewn over the floor. The emotions I run through correspond to those I would have felt if I had watched the whole episode without the chance of interfering. My image vision of the books being thrown about is a vision of the past because it forms together with an actual datum a totality resembling a view of that fairly long drawn out series of events which (supposedly) ended in the scene of which that datum is an actual view.

A variant on this way of experiencing a belief explicitly about the past would consist in experience of a rush of successive images the last of which is closely similar to a datum I am experiencing, and where in some way or other that last image is treated as being one with the datum, that is the reaction to the image series and in particular to that member of it is at the same time and equally a reaction to that datum.

Thus the imagist-mentalist will cope with the time-element in our belief experiences much as he did with the space element. A group of images sufficiently united to form an image field may, or perhaps must, have a time dimension. It will be spread across time, and will often be a changing image field. We may then call it an image sequence. What is by clock time a very briefly enduring image sequence may resemble some long and elaborate datal sequence, in virtue of the sort of developments which occur in it. If it is reacted to as though it were such a datal sequence it constitutes experience of belief in the existence of such a sequence. If this were all, it would be belief in a series of events not placed in any time relation to the data being experienced within the same specious present. But if it terminates in a datum within the same specious present, or in an image which is treated as one with such a datum, then it constitutes belief in the existence of a series of views of events terminating in a view of an event such as one now actually has a view of. Thus it constitutes belief in the existence of a vision (experienced or otherwise) of a portion of history terminating in an event being witnessed within the same specious present.

If the images succeed a datum within the same specious present and the datum and images are reacted to as though they were a datum of that sort followed by data similar to the images, then we have a belief about the future.

(ii) Are any two experiential particulars in real time relations, or are they only so when they belong to the same experiential flow?

We have taken it that real *spatial* relations hold between the elements of one datal field, but not between elements in different datal fields. A portion of public physical space is composed, on present assumptions, of a whole lot of different views of that portion of space. Their all being views of the same place turns upon their forming a special sort of ideal group, that is, a group related by ideal relations of just overlappingness, etc. It appears senseless to talk of different views as having relations one to another not turning on their intrinsic qualities. As a consequence of this, when I treat an appearance of a bush and a tiger image as being the appearance of a bush in front of an appearance of a tiger, although there may be a view of that kind, it cannot be supposed that there is in some sense a tiger appearance behind that particular bush appearance. There is at most another view of a tiger behind a bush, which latter bush appearance fits into the same ideal group as does the bush appearance actually experienced.

Suppose now that I experience a sequence of images and data and treat it as a sequence of data. Let us suppose that within my own experience no data like the images occur in the relevant time relations to those data which belong in the sequence with the images. I treat this image and datal sequence as though it actually were a set of data in a certain temporal pattern. Is it possible that those very data do belong to a set of data in such a temporal pattern? If they do – but that is what may well be impossible – then I am imagining them and treating them as being in a context in which they actually are. If not, then there may be data just like them belonging in a context such as I treat these as belonging in, but these themselves are not in it. Or rather, they may belong in such a context in an ideal sense, but not in a real sense. That is, there is a view of a series of events terminating in the view of a certain event such that these data are, in virtue of the ideal relations, a view (of just the same kind) of that same event.

Let us suppose that we take the line that the data belonging to different experiential flows cannot be in real time relations. Then just as the unexperienced views of objects must be supposed to be of a certain spatial size, though we cannot know what size, so equally the unexperienced views of objects, scenes, or events, must be supposed to be of certain temporal lengths, though we cannot know what length. Public time will be a matter of the ideal relations holding between these different flows, as public space is a matter of the ideal relations holding between the different views.

Even if time relations between different flows are only ideal, time relations within the same flow are real, and the experiences of a man from waking to sleeping will constitute one flow. In the case, then, where I experience a belief about the occurrence of an experience of mine since I last woke or before I next go to sleep, the group of images and data which constitute my symbol for the fact will contain the very data which occur in the symbolized fact (supposing the belief is true). The spatial analogue for this would be where an image is so related to a datum that they form a simulacrum of a part of the visual field including that datum and other data.

Perhaps temporal relations between different experiential flows can only be analysed in causal terms. But does not a causal relation presuppose a real temporal relation? I leave this open.

(iii) *Substitutes for the earlier-later relation:* Could not some relation other than that of being earlier than – or more strictly, being an image which is earlier than – serve to imitate the relation of *being earlier than* between data?

On the face of it, it is difficult to see how any non-temporal relation could be like a temporal relation. However, there is no reason why the imagist-mentalist who is prepared to be flexible as to the amount of resemblance between symbolizing fact and symbolized fact should not allow that in this respect resemblance between symbolizing and symbolized fact might fail. For example, one might have the habit of representing a temporal series of events in imagination by an image field in which a series of scenes were imaged, one in front of the other, somewhat like a set of postcards standing in front of one and receding into the distance, so placed that each one can be seen, the more distant ones representing the earlier events.

I think the imagist-mentalist should allow this, though it would be a step towards what might be called substitute-mentalism (on analogy with substitute-activism). Distinguishing of the relevant objective would be moving into the hands of the reaction experience and away from the hands of the intrinsic character of the symbolizing fact.

Another way in which temporal relations might be imitated within the symbolizing fact may suggest itself if we take another look at the notion of the specious present.

The interpretation put upon the expression 'specious present' in this book has diverged from some traditional accounts. For us the specious present is a time-extended tract of experience of a specially unified sort. The elements within it are real time relations. But the specious present is sometimes understood as being something which occurs at each instant and is not time-extended, but within which, all the same, something analogous to time-relations occurs, from which we get our concept of time. Sensations are supposed to start with a certain degree of vividness and gradually become fainter and fainter in a special sort of way. (Or it may be that they commence in a dawning form, reach maximal vividness, and thereafter become fainter.) At each instant relative degrees of faintness will represent (in some sense) the temporal relations between two sensations.

This certainly seems a correct account of an aspect of our

experience, but I do not think it really describes what is involved in witnessing movement and change. The experience I call seeing a pendulum swinging, surely, takes the same length of time as does the swing I am seeing. An instantaneous experience, if such a thing can be talked of at all, may contain sensations of varying degrees of vividness but it will not be an experience of any temporal relation, and a property which specified the characteristics exemplifiable in an instant would not be the specification of any time-relation.

Having admitted, however, that there are present 'at each instant' echoes or fading versions of earlier sensations, it might well seem that the relation of Being fainter than – in this particular sort of way, might, if exemplified within a group of images, form a peculiarly suitable imitation of the relation of earlier than. Yet I am doubtful whether this could play much part in our imagination of time extended events. The fainter images would be so faint that they could hardly feature in an image scene to which we could in any definite way respond.

(iv) Let us now discuss the type of specifying properties likely to figure in belief experiences about the past and the future, concentrating first on the past.

If I see a hideous office block, my experience of belief that there was previously a beautiful Victorian Gothic structure there, may consist in experiencing an image resembling such a Gothic structure being pulled down and such an office block being put in its place, terminating in the view I now have, and I may react to this whole fact with those mixed feelings of impotent rage, dismay and insecurity with which I would have witnessed the totality of the fact believed in.

There are one or two remarks to be made about this example.

The question arises in the first place whether I did or didn't witness any of the earlier phases of this process in which I believe. Let us presume that I did not, that hitherto I have not visited this spot, but have read about, or somehow inferred, this history.

In point of fact I never have had an experience falling within one specious present of any such history as I now believe in, or of any other of comparable length and complication. If therefore we say that my reactions are those which I would have had if I had experienced such a history within a single specious present, this is a *counterfactual* the basis of which *in fact* is to some extent problematical. But perhaps it can be said that my reactions to the histories short enough to be experienced within a specious present, display reaction habits which would yield these results if such circumstances came about.

It might be better for the imagist-mentalist to put less emphasis upon the specious present, or to insist even more strenuously than heretofore on the fact that what counts as a specious present is only an experience with a very high degree of unity, and that some degree of that unity may belong to a tract of experience of very great extent (perhaps several years?). Perhaps he might even claim that in some way several tracts of experience can belong together, even though there come in between them in time tracts of experience not belonging to this same unified group. Thus my various non-continuous experiences of seeing an event such as that in our example might have evoked emotional reactions of a kind which are all brought together in a short spell in the case of the belief experience.

The essential claim of the imagist-mentalist is that in an example such as the present I react to the totality made up of the present view of the office building and the imaged history of the site, as I would have done to such a history, or to the view of such a history, if I had experienced the whole of it. That some such account of what may happen is acceptable seems clear to me, but that it involves appeal to a rather hefty counter-factual cannot be denied. Still more will this be so, if we take a case where an outline of the history of the solar system, or even a long period of human history, is envisaged.

Let us now suppose that I have witnessed a series of representative events from this history of this site. Then I will have lived through a series of feelings such as are now run through in a moment. Thus memory recapitulates in a moment in response to an imitation of past events witnessed by that consciousness the emotions lived through in response to them, while belief about the past which is not memory constitutes an imitation of past events not witnessed by that consciousness together with a rehearsal of the emotions which would have been lived through if those events had been witnessed. The witnessed or unwitnessed events are only imitated in each case, but the emotions are actually lived through.

Where the specifying property for a certain sort of sequence of events is verbal, words will be uttered publicly or privately such as actual witnessing of the events believed in would have prompted. However the imagist-mentalist might in this case have to allow that sometimes in believing, the specification properties for a type of situation are only directed at the images symbolizing such a situation in a characteristically modified form.

Presumably the specifying property involved in a belief about the past may be that possessed by the experience accompanying certain sorts of action. For sometimes action will take place, and thus normally experience of that action, when an image and datum group similar to a certain time-extended datal group has been experienced, such as would have taken place at the termination of experience of such a time-extended datal group. The spatial direction of the action will be determined, in the way discussed before, by the 'spatial' location of imagery and data. Thus I might have the experience of spitting at the building, or putting dynamite beneath it.

It may be suggested that if I had actually experienced the earlier stages of some processes which I may now imagine, I would have interfered with them, and that hence I would try to interfere with the earlier stages of the image sequence, if the reaction was really transferred. Yes, but if I had successfully interfered, the events believed in would not have taken place, yet it is believed that they did take place. So if the image series is to reproduce the believed in series, the series must not be interfered with. What is reproduced then are the experiences in reaction to it of one who does not interfere (presuming no such interference is believed to have taken place). If my non-interference would have produced a feeling of frustration that may be reproduced; but to introduce myself as interfering would simply alter what is believed in.

Let us now turn to belief in the future.

We are concerned, still, solely with existential beliefs. Now many beliefs about the future are of a conditional character. Hence it is only a limited type of belief about the future with which we can yet concern ourselves. Still, we do have some 'absolute' beliefs about the future. Indeed I have a confident belief in the continued existence into the future of most of the material objects which surround me. Yet how often are such beliefs experienced in the way the imagist-mentalist is concerned with? Normally they are just facts to which our behaviour is adjusted without their being consciously thought of. Consciousness is concerned rather with that which stands out in contrast from the dim background of material constancy.

There is a difficulty in allowing that belief experiences about the future occur answering to the imagist-mentalist's account. If I see a present event bathed in the light of its imaged future I may *feel* about it and *utter words in response to it* just such as I would have done had I had an experience which actually comprehended the whole sequence of events in the specious present. The shepherds perhaps felt towards the baby Jesus, together with an image of the sort of coming glory they believed in for him, those feelings of awe, honour and gratitude which an actual experience of such a series of events would have produced. But what of the actions prompted by the symbolizing fact, or of the experience of such action? In some cases this may be straightforward enough. In bowing to the baby Jesus the shepherds perform an action as near at any rate to bowing to the destined future king as possible. Sometimes even more practical actions may seem to answer to this account. If I believe that there is going to be an explosion and image the coming event at a certain place, I may start running from that place as I would have done had the actual explosion been observed there.

But what of cases where a vision of the future prompts avoiding action which would be too late once the envisaged event took place, and hence would not be prompted by it? If, for instance, I see a child playing near a parapet and envisage its falling over, I pull it away. I do not send for the doctor or undertaker, as I would in response to the event envisaged.

To bring up these cases against the imagist-mentalist shows a misunderstanding. To believe that an event will take place is incompatible with taking steps to prevent it. We have here belief that an event will or would take place, if something is not or were not done. Such conditional beliefs are not supposed to be covered by the present account. If one believed that the child definitely was going to fall one might send for the doctor or the undertaker. Where one simply believes that something is to happen, feeling, speech, and action will naturally reproduce what the event itself will or would prompt.

Even so, it may be said, any active reaction on one's part now will be directed on an earlier phase of the event, whereas actual experience of the event would lead rather to action on its later phases, and in some cases this must make a difference to the action in question.

The validity of this point may be acknowledged, and it calls for emphasis on something which the imagist-mentalist should bring into his account. When an image occurs as a symbol any action it evokes will be directed on to those aspects of the environment which will be in certain relations to that which the image symbolizes, if such a symbolized thing actually exists. It will not be directed on to the image itself. The same goes, naturally, for the experiential aspect of the action. This condition being allowed for, there may be some aspects of the action which the symbolized thing would evoke, which simply cannot be reproduced, because the thing in question needs to be present for that action to take place. If comparable action does take place, it will be action related to the present data as action in response to such a datum as is believed in would have been related to such data.

A belief in the occurrence of some future event in the material world may leave it open whether or not I am to witness that event.

Thus I may imagine in a believing fashion certain future events, and not positively put them in a context of feelings and activity such as imply my own witnessing of them. In that case, we have one settled fact about the future and another unsettled fact. There can be no question of my trying to avoid the occurrence of the settled fact, but my belief in the settled fact may bring about activities designed to settle the unsettled fact. However, the unsettled fact will be an object of purpose, not of belief, and we are not concerned yet with my purposing of future events as opposed to my believing in them.

Suppose the experience of data of a certain kind is frequently followed by pain. Then certain feelings which we may call apprehension may regularly occur in response to the experiences of such data, and not otherwise (apart from the image case shortly to be mentioned). This apprehensiveness will then be a specifying property for that kind of datum. Suppose now I have an image resembling such a datum and respond to it with an apprehensive feeling. That will constitute a belief that a datum of the kind in question exists now.

In neither such case is there anything which the imagist-mentalist would call belief about the future. What is called apprehensiveness is a certain quality of feeling. One cannot find any 'intentional' aspect to feelings of this character. Use of the *word* 'apprehensiveness' for this quality implies a certain view about the causal background to its exemplification here, namely that when pain occurs it produces a tendency for experiences of such kinds as preceded it to be greeted in future with feelings of that quality. Our language for referring to this quality can hardly avoid identifying it for public purposes as a quality playing a certain causal role in our mental life. But the quality which plays this role is an intrinsic quality in its own right, and we should for present purposes take 'apprehensiveness' as simply a name for this quality.

Now it may well be that in virtue of its causal role the occurrence of a feeling with this quality in response to certain data may from some points of view be called an experience of believing that pain is to come. If he refuses so to call it, the imagist-mentalist may be further from ordinary language than one who does so call it. But the point he is making is correct enough, that it is a response to the present data, causally explicable by the sort of consequences such data have had in the past, but that all the same it contains no envisagement of the future, no bringing home to oneself of the existence, or fancied existence, of certain events in the future. One who wishes to explain what it is for a mind at a given moment to *grasp* the character of unexperienced events in various relations to its present data, should not regard it as an instance of what he seeks to explain. *Envisaging* expected pain would be different.

3 ALTERNATIVE VIEWS OF MATERIAL OBJECTS

As was said in the first chapter, there are three different sorts of thing which a man might be believing, in believing that his sense-data are appearances of material objects. (1) He might believe that they belonged to groups of sense-data of a certain kind many of which really existed, though without being experienced by any-one. (2) He might believe that they were signs that the existence of various other sense-data could be brought about if he took certain steps. (3) He might believe that his sense-data were signs of events in a medium of which he could not know the intrinsic character, though he could know that the events satisfied certain formal conditions. We may amplify on this by saying that the belief will be to the effect that his sense-data are signs of the changing relations of one enduring, though not unchanging, thing (his body) to other things of essentially the same kind.

The suggestion may well seem strange that in believing in a material world we are probably really believing in different things from one another. It may seem less strange if we bear in mind the distinction between having a belief, that is a certain disposition, and experiencing a belief at a particular moment.

There are various different sorts of dispositions which might reasonably be called beliefs, so that there is no one answer to the question 'What is it for a man to believe something in the dispositional sense?' But one thing which might be meant would be something which had nothing to do with consciousness, but which concerned adjustment of an animal organism to there being a fact of the kind it is said to believe in.

A theory about such believing might follow in some respects the lines common to imagist-activism, imagist-mentalism, substitute-activism, and substitute-mentalism. It might say that to ascribe a dispositional belief in the existence of things of a certain kind to an organism is to say that the organism's behavioural tendencies are such as they would be if it were in contact with such things, and that their present character is due to past contact with such things or with their elements. The contact in question covers any sort of close causal exchange. To say that it believed in the existence of such a thing would be to say that though such a thing was not causally linked to it, its behavioural tendencies were as though such a causal link held. This is vague, but sufficient for our purposes.

Such a use of 'belief' is a perfectly proper one, and it is clear that where 'belief' is thus used, it cannot be proper to say that different people believe in different things in believing in material things. Whatever the realities be which best answer to that title, it will be in these realities, in some part of their true nature, in which each one of us believes, for it is to these realities, in some part of their true nature, to which our organism, which is one of those realities, is adjusted to the extent that it is adjusted to them at all. Even a false belief will be a mistimed adjustment to things of a kind which there really are, or inept combination of adjustments to things of a kind which there really are, and cannot therefore involve a radically mistaken 'notion' of the stuff or status of material things. This explains a certain oddity in saying that we may each believe in the existence of things of very different kinds, when we are said to believe in material objects.

There are doubtless other senses of 'believe' not so purely behavioural, of which the same thing could be said. If the question: 'What kind of fact is this conscious state directed on?' is equivalent to the question: 'What kind of fact is this conscious state a symptom of the organisms's adjustment towards?', it is, once more, a question to be answered by arriving at a correct metaphysics of whatever reality can best be called the material world, and not be examining the state of consciousness itself.

When one asks what the common sense view of the material world is, one may mean many things, but what I have meant by such a question concerns the nature of that which is believed by 'ordinary' people in such perhaps not very common moments as some conscious envisagement of the world occurs in them. My answer is that there are at least three different common sense views of material objects, experienced by different people or by the same people at different times.

What is my evidence for this? On such a matter there can hardly be scientific evidence. The differences need not be reflected in differences in language at any ordinary level, for speech for the most part may be one of those carryings on of the organism having nothing especially to do with our few precious moments of belief experience. It is only sometimes that speech is associated with a bringing home to oneself in consciousness of the character of the realities talked of. Apart from one's own case, then, one can only gather impressions from various sources. Methodical questionnaires might achieve something, indeed, but they would be difficult to conduct. Still, philosophical writings give one a rich field in which to gather impressions on this matter. For what the philosopher is often attempting is precisely to bring about satisfactory belief experiences in himself and others on these matters. Since philosophers of the less speculative kind are simply 'ordinary' men of a rather specially reflective kind, it is not to be supposed that the belief experiences one judges them to be exhibiting, are different in kind from those which come from time to time to ordinary folk.

Having said this, I should put out the *caveat* that members of civilizations other than our own may have belief experiences in these matters of types which do not receive much reflection in Western philosophy.

Our first view will do as an idea of the world to flit into the mind and guide one's feelings as one's organism in its true nature moves about (in some sense) in its true environment, but if it is pinned down in reflective moments and developed into a carefully thought out scheme it becomes increasingly unacceptable. Surely a variety of arbitrary facts about our sense organs determine the sense-data we experience, while other animals receive different sense-data. To believe that sense-data of the kind we humans get are, and sense-data otherwise endowed animals do or would get are not, selections from a realm of largely unexperienced sense-data is strangely arbitrary. Again one may ask what 'size' the fields are to which the sense-data belong. If they are of limited size, then one must suppose that what determines a host of sense-data to be 'views' of the same object, and thus to constitute that object, are solely the ideal relations between them. Yet it is hard to accept that the unity of a material object is not more real than this. The less readily imaginable alternative is the supposition that all un-experienced sense-data belong to one vast field, such as the sensorium of Berkeley's God, but without the thought-processes which would make of it a mind.

We have talked mainly of visual sense-data. Now a world composed of largely unexperienced sense-data of one of the non-visual kinds is conceivable. Some people may imagine the world as composed of somatic feelings, so that one's own body is regarded as a group of bodily feelings and other bodies as com-posed of other such groups. Indeed it may be taken for granted that hardly anyone will suppose the unexperienced world to be composed solely of data belonging to one sense. Even the inveter-ate visualizer will, indeed, suppose that the groups of sense-data which make up a material object contain tactile data as well as visual. Yet if a world of unsensed data is to be conceived of, it is, probably mainly the visual data which are present to imagination. Some senses, at any rate, hardly supply much material for compos-ing a world. Auditory data may be supposed to exist unsensed, but only as accompaniments to a world mainly composed of other elements.

Thus the conception of the world as composed of unexperienced data will probably find its home most naturally in the belief experiences of strong visualizers. Weak visualizers are more likely to experience beliefs answering to the categories (2) or (3). Indeed according to imagist-mentalism one must have visual images if one is to experience belief in the existence of unsensed visual data. The position would be different if one moved on to substitute-mentalism.

We have confined ourselves to view (1) so far and for good reasons. But we must ask now whether imagist-mentalism can account for belief experiences which exhibit rather views (2) or (3). However we must leave view (2) aside until we have said something about belief in conditional propositions. Let us turn then to the third view.

One can quite easily experience data in which variations of a certain sort in individuals of one kind correspond exactly to variations of a certain other sort in individuals of another kind. Anyone who follows a musical score as he listens to music is experiencing such a relation of concomitant variation. It is realized also in the relation between our kinaesthetic sensations and certain aspects of our visual sense-data.

A musical child watching a piano being played for the first time may notice that the property of being a striking of the note so many places to the right or left on the piano of the last note struck, corresponds to being a sound so many semitones higher or lower. Thus relations of concomitant variation are to be met with in sense experience.

The relation of concomitant variation is a special case of the relation of isomorphism. Two groups of elements are isomorphic if and only if (i) there is a certain relation such that it connects a member of each group with just one member of the other group. The elements thus related may be said to correspond, and the relation may be called the element-relating relation. (ii) There are two relations, call them R and S, exemplifiable to different degrees, such that if an element in the first group is related to another such element by a greater (or lesser or equal) degree of the relation R than it is to another such element, then the corresponding element in the second group is related to the element corresponding to the second element in the first group by a greater (or lesser or equal) degree of relation S than it is to the element corresponding to the third element in the first group. These two relations may be called the corresponding relations. (iii) Usually a member of the first group is R to some other member. N.B. Extension of these conditions to cover relations of more than two places should be understood.

In the piano case the element-relating relation is *Being a striking of a note which is simultaneous with the occurring of . . . which is a sound* and the corresponding relations are *Being so many notes up to the right* and *Being so many semitones higher than. Being so many notes to the left* and *Being so many semitones lower than* may be regarded as the same relations as these first two, realized to a lesser degree. The relations playing these roles could be very different. The element-relating relation might be rather some quasi-ideal relation resting on the role the elements play in their respective groups.

Being isomorphic may be regarded as syncategorematic on the two groups being in one to one correspondence in virtue of relation E (the element-relating relation) and being respectively a group whose members mostly are R, or mostly are S, to some other member, R and S being relations. Alternatively, it may be taken as nonsyncategorematic (apart from the syncategorematicness of every universal exemplified by an aggregate *qua* aggregate) and merely signifying that they are isomorphic in the first sense *qua* something or other.

We may also introduce the expression 'richly isomorphic' in this way: One group may be said to be richly isomorphic to another group if there is one element-relating relation which combines with a whole number of different corresponding relations to determine an isomorphism between the two groups or between subgroups of each which, taken together, leave no member out. In one sense the two groups are only richly isomorphic *qua* a certain element-relating relation, in another sense they are richly isomorphic provided they are richly isomorphic *qua* something in the first sense.

For two series to be related by concomitant variation is for them to be isomorphic groups where simultaneity or some close temporal relation is included in the element-relating relation. Here again there is a syncategorematic and a non-syncategorematic sense of 'varying concomitantly'.

We may talk of the element-relating relation and the corresponding relations as constituting the key to an isomorphism or concomitant variation. Where there is a rich isomorphism between two groups, a certain element-relating relation will combine with different corresponding relations to make up a whole number of different keys to isomorphisms between the two groups or between subgroups of each.

It is evident that one might learn to notice that two sequences were isomorphic according to a certain key (or a key of some general sort) without having the power in general to notice that two sequences were isomorphic according to some key. That is, one might have a specifying property for a certain type of isomorphism without having a specifying property for isomorphism in general.

Suppose now that when a man experiences sequences of data which vary concomitantly according to a key of some general sort, he often responds with an experience which is R to the two sequences. Suppose that thereafter he experiences a sequence of data and a sequence of images which, though they have an isomorphic relation of a similar sort to one another, do not have an isomorphic relation of exactly that sort to one another. If he then responds to these two sequences with an experience which is R to them, he will be believing in the existence of a sequence which is isomorphic according to a key of the initial sort to the sequence of data.[1] If the sequence of images is not treated as though it were a sequence having any sort of intrinsic character, if none of its intrinsic qualities is obliquely specified in place of certain other similar intrinsic qualities, no belief will be experienced about the intrinsic nature of whatever sequence it is which, if the belief is true, is isomorphic according to a key of some general sort. It may also be that the image sequence is in that very same sort of isomorphic relation to the data which its relation to the data symbolizes. For if the image sequence is treated as though it were a sequence of some other sort, such as one composed of much less vague and vacillating components, that will suffice to establish that the fact in which it occurs is taken as a symbolizing fact rather than as a fact in its own right.

It should now begin to be clear roughly how an imagist-mentalist might explain the experience of believing in material

[1] It is to be noted that whether it is or is not possible for one's sense-data to be in real relations (other than negative ones) to things outside one's consciousness, since isomorphism can be a purely ideal relation, he can be coherently believing that there is a sequence isomorphic to this sequence, not simply to an exactly similar sequence.

objects in the third sense. In its essentials it will be a matter of believing that there is a sequence of events of some largely unknown sort which is isomorphic according to a key of some only very generally specified sort to the sequence of my sense-data.

However, it is not true that nothing is settled regarding the character of this believed in sequence. Its character as a sequence of total events each of which contains all along some more or less constant element – my body – is distinguished. Certain formal properties which belong to it or to its elements may also be distinguished, though what these are admits of variation. One can image this easily enough by an image resembling a series of views all of which contain the view of a certain human body. The only characteristic of this series of image views which need be obliquely specified is its containing one continuing element. The sensible character of the images need not be regarded.

However, we cannot quite leave it at that. If the image sequence really does contain a constant element, reacting to it as though it constitutes such a sequence will be simply noticing that it does so, not believing that there is something which does so.

It may be answered that the two sequences, the datal sequence and the image sequence, are being treated as though they were a pair of sequences in an isomorphic relation of a certain kind, in which the second contains a constant element, and that this they are not, since it has been stipulated that they are only in a similar isomorphic relation. To this one may add that the image sequence may be treated as though it were something of a less fragmentary and imagy sort than it is, treated indeed in a manner originating from one's treatment of data, but that all treatment of data as having certain sensible characters, such as distinguish a datum of one sense modality from one of another are absent.

This account seems to need supplementation by introducing some more definite rejection of the sensible character of what is believed in. For though one might perhaps just not believe that the believed in sequence had any particular sensible character, it is perhaps unlikely that such a belief would just be absent. Visual images are almost bound to be treated as visual unless their visual character is specifically discounted. Likewise with the other senses – for we must not assume that the images which symbolize this unknown sequence are visual. They might, for instance, contain as their constant element an image of bodily feeling and as their varying element various tactile sensations. They might even be auditory, containing one constant note with various other changing sounds combining with it.

We have not yet spent much time on the question how the imagist-mentalist should deal with negation. Maybe he should allow for an experience with a specifying property to emerge only somehow to be rejected. If he does allow for this, then we can suppose that all sensible characters – meaning by this such characteristics as distinguish phenomena of one sense from another, as opposed to those more formal properties exemplifiable by them all – are consciously denied of the sequence believed in. That is, whether it is visual, tactile or whatever, the specifying properties for visualness, tactileness, and so on all emerge only to be rejected. What we are left with is the treatment of the image sequence as though it had certain formal characters – such as we often meet with in our sense-data – but lacked all sensible characters. It is not, of course, treated as something which lacks any intrinsic and non-formal quality, which would be absurd, it is only that each such quality experienced by us is rejected. Note also that each such separate property it is treated as lacking is lacked by many things within our experience.

Even if an image lacks all ordinary sensible characters, it will have an intrinsic character of its own which must be specified and rejected.

We have so far spoken of a belief experience in which the symbolizing fact contains a sequence of data and a sequence of images, and they are treated as having an isomorphic relation of a certain kind, perhaps different from that which in fact they have. However, a belief experience of the kind in question is at least as likely to contain two sequences of images, one of which is treated as though it were a sequence of data with a definite sensible character, and the other of which is treated as a sequence isomorphic in the same way to the first, and having certain formal properties, but treated as though it lacked each of the properties of visualness, tactileness, and so on.

So the imagist-mentalist can account for moments when there enters consciousness not the belief that our sense-data are selections from a world of largely unsensed data, but the belief that our sense-data register changes in the relations between a certain enduring object we may call our body and other objects of essentially the same kind. Concerning the formal properties of objects of this kind, which we may call bodies, a good deal may sensibly be believed – concerning their intrinsic qualities little or nothing. Such beliefs are certainly experienced by many people who have explicitly reflected on the matter. Such reflective persons will then conceive the human being as one body among others, which makes adjustments to the bodies directly acting on it and after a time comes as it were to adjust itself as though to bodies which are not in fact acting on it. He will then describe the latter 'as it were' adjustments as the beliefs of that *body* or organism about its environment, and the propositions said to be believed in will describe the world as conceived – perhaps correctly – in the consciousness of these reflective persons. But the consciousnesses attached to most of these organisms may have no experience of belief in such propositions. On the other hand, they may do so. The view of the material world in question may be that present in the consciousnesses of quite unreflective persons, in so far as they can be said to experience belief at all. In some ways this belief is more complicated to experience than the belief in unsensed data, but the states of the human brain which give rise to consciousness are complicated enough and there is no reason why the consciousness should not be very complicated even at an early stage of individual or racial development.

The determinate forms of this general theory believed in by different people may differ, especially as regards (i) the sort of element-relating relation supposed to be in question (ii) the sort of corresponding relations in question. Under (i) one might ask whether simultaneity was included in this relation. Probably ordinary thought will suppose the material events to be simultaneous with the corresponding sense-data in the way in which one sense-datum may be simultaneous with another. Reflection may lead us to abandon this, not because of time-lag considerations to do with the speed of light or sound, but because such simultaneity is a real relation of a kind which may well be supposed incapable of joining an event in my consciousness to one outside it. We may then suppose that some unknown relations, somehow comparable to the time-relations found within consciousness, link events within consciousness to those outside.

As regards the corresponding relations we may suppose there to be a great number of pairs of them, so that for any one element-relating relation there is a rich isomorphism between sensory events in consciousness and the relevant events outside consciousness. The most important of the corresponding relations on the side of the material events will be those which put the material events in a unitary spatio-temporal scheme. The problem here is rather what the corresponding relations are on the sensory side, but they are, roughly, those which go to make up what may best be called sensory space and time. It is clear that we conceive of a much larger set of things in the corresponding material relations one to another than we ever experience in the corresponding sensory relations. That is, the events believed in as isomorphic to our sense-data are taken as being parts of a much larger field of events linked by the corresponding relation on their side of the isomorphism.

In saying that our images distinguish such objectives as we have just vaguely hinted at we suppose that we may experience joint sequences of images which are isomorphic to one another in virtue of a certain definite element-relating relation and of certain corresponding relations. The images are however treated as we treat things of a less vague and fragmentary character and as we treat a field displaying a richer and more complex set of relations, and those belonging to the second sequence are treated as lacking each of the sensible characters they actually have and as lacking each of the sensible characters which data ever have. Moreover, the ordered pair of the sequence of images symbolizing the data and the images symbolizing the material world are treated as we treat isomorphic sequences in which the second is the more steady and definite and rich in the complexity of the relations exemplified. That is, we react to them in three ways at once: we treat the one sequence as a sequence of data and the other sequence as something which has the formal but not the sensible character of data, we treat them as isomorphic in a certain way, and we treat the latter as the more steady, definite and complex. Our treating them in these three ways constitutes our belief that something of a certain formal nature exists related to our sequence of data by a certain set of relations (met with in our experience) and specified by certain properties. Having once conceived this non-sensory sequence of events to which the course of our sense-data is isomorphic, we then of course extend our conception of the former course of events by supposing it linked to an indefinite set of further events by the *corresponding* relations on the material side. Above all, the relations which correspond to the sensible spatial relations met with in consciousness are supposed to link a much larger set of objects than they do within consciousness.

It may be said that the specifying properties and relations for the various formal relations and isomorphisms in question must be of a verbal nature. It may be said that it is only by having among one's experiential responses, tendencies to experience utterance of such sentences as 'This is a map of that' or 'The fluctuations in this quality correspond to the fluctuations in that quality' that one could have a way of noticing the presence of isomorphic groups or sequences.

Even if this were so, its being so could not be a necessary truth, unless indeed we call any organized set of specifying properties a language. If it were so, as a matter of contingent fact, that need not embarrass the imagist-mentalist. But there seems no reason to believe that it is so. We should not be too sceptical of the complexities of conscious thought possible in virtue of specific emotional and action-experiential universals which mark for us the universals exemplified by our sense-data and which when applied to images make them symbols of the exemplification of such universals. That we should feel in a certain way about isomorphic sequences met with in our experience, and transfer this feeling to pairs of image sequences in the way required to constitute belief in non-experiential sequences which are isomorphic to experiential sequences is not in any way improbable. But non-verbal believing is hard for most of us to introspect, because our philosophical preoccupations fill our consciousness with words which drown the more primitive non-verbal mental states.

The imagist-mentalist, indeed, attaches no sense to thought without symbols; he also claims that images, treated or felt about as things other than what they really are, are the only symbols in the most important sense of the word; but how far the treating of images as what they are not may consist in verbal reactions to them, and how far in emotional and action-experiential reactions he will leave open as in empirical question.

4 NON-EXISTENTIAL BELIEVINGS: (I) TRUTH-FUNCTIONS OF SIMPLE EXISTENTIAL PROPOSITIONS

Negative universals as well as positive universals may occur in facts noticed or intended. Objects lacking a certain character may often evoke a response of a certain kind, never evoked by objects with that character. Yet a negative property is liable to be so constantly experienced that its frequent evoking of a certain response may seem unlikely. I am far more likely to have a specifying property for an H which is not-F, than simply for something which is not-F. Moreover, the more usual it is for Hs to be F the more likely it is that I shall have a way of specifying non-F-ness conjoined with H-ness.

May the specifying universal for a negative universal be itself negative? A superficial glance at the subject may make us feel that where G specifies F, non-G specifies non-F. However this is wrong. To say that G specifies F is (roughly) to say that F data often evoke G experiences, and non-F data if they evoke experiences at all evoke only non-G ones. But it is not to say that every datum which evokes a non-G experience is non-F. Not every F datum I experience need evoke a G experience. Thus if non-G is to specify non-F it must be true that every F datum evokes a G experience.[1] (A fairly similar point can be made if *noticing* is defined in terms of counterfactuals.)

The more straightforward case is where a negative characteristic is specified positively.

It seems that this may take two forms. One form arises where there is some characteristic modification of a specifying property for a positive universal which produces a specifying property for the corresponding negative universal. A verbal specifier for any positive property may become the specifier of its negation, for instance, by becoming itself preceded by 'not'. Or, more interestingly, an emotional property which specifies F-ness may pass into what we might call a frustrated version of itself and become a specifier for non-F-ness, and an active-experiential property may pass into an inhibited sense of its earlier stages.

Put more precisely, what is intended is this. There may be a Platonic relation N such that one may represent many an universal by referring to it as the universal which is N to some other universal. It may then be true in general that where one universal specifies a positive universal, the universal which is N to it

[1] Moreover it is only if G is simple that non-G is a natural property and hence capable of being a specifying property. G may be a natural property without its negation being one. See p. 78.

specifies the corresponding negative universal. For instance, the experience one has when one's body is set to act in a certain way and does not, may always be in a certain relation N to the experience one has when one's body does act in that way.

The less interesting case is that where the conjunction of some particular negative property and a certain positive property acquires a certain specifier which is not in any characteristic relation to the specifier for the conjunction of the corresponding positive property with that same second property.

The way in which these various specifiers for negative universals may be carried over into believings does not appear to pose any special problems.

But what of beliefs expressible in sentences where negation applies to whole sentences and not, on the face of it, expressible in sentences where only predicates are negated?

Such negation may be divided into two kinds. (1) The negation of existential sentences, producing sentences of the character 'There are no Fs', 'There is no F', 'There is no pair of R-related objects', etc. (2) The negation of certain compound sentences.

Let us attend, first, to the negation of existential sentences.

A great many sentences of this kind report the fact that some specified object does not contain any object of a certain kind. This failure to contain a such and such is an intrinsic property of the thing in question, and if the thing is experienced this failure will be experienced and may be noticed.

It may be noticed that my visual field does not contain a red circle. It was a property of this kind which Old Mother Hubbard discovered in the cupboard.

It is arguable that all the most usual negative existential beliefs are of this kind, and that they pose no special problem for the imagist-mentalist. It may be urged, for instance, that by 'Unicorns do not exist' one usually means 'The earth and its immediate environment does not contain unicorns', and that this is on the same level with any other predicate ascribed to the earth.

But this does not really dispose of the problem of negation. For one thing it does seem intelligible simply to deny that there are unicorns, as opposed to simply denying that some specified region contains them. If one could explain the property of being a universe perhaps one could then equate this blanket denial with the assertion that the universe does not contain unicorns, but the notion of being a universe itself seems to demand definition in terms of there being nothing not included in the object in question.[1] For another thing, negation may seem required if we are ever to specify some particular object. To believe in the existence of the cupboard of which this sense datum is an appearance is to believe that there is a cupboard of which this is the appearance and there is not any other cupboard of which this is an appearance.

It does seem that negation cannot be completely accounted for without the introduction of some notion of disbelieving or rejecting an objective. This might sometimes consist (so the imagist-mentalist might suggest) in the having of imagery similar to a certain situation and there occurring in response to it an undeveloped form of a specifying experience for some state of affairs similar to that image state of affairs, developed, however, far enough to make it unambiguous what state of affairs is in question, and then a feeling on the part of the mind of detachment from this incipient belief experience, an experience of a sort of alienation of this undeveloped belief experience so that it stands apart from all those belief experiences which have any powerful effect upon one's subsequent experience.

The sense of alienation or psychic distance is an experiential quality in its own right. The point must be acknowledged that such a quality can only be regarded as the distinguishing mark of disbelief if it is true that an undeveloped belief experience having this quality does not leave those effects on subsequent experience which a proper belief experience would have done. Its role becomes even more marked if subsequent experience, and indeed such present experience as is not marked by this quality of distance, has characteristics which actually conflict with the proper development of the specifying qualities for the objective said to be disbelieved, as a state of mind diffused with calmness conflicts with the development of turbid anger.

The imagist-mentalist will hardly want to deny that some sort of private or public negative symbol is likely to develop at an early stage in a mind's development, so that the co-presence of

---

[1] The universe may be defined as that which is a part of nothing. But if being a part of nothing is a property, it is one which could not be noticed, and could only be taken account of by one's disbelief that there was anything else.

this symbol with an incipient form of belief in something will be a sign of a readiness to experience disbelief – in the full sense indicated – in the objective in question, and an unreadiness to experience belief in it. But experience involving this symbol will be a substitute for that more radical sort of disbelief we have attempted to describe.

A word now about beliefs the full expression of which requires a definite description. Normally the experience of believing in *the* such and such may be supposed to be an experience of believing in the existence of *a* thing of a certain very fully specified sort. Suppose I believe that the house of such and such a kind contains no cat. To experience belief that there is a house of such and such a kind which contains no cat, leaves it open that there is also a house of such and such a kind which does contain a cat. Thus 'The F house does not contain a cat' is neither equivalent to 'The F house without a cat exists' nor to 'An F house without a cat exists'. Yet we may take it that for the most part much the same belief experience will be the nearest we ever get to experiencing belief in any of these things. If that is so, what distinguishes belief experiences in the three different things, will be the readiness or unreadiness for the rejection of certain other beliefs in each case. For instance, if what I am believing is that the F house does not contain a cat, I will be ready to reject the idea that there is an F house which does contain a cat.[1]

Something should be said regarding disbelief in conjuncts.

To experience belief that P and Q, is to experience belief that P and belief that Q in the same specious present, but to experience rejection of P and Q cannot be identified with simultaneous experience of the rejection of each.

Here as in previous cases it must be insisted by the imagist-mentalist that essentially the same thing can be achieved by very different processes. The essential thing would seem to be that belief in two objectives should have coalesced into a highly

---

[1] A more complete discussion of this topic would require some account of our attitude to the identity of indiscernibles. In so far as it is the identity of material objects (as opposed to experiences) which is in question there seem rather good reasons for accepting it, at any rate on certain of the views of material objects which we have canvassed. That being so, to believe that there is only one F house will be to believe that there is an F house, and for all other predicates than F, to be ready to disbelieve that there is both an F house answering to this predicate, and an F house not answering to this predicate.

unitary experience which can then be rejected, without this rejection amounting to the rejection of either individual belief experience taken separately.

The most straightforward case will be where one can say that the F-ness of one thing and the G-ness of another thing has its own specifying property, which is not the mere conjunction of the specifying properties for each of F and G separately. Thus when I have an F-like image and a G-like image at once and react to them with this specifying property for there being one thing which is F and another thing which is G, I am experiencing one belief that there is an F and a G, rather than merely experiencing two beliefs. If an incipient form of this belief experience is rejected, then there is no reason why belief in one of the separate components of the conjunct should not continue to flourish. What we have then is belief that either there is no F or there is no G.

So far we have described belief in the existence of things of a certain kind, belief in the existence of things not of a certain kind, belief in the non-existence of things of a certain kind (or not of a certain kind), belief in the existence of things of one kind and the existence of things of another kind, belief in the non-existence either of things of one kind or of things of another kind.

This last is equivalent to believing that of two types of things, things of at most one of the types exist. But there are two other sorts of thing of a disjunctive kind which may be believed. One may believe that of two types of things, things of at least one type exist. Or with regard to either of the types, one may believe that things of that type don't exist without things of the other type existing.

To believe that at least things of one of the two types, F and G, exist is to believe that there exists something which is either F or G. *Being F or G* is what we earlier called an artificial universal, and we have insisted that a specifying property cannot be of this type. This is not to deny, however, that a specified property may be of this type. If I respond to things which are F or G with an H experience, and would not do so unless they were F or G, I may perhaps be said to be noticing that they are F or G. If subsequently I respond to an image which is F-or-G-like with an H experience then I may be said to believe that something is F or G.

Presumably, being F-like or G-like is a sufficient but not a necessary condition of being F-or-G-like.

Is there something rather artificial about this treatment of the matter? It is difficult to avoid feeling so. Perhaps the imagist-mentalist will have our consent more willingly, if he says that believing in the existence of an F or G, involves having imagery which shifts from being F-like to being G-like and back again, but evokes the same specifying response for F-or-G in either case.

Let us now turn to believing that a thing of one type doesn't exist without a thing of another type existing.

This is not a matter of believing that anything which is F is also G. That could be explained simply as disbelief in the existence of a non-G F. What we want is a denial of F-ness being exemplified without G-ness also being exemplified, whether together with or separately from F-ness.

It would seem that the imagist-mentalist would have to deal with such a belief by saying that it could only be experienced as the rejection of a total state of mind in which the existence of an F is believed in and the existence of a G is disbelieved in. Rejection of this total state of mind would be the same sort of thing as rejection of the other belief states we have described.

If 'P' is 'There is an F' and 'Q' is 'There is a G', we have now in effect described how one could experience the belief that $P \supset Q$, that not-$P \supset Q$, that $P \supset$ not-Q, and that not-$P \supset$ not-Q. That is, we have described believing that Fs don't exist without Gs, that at least a thing of one of the two types F and G exists, that a thing of at most one of these types exists, and that Gs don't exist without Fs. It should be borne in mind that negative properties are possible substituends for 'F' and 'G' here.

This account has been sketchy, but it has perhaps served to indicate how the imagist-mentalist might try to extend his account of believing, to cover believings which are not simply in the existence of things of a certain kind, where these are truth-functions of such simple existential matters.

5 NON-EXISTENTIAL BELIEVINGS: (2) BELIEF IN COUNTERFACTUAL CONDITIONALS

A counterfactual proposition may be defined for present purposes, as a logically contingent proposition which says that if things had been otherwise than they are in one specified way, then they would (or: would not) have been otherwise in some other specified way. The times to which counterfactuals refer may be past, present, future, or unspecified.

Philosophers who have accepted some form of the verification principle have found counterfactual conditionals problematic, since, on the face of it, 'If p had been so, then q would have been so' is unverifiable.

To meet verificationist worries over counterfactual conditionals, one can imagine an acute philosopher arguing as follows.[1] It is only if we take 'If p had been so, then q would have been so' as logically implying the falsehood of p that we can call it unverifiable. But the kind of conditional statement which we should deal with first, is one which does not imply (separately) any of 'p', 'q', '-p', and '-q', but which is at the same time distinct from the material conditional in that it is not implied by -p. This kind of conditional is best called the subjunctive conditional. We may write it 'pSIq'. Thus 'If X had occurred, then Y would have occurred' taken in a sense in which it is not implied either that X did or that it did not occur, is written 'X occurred SI Y occurred'. Such a proposition is certainly in principle both verifiable and falsifiable. It is verified if both of 'p' and 'q' are found to be true, and it is falsified if 'p' is found true, and 'q' is found false. Of course if 'p' is false, it follows that the proposition 'pSIq' will not be decisively verified or falsified. But it does not follow that the proposition is in principle unverifiable. Compare the proposition 'There is a stain under this carpet'. If the carpet is never moved, it follows that the proposition will never be conclusively verified. But it does not follow that the proposition is itself in principle unverifiable.

Let us now turn back to counterfactual conditionals, as opposed to subjunctive conditionals. We may write the counterfactual conditional with the same antecedent and consequent as that just under discussion thus: 'pCFq'. This is taken as implying, that is, as asserting, the negation of 'p'. There may also be a type of conditional sentence which in some sense implies negation of its

---

[1] Cf. 'The Problem of Contrary-to-fact Conditionals' by John Watling (*Analysis*, March 1957). The view I attribute to an acute philosopher is in my mind as a result of discussion with John Watling, but whether it is precisely his view I am not sure.

antecedent without asserting it, but it will be simpler to concentrate attention solely on the question whether this is asserted, for that is all that is really relevant from the point of view of verification and truth. If I write 'Hitler invaded England CF Germany won the war', this is equivalent to 'If Hitler had invaded England, then Germany would have won the war' in a sense of this sentence in which it is taken as asserting that Hitler did not invade England.

One might say that whereas 'pSIq' is in principle verifiable 'pCFq' is in principle unverifiable, (though it will be falsifiable by the negation of 'p'). However our acute philosopher would argue that 'pCFq' is simply the equivalent of 'pSIq and not-p', and is therefore simply the conjunction of two separately but not jointly verifiable propositions. In this respect it is comparable to 'There is a stain under the carpet, but the carpet will never be moved'. Such propositions have not usually been regarded as problematic by the verificationist.

Whether our acute philosopher is right or not in suggesting that these considerations show that there is no need for the verificationist to seek an extensionalist reduction of subjunctive conditionals, these propositions still pose a problem for anyone who is prepared to say some such thing as that it is facts or fact-properties which determine whether a sentence is true or false, or whether a belief is true or false.

The difficulties seem especially great for the imagist-mentalist and indeed for any imagist. Can an image fact resemble a conditional 'fact' (if we suppose the word extended to cover some such mysterious things)? How else can the imagist explain belief in a conditional 'objective' (an essential property of a conditional 'fact')? Can one perhaps experience image conditional 'facts' which may symbolize non-image conditional 'facts' by resembling them and being reacted to in the same way? But what sense could be attached to saying that one experienced the 'fact' that if one universal were exemplified, then so would another be? Yet imagist-mentalism can offer no account of belief in a certain kind of state of affairs where experience of a state of affairs of that kind is an absurdity. Belief in non-sensorily conceived material objects is no exception to this, for what one believes in is the exemplification of positive and negative universals of a kind which are not intrinsically unexperienceable even if they are not actually experienced in those combinations.

The problem concerns the nature of the 'objectives' (or whatever plays a similar role) which must be exemplified in order that a conditional belief or assertion shall be true. On our acute philosopher's view it would seem that one 'objective' the exemplification of which is sufficient to make 'pSIq' (and a belief expressible by it) true, is the objective *that p and q*. Unless this is the case it would not be true, as our acute philosopher takes it that it is, that 'pSIq' can be verified by finding that both p and q are exemplified. Thus we can say that the exemplification of the compound objective *p and q* is a sufficient condition for the truth of 'pSIq'. But our acute philosopher also holds that if 'p' is not so, it is still possible for 'pSIq' either to be true or false. That is, its truth-value when the objective p is not exemplified is settled by something other than those objectives which settle the truth-values of 'p' and 'q'. Thus whatever it is which can make 'pSIq' true when 'p' is not so, must be something other than any truth-function of p and q. Let us call the 'objective', whatever it is, which can make 'pSIq' true when p does not hold 'pXq'. (Since it is bound to have something to do with p and q, a representation of it which incorporates their names cannot be unsuitable). Then 'pSIq' can be true on the basis of two quite different 'objectives' holding, one the objective *that p and q,* the other the 'objective' *that pXq.* Likewise it seems that it can be false for two quite different reasons. It may be false because p is true (holds) without q being true, or it may be false because not-p is true without pXq being true. Thus 'pSIq' is equivalent to 'p and q *or* not-p and pXq', the 'or' here being the usual truth-functional non-exclusive connective.

It is evident that 'objective' pXq can hold without objective *p and q* holding, but can objective *p and q* hold without 'objective' pXq holding? One may ask likewise whether *p and not-q* is compatible with pXq. 1) If the answer to both these questions is affirmative, then we must certainly regard 'p and q *or* not-p and pXq' as supplying a proper analysis of 'pSIq'. Of course, the crux of the problem of analysing 'pSIq' will still lie in analysing 'pXq'. 2) If, however, one could establish that exemplification of *p and q* required the exemplification of pXq and that *p and not-q* similarly excluded the exemplification of pXq, then it might be that 'pSIq' would be better analysed as equivalent simply to 'pXq', than as equivalent to 'p and q *or* not-p and pXq'. (However, if by any chance it turns out that *p and q* implies pXq and that *p and not-q* implies *not* (*pXq*) only because pXq is reducible to something of the form (*p and q*) or (*not-p and pYq*), that will show that it was really with pYq that we should have been concerning ourselves, under the title of pXq – for it will really be pYq which settles the truth-value of 'pSIq' whenever p does not hold.)

The cases which primarily interest us are those where 'p' and 'q' signify existential objectives. So let us suppose that 'p' is 'There is an F' and that 'q' is 'There is a G'. If we take the line that *p and q* entails pXq and that *p and not-q* entails *not*(*pXq*) (and that 'pXq' is not reducible to something of the character '*Either* there is an F and there is a G *or* there is not an F and pYq' in which case pYq would really be our pXq) we are supposing that the objective that things of a certain two kinds exist determines some 'objective' of a radically different character, which is not a matter either of there being anything of a certain type, or of anything being of a certain type, and also that the existence of a thing of a certain one of the types without one of the other would have ruled out the holding of any such 'objective', the *would have* here in question being logical. It is not easy to conceive what sort of determination this might be, or what sort of 'objective' it might be that is thus determined.

Since this is so difficult to conceive, let us for the present take the alternative that *p and q* does not determine pXq, and that *p and not-q* does not perhaps exclude it, but that 'p and q' entails 'pSIq' simply because 'pSIq' is equivalent to 'p and q *or* not-p and pXq'.

Having got so far, it represents itself as a possibility that 'pCFq' is equivalent to 'not-p and pXq'. If that were so, 'pCFq' would be more basic than 'pSIq' which would be properly analysed as 'p and q *or* pCFq'. One who asserted 'pSIq' would be claiming that one or other of two quite different kinds of 'objective' hold, whereas one who asserted 'pCFq' would be definitely asserting each of two objectives, namely not-p and pXq. A much more definite claim would thus be being made by 'pCFq' than by 'pSIq'. I suggest, then, in opposition to our acute philosopher, that the counterfactual conditional is more fundamental than the subjunctive conditional.

It will be well therefore to concentrate attention on 'pCFq' and 'pXq'. These are both conditionals of a kind the truth of which could never be settled by anything so simple as the truth of both antecedent and consequent. Could the two of them possibly be assimilated, that is, could 'not-p and pXq' be regarded simply as a redundant expansion of 'pXq' which entails 'not-p' on its own (without being the mere conjunction of 'not-p' with something else which does not entail it)? It does not seem so strange to allow this possibility as it was to allow the possibility that 'pXq' might be entailed by 'p and q' without merely being its disjunction with something else not entailed by it, and that 'pXq' although compatible with each of 'p' and 'not-p' is not compatible with 'p and not-q'. We need not, then, assume a distinction between 'pCFq' and 'pXq'. Moreover, if there is a distinction, 'pCFq' seems the right one for us to attend to first, since a conditional which leaves p open as a possibility but which is not entailed by 'p and q' seems further from ordinary ways of thinking than one otherwise similar which denies the holding of p.

We should be clear, to begin with, that in 'pCFq', 'p' and 'q' may refer either to the time of speaking, or to an earlier, or to a later time. 'If he were in that swingboat, he would be being sick', 'If he were in that swingboat, he would be about to be sick', 'If he had been in that swingboat, he would have been sick', 'If he were to go into that swingboat, he would be sick', are examples of various different tense possibilities. One may ask about the last one, however, whether it really does imply, 'He will not go in that swingboat', that is, whether the whole sentence is not really of the form 'pSIq', rather than 'pCFq'.

It would not go against anything we have said if we were to say that it is of the form 'pSIq'. For we could still say that 'pSIq' is analysable as 'pCFq *or* p and q'. One might bring this out in ordinary language, or in something approaching ordinary language, by saying that 'If he were to go on that swingboat, he would be sick' means 'Either he will go on that swingboat and be sick, or it will be true that if he had done so, then he would have been sick'. This would bring out the point that there are two quite different circumstances in which the sentence, if it is supposed that it leaves it open whether he will go on the swingboats or not, may turn out true.

But is it true that 'If he were to go on the swingboats, he would be sick' does imply that he will not go on the swingboats? Possibly the answer is this. It does have some such implication in a loose way, in that it is a form of words which suggests that the speaker does not expect the antecedent to be false. But if the antecedent does turn out false, the original assertion will not therefore be thought of as exactly false. It may still be regarded as true, if it is supposed that if the antecedent had been true, then so would have been the consequent.

However it may be with such conditionals with future subjunctive verbs, it seems clear that a conditional with future indicative verbs is normally in effect, of the form 'pSIq', that is, on our present assumption, implicitly of the form 'pCFq or p and q'. Thus 'If he goes on the swingboats, he will be sick' means 'Either he will go on the swingboats and be sick, or it will be true that if he had gone on the swingboats, then he would have been sick'. Most conditional claims about the future, and doubtless most of our belief experiences about the future, are of this disjunctive character and envisage one of two quite different possibilities, one that of the antecedent and consequent both being true, the other that of the antecedent being false, but being in that relation to the consequent, whatever it is, which a counterfactual concerns.

Let us now turn to the question as to the nature of that relation. What is the kind of state of affairs or circumstance, signified by 'pCFq'?

It is easy to go on worrying at this question in an endless fashion without appreciating that a definite decision on a certain point has to be made, which no amount of complicated logical manipulation will assist one in making. Either one must take it that somehow the way things are settles[1] the truth-value of a counterfactual, or one must say that this is not so, and that the way things would be if they were otherwise in a certain way is irreducible to a truth about how things are.

The trouble is that there are grave objections to either course.

On the one hand it may well appear self-evident that however things are, they cannot *entail* a truth about how they would be if they were otherwise.

If one takes this line, there will be little point in pursuing the detailed attempts of writers such as Nelson Goodman and R. Chisholm to find a satisfactory formulation of counterfactuals in terms of how things are. At the most they would be saying something about what would be the best evidence on the matter.

---

[1] Readers steeped in modern philosophy may find it hard to grasp the sense of *settle* here in question. I do not mean – is what makes human beings arrive at their decisions as to its truth-value, I mean – be what gives it the truth-value it actually has, whether this is known to anyone or not.

Their attempt to give the meaning of a counterfactual will be doomed from the start.

There is, then, on the face of it, good reason for thinking that the state of affairs which makes a counterfactual true is *sui generis* and not reducible to some complicated 'actual' state of affairs.

Yet there are good reasons for taking the other view as well. What sense does it make to talk of there being a state of affairs which is not actual? If there is, in any sense of *is*, something which makes a counterfactual true this must be something actual. However mysterious an entity one supposes, there will be the same logical gap between the existence of such an entity and the claim made by a counterfactual, as we have already spoken of.

Faced with this dilemma, I must give it as my own view that we should look for that which makes a counterfactual true in the actual. It hardly makes sense to look elsewhere[1]. Yet some explanation needs to be given of why we are left with such a feeling of a gap. I shall attempt at a later stage to offer some such explanation.

There would seem to be two main ways in which one may try to find the truth-determinant of a counterfactual in the actual. According to the first, 'pCFq' says something like, 'p is false, but there is evidence for $p \supset q$ which is not evidence for any of p, not-p, q, and not-q, considered independently'; according to the second 'pCFq' says something like 'p is false, but there are laws of nature which together with certain particular factual truths such as do not entail any of p, not-p, q, and not-q, taken separately, entail $p \supset q$'. The two main lines of approach which have been deployed amount to attempts to elaborate on one of these hints.

The trouble about the first approach is that it makes 'pCFq' too much a statement about human knowledge. Anyway, must the evidence be known to the speaker, or to people in general? If the latter, must all of it be known to one person, or may it be the sum of knowledge distributed among all people? Or is it enough that the knowledge be *available*? But can availability be analysed other than by appeal to counterfactuals? However these questions are answered the root objection remains. If I say 'If the patient

---

[1] The realm of universals might in one sense be called an unactual world, but it is clear that the inhabitants of this realm, considered apart from their exemplification by particulars, only determine necessary truths, never contingent truths, such as are the counterfactuals of our concern.

had been given drug X, he would have survived', what I claim to be so is something for which one can, of course, look for evidence, but surely its truth-value *might* actually be settled by facts beyond all human knowledge now and for ever.

The second approach requires us to explain what a law of nature is, without employing the concept of a counterfactual truth. A law of nature, by one taking this view, will be 'a statement to the effect that whenever and wherever conditions of a specified kind F occur, then so will, always and without exception, certain conditions of another kind, G.'[1]

The difficulties in supplementing this definition so as to distinguish laws of nature from accidental generalizations which happen to be without exception has given rise to a vast literature. Even if we suppose this done, difficulties remain, if 'pCFq' and equally 'pCFnot-q', which should be incompatible with it, is not always going to be generable in some trivial way. But let us assume these difficulties also resolved.

What I think objectionable about this account is that it implies that the whole of past time and the whole of future time are as relevant to the truth-value of 'pCFq', as are nearer times. Suppose I say that if I had put a certain piece of wood on the pond this morning, then it would have floated. Doubtless my belief in this rests upon belief in the general truth that wood floats, and doubtless I should be able to see this truth as derivable from other more ultimate 'laws'. But do I really have to regard it as essential to the truth of my claim that these 'laws' will hold for ever and ever . . . and ever?

Doubtless *natural law* may for some purposes be suitably defined as a universal statement true of all times. But it is at least possible that what for all intents and purposes are natural laws for trillions times trillions times trillions of millennia should eventually change. If the idea of really endless time is grasped I cannot believe that there is anything in science to make us confident that the most fundamental habits of the universe will not one 'day' change, or never did so one 'day' in the past.

My objection is not that one could never have logically adequate evidence for claims about all future time. Philosophers are still far too obsessed with the question of the evidence for basic beliefs (as shown in their rejection of the more straightforward

[1] C. G. Hempel, *Philosophy of Natural Science*, p. 54.

analyses of these beliefs on the ground that if these analyses were correct there could be no evidence for the beliefs); all belief and so-called knowledge involves a leap of faith, and one may have this sort of faith in the perpetuity of natural law. All I am saying is that my firm belief that if I had put the piece of wood in the water, it would have floated, seems compatible with not having a firm belief that wood will float a trillion, trillion, trillion years from now in some remote planet, or not believing that the ultimate laws which underlie this generalization about wood will last forever. For this reason, I must reject the present account of counterfactuals.

What can I put in its place? Only something absurdly vague, yet which still seems to me more satisfactory than what is offered by either of the other accounts.

I suggest that 'pCFq' means 'P is not the case but among all logically possible but non-actual universes there is one which includes p and q, and which is more similar to the actual universe than is any logically possible universe which includes p and not-q'. By 'being the (actual) universe' we had better understand here simply 'being some vast aggregate of particulars to which every particular which can ever concern me belongs'.

Any property which could (logically) be the total nature of a universe can be called a logically possible universe. The nature of the universe is itself the one logically possible universe which is actual, in the sense that it is exemplified. If there is no such thing as 'p' asserts that there is (or is not any such thing as 'p' asserts that there is not) this is something which could be deduced from that one logically possible universe which is actualized. Each other logically possible universe will either imply what 'p' asserts or will imply its negation. Among those which imply it, some will and some will not imply what 'q' asserts. In saying 'pCFq' we claim that there is one such possible universe, or universe-nature, which implies p and q and which is more similar to the universe-nature actually exemplified than any which implies p and not-q.

It should be realized that this leaves open the possibility that both 'pCFq' and 'pCFnot-q' are false. This seems to me consonant with Common Sense. Sometimes it is neither true that if such and such had happened, then so would such and such, nor true that if such and such had happened, then so would not such and such. If I say 'If I had gone to London yesterday, I would have met X', this may be no more true than 'If I had gone to London yesterday, I would not have met X'. We might ordinarily say that they were both neither true not false, rather than both false, but I don't think that there is much in this. The point is that neither is true.

A strong degree of similarity between the actualized possible universe including not-p and an unactualized possible one including p will depend on all sorts of different factors. If the actualized possible universe does not contain laws of nature lasting through all time, then to keep as near as possible to it a universe with p will have to conform to the regularities which hold in the region where p or not-p is to be found.

The obvious objection to our account is that there cannot be an exact measure of degree of similarity. However, what our account demands is that there be sense in talking of one property being objectively more similar to a second than a third. It does not matter that for many pairs of properties it is not true that a certain other property is more similar to the one than to the other, provided it is sometimes so. Wherever the actualized possible universe is not more similar to one with p and q than to any one with p and not-q, 'pCFq' and 'pCFnot-q' will each be false. All we claim is that sometimes one of them may be true. Anyway we only pretend to give a hint as to the meaning of 'pCFq', which seems less objectionable than the hint contained in the other two suggested accounts we have mentioned.

If our suggestion is accepted, we can now say that 'pSIq' means 'Either p and q are both the case, or p is not the case but there is a logically possible universe containing p and q more similar to the actualized one than is any logically possible universe containing p and not-q'. It may be true by p and q both being true, or it may be true in virtue of the similarity relations described holding between the actualized possible universe and unactualized possible universes.

In discussing whether subjunctive conditionals or counterfactuals were the more basic sort of proposition, we found ourselves inclined to hold that 'pSIq' was equivalent to something of the form 'p and q *or* not-p and pXq', where pXq was not entailed by *p and q*; and where, unless perhaps pXq entailed not-p, its negation was not entailed by *p and not-q*. Our reason was, roughly that it seemed that when p is not true, that which settles the truth-value of 'pSIq' must be something so radically different from what settles its truth-value when p is true (namely *p and q* or *p and not-q*) that the holding of logical relations between them seemed problematic. If the account we have now arrived at is acceptable, our expectations, I am inclined to say, are vindicated in their spirit if not in the letter. Our account does imply that the sort of fact which settles the truth-value in the one case is fundamentally different from that in the other. One would surely be twisting things if one tried to say that 'p and q' only entails 'pSIq' because if the actual universe contains *p and q* then, since nothing can be more like it than itself, there is a possible universe more like the actual universe than any logically possible universe containing *p and q*. One could indeed by this device simply analyse 'pSIq' as 'There is a logically possible universe containing p and q more similar to the actualized one than is any logically possible universe containing p and not-q' (which is, one might think, what pXq has become), and thus make 'pSIq' more basic than 'pCFq', but it would disguise the fact that 'p and q' entails 'pSIq' in its own right, so to speak, and not simply via this queer and tautologous intermediary. So far as the letter goes, then, our analysis does not provide us with quite what we expected, for our 'pXq' might be thought of as being itself entailed by 'p and q' (and as having its negation entailed by 'p and not-q'). On the other hand, our sense that 'pXq' would not really offer a proper analysis of 'pSIq' on its own, and that pSIq is true or false on radically different grounds when p is true and when it is false, is conformed to by the present analysis, and that sense led by a not unreasonable train of thought to these expectations. Besides it seems somewhat forced to regard our analysis of 'pCFq' as the conjunction of 'not-p' and another logically independent 'pXq'. One might equally regard them as jointly constituting 'pXq'.

Presumably an experience of believing that pCFq, as we have described it, very seldom accompanies affirmation of the counterfactual sentence in question. There is another experience which much more often goes with it, which might be better called the experience of believing a counterfactual. The only trouble is that this experience is not really cognitive, and cannot be called true or false. What we have described is the nature of the only proper *belief* which such a sentence can express.

What would it be like for the belief we have described to be experienced, granted that it is not very common for this to happen?

We must first explain what it would be like to believe that some actual situation is more like some one non-actual situation than like another. Such beliefs are clearly quite common. We may have never seen a unicorn nor a dragon, nor believe in their existence, but we can agree that a horse is (fitted to be) more like a unicorn than it is (to be) like a dragon.

What happens here, according to the imagist-mentalist, is that we consciously reject belief in something but that the thing is envisaged with sufficient clearness for us to take in the ideal relations which such a thing would have to a thing of some other kind which we envisage, believingly or otherwise. Thus one can envisage there being a unicorn in a certain field and envisage there being a dragon in that field and believe that there is a horse in that field, and one can *take in* the greater similarity of the universals involved in the first and third situation than that holding between the second and third situation. In its most developed form such 'taking in' will consist in a feeling of bafflement at the attempt to imagine instances of the three universals, such that the first is not more like the third than is the second.

Now one could notice that some situation had a certain property F, and believe that there was a certain unexemplified property G more like it than any determinate of some very general determinable could be. One would do this by noticing the F-ness of the situation, thinking of the existence of a G but rejecting the idea, and then having these two experiences: first one finds that a G is necessarily very like an F, secondly one finds that there could not be an H (where H is very indeterminate) as like an F as a G would be bound to be. Having the first experience would consist in being baffled at the attempt to think of an F and a G which are not very similar to one another, the second would consist in being baffled at the attempt to think of an H, an F, and a G, where G is not more like the F than the H is.

If, *per impossibile,* someone could notice the nature of the universe as being F, he might then think of, without believing in, a G universe and think of an H universe, and find himself baffled at the attempt to do this without making the G universe more like the F universe than is the H universe.

The nearest approach to actually noticing that, as opposed to experiencing the belief that (and that is difficult enough) pCFq, would be made by God if he noticed the total nature of the universe, F, which excludes p, and thought of a certain nature G which implied p and q, and was baffled at the attempt to think of a nature implying p and not-q,[1] such that a something with this nature would be as like an F as would a G.[2]

If one can make any sense at all of the idea of noticing the character of the universe, one can, I suppose, make sense of responding to the universe in this fashion. The imagist-mentalist may claim that some blurred image may be treated as though it were the universe, and a fragmentary version of such a reaction may be made to it.

But what is it to treat an image as a universe? It must be to treat it – for the moment – as though it contained everything that could ever concern one. There is no difficulty in treating an image as rather vast and comprehensive. To treat it in this way to the maximal extent one can, will be to treat it as a universe.

It is to be noted that to treat an image as the universe and as F would have two stages. First one would treat it as vastly comprehensive so that nothing one was concerned with lay outside it. Second, one would treat it as F. Being F must not be supposed to be a property which only a universe could have. For in imagining an F and a G and an H together, one is bound to be imagining that the F is not a universe (for the G and the H will lie outside it).

Doubtless this all sounds somewhat phantasmagoric. It may be admitted that a belief experience like this is pretty far from the cases with which imagist-mentalism copes most easily. But the imagist-mentalist may say that if we try to bring home to ourselves, really to experience belief in, some of the sentences which we casually affirm in day to day life, we just do find ourselves in such dizzy regions as this. For that very reason, he may say, philosophy is a vertigo-producing subject, for it does prompt us to realize in consciousness beliefs which we normally never do.

As already remarked, those conscious states, which counterfactual affirmations are more often associated with, are of quite

---

[1] 'Being of a nature which implies p and not-q' is the value which H takes here.

[2] One may need to say, perhaps, that for God it would not be the universe, for his reactions to it, which concern him, would lie outside it. But at least he could find that all this held with regard to something very vast and comprehensive. If we can imagine something very vast and comprehensive as having this character, perhaps we can be said to imagine the aggregate of all that concerns us as having this character.

another kind to which we shall now turn. But if we want to give cognitive content to counterfactuals, they must, so it seems, be interpreted in some such way as we have now indicated.

6 DESIRE AND SUBJUNCTIVE CONDITIONALS: THE FEELING THAT A THING IS IMPOSSIBLE

It is doubtful if there is in ordinary language any single concept of a voluntary action, and to attach a precise concept to this phrase is bound to appear eccentric. But certain movements on the parts of a conscious organism are called its voluntary actions for such reasons as that it is supposed that at least in a dispositional sense the organism is aware that it is making movements likely to have such effects as those movements are likely to have, and is not discontented with this situation, and perhaps that such movements would not have occurred unless such contentment was likely. What kind of action those movements constitute an instance of is not so much a matter of the geometric character of the movements, as of those likely effects of which the organism is supposed to have dispositional awareness. Among these reasons, it is to be noticed, there is a counterfactual element.

There is no need for a so-called voluntary or deliberate action to be preceded by anything which can be called a volition. None the less voluntary actions sometimes are so preceded.

A volition, an act of will, or the experience of willing something or deciding to do something (all of which may be identified), may be considered as bearing to the having of a certain purpose somewhat the same relation as an experience of believing something has to believing something in a dispositional sense. Both of them are the fruition into consciousness of what is otherwise merely a physical habit of an organism.

In our section on belief in necessary truth we ascribed to the imagist-mentalist the view that sometimes the specifying property for a certain universal occurred first, and was then followed either by the specified property or by an image-property such as imitates it. It may be that a certain feeling tends to go with the specifying property when such a 'fulfilment' of it is likely to follow. We have here, then, one thing which might be called a volition, or act of will.

However one will not really know what one is willing, one

will not be envisaging the object of one's desire. Just as a fully realized belief must, according to the imagist-mentalist, include such envisagement, so, we may take it that he will insist, must a fully realized act of will or desire.

Until a man *decides* what to do, he normally does not *know* what he is going to do. Once he has decided what he is going to do, he does have a firm belief as to what he is going to do. My suggestion, on behalf of the imagist-mentalist (which has also been made by others, as well, of course) is that the coming to the decision is to be identified with the forming a definite belief as to what one is going to do. However it is not merely a belief. It is a belief one is happy in the experience of, it is a pleasurable, or at least a contented, belief experience. Moreover, it is a belief one would not be experiencing unless one liked doing so. The fact that it is pleasurable is the major determinant of its being what I believe. It is indeed a voluntary belief in something like the same sense as that in which a movement may be a voluntary action. There will not normally be a previous volition to believe. But another point needs to be added concerning those pleasant belief experiences concerning the future which we most readily call volitions. They all answer to some description such that belief experiences answering to that description have a strong tendency to be true. For each human mind the description actually in question is roughly that of being directed on objectives concerning the future movements, and the effects of the future movements, of a certain body, that body which is connected with that mind in a large variety of ways which we sum up by saying that it is the body to which that mind belongs and *vice versa*. But we can conceive of minds for which the description in question would be different.

When I am wondering what to do, what happens in consciousness, to the extent that it is a conscious process, would seem to be something like this. A series of faint and wavering beliefs in incompatible objectives to do with my future doings flits through my mind, and gradually one belief emerges as the pleasantest. When I settle down to a pleasing belief in that objective I have willed that objective. If willing is simply defined as the having of pleasant beliefs about the future, where the pleasurableness of the belief is causally connected with its being sustained, it would be true of me that I sometimes will things which are notoriously outside my agency. All wishful thinking is willing in this sense. But it is equally true that considered from every point of view but that of its likely truth-value willing is simply wishful thinking. For one might describe wishful thinking as occurring when a contest between incompatible believings is won by the pleasantest belief experience simply because it is the pleasantest and irrespective of any consciousness of evidence in its favour.

When we talk of the most pleasurable incipient belief experience of a set of incompatible incipient belief experiences ousting the others, we should take this as covering the case where the least unpleasurable one ousts the others. Often we can form no picture of the future which is not gloomy. To the extent that the picture we finally accept is accepted simply in virtue of being the least unpleasurable we have wishful thinking as much as where it is because it is the most pleasurable. Where such wishful thinking is on matters where wishful thinking tends to turn out true, we may call it *willing*.

Various incipient believings about his future doings run through the mind of a man who is wondering what to do. The fate of each such incipient believing will be either to give way to a pleasanter, or less unpleasant, alternative, or to gather strength from its delightfulness, or on balance least unpleasantness, and become a settled belief and act of will. But there are other possibilities, above all there is the possibility that while its comparative pleasurableness as an act of imagining remains strong, it dies down as a belief and is replaced by experience of belief in some incompatible objective which is far less pleasing. That is, it is not really felt about as something which is going to happen although the image remains before the mind with a faded version of the specifying experience just sufficient to make it the imagining of a definite situation. In such a case the pleasure principle has clashed with the reality principle and the latter has proved stronger. We have then the experience, which may be described as that of the impossibility of a certain objective, where an incipient believing retaining its own delightfulness, or slighter unpleasantness, fades away dismally to a mere imagining in the presence of a less pleasing belief in some contrary objective. For instance, an incipient believing may develop which envisages me as going and demanding, and in consequence receiving, from my employer a much larger salary than that which I receive. But though the incipient believing is pleasant it simply does not develop into a belief, and simply arouses unpleasant incipient believings in situations incompatible with it, such as my being spoken to contemptuously after my having made my request, or my not making the request at all. Which of these two incipient believings wins the day and becomes a believing proper will however depend upon which proves the pleasanter.

The experience of impossibility may, however, take a milder form. It may simply be that an incipient pleasurable believing fades into a mere imagining accompanied by belief in its contrary, without believing the contrary actually being unpleasant. If the idea of flying like a bird begins to enter my head it meets some such fate as this, where it would be too strong to say that it was found actually unpleasant to believe its contrary. Suppose I am in a train which stops out in the open country and I am late for an appointment. I might look out of the window and imagine myself flying on ahead (without mechanical assistance) towards my destination. This may be a pleasant imagining but it hardly even begins to be a believing, being met immediately by a less pleasing belief in some contrary of it.

Willing, we have said, is wishful thinking on matters concerning which wishful thinking tends to turn out true. One might say rather that it is wishful thinking which tends to make itself true. The question of the causal efficacy of the mental act of willing is a difficult one, but there is clearly some sense in which in successful willing the world conforms itself to the pleasing belief rather than the pleasing belief to the world, as in the case of believing dominated by the reality principle.

In general, processes of thought where what is believed is settled by the degree of pleasantness attaching to believing it, have little tendency to lead to truth. Neville Chamberlain's belief that Hitler would keep his word did not make this more likely. However if I have a pleasurable belief that I shall call on a friend tomorrow, which is sustained simply by its own pleasantness, that makes it more likely that I shall call on him, and so we call it 'willing'.

When I consider the future, when I start forming pictures of what will come after the present moment, my belief in what a picture symbolizes may wax and wane irrespective of the degree to which, when seen in the shifting context of other pictures symbolizing things I believe in, it is pleasing or displeasing. What may seem to influence whether I believe or not may rather be the customariness of the complex which those various pictures form together. We may say in such cases that the reality principle is in control. In other cases, however, whether I continue to believe in that which a certain picture symbolizes may seem to turn precisely on the degree to which I find it more pleasant than its alternatives when combined with pictures symbolizing the other things I believe. We may say in such cases that the pleasure principle is in control, and that I am engaged in wishful thinking. There is a limit to how far a belief can be completely confident and completely pleasure-determined without its gathering a certain claim to be described as willing. Such wishful thinking as would never be called willing tends to possess a certain uneasy diffidence, and also to require some basis in the reality principle if it is to be sustained. If someone believes, and with complete confidence, either that it will rain or that it will not, according as to whether it proves pleasant to him to believe one or the other, we may feel inclined to describe him as willing it to rain or not, though we will hold that it is an intrinsically impotent willing. For a normal person thinking is only completely wishful where it is also to some degree effective. Thus the two criteria of being an act of will (1) being a piece of *completely* wishful thinking, (2) tending to make itself true, normally, but by no means always, go together. Where we get (1) without (2), we get something which is the same as willing in its intrinsic character, but different in its effects or as a predictor of the future. We may say that from an internal point of view this is willing.

The use of the phrase 'wishful thinking' is somewhat complicated by the fact that it is normally a derogatory term.

Faced with someone who (apparently) envisages with pleasure a certain future state of affairs in a more or less believing fashion, the outsider may take the state of affairs to be of a type such that pleasurable belief in it on the part of the individual in question is in itself good evidence in favour of the likelihood of this state of affairs coming about, or he may not take this to be so. If he does not so take it, he will condemn it as wishful thinking if he judges that it is pleasure-determined rather than reality-determined. Where what will happen is independent of how we picture it, it is better that our picture should be determined by our experience of how things have been in the past, than by what we find it pleasurable to picture. Thus in this kind of case we will be more likely to call it by the somewhat derogatory title of wishful thinking, the more strongly it is believed. On the other hand, where the state of affairs is of a kind such that the more firmly it is believed in with pleasure, the more likely we hold that it is to be actual, we will dismiss its envisagement the more readily as mere wishful thinking the more weak the belief is. We will then be regarding it as mere pleasurable imagining rather than the firm believing required if the state of affairs is to become actual.

Thus my thought that I shall give up smoking may be condemned as mere wishful thinking, either in contrast to a full-fledged act of willing because it lacks the requisite confidence to be effective (is too shot through with tendencies to believe the opposite), or because it is too confident in the light of the evidence that I never will give up smoking.

In primitive states of mind, which some of us perhaps remember from our adolescence, the distinction between the realms in which willing is appropriate and the realms in which it is not, is not well observed, indeed willing and mere believing slip into each other, in a way in which what we have been saying should make easier to understand than it often seems. Many people, especially adolescents, in matters such as religion (where immediate falsifications are not likely to give the system a shock) do not distinguish at all clearly between asking themselves whether a certain picture of the world is true or whether it is one they enjoy contemplating. Now if one had control of the nature of the world, indeed to the minimal extent that in certain areas one does so (at least in the sense that things have a tendency to take the form we have willed) a failure to keep the two sorts of mental process apart would be quite appropriate, for that will turn out true which one does in the end find most desirable.

It is tempting to say that we learn by experience what kinds of thing can be affected by wishful thinking, and what kinds of thing cannot, and that we learn to desist from wishful thinking in the latter regions. Perhaps this is true in a sense, but the learning in question must not be thought of as another stream of thought guiding the stream of thought which is being explained. It is simply that in the former regions pleasure-determined belief is reinforced by reality-determined thought pointing in the same direction, while in the latter regions it is gradually swept aside by reality-determined thought pointing in opposite directions.

In a fully civilized adult the pleasure principle would be confined to settling what is to be believed about the future movements of his body, and about all situations which the reality principle cannot select between until the future movements of his body are settled. I do not mean that what one wills is always primarily a movement of one's body. One wills one total situation as against other total situations. But what marks off these total situations from others which one does not will, is that the reality principle will not let the remainder of them be believed in, as being uncustomary, unless some at least roughly specified movements of one's body are part of what is believed in.

This gives us a background to understanding what sort of experiences may constitute such feelings as that something is impossible, is necessary, or is possible. Affirmation of subjunctive conditionals is probably more closely associated with a tendency to experience such feelings than with a tendency to belief experiences of the kind described in the previous section. This serves as some explanation of our sense that such belief experiences do not really contain the apprehension of the essential matter involved in a subjunctive conditional. If I say 'If I put my hand in that fire, I will experience pain', I am liable to feel the impossibility of putting my hand in the fire and not feeling pain, and this seems something different from merely believing that either I will put it in the fire and experience pain or that the world is more like one in which I do this and do feel pain than like one in which I do this and don't feel pain.

Among the things that we learn from experience are new views as to what objectives are successfully willable and what are not. I am not thinking of one's learning that one can move one's hand without moving the teapot but not the teapot without moving one's hand (or at least some other part of one's body). It may be very misleading to suggest that one *learns* this. It is rather that nothing ever prompts the belief, neither the reality principle nor the pleasure principle, that the teapot is going to move unaided.

I can only will that which I am able to believe, for willing is a form of believing. If the reality principle (or some other cause) makes a thing unbelievable, then I cannot will it. But it sometimes happens that if the pleasure principle worked quite alone, a certain objective would be willed, which in fact the reality principle stops our seriously believing and hence willing. Suppose such a belief begins to dawn, but instead of developing into a belief it remains simply a pleasurable imagining, while a decidedly unpleasurable belief in the opposite develops. Then it is that I feel a kind of frustration which might be called the sense of impossibility.

One might suggest that the sense of (natural) necessity is to be identified with living through a belief the strength of which remains complete in spite of changes in its pleasurableness. The sense of an objective as being willable is to be identified with living through a belief the strength of which varies directly with its pleasurableness and inversely with its unpleasurableness. One might also say that if one has some inclination to believe p and some to believe not-p, and neither inclination is very strong, and if the strength of the inclination either way is independent of any change in the pleasurableness or unpleasurableness of either belief, then one is feeling that p is possible, but not, in one's own case, willable.

One may distinguish feeling that an objective is necessary, willable, or possible, from noticing that one has so felt it. That an objective has over a certain period been believed in with a degree of assurance that has risen with the pleasurableness of believing it, and sunk with the unpleasurableness of believing it, is presumably something which can be noticed. That is, there might be a distinctive sort of experience that is called forth by events having this character. Such a distinctive experience might be that of saying something like 'It's up to me', or it might be a peculiar sort of joy at one's own potency in a certain matter. Equally one might notice in some way that one has experienced an objective as necessary or as possible but not willable.

We have now an adumbration of an account of what it is to regard an objective as necessary, or as willable, or as possible but unwillable. We have three different ways of 'treating' an objective, which might be described in these terms.

Can one say that these ways of treating objectives constitute belief experiences to the effect that certain things are possible or impossible, within one's power or not within one's power, and so forth? If so, these believings could surely be said to play a part in bringing home to one what is involved in assent to a sub-junctive conditional.

But before one enters on such a beguiling path the following point must be considered. Beliefs are normally classified as true or false, and our development of this platitude has led us to say that a belief is fitted to intend a fact, and either actually does so, or actually doesn't do so. Yet if our feeling that an objective is necessary, impossible, willable, possible, or what not, is to be analysed in some such way as has been indicated, nothing at all has been said, and it is not at all clear what on earth is sayable, re-garding what it is for such a feeling to be true or false, or in what sense it is fitted to intend a fact (or anything at all like a fact) and either actually does so or does not.

If believing that an objective is necessary is having a strong belief in it which does not vary its strength with variations in its pleasurableness, it is not clear how any question can come up as to its truth-value which is not simply the question of the truth-value of the objective felt to be necessary. But clearly one would not want to say that any belief that an objective was necessary was shown to be true when it was found that the objective in question was actualized. Similar remarks apply to the other feelings which seem expressible in these modal terms.

Nor is the position in any way eased if we identify belief that an objective falls under one of these modalities with noticing that one has felt that it does so. Noticings cannot be divided into the true and the false, and apart from this the correctness or incorrect-ness of the claim that one has felt an objective to be necessary or otherwise could not be identified with the correctness or in-correctness of a claim that it was necessary or otherwise.

The conclusion to be drawn from these considerations would seem to be as follows. There are various experiences which may be described in such ways as a feeling that something is impossible, is within my power, is not within my power, and so on. We have thrown out some hints as to what these feelings may sometimes amount to. It is not unreasonable to regard these feelings as in a certain sense serving as bringings home to oneself in conscious-ness of what subjunctive conditionals, in particular ones concern-ing the future, amount to. If we looked further into the nature of the feeling of regret, we could probably say something of the same sort regarding its connection with the affirmation of counterfactuals about the past. We cannot however regard these feelings as belief experiences proper for no sense can be given to calling them true or false. So far as a definite cognitive meaning is attached to subjunctive and counterfactual conditionals it is one which we can only bring home to ourselves in terms indicated in the previous section. Yet it is with the feelings discussed in this section rather than the belief experiences discussed in the previous section that these conditional sentences have more often to do, hence a sense of dissatisfaction is left with the elucidation of their meaning which sees them simply as concerned to assert that objective belief in which is experienced when we have these belief experiences.

7 DIFFICULTIES OF PHENOMENALISM

In the last two sections we have argued on behalf of the imagist-mentalist that to experience belief in a subjunctive conditional or counterfactual conditional may take two forms. What one may experience in the case of a counterfactual, is the belief that though the antecedent is false, the world is more like one in which antecedent and consequent are both true, than like one in which the first is true and the second false, while in the case of a subjunctive conditional one will believe either that this is so or that both antecedent and consequent are actually true. But there is an alternative form which experience of belief in pSIq may take. It may take the form of giving up the willing of p and not-q in spite of the pleasantness of believing in p and not-q. We have hinted that there are further mental occurrences which might be called experience of belief in pSIq or pCFq, but which like this last one could not properly be called true or false. For instance someone whose initial sadness that q is false passes into a sadness that p is false may, under certain further conditions, be said to be experiencing belief that pCFq.

Now if my belief in material objects takes a phenomenalistic form, then my experiencing the belief that a certain sense-datum is the appearance of a material object of a certain kind consists simply and solely in experiencing an indefinite number of beliefs to the effect that if certain further sense-data (usually of myself in action in a certain way) are sensed, so will certain other ones. Doubtless only some of the conditional beliefs in which the material object belief consists are actually experienced, but one may suppose that the rest exist as especially active dispositions (where 'disposition' must be interpreted concordantly with the remarks on counterfactuals in section 5). This is comparable to what we have said with regard to other forms which the belief in material objects may take. That is, only belief in a fragment of the totality which one is said to believe in is ever actually experienced. Total realization of what we believe in consciousness is a sort of ideal rather than something which actually occurs.

It may be granted forthwith that the person who affirms material object sentences normally is ready for, and to some extent actually experiences, those mental states of the not strictly true or false kind, which we have said may be called belief in subjunctive conditionals, where the subjunctive conditionals are those to which philosophical phenomenalism will reduce the material object affirmations. To this extent material objects may be said to be conceived phenomenalistically by many people on many occasions. But in so far as these are the 'belief' experiences mainly associated with the affirmation of material object sentences, nothing is really *believed* in the proper sense in a conscious way at all. A man who reflects on just what the truth of certain material object sentences really amounts to must pass on to a proper belief experience.

It seems very unlikely that what he will pass on to will be experience of belief in subjunctive conditionals as described in section 5, and much more likely that he will either experience belief in unsensed data, or in the existence of causes of sense-data of a partly unknown kind in the manner of section 3.

There are two reasons why it seems less likely that he will pass on to belief in subjunctive conditionals as described in section 5. First, it is a very much more recondite thing to believe than either of the other two. One has to be very sophisticated to experience such a belief. If it seems ridiculous to say that one must be sophisticated to experience belief in subjunctive conditionals, that is because one is thinking of those emotional experiences with which subjunctive conditionals are associated, and which are not especially for the sophisticated.

The second reason is this. If one experiences the idea that the world is more like one in which p and q are true than one in which p and not-q are true, one must suppose there to be some features of the actual world which make this so. One does not have to envisage what these features are, but one must hold that there are such features. Now someone who took a purely phenomenalist view of the world would not believe in the actual existence of anything except streams of animal consciousness. The existence of objects would lie in the fact that certain sense-data were sensed by such animal minds together with the fact that the totality of facts about these streams of consciousness constituted the world more like one in which various further successions of sense-data were sensed than like ones in which certain other successions of sense-data were sensed. But if one thinks it through, it will suggest itself that such a world simply would not contain enough for such resemblances between the actual and one possible world rather than another to hold. To take one simple case. It surely may be the case that some sense-datum has been experienced and that the person judged it to be the appearance of an X, while really it was a Y, and yet that no sense-data have been or ever will be *experienced* which make the world more like one in which certain further steps were taken and X-type sense-data were sensed rather than one in which certain further steps were taken and Y-type sense-data were sensed. Yet unless this is so, the phenomenalist can attach no sense to supposing that it may really have been a Y rather than an X. It is no good saying that if certain conditions had been satisfied, then sense-data able to settle the matter would have been experienced, for it is precisely with the content of such a conditional that we are concerned. The truth surely is that we suppose that one of these two is true, either that if the further steps had been taken, X-type sense-data would have been sensed or that if further steps had been taken Y-type sense-data would have been sensed, because we suppose that something outside the realm of sensed sense-data, settles which of these is so. It is most unplausible to say that things are always settled one way or the other by actually sensed data. But if it is not settled by sensed data, and we draw back from any assertion regarding the actual existence of anything else, we must suppose that in many cases there simply is no truth as to whether a certain sense-datum was an appearance of an X or a Y, if of either.

It may be that sometimes an ordinary man who believes that a sense-datum is the appearance of an X experiences belief that there are sensed data which make the world more like one in which certain steps lead to X-type data than one in which they do not, but it is more likely that if his belief has this conditional element he supposes vaguely that the basis for the conditional lies partly in the existence of things unsensed by anyone. But then, according as to whether these unsensed things are data or some non-sensory cause of data, he is in effect taking one of the other two lines.

It seems proper to conclude that though doubtless some of the belief experiences prompted by affirmation of material object sentences may be of a somewhat phenomenalistic kind, it is most unlikely that anyone who really brings his material object beliefs into full consciousness will find the character of what he believes mainly phenomenalistic.

8 BELIEF IN OTHER MINDS AS CONCEIVED BY IMAGIST-MENTALISM

In discussing the character of an experience of belief in the mental states of others it will be very much simpler if we take these mental states as being specified in a way which leaves any intentional character they may have on one side. It will be simpler, for instance, if we consider believing that other people have certain sensations, pure feelings, or images rather than that they experience or have certain beliefs, desires, and so on. This will allow us to deal adequately with the basic problem of the otherness of other minds. If there remains a special problem in believing in the occurrence of a belief experience (as opposed to a sensation, pure feeling, or image) it will not be particularly a problem of *other* minds.

Our concern is with what our believing in other minds consists in, that is with what we believe and how we believe it. Our concern is not at all with what justification we may have for such believing.

To discuss our topic at all completely I should have to go into the various problems that there are concerning the analysis of propositions about other minds, or about minds generally. This I cannot do here, however. I can only say that, on my view, there is to a man both a physical organism and a consciousness or stream of consciousness, the concept of which is not identifiable with any concept analysable in physical terms. Statements said to be about the mind have implications both as to the likely movements of the organism and as to the likely contents of the consciousness, so that the mind (of ordinary speech) cannot simply be identified with the consciousness. (We may, however, ourselves, out of long philosophical habit, occasionally use 'mind' to mean 'consciousness'.)

Sometimes, when I specify another person it does not seem far wrong to say that I am specifying him as the consciousness associated with a certain physical organism.

We may concentrate attention on such cases in which my belief that a certain someone is (for example) in pain, is the belief first that there is a certain material object, his body, and secondly that there is a certain stream of consciousness associated with that body as is my consciousness with my body, which stream of consciousness now contains feelings of pain. In saying that the consciousness in which I believe is a consciousness associated with a certain body as the consciousness which, in one sense of 'I', I am, I am not entering into the question whether this belief is justified by an argument by analogy, or by some other argument, or by no argument at all, being a spontaneous and indispensable but logically unjustifiable conviction.

I can no more enter deeply into the question of the consciousness-organism relationship than I can into the mind-body relationship, beyond remarking that any consciousness such as I normally think myself to be in contact with is linked with some one animal organism by a number of different relations. There is no precise answer to the question what is the minimal subset of these relations which must link a consciousness to an organism in order that it be the consciousness of that organism.

Among these relations two stand out as especially important. One is that the consciousness contains sense-data which are appearances of physical things from the position occupied by that organism. The further explication of this clearly turns upon the view of the sense-datum physical object relationship taken. But whatever view is taken one may say first that believing in the existence of a consciousness, associated with a physical organism in this way, will be a matter of believing in the existence of a consciousness such that the kind of sense-data it experiences at any time are a function of the relations which that body is in to other physical objects, and secondly that in all ordinary cases I will believe that the sense-data in question are of very much the same kind as I would experience if my body were in the situation in which that one is. So far as their intrinsic nature goes I will believe that they are of a type capable of being co-members with various sense-data of mine of such types as according to the unsensed-sense-data view actually make up the material world. Indeed on that view they actually will be co-members of such groups, and even on the causal view your sense-data and mine will be such as are fitted to be co-members of such groups.

The other main relationship which certainly normally holds between a body and the consciousness which is the consciousness of that body, and in the absence of which one would be disinclined so to describe it, even if the first relationship held, may be very roughly indicated as follows. The consciousness must tend to be pleasurable in so far as that body is prospering and unpleasurable in so far as that body is doing badly. But what is it for an organism to prosper or do badly (since it clearly cannot be defined here in terms of the feelings evoked in the consciousness of that organism)? This could only be answered by an analysis of the sense in which biological organisms are teleological systems quite apart from any connection which they may have with thoughts and consciousness. One may say roughly that there are certain types of situation which an organism's movements tend to get it into and keep it in so far as circumstances allow, and certain other types of situation which its movements tend to get, and keep, it out of so far as circumstances allow. The organism is prospering to the extent that it is in situations of the first type and out of situations of the second type and doing badly if the converse is so. Now a consciousness the state of which was painful to the extent that an organism was prospering and pleasurable to the extent that it was doing badly, simply would not be the consciousness of that organism, even if it perceived objects from the point of view of that organism.

A third relationship, connected with this one, which also has some importance is this. If a consciousness is capable of wishful thinking, in the sense explained in an earlier section, then, if it is the consciousness of a certain organism, there will be a tendency for it only to think wishfully that a future situation to do with the movements of that organism is going to occur if it actually is going to occur. One would be a bit uneasy in regarding a consciousness capable of wishful thinking as the consciousness of a certain organism unless this relationship held.

Whether there could conceivably be a consciousness related to an organism by the first relation and not by the other relations is a point we must leave unsettled. Certainly I do not believe that there is such a consciousness, and I do not believe that others believe that there is; moreover if there were (I do not say, if I knew that there were, for nothing which I could experience would make me believe that there were), it would not be what I call the consciousness of that organism, nor, I believe, what others, apart from itself (which unknown to us all would be attaching very strange meanings to our apparently shared vocabulary) would so call.

In a typical case then in which I believe that someone else is in a conscious state of a certain kind I believe that there is a human organism in a certain situation and that there is a consciousness associated with it by these three relations, and perhaps by others we have not mentioned, and that this consciousness includes a state of the kind in question.

It is to be noted that these relations between the consciousness and the physical organism together with its environment are, with the possible exception of the temporal relations, ideal relations. That is, granted that there exists a phase (of a certain sort) of a conscious stream (of a certain sort), and granted that there exists at the same time a physical organism (in a certain situation), it follows from the intrinsic natures of each that the consciousness is the consciousness of that organism. There cannot be real relations between the consciousness and the material objects in question. (At least, if the consciousness contains parts, i.e. sense-data, which are to be considered as parts of the material situation, they are such parts in virtue of their ideal, not their real, relations to other sense-data.) Let us suppose now that the expression 'G' stands for an elaborate complex of intrinsic properties possessable by a stream of consciousness, and that the expression 'F' stands for an elaborate complex of intrinsic properties possessable by an organism together perhaps with some portion of its environment,[1] and that these two sets of properties are such that an

---

[1] Actually on the causal or representative view of our conception of physical objects 'F' cannot really, it would seem, stand for a complex of

organism possessing the one set is fitted to have a consciousness possessing the other as its consciousness and vice versa. The question I want to raise now is this. Suppose I believe that there is an F organism and that there is a G consciousness, does it follow that I believe that there is a consciousness which is the consciousness of that organism, or is it required further that I believe that the relevant ideal relations hold between them? This latter point is something logically implied by the former two ones, but someone might say that it was a logical consequence which had to be specifically believed in its own right. But I think that this is an artificial insistence. To all intents and purposes one must allow that someone who believes in an object of one kind and simultaneously believes in an object of another kind, believes in the holding of all those relations between the two objects which follow from their being of those kinds. I am talking here of what a man can be said to believe, rather than of what he can be said to experience belief in at a given moment, in the fullest sense. If he believes in the existence of the objects of the two kinds then the holding of these relations between them is implicit in what he believes, and he may be said to believe in their holding more or less explicitly according as to the degree to which he takes account of them. It hardly makes sense to talk of his not taking account of them at all.

We have already seen that the nearest one ordinarily comes to experiencing belief in the sort of things one is normally said to believe in, is that one experiences belief in some fragment of the total, while one is in a state of specially high readiness to experience the remaining fragments. Thus in the case of believing that a certain organism is enjoying a certain conscious state, or what is the same thing that a consciousness which is *its* consciousness now contains certain elements, the most that I ever actually experience may only be a fragment of all that we have seen to be involved in this being the case. I may have a fragmentary version of that experience which would be a completely realized belief in the existence of such a material organism and I may have a fragmentary version of belief in the existence of a

intrinsic properties. But it may stand for properties of an organism and its environment which are compatible with there being no consciousness attached to it. If this is so, 'quasi-ideal' should be substituted for 'ideal' later, but the argument is not substantially affected.

certain stream of consciousness now in a phase of a certain kind, such as is fitted to be the consciousness of that organism. My experience will be describable as belief in the objective that this organism is in this conscious state, because there is a certain readiness to produce the remaining elements in the picture so far as occasion may demand.

Let us consider this with respect to a case where I believe regarding someone I am actually looking at that he is in pain. I suggest that a form which this may take is that I have imagery as of sense-data such as I would see if I occupied his position, and these sense-data are imagined as being 'united' with an experience of pain.

As I look at you, then, I may experience imagery resembling the field of sense-data I would experience if looking at the world from your point of view in particular, probably, the visual field. There will be a certain intrinsic character which such a visual field must have which we may call H-ness. There is no new problem for us in describing my belief in the existence of an H visual field, for it is what we have been concerned with in a large part of our previous discussion. But, of course, simply to believe in an H visual field is not to believe in another mind. For often belief in the material world is largely a belief in the existence of such unexperienced visual fields. In order that the H visual field which I believe in be taken as an element in the experience of another mind, it must be supposed to occur as part of a larger totality which includes more specifically mental factors. One such factor is pain. The least we require then, if anything approaching belief in another mind is to be experienced, is that the H-like visual image field which I experience should be part of a larger image totality which I experience which contains pain-like elements which are treated as pains.

This confronts us with some questions. First, we may ask whether and how an image can really be pain-like, and how a pain-like image can be treated as though it actually were a pain. Second, we may ask how we treat certain images which are 'part' of some larger image complex, as though they were experiences which were parts of a consciousness and what the sense or senses of 'part' in question are.

(1) To deal with the first question, we must ask how it is that one may *notice* regarding an experience that it is painful. The

possible specifying properties for painfulness may be quite various. For most of us there are certain words with which we tend to react to pain: 'Ow', 'Oh my God', 'I can't stand this', and so on. More important are such reactions as having experiences of the type one has when rubbing the region to which the pain in some sense belongs, feeling another sort of pain directed at the first pain (the pain of objecting to the first pain) which turns into a feeling of relief immediately the first pain stops, the experience of tears starting to the eyes, and so on. To believe that a feeling of pain exists, as opposed to feeling pain oneself, will (on the imagist-mentalist view) be to react in such ways as this to an image which is pain-like without actually being painful.

This brings us to the question concerning the possibility of an image which is painful-like without actually being painful. Many, I believe, would dismiss this idea as absurd. But I do not think the case is really very different from that of an image which is like a red sense-datum, without being a red sense-datum. An image resembling a red sense-datum certainly is *red* in a permissible sense of the term. Let us italicize 'red' when it is used in this sense. Merely experiencing a *red* image and reacting to it as something *red* would not constitute believing that there exists something *red*. It would constitute noticing that something was *red*. In order to get a case of believing, the image must be treated as having a property which it does not have, e.g., as having the property of being a *red* sense-datum, or simply as having the property of being red (in a sense of 'red' applicable only to sense-data). If then the *red* image is treated as being a *red* datum the whole affair constitutes belief that a red sense-datum exists. The situation with pain, or painfulness, is analogous. There are experiences which can be called feelings of pain, or painful feelings. There are other experiences which are related to these painful feelings much as *red* images are to *red* sense-data. Let us call these experiences image-feelings *of pain*, or *painful* image-feelings. Both feelings and image-feelings may be *painful*, but an image-feeling cannot be a *painful* feeling, and in a more limited sense of the word 'painful' applicable only to feelings, it cannot be called painful. To experience a *painful* image-feeling and to react to it as though to something *painful* would be to notice its *painfulness*, not to believe in the existence of a painful feeling. On the other hand, to experience a *painful* image-feeling and to react to it as though it were a *painful* feeling, as though it were painful, would be to believe that a painful feeling exists.

It is in vain to ask whether the image-feeling is really painful or not. It is really *painful*. As such, it really resembles a *painful* feeling. But there is a sense of 'painful' in which it is not really painful, for there is a sense in which 'being painful' implies 'being a feeling and not an image-feeling'.

There does not seem to me much doubt that I find among my experiences ones which can be regarded as imitation feelings of pain in much the same way as an ordinary visual image can be regarded as an imitation sense-datum. I use the word 'imitation' here just as a stimulus to introspection, not as an explanatory concept. Whatever the relation is between a red image and a red datum I find the same relation between experiences I call image-feelings and experiences I call feelings.

But the question may still be pressed as to how I can treat a *painful* image-feeling as though it were a painful feeling.

There is some difficulty, indeed, in the idea of someone simply having an isolated *painful* image-feeling and responding to it with experiences of a pain-specifying sort. With regard to some such specifying properties the difficulty amounts to a logical impossibility. Confronted with a pain-like image one could direct a saying of 'My God' at it, one could direct a painful feeling (of a kind other than that to which it was akin) at it, but if it had no sort of location, one could not have an experience of the type one has when rubbing *its* region. Perhaps however there might be some feeling, lacking spatial direction, which occurs when one is about to rub, which could be reproduced. Anyway, one could have an experience of the type one has when crying. But even if such a belief which would be merely to the effect that a painful feeling exists, and which does not specify any context for it at all, is one which someone conceivably might experience, this can hardly be regarded as a very usual occurrence.[1] We do not often experience belief in that which is logically *simplest*, even if it is also true that what we actually experience belief in is, if we

---

[1] The attempt to experience such an imagistic belief may show one the important truth that one cannot just experience imagistic beliefs at will. This explains why some people find such a thing as contextless pain logically impossible. But they have not used the right technique for inducing such a conception.

abstract from all consideration of that which we are ready to experience belief in, always logically *simpler* than that which we would ordinarily be said to believe.

Suppose that one experiences an image complex which contains an H-like visual image field and a pain-like image feeling, and which as a whole resembles, or is fitted to resemble, a mind of one experiencing an H visual field, and in pain. The believing person reacts to the H-like visual image field, as though to an H visual field, and he reacts to the pain-like image-feelings as though to painful feelings. Can we now make sense of the idea that this reaction to the pain-like images consists in an experience as of rubbing their region? This depends, of course, on whether in any sense the pain-like image-feelings stand in local relations of any kind to the believer's own sense-fields. It does not seem absurd to allow that they may do so.

Things might be put more exactly if we said that one of the specifying reactions to painful feelings was the experience of applying one's visual hand to that region of one's visual field with which the painful feeling was most closely associated, in a rubbing manner. This reaction can then be transferred to a pain-image provided there is some region of one's visual field with which the pain-image is most closely linked. Now of course when one is in pain the painful feeling is normally most closely linked with a part of one's visual field occupied by a visual datum belonging to one's own body. This does not preclude that a pain-image should be most closely linked with a part of one's visual field not so occupied, but occupied instead, for instance, by a visual datum belonging to someone else's body (we do not say: believed to be so occupied).

Of course, rubbing is just one possible reaction to pain, and in fact only to pain of a certain sort. Still, it does seem possible that some pains are noticed by an experience of rubbing, or possibly by the early stages of rubbing which may not continue always to its usual end. It then becomes possible that a belief that a pain of that kind is occurring may consist in an image-feeling resembling such a pain evoking an experience of rubbing, or at least the initial stages of it, directed at the region most closely associated with the image.

It is not claimed by imagist-mentalism that the specifying properties for a given universal need be the same for all those capable of noticing or believing in the exemplification of that universal. It is not even claimed that the reactions which play this part in a person's life may not alter as time goes on. The response to a universal which serves as the noticing of it can be a conditioned response, for instance, only set up for some people, and it may be set up late in life. So the imagist-mentalist does not have to find some reaction to pain, the transferring of which to pain-images always plays a part in believings about pain. It may differ a great deal from person to person, and from time to time in one person's life.

It is very possible that many of the reactions which play this role, though they have their own intrinsic natures, are only describable in question-begging terms the applicability of which to them is dependent on various relations they stand in to other things. For instance, there may be a special kind of feel which often occurs when someone is about to move his hands in a certain way, and which thereby tends to be described to oneself as an impulse to move one's hands in that way. This feel, however, has its own special quality, call it J-ness, and it may be in J feelings that we should locate the noticing of some property or other.

Noticing reactions to pain most often take the form either of objecting to it or of attempting to relieve it. The expressions 'object' and 'relieve' or 'attempt to relieve' seem to be intentional in character. To object to something, one might say, is to wish *that* it was not there. To relieve something is to act in a manner which one *believes* will remove it. Now it is not false that we react to pain by objecting to it or by attempting to relieve it. On the other hand the experience which is my objecting to a pain or which is the experience of my attempt to remove it will have its own intrinsic character. It may be that a certain kind of experience J tends to occur in response to pain *because* the occurrence of J (or at least its neural correlate) tends to cause the removal of pain, or tends to occur when causes of such removal are afoot. This may supply at least part of the justification for describing these J experiences as attempts to remove pain. Something more complicated of essentially the same sort may be true of such experiences as are describable as cases of objecting to that at which they are directed. But the *because* above occurs in the language of an outsider explaining the situation with the use of some basic principle to some such effect as that if a certain kind of experience, or a certain kind of neural situation, occurring after a pain, or after a neural correlate of pain, has been frequently followed by cessation of the pain, then it will tend to occur more frequently in future after pain.

Experiences of a type which, when directed on to pains, constitute in this way cases of *objecting to* or *attempting to relieve* the pain, may, by being directed on to pain-like images occurring in a certain context, constitute belief in the existence of pains in a certain context.

(2) We have said nothing concerning the way in which the visual field and the pain image are united nor as to how such unity serves to symbolize that the H visual field and the pain, together perhaps with other imagined elements, belong together in one consciousness.

What is required is that the H visual field and the pain-like image-feelings should be elements in a complex similar to a consciousness, and that this complex be responded to by the believer as he would respond to a consciousness. But various difficulties, great and small, seem to cluster around such a requirement.

A preliminary point concerns the other elements, if there are such, in the consciousness-like image complex to which the H-like image field and the pain-like image-field belong.

Even if a human consciousness would always contain more than merely the experience of an H visual field, and a feeling of pain, it might still be possible for an image-complex containing only an H-like visual image field and pain-like image feelings to symbolize a phase of human consciousness. For such a complex might still be pretty like a possible phase of human consciousness, and if it was reacted to in the same way as a phase of consciousness of the relevant kind is reacted to when noticed, it could serve to represent such a phase. On the other hand it is possible that a typical imagistic belief experience in the objective now in question would contain a complex rather more like a phase of human consciousness than this. It might, for instance, contain as well as the H-like image field and the pain-like image-feelings a rather blurred image bearing some resemblance to the mass of bodily feeling, thought, sensation, and what not, which is normally included in a phase of human consciousness. This complex will be well fitted to *resemble*, and to be reacted to as though it *were*, a phase of consciousness including an H visual field and pain.

But two questions stand out. First, must there not be some totalistic quality of this complex in virtue of which it is mind-like. Second, can one ever in fact notice a fact containing the universal, *Being a mind* (or rather *consciousness*), as this account might seem to require that one can?

Turning to the second question first, we may point out that the difficulty really arises because one can hardly allow that an experience of noticing can be directed at itself, or even at a totality of which it is a part. From this it would seem to follow that a phase of human consciousness can never notice its own possession of certain properties, for the noticing itself will be part of that phase of human consciousness and hence part of what it itself is directed at. However, an act of noticing could be directed on to the totality which contained everything at present in consciousness except the noticing, and this totality is a phase of human consciousness. It is not indeed a *total* phase of human consciousness, but it perfectly well could have been. It only fails to be such because of the existence of the act of noticing compresent with it, and there is no need for there to be such an act of noticing. It is as though one said that one could never see the whole group of people in a certain room, if one could only see the people in the room by being in it, and could not see oneself. True, one wouldn't then be able to see the *whole* crowd of people in the room, but one could see a crowd of people in the room, and what is more, such a crowd would be in itself perfectly fitted to be the whole crowd of people in the room. Its incompleteness would not be essential, as is the incompleteness of a man who has lost his legs. Since then one could notice concerning something that it was a phase of consciousness containing an H visual field and painful feelings, by reacting to it in some distinctive way, it makes sense to talk of oneself as reacting to an image complex which is similar to such a mind-phase as though that were what it actually was.

There remains the problem of the kind of unity holding between various elements such as certain sense-fields and pain-feelings in which I am believing when I believe that they compose one consciousness. Even if we are satisfied with talking of some such relation as compresence (which is perhaps just that relation in virtue of which two elements belong to the same specious present) and claim that what we notice is the relation of compresence holding between each of these things and each other there is a problem as to how this relation can really be noticed. For we never come across any two particulars between which it does not hold. There is thus in our experience no contrast between the holding of this relation between two particulars and its not holding. This makes it difficult to see how it can be noticed. Moreover under these circumstances one may ask what the difference would be between a property being a specifying property for this relation, and its simply being a specifying property for two-ness, or several-ness.

A partial explanation may be that the relation of compresence admits of degrees. A property of experience, which varies in its intensity with the degree to which particulars upon which the experiences are directed are in a certain relation, might constitute the noticing of this relation, and of the degree to which it holds. On this criterion an inclination to use the words 'illegitimate abstractions when separated one from another' is, in the probably peculiar case of the present writer, a specifying property for the relation of compresence, for I find myself inclined so to speak of certain pairs of elements in my mind more strongly than of others. Of course there are lots of other properties which may serve to specify this relation as well, both in my own case and in that of others.

It will not therefore be merely compresence holding between various images that makes them as a group resemble a phase of consciousness more than do any images which occur within one specious present, for any two elements in one consciousness are (by definition) compresent to some extent. What is presumably required is a specially high degree of compresence between them which evokes a specifying property for compresence. Moreover it is not any group of very compresent images which resemble a mind-phase; certain ingredients must be included, resembling pain, care, worry, grief, joy, or something of the sort.

The complex of an H-like visual image field, a pain-like image, and vague blurred images, is fitted to resemble a phase of consciousness including an H visual field and a feeling of pain. The experience of such an image-complex, together with a response to it as though it were such a phase of consciousness, constitutes the experience of believing in the existence of such a phase of consciousness.

Certain behaviouristically minded philosophers have raised difficulties as to the very possibility of one's having the notion of another mind or consciousness on mentalistic principles. For, they say, my experience would seem to give me no opportunity for forming a concept of *pain* distinguishable from a concept of *my pain*. In part we have implicitly dealt with this point, but there is more to say on it.

In a much admired passage Wittgenstein says: 'If one has to imagine someone else's pain on the model of one's own, this is none too easy a thing to do: for I have to imagine pain which I *do not feel* on the model of the pain which I *do feel*. That is, what I have to do is not simply to make a transition in imagination from one place of pain to another. As from pain in the hand to pain in the arm. For I am not to imagine that I feel pain in some region of his body. (Which would also be possible)' (*Philosophical Investigations*, §302).

Norman Malcolm, in his discussion of Wittgenstein's *Philosophical Investigations* contained in *The Philosophy of Mind*, edited by V. C. Chappell, explains the point by saying that it is an attack on the idea that I learn what pain is by perceiving my own pain, an idea which is more or less the one I support. The point, says Malcolm, is that 'if I obtain my *conception* of pain from pain that I experience' then 'for me it will be a *contradiction* to speak of *another's* pain'.

My view is that I do indeed obtain my conception of pain from pain that I experience, as I do all my basic empirical concepts from things that I experience. I learn to react to things of a certain *kind* by directing at them a certain word, which word is then my name for that *kind of thing*.[1] I can only react to things which I experience. Suppose, in a somewhat simplified way, that I learn to react to painful sensations by saying 'That is painful' fixing my attention on the sensation by means of the word 'That'. I am thereby noticing a fact, the painfulness of *that*. I am not necessarily noticing a fact very appropriately represented by 'I am in pain' or 'That is my pain'. It will only be appropriate for me to say 'That is my pain'

---

[1] The word 'kind' is an interesting one from the point of view of the theory of universals. Mostly I so use it that a *kind of thing* is a property, a way in which one thing can be like another thing. This is my usage here. In this usage there is a great difference between talking of a thing of a certain kind and talking of a certain kind of thing. Ordinary language is rather confusing here. Naturally we find it easier to say: 'He is the kind of man we need' than 'He is a man of the kind such that we need a man of that kind'. One may note also that 'is a kind of' often names the Platonic relation 'being a determinate of', as in 'A cat is a kind of mammal'.

when I contrast my pain with someone else's pain. But Malcolm and Wittgenstein might ask how a distinction can be drawn between 'That is my pain' and 'That is a pain', since the one can never be called for without the other being called for. Yet if they cannot be distinguished 'There is a pain which is not mine' would indeed seem to be a contradiction.

My answer is that there probably is a use of 'I am in pain' and 'That is my pain' where the personal pronoun is really quite vacuous. One can take it that 'That is my pain' might express the noticing of a fact comprising simply a certain particular and its quality of painfulness and containing nothing corresponding to 'my'. On the other hand, 'That is my pain' may represent a fact more explicitly represented by such a sentence as 'That is a pain and it is compresent with these other experiences'. This latter, we have argued, is a fact of a kind that can be noticed. We can have a specifying property for compresence which is more or less intense according to the degree of compresence. Let us now consider whether I am able to notice such a fact as 'These experiences are *not* compresent with an experience of pain'. This is a case of noticing the presence in something of the negation of a relational property of type three. It does seem that in some cases there is a genuine universal, such as can be noticed, which is the negation of such a relational property. That is, one can sometimes *notice* facts of the form 'x fails to be r to any f'. It seems reasonable to talk of someone noticing the failure on the part of a certain experience to be compresent to anything of a certain kind.

Noticing the negation of a relational property of type three might be accounted for in some such way as follows. To notice a fact of the form 'x is r to y which is an f' will always be a matter of having experiences in response to x and y respectively of certain sorts, say J and K, which are in a certain relation, say S, to one another. Now there may be a Platonic relation N such that for certain series of three universals, consisting in two properties and a relation, there is a property which is N to this series. Perhaps then it may be true of someone in general that he will respond to an experiential particular with an experience which has a property which property is N to certain universals, j, k, and s, if and only if (1) j, k, and s, serve for him as specifiers of a certain objective of the form 'x is r to y which is an f'; (2) the experiential particular in question now fails to be R to any F (where R and F are the values of 'r' and 'f' in the relevant objective under (1)). In these circumstances he may be said to have noticed that the particular is not R to any F.

Let us suppose then that a man notices concerning various experiences that they are not compresent with any pain. This is as much as to say that he notices that *he* is not in pain. And let us suppose that at the same time he experiences a pain-like image-feeling and responds to it as though it were a pain. That is as much as to say that he believes that a pain exists. If we put the pain-image feeling in an appropriate context and supplement the responses to it in an appropriate way, we get the belief that a consciousness of a certain sort contains pain. This combined with the noticing that one is not oneself in pain may reasonably be said to amount to the belief that someone not oneself is in pain.

It was said above that there may be a quite vacuous sense of 'my' in which 'That is my pain' and 'That is a pain' are indistinguishable. This contrasts with such non-vacuous senses as occur where 'That is my pain' means 'That is a pain and is compresent with these experiences' or 'That is a pain and is compresent with these experiences which are views of the world from such and such a point of view' or something else of approximately this sort. If 'my' is used in this vacuous sense there is no harm in saying that when I believe in the existence of pain in compresence with a view of the world from your point of view I am believing in the existence of my pain in such a context. But this is perfectly compatible with the fact that the consciousness which contains the belief that my pain is going on in that context does not itself include the portion of 'my' pain believed in, that is the belief-experience is not compresent with any such pain as it is a belief in. In this vacuous sense of 'my' it may be true that in believing in other people's experiences I am believing in the existence of experiences which are my experiences in all sorts of contexts not compresent with my (in a less vacuous sense of 'my') belief experience in them. It may even be that there is a peculiar sense of 'my', appealed to in certain mystical Hindu sayings, which is not completely vacuous but which stands for a special 'first-personal' quality of being ranged round a centre, in which every *mental* event may be presumed to have a quality of my-ness. Thus when in one consciousness there exists a belief in the occurrence of pain in another consciousness it may be a belief in the occurrence in that other consciousness of pain with a quality of my-ness. But both the vacuous and this rather mystical sense of 'my' and of other first-personal pronoun words are to be distinguished from the use of personal pronouns in such utterances as 'His consciousness contains pain and mine does not'. In this sense 'His' will be subjectively equivalent[1] for the speaker to something like 'The consciousness which contains a view of the world of that kind or from that place' and 'My consciousness' will be subjectively equivalent to something like 'The total set of experiences compresent with these experiences'. Where the expressions are understood in this way there is no difficulty for the imagist-mentalist in describing the difference between the states of mind involved in assent to 'His consciousness includes pain' and 'My consciousness includes pain'.

It may be suggested that what we have indicated is the possibility of a state of mind in which one experiences the belief that the consciousness answering to a certain description includes pain and at the same time notices the absence of pain from one's own consciousness, but that this still does not give us the experience of believing that a consciousness other than my own contains pain. For this what is required, it may be said, is the belief that there is a feeling of pain in a consciousness of a certain sort, which feeling of pain is not compresent with these experiences. It is hard to say whether the extra ingredient said to be required in order that a belief in a pain not my own should be experienced, really is required. But there is no great difficulty in supposing that belief in this extra ingredient might be experienced. For if I have a specifying property for compresence, I can respond to two experiences with an experience which has a negatively modified version of the specifying property. This will be to treat them as not being compresent. In fact of course they will be compresent, but they are treated as though they were not. There may even be an actual relationship between the image complex which symbolizes another mind and other experiences in my mind which has a certain suitability for symbolizing non-compresence. A certain sort of wholeness may belong to the collection of images, such as belongs to all the contents of my consciousness taken together, but such as does not belong to the collection of that collection of images and the experiences (not the totality of all my present experiences),

[1] See p. 149.

which are treated as not being compresent with it. That is a certain sub-group of the contents of my consciousness may be unlike various other such subgroups in having a unity akin to that belonging to the group of all my experiences.

We may sum up what the imagist-mentalist says about believing in the existence of other minds as follows. In most typical cases the belief that the consciousness of another person is in a certain state consists in the belief that there is a phase of consciousness which contains a vision of the world from a certain point of view, the point of view occupied by the body of that person, that it is a phase of a stream of consciousness which has followed the fortunes of that body both in the sense that its sense-data have signified the varying relations of that body with other things and in the sense that it has been joyous or sad according as to whether that body has prospered or otherwise, and finally in the belief that this present phase contains certain specified features. In all this there is nothing which could not be symbolized by imagery fitted to resemble such a state of affairs. In fact, however, it is only in a few elements of this whole that belief is ever likely actually to be experienced. Most typically, probably, it will take the form of an image complex fitted to resemble the present phase of consciousness in question in respect of the sense-data and feelings it contains, which is treated as though it were a phase of consciousness of that sort.

Two further comments on this seem called for. First, there is no difficulty in allowing for belief in streams of consciousness which in certain or all of their phases are not in this sort of connection with a body. One could believe in the existence of a phase of consciousness containing elements of a certain kind, without regarding any of these elements as visions of a physical world. In particular, a Berkeleyan world of spirits is not logically incoherent, however incredible. My belief in another person might be a belief in the existence of a consciousness containing perspectival variants of the sense-data I am now experiencing without my taking either his sense-data or mine as appearances of an actually existing physical world.

The second comment is this. It would seem to follow from imagist-mentalism that, if I really experience belief in the existence of painful feelings in your consciousness, I must have an attitude to those supposed feelings not altogether different from what I have to painful feelings of my own. Someone who always tries to relieve his own pain, and whose way of noticing pain consists in experiencing incipient relief activities will be bound to experience incipient relief activities when he believes in another's pain. Otherwise he would not be treating the image-feelings which symbolize that other's pain as pain. It would seem to follow that, unless he is hallucinated, relief activities really will be incipient in him on those occasions. Now doesn't this go against the obvious fact that people can believe that others are suffering and not feel inclined to do anything about it?

One may remark first that many people who might be said to know that other people are suffering really do not bring home to themselves, do not really experience belief, in that suffering. If they really realized in consciousness what was going on in that other person's consciousness it may well be that they would not be indifferent. In the second place there may be various different experiential responses which serve a given individual in the noticing of pain and only some of these may be carried over to belief in the existence of pain in other consciousnesses. In the third place, one's attitude even to one's own suffering is not as simple as all that, as the phenomenon of masochism makes especially obvious. Therefore if someone delights in another's suffering this may well in fact repeat something to be found in his attitude to his own suffering. It seems reasonable to say that I am not really taking a feeling-image as a symbol of another's pain, unless I respond to that image in a way derived from my response to my own pain. In itself it is just a certain mental event with its own character. If it symbolizes an occurrence of another (even if a similar) type, that must be because it is treated as though it were of that other type. On the whole it seems to me that the basis of ethics must be sought in our ability to form images of the feelings of others, that is to treat certain images which belong to certain image complexes in our own minds, as though they are mental events of certain other but similar kinds occurring in contexts similar to but different from the context provided by that image complex.

XIII

MERITS AND DEMERITS
OF IMAGISM

We have now surveyed in outline the main features of a theory of
believing which we have called imagist-mentalism. We have
neither accepted nor rejected it. If we are now to turn to a more
decisive summing up of its merits and demerits it is important
that we keep in mind the nature of the claim which the theory
makes for itself. It does not propose an analysis of the exact
meaning of sentences in ordinary language containing the word
'believe', though it may not be without implications for such an
analysis. Rather it sets out to analyse a concept for which there is
no one ideal word in ordinary language. The concept in question
is that of believing something to be the case, where this refers to an
event in consciousness which takes place at a certain time. It
could be described as an act of consciously assenting to a proposition, if it were not that this way of putting it has an unduly
linguistic air. We have chosen for the most part to call it the
experience of believing something. But perhaps it would in some
respects be more natural to talk of it as thinking at some particular
moment that something is the case, where the thinking in question
is something fully conscious, and not simply some bodily reaction.
Our choice of terminology has already been explained at greater
length.

Is the imagist-mentalist analysis of this concept successful?

It does seem to me that it describes something which sometimes
takes place in my own case, and in that of others, and that this
something is at least one of the main forms which the experience

of believing something may take. My only doubt is as to whether there may not be other sorts of experience which should also count as experiences of believing something.

In our discussion of imagist-activism we considered the possibility that an activist might drop the image element in the situation altogether without trying to replace it by anything else at all, and might identify believing entirely with behaving as one would if experiencing the thing believed in. Such a theory was seen to amount to a turning of one's back upon the notion of a belief experience altogether. We moved on, therefore, to a second alternative theory which we called *substitute-activism* where the image element was not just dropped, but was replaced by the more general notion of experience of a substitute object, whether that substitute object resemble that which it substitutes for or not.

Might not a mentalist present a similar critique of imagist-mentalism and say that what is important in believing in the existence of a situation of a certain kind is that one feels the way one would, or has other experiences such as one would have, if a situation of the kind being believed in were being experienced? If no object is introduced to play the role of the image we have a theory similar to the first theory above which might be called just-as-though mentalism. If however he says rather that believing is reacting to *some object* given in experience, as though it were an object of some other kind, for which other kind of object it thus acts as a substitute, he would be advancing a theory similar to substitute-activism which might be called substitute-mentalism. The substitute-mentalist would allow the belief experiences described by the imagist-mentalist as one type of belief experience, but would regard the similarity holding in such cases between substitute and original as inessential to full believing.

The difference between the imagist-mentalist, the substitute-mentalist, and the just-as-though-mentalist is not very sharp, for each may admit the occurrence of experiences answering to the descriptions which feature in the theories of the others, and may admit that they can reasonably be described as belief experiences. All that divides them is the imagist-mentalist's claim that image belief experiences are in some way more full and satisfactory than the others, and the substitute-mentalist's similar claim regarding his more inclusive class of favoured belief experiences.

On this point I support the imagist-mentalist. It does seem

proper to say that someone whose feelings are in response to images which actually resemble some absent situation, which, if it had been present would have evoked such feelings, is believing in the absent situation in a more complete manner than one who has those feelings in response to something not at all similar to the absent situation, or not in response, properly speaking, to anything at all.

The most familiar type of belief experience which is not imagistic is doubtless that which consists in the 'imaging' or uttering of certain words. (It has already been explained in Chapter X that to think in word images is in an important sense not to think in images.) Thus the main advantage which the other two mentalisms, especially substitute-mentalism, may be thought to have over imagist-mentalism will probably lie in their capacity for dealing with word believing.

The imagist-mentalist says that the image fact symbolizes the fact intended (if there is such a fact) both because of its similarity to it and because it evokes the same experiential reactions as such a fact would have evoked if experienced. The substitute-mentalist holds that the symbolizing fact need not contain universals similar to those in the symbolized fact, and it is enough if it produces the reactions which a fact such as the symbolized fact would have done. In particular, the universals figuring in the symbolizing fact may be word types, which will, in most cases, be quite unlike any universal figuring in the fact symbolized.

Does the substitute-mentalist need to put any limitation upon the kind of fact which could serve to symbolize some other kind of fact? Is there some ideal relation which must hold between symbolizing fact and symbolized fact, as, according to all variants of imagism there must be the ideal relation of resemblance of a certain sort? May not some restriction be implied in the demand that the symbolizing fact be obliquely noticed by an experience of a kind which would have served for the noticing of the symbolized fact? Does not this mean that the symbolizing fact and the symbolized fact must share whatever is required (for instance, *structure* at the least) in any fact which is susceptible of being responded to by an experience of that kind?

The substitute-mentalist will claim that just as one may feel about the quality of certain images one is experiencing what one would feel about the similar quality of certain data if one had been experiencing them, and that this constitutes one's believing in the existence of data of the latter quality, so one may feel about the verbal quality of certain experiential particulars presented to one, as one would feel about the quite dissimilar quality of certain data if one had been experiencing them, and this likewise constitutes believing in the existence of data of the latter quality.

Words played quite a part in our illustrations of imagist-mentalist type belief-experiences. Word-universals came in, however, not as components of the symbolizing fact but as the specification universals which might be turned on images in place of the data believed in. Some readers (probably substitute-mentalists in effect) may have felt that once words were brought in, the image fact exhibited itself as merely an irrelevant side-effect of the understanding use of words, which might have been altogether absent, without any lessening of the fullness of the belief experience.

On the face of it there seem to be two different functions which the substitute-mentalist would allow words as capable of fulfilling in belief experiences. On the one hand he would allow that they could play the role allowed them by the imagist-mentalist, as the specification experiences which transform images resembling certain kinds of data into actual symbols of data of those kinds. On the other hand they can replace images and be themselves symbols, obliquely specified in their turn by some further specification experience.

It seems that the substitute-mentalist should be able to distinguish these two different roles even when words occur without images in both cases. They might sometimes be the specifying properties for facts of certain kinds occurring in the absence of such facts or of any symbols for such facts, and constituting therefore beliefs of the just-as-though-mentalist type (which the substitute-mentalist allows as an inferior sort of belief experience), and at other times they might be symbols themselves obliquely specified by further experiences directed on to them. But this distinction would usually be somewhat artificial. If I respond to the verbal description of an event with feelings such as I would have done to the event itself, the verbal data I am experiencing are being treated as though they were the event itself, and thus symbolize that event, but it may also be true that those verbal data are experiences of a kind with which I would have reacted to the event itself, and in doing so have been noticing its character, in which case my experience of them *in vacuo* can be regarded as the occurrence of a specifying property for a certain kind of event without anything being specified thereby either directly or obliquely, so that they can be regarded as a sort of inferior belief experience from the point of view of substitute-mentalism. The substitute-mentalist should be content to say that some verbal experiences may be better seen in one way, and some in the other way, without insisting on an absolute distinction between the two.

The main point of substitute-mentalism is that words are taken as capable of substituting for things just as well as are images. The theory does, however, point to the following differences between words and images. The image fact is a substitute for the fact believed in, and not a fact of a kind which could have played any part in the noticing of the fact believed in, while the verbal fact as well as being a substitute for the fact believed in, is a fact of a kind which might have served in the noticing of the fact believed in. The words have their symbolic function in virtue of association with the sort of thing believed in. The images do not have their reference in virtue of this, but rather in virtue of their likeness to the sort of thing believed in. Note that their referring as they do does not consist in their having this likeness – it consists in their being reacted to in the same way. But that they are reacted to in the same way arises from their likeness to, not from their having been associated via social conditioning, or any other such thing, with experience of, the facts in question.

2 LINGUISTIC MEANING AS CONCEIVED BY IMAGIST-MENTALISM AND SUBSTITUTE-MENTALISM RESPECTIVELY

Before we can really decide what is at issue between imagist-mentalism and substitute-mentalism we must try to be clearer as to how the imagist-mentalist views language.

Imagist theories of believing or thinking have often involved the view that real thinking is image thinking and that the use of language is solely for communication of what, once communicated, is thought of by both parties in images. Or, if it has been allowed that much private thinking goes on in words, it has been held that the significance of this inner verbal monologue lies solely in its being a sign that the thinker is ready, if need be, to form certain image thoughts. Or, perhaps more subtly, it has been thought of as an in some sense meaningless device by which the image thinker can pass from one reasonable image belief to another.

The imagist-mentalist need say no such thing. He can admit that linguistic activity is a way of responding to and acting on the world, the explanation of which has nothing particularly to do with imagery. He does urge, however, that as long as one is thinking solely in words without experiencing image beliefs one is, in an important sense, not bringing into full conscious realization the nature of what it is one is believing in, or thinking of.[1]

We have identified the pragmatic meaning of an utterance with what the linguistic habits of the group of the individual allowed one to infer from it regarding his propositional attitudes, e.g. his beliefs.

The sense of 'believe' in question here is a dispositional one, not the occurrent experience of believing which imagist-mentalism has analysed. The imagist-mentalist does not so much tell us what it is to believe something, as say: 'Granted that a man does believe something, I will tell you what it is for that belief to become fully conscious, which normally it is not.'

The imagist-mentalist might say that there are various different senses of 'believe', in a dispositional sense, possible, and that they yield different senses of pragmatic meaning. Perhaps he will emphasize the importance of a sense of 'believe' in which one will believe something if and only if there is in one a certain readiness to experience belief in that something in the full imagistic sense. To know the meaning of a fact-stating utterance in the sense of meaning associated with this sense of 'belief' will be to be able to infer from the occurrence of that utterance and the general linguistic habits of the speaker or his group, all that can be inferred therefrom about the belief experiences, which the speaker is ready to have if appropriate circu⸻ ⸳⸳⸳ances occur. If there is someone in whom there is no readiness for such belief experiences at all, then in that sense of pragmatic meaning his utterances will have no meaning at all. But they may still have pragmatic meaning, in

---

[1] The following point should, however, be borne in mind in this connection. An enormous amount of human solitary thinking (the evidence for this is of various kinds) consists in mulling over past or projected conversations in which one is a participant, and of hypothesizing about the conversations in which one has not taken part. Where this consists in experiencing word images and treating them as symbols of conversations in which those words occur, one will have a sort of thinking which answers to the fullest demands made by an imagist-mentalist of a belief experience.

senses of pragmatic meaning associated with purely behaviouristic senses of 'believe'. Differences between philosophers about the meaning of various utterances may turn in part upon the tacit appeal to different senses of 'believe'. Certainly if one starts out with a behaviourist sense of 'believe', one may have difficulty in the idea of sentences about minds having any but a behaviouristic meaning. If what someone believes is made rather a matter of what he is ready under certain circumstances to envisage to be the case, one is liable to say something quite different about the meaning of these utterances.

With much of this the substitute-mentalist will be in agreement. He will accept that there is an important sense of 'believe' in which what someone believes is a matter of the belief experiences someone is liable, under appropriate circumstances, to live through, and that there is an important sense of 'pragmatic meaning' associated with this. But he takes a broader view of what constitutes a belief experience.

According to the substitute-mentalist, the utterance of a sentence may be related to belief in a certain situation in two quite different ways. It may simply be a sign of a readiness for experiencing belief in that situation, or it may actually constitute the experience of belief in that situation. It might even be a sign of a readiness for believing in a situation of one kind, and be a believing in a situation of another kind. It is especially likely, perhaps that if it is the believing in a situation of one kind, it will be a sign of a readiness for believing in a whole complex of situations of which the situation it actually is a believing in, is just one. The meaning of the utterance is a matter of the belief experiences it is a sign of the readiness for, not a matter of the belief experience it may actually be. There need be no assumption that most fact stating utterances are belief experiences at all.

If utterance of a sentence constitutes an act of believing in a certain objective (that is, if the sentence as then occurring is fitted to symbolize a fact exemplifying that objective), the sentence, in that utterance of it, may be said to *embody* belief in that objective. The objective, belief in which is embodied by a sentence, will not normally be the same objective as that signified by the sentence. For instance, a material object sentence, one which makes a certain claim about physical objects, might embody a belief in the existence of a certain sense-datum, that is, it might be responded to just as though it were such a sense-datum, and yet the utterance of that sentence be a sign of readiness for having belief experiences in some much more complicated objective which (or in any of a set of objectives the conjunction of which) would be the objective signified. If we take someone for whom the material object sentence can best be said to signify some complex objective about unsensed sense-data then the objective, belief in which is embodied in that sentence, will be an element in the objective signified, but if we take someone whose more carefully meditated belief experiences about the material world are of the type discussed in Chapter XII, section 3, then it may be that we should say that the objective signified by the sentence does not include the objective, belief in which is embodied, as an element. To say this is to take it that the objective signified by a sentence is that which one can take it as a sign the speaker would experience belief in if he was taking maximum care to think cogently and realistically.

3 FINAL ADJUDICATION BETWEEN IMAGIST-MENTALISM AND SUBSTITUTE-MENTALISM

Substitute-mentalism agrees with imagist-mentalism that in order to believe in an absent situation I must experience something which works on my feelings, or otherwise affects my experience, in the same way as would experience of the absent situation. But it claims that there is no need for the substitute situation which is experienced to resemble the absent situation. Actually we saw that in some cases imagist-mentalism was forced to move in this direction itself, and that the resemblance might become more and more attenuated. The difference between the two theories is really one of degree of emphasis, coming perhaps in the end to this, that imagist-mentalism wants to say that in some sense the belief experience is more full and satisfactory the closer the resemblance is.

The imagist-mentalist might defend this judgment (which is partially a value judgment) as follows.

When I experience belief in a certain situation I experience some situation other than the situation believed in but treat it as though it were a situation of the kind believed in. Now the whole experience of experiencing the substitute situation, and reacting to it in the relevant way, can be regarded as a substitute for experiencing the actual situation and reacting to it in the relevant way. But presumably the more alike one thing is to another the better substitute it makes for it. Now surely the more alike the substitute situation is to the actual situation then the more the whole experience to which it belongs is like the whole situation for which it substitutes, and thus the more perfect an example of the phenomenon of believing it is. And of course this is going to be so to a greater extent if the substitute situation is an image rather than (say) a sentence.

Moreover there is also this to be said. We have pointed out periodically that there may be for a given person more than one type of experiential response which serves him for the noticing of a given universal. When he experiences belief in the existence of some instance of that universal there may occur just one of the noticing responses for that universal, or there may occur more than one. The more of them there are present, the more complete the belief experience, for the more one is responding as though one actually were experiencing an instance of that universal. Now it seems likely that some of the responses which serve for noticing that a thing is an instance of a certain universal can only be directed on to something which is an instance of a pretty similar universal, while there may be other responses which can be transferred to instances of pretty unlike universals. Clearly so long as the substitute situation in a belief experience is a linguistic item rather than an image, the obliquely noticing responses will all be of the latter type. But if the substitute situation is an image not only will those responses be possible, but so will those of the other type. Thus something which we can recognize as a more complete type of belief is possible where the substitute situation is an image.

In accepting this we are not denying that up to a point verbal experiences can actually be belief experiences. We are only saying that an image experience is capable of being a more completely realized belief experience. Someone who did not have images would never live through belief in its most complete form, and would miss indeed *one* of the main things which language can do for us, which is to conjure up in our minds images of absent situations.

These considerations are especially important where what is believed is something about the experiences which some person has undergone, is undergoing, or will undergo.

If I read an autobiography I may for much of the time simply be the recipient of information which is stored up for possible use in the future. There may be virtually no bringing home to myself in consciousness of the character of what I am learning. My conscious state may be that of following what is being told, and no more. In the experience of following what is being told, I experience the words with a special sort of acquiescence which is the pathetically impoverished sign in consciousness that my brain is storing some rich stock of information. As far as this particular phase of consciousness goes its character contains little that corresponds to the character of the information, except for some very abstract structural relations between the sensible character of the verbal images or data I am experiencing and the information they convey. Otherwise there is just the somewhat characterless feeling of acquiescence, jolted occasionally into a more troubled feeling if the grammatical structure or the vocabulary of what I am reading faces the brain with some difficulty in 'digestion' of the signals it is receiving. Certainly the rhythm of the events in my consciousness may reflect the grammatical rhythms, and even the 'meaning rhythms', of the text, but exactly the same conscious states might have gone with the perusal of a text having quite different specific meanings. This sort of thing would be admitted by many philosophers who without being complete behaviourists have minimized the importance of consciousness and have emphasized that the meaning of what someone says, or the meaning he attaches to what he hears or reads, is not a matter of concurrent, or they would say of later, events in consciousness, but of the behavioural dispositions produced. Consciousness, such philosophers say, exists but is without importance, meaning perhaps by consciousness to refer not so much to the experience of sense-data, but inner feelings and images which cannot count as perceptions in a straightforward sense of outer things. One would be inclined to agree with them if consciousness was always as impoverished as this, and one may agree that consciousness actually is as a rule much more impoverished than it has often been represented as being in philosophy and psychology of the past. But surely consciousness can do better than this, the meanings absorbed so drearily can leap into vivid consciousness, the brain may be an instrument making sweet and complex music rather than a machine with a single toned hum?

Yes, something more than this dull feeling of acquiescence may occur in consciousness as I read. The words may be responded to by an immense array of subtly varying feelings, such as prose can only put under such general headings as 'indignation', 'fear', 'sadness', 'excitement', 'disgust'. The experience of uttering (outwardly or inwardly) the words takes on all sorts of emotional tones, and evokes other experiences with further emotional tones. So far there need be no imagery. The words are reacted to as though they were the experiences they describe, or a large element of them, thus embodying belief in the whole or in part of the objectives they signify. One reads: 'I saw a dark figure crouching in the doorway'. One may experience no visual image like the visual sensation the autobiographer experienced, but one reacts to the words as though they were a certain type of visual sensation, occurring in a certain context which has been set by what preceded. Perhaps one feels a shudder of fear. This stage comes much nearer to real consciousness of the situations described. But having allowed that we have here a much greater entry of what has been described into consciousness, can one deny that one has a much greater entry still, indeed the maximum entry conceivable, if imagery resembling the situation described is evoked, and if the feelings are in response to these images rather than to the words? But this is precisely what the imagist-mentalist calls a real belief experience.

An interesting situation arises where what is described are the emotions of the autobiographer. Here one needs to distinguish between onlooker emotions and the emotions described. For one to believe in the existence of the emotions described, it would not be enough merely that I should have emotion-images like them. My feelings in response to these emotion-images must be such as I have to such emotions in myself when I come across them and this may diverge – though of course it doesn't have to – from the emotions the autobiographer has in response to these emotions. For instance I may be shocked by emotions which he is not shocked by. Moreover, where the words themselves serve as the symbols in the belief experiences I have while reading, I may be shocked by the words themselves rather than by an image of the emotion described.

It is books written with a certain vividness or at least a fair amount of concrete detail which most readily evoke genuine belief experiences in the reading of them. But there is some sense in which I could not be said to understand any book at all of a fact stating kind, if my acceptance of what it said did not produce some sort of tendency for envisaging certain supposed absent situations in the way described by imagist-mentalism. Or perhaps if the reading of a book produced an adjustment in my behavioural dispositions of a sort which would be helpful biologically if P is so, and unhelpful if P is not so, I, considered simply as a physical organism, might be said to have understood and accepted the contents of the book, namely P. But I, considered as an individual consciousness, would not have understood it, unless there was some tendency for P to be exhibited in imagery and treated as a reality in the manner described by the imagist-mentalist.

One may also say that an English man who reads about a famine in India may have the words to some extent embody a belief in the occurrence of hunger pangs in certain contexts, for he may react to the words with feelings of sympathy – but it is not such a completely realized belief as that which occurs if he actually imagines the hunger pangs or the scenes of misery which supply their context. Moreover if he does not really know what hunger pangs are like in the sense that he cannot really approach the imagination of them, then there does seem a sense in which he cannot really believe in their existence. He can only believe that certain visually conceived scenes which of themselves perhaps have a certain tendency to evoke pity, are connected with what he conceives of in a general way simply as unpleasant sensations. This feeling, that one can only in the full sense believe in the existence of something if one knows what it is like, seems to rest upon the idea that belief in the fullest sense demands a reproduction in imagination of the thing believed in.

We are now in a position to sum up our conclusions on the question whether one cannot say that verbal experiences are just as capable of functioning as real acts of belief as are image experiences. We have found that a verbal experience certainly can function to some extent as a real act of belief. On the other hand, image experiences, at their most complete, are more complete acts of belief than a verbal experience can be. A being who used words as we do, but had no imagery, would lack the capacity for a type of experience which it is one of the chief values of words to provide. In an important sense of the words he would never really *know* what was being talked about. One could say much the same about such belief experiences as may appear to consist in specification experiences without symbolizing imagery or words. The specification experiences would be feelings in the dark which lacked all knowledge of their object. Our support goes, therefore, to a modest form of imagist-mentalism.

4 DIFFERENT SENSES OF 'BELIEF' CONSIDERED AS A DISPOSITION

It is not an aim of this book to supply any account of the different senses of 'belief' taken as referring to a disposition. Its concern is to identify what we call conscious acts of believing and to say something about their nature, and this does not presuppose a theory of believing as a disposition. It would be unsatisfactory, though, if nothing were said about the more usual sense of 'belief' as referring to a disposition.[1]

We have indicated that there may be a behaviouristic sense of 'belief' according to which to say that an organism believes something is to say that it acts as though it were in the presence of that thing, or rather, it has a disposition to act as though it were. The difficulties of such a view in dealing with belief in the past and future need not now concern us. Perhaps it could speak of the organism as behaving as though it had been in contact with things when it was said to believe things about the past, and as though it were going to be in contact with them when it is said to believe things about the future. On the face of it this implies that its beliefs regarding its own past and future are always correct. But in spite of difficulties we may suppose that some theory satisfactory in its own terms is constructible along these lines. Behaviourist accounts of belief of quite different types are also possible, but we shall take it here that a purely behaviourist account of belief is going to follow some such lines as those here indicated. (Cf. Chapter XII, section 3.)

What the imagist-mentalist might propose is this. In one

---

[1] Another common sense of 'belief' may be said to be one in which it is equivalent to 'proposition' or 'objective'. If so, it needs no especial comment. But note that in such statements as *The belief in a future life* is on the wane' or even *The belief that there is a future life* is on the wane' the subject expression can better be taken as representing believing in or that, etc., considered as a dispositional property than as representing a proposition or objective.

important sense, whether someone believes that something is the case is to be answered simply by reference to his behavioural dispositions as indicated on this behaviourist analysis. But of someone who believes something in this sense one may ask whether his belief ever becomes conscious. That is, is it ever true of him that he experiences an image belief, or, failing that, at least a belief of the substitute-mentalist kind, in the situation to which his behaviour is adjusted? He might add that only if this had at some time happened, or was liable to happen again, could he be said to have this belief in a fully conscious way. It would be appropriate to add that this was only one sense of the phrase 'in a fully conscious way', in which it marked an important point, but that there might also be other reasonable uses, perhaps even purely behaviourist ones!

There is a point in this connection, already made, which is of considerable importance, namely that certain sorts of questions about what people believe can only be pressed to the extent that they believe things in this fully conscious way. If one asks how people ordinarily conceive of material objects, what they really believe when they make material object statements, then if one takes belief in a purely behaviourist sense, one cannot really distinguish this question from a question regarding the true nature of the material object situations to which people are adjusting themselves more or less successfully. If one does want to distinguish the questions, it must be because one supposes that people hold these beliefs in a fully conscious way, and one's queries concern the character of the objectives on to which their belief experiences are directed. If in fact for the most part people believe precious little in a fully conscious way, it is no wonder that attempts to answer this question are hard to judge for success. What one is doing, perhaps, is asking what they would believe in a fully conscious way if prompted to do so, and it may be that the answer differs considerably from person to person. As a matter of fact whether someone can actually be said to be having a belief experience in something would seem to be a matter of degree, so that while it might be absurd to say of someone that his beliefs about material objects never rose to consciousness, the consciousness might normally be so slight that it would not be directed onto one of the possible objectives much more determinately than on to another. At any rate the purely behaviourist sense of believing will give a sense to saying that someone believes that there is a dog in the garden as opposed to a cat, but not to saying that someone believes in a dog as consisting in a set of actual but largely unexperienced sense-data rather than that he believes it as consisting in some cause of certain sense-data knowable only as such a cause.

We have then two very roughly indicated senses of 'belief' taken as referring to a disposition. First we have the purely behaviourist sense in which to believe in the existence of something is to be ready to adjust one's behaviour as though one were actually in causal interaction with such a thing. In perception, physically considered, signals reach the brain, which signals are the result of a process originating in the presence of certain objects in the environment, to which objects useful behavioural adjustments then occur, useful in the sense that they aid preservation of the organism. Belief can then be conceived as a process whereby some internal substitute for stimuli which prompt such signals is ready to occur and to modify behaviour in the same way that such signals would have done, in a manner which will be useful if there are objects of a certain kind in much more remote areas of the environment, and not otherwise. The organism is then said to believe in such objects. What is talked of here as an internal substitute is internal in a simple physical sense.

Belief of this behaviourist kind may however be associated with a readiness for experience of belief in the existence of things of a certain kind. Presuming that in some way or other the objects in which belief is experienced occupy, in the environment they are believed to occur in, a place corresponding to that which *the actual objects* behaviouristically believed in occupy in their environment, one may say that the objects in which belief is experienced are *the actual objects*, as conceived by that consciousness, perhaps quite correctly conceived so far as the conception goes. When this association exists[1] one may say that there is a fully conscious belief (dispositionally speaking) in the existence of the objects concerned, whether conceived more or less adequately.

---

[1] Actually more than association with a mere readiness for such a belief experience is required if the dispositional belief is to be described as conscious; such a conscious belief experience, or at least the adumbration of one, must have actually taken place, though thereafter only a readiness is required.

But might there not be a disposition to have belief experiences in something without there being any behaviouristically analysable belief in that something, and, if so, would not there be a dispositional belief of a nonbehaviouristic kind in that something? Or even without assuming that they might exist independently, might there not be a purely mentalist conception of belief as a disposition, lacking the behavioural component which we have associated with it above?

To say that a man had a non-behavioural dispositional belief of an imagist-mentalist kind would perhaps be to say that there was some sort of potentiality within him throughout the period he was said to have the belief, for imagery of a kind resembling the kind of situation believed in, and for reacting to such imagery as though it actually were a situation of the kind believed in.

This potentiality can hardly consist merely in the fact that there are *some* circumstances under which he would experience belief (in the imagist-mentalist sense) in the kind of situation in question or in its elements, for this would be true of many people who could not be talked of as having the belief. There are presumably some possible circumstances under which I would experience belief in the existence of the Loch Ness Monster, but that does not make it appropriate to say that dispositionally I believe in its existence, especially as it is equally true that under some possible circumstances, I would experience belief in the monsterlessness of Loch Ness.

Perhaps the most hopeful course would be to say that someone has a dispositional belief (of the mentalist kind) in something, if and only if it is true of him now that there are numerous trains of thought which if they were actualized in him without his having the opportunity to collect more evidence on the matter would lead him, if carried on at sufficient length, to experience belief in the something in question.

Suppose for instance that I am said to believe that Mr Y had angry feelings on a certain occasion. My having this belief might involve my having some belief of the more basic sort, 'Angry feelings occurred in a mind having such and such visual sense-data'.

To say that I believe this in the imagist-mentalist dispositional sense is to say that if I meditate at length on certain themes, most obviously upon the question of the kind of man Mr Y is, and of his relations with other people, my meditations will eventually involve my having imagery of a mind-state comprising angry feelings and visual data of a certain kind (the kind he could be expected to have had on that occasion).

Perhaps we may generalize from this case and say that for a man to believe that P in the present sense of 'believe' is for it to be true of him that if he meditates at length on that part of reality in which P will occur if it does occur, he will at some stage experience an imagistic belief that P.

To this the following objection may be raised. Surely a period of meditation may give rise to beliefs which were not held at the beginning, as the process merely of being questioned in a certain manner led Meno's slave to form fresh beliefs, fresh at least, as even Socrates or Plato would admit, in this life. Meditation may surely lead to belief for the first time in certain contingent propositions as well as necessary ones.

This objection will be quite final if we understand a period of meditation as possibly including observation of various facts which supply evidence for or against there being a fact of the kind believed in. We must take it then that 'X believes that P' implies not just 'A sufficient length of meditation on that part of reality in which P occurs, if it exists, will lead to X experiencing belief in P in the full imagistic way', but also implies it when 'which does not include the observation of any facts supplying evidence in favour of P' is inserted after meditation.

It is, however, pretty unclear what this qualification excludes. It is tempting to remove all ambiguities by saying that the period of meditation must include no observation of facts at all, or at least no observation of new facts. But this would be quite unhelpful, at least if observation of new facts is equated with experience of new facts. Any period of meditation involves the experience of new facts, for all experience is of new facts, and meditation is presumably a form of experience. An alternative interpretation of 'observation' would make it equivalent to noticing, and it would seem indeed that there can be tracts of experience, possibly even of meditation, which do not involve the noticing of any facts. But then it seems that mere experience of facts, as opposed to observation of them, may sometimes produce what we could call beliefs rather than the bringing to consciousness of beliefs already held.

Perhaps we must use the old distinction between experience of internal facts and of external sense-datum facts. Then we can say that the period of meditation must not include the experience of any external facts such that experience of them plays an essential part in producing the experience of believing in P.

But surely such a period of meditation may produce new beliefs, as opposed merely to bringing old ones to consciousness.

It may be that we are making the matter more difficult than it may be by a failure to note the following possibility. Is it not plausible to suggest that in order that someone be said to believe in P in the imagist-mentalist, though dispositional, sense of 'believe' now in question, he must already have had at some stage the experience of believing in P, so that belief in P is a matter of having experienced something approaching belief in P in the past and being ready to experience it again after a suitable phase of meditation?[1]

We might need, however, to add the requirement that the various objectives in which we have experienced belief during the period in which we are said to have believed in this objective in the dispositional sense, should be reasonably coherent with this objective.

The imagist-mentalist might explain this sense of 'belief' further by saying that by 'meditating upon a certain part of reality' he meant 'experiencing beliefs about elements of that part of reality'. He would then be saying that if one still believes that P, it must be true of one that if one has (as one is capable of having) a sufficiently long train of genuine belief experiences concerned with that part of reality to which P, if it exists, belongs, one will end up by experiencing a genuine belief in P itself. There would be no circularity here, simply an explanation of believing

---

[1] We have long allowed ourselves to talk of a component objective as the object of a belief experience when some component of it is so (in the strictest sense) and there is a strong readiness to experience belief in the rest (cf. p. 192). If we should readopt the strictest sense it would be inappropriate to say that everything in which I have such a dispositional belief as is now in question must have been the object of a belief experience. In any case the readiness for believing the remaining components of the compound fact offers an example of a dispositional belief which may hold without ever having been consciously believed, and the nature of the readiness for experiencing belief in them may still pose some problems.

in the dispositional sense in terms which included experiential believing twice over rather than only once.

Perhaps a mind, or rather a consciousness, which was disembodied, might have beliefs solely of this non-behaviourist sort. But this is not to say that the consciousness belonging to an organism could have one set of beliefs from a mentalistic point of view, while the psycho-physical entity consisting in the organism and consciousness together had quite different beliefs from a behaviouristic point of view. It seems reasonable to insist, in accordance with the sort of thing we have already said about the relation between an organism and its consciousness[1] that there are certain conditions which a consciousness must satisfy to be the consciousness of that organism. Among these conditions is that a certain correspondence exist between what the consciousness may be said to believe mentalistically speaking, and what the organism may be said to believe behaviouristically speaking.

It would be over simple to say that the beliefs must be just the same, or rather that their objectives must be just the same. In fact a rather interesting reciprocity seeems to hold between the two. In order to decide exactly what objectives an organism can be said to believe from a behaviouristic point of view one may have to borrow from events in consciousness, that is there may be various alternative objectives which the organism could equally be interpreted as believing, and decision between them may only be possible when consciousness is taken into account. Equally the exact converse may be said, and the vagueness with which consciousness specifies its objectives, may be something which from the point of view of an outsider (though hardly from the point of view of that consciousness) is made determinate by the physical environment with which the organism is interacting. It is worth remarking perhaps that consciousness is doubtless in one sense secondary, in that the basis for the dispositions which figure in a mentalist dispositional sense of believing must presumably be physical.

On the whole it seems clearest to regard the concept of believing, considered as a disposition, as concerning, like most mental concepts, both behavioural and experiential dispositions, in a way which it is difficult to sum up by any neat formula.

[1] See pp. 301–3.

5 'IMAGELESS' BELIEF EXPERIENCES

What should the imagist-mentalist say about persons who claim that imagery plays little or no part in their mental life? It would seem that he must say that such people never or seldom bring their beliefs to full consciousness, and even that in a certain sense of believe they can hardly be said to believe things at all. This remark is likely to be resented or ridiculed by such persons.

In discussing this matter we should make it plain from the outset that we are not here concerned with the objection that a public language cannot refer to anything with the essential privacy of imaging and that hence believing cannot, as a concept expressible in a public language, have to do with such private events. We are concerned with the claim that there are persons of whom it might be odd to say that they never brought their beliefs to consciousness but of whom, if their own report be accepted, it must be said that they do not have imagery, or at least do not have it as often as they would be said to bring their beliefs to consciousness.

This subject is closely linked with that of imageless thought over which there was, in the days of introspective psychology, a good deal of controversy.

If one says that at a particular time someone went through a process of imageless thought there would seem to be several different things which on the face of it might have taken place conformably with this description.

(1) Someone writing a letter, working in clay, mending a fuse, indeed anyone acting intelligently in the full physical sense of acting might be said to be going through a period of imageless thought if they had no imagery of any kind during that period. Normally however they will be experiencing sense-data belonging to the activities in which they are engaging, and will be having certain feelings in response to these sense-data. Such people might be said to be thinking in sense-data rather than in images (or words). It is not such thinking which is usually characterized as imageless, though the expression strictly taken is quite apt to these situations.

(2) One's experience in speaking or writing coherently, when no imagery is evoked, could be called imageless thought. Granted the various possible uses of 'image' this description is not very

clear, but it does not seem that any experience of, or accompanying, speaking or writing represents the sort of thing most typically described as imageless thinking.

(3) Is solitary thinking in words a form of imageless thinking? If the words are imagy in quality there is a sense in which the thinking is, and a sense in which it is not, imageless thinking. (Cf. pp. 227–9). But though in a sense solitary thinking in words (datal or imagy) is imageless, it is not what is most typically intended by the phrase 'imageless thinking'.

(4) By imageless thinking might be meant thinking where no sort of experience or object of experience occurs at all in such a way as to be described as the vehicle of thought, or the 'stuff' in which thought goes on. Such thinking is indeed possible. The person who solves a problem in a period of dreamless sleep, as witnessed by his waking up with the answer to a problem he went to sleep meditating on, has gone through just such a process of thinking. Yet it is not of such problem solving in sleep that those who talk of imageless thought have been talking. Their concern has been with something which occurs in waking hours. However there is no reason why such a thing should not go on in waking hours. Suppose you set me a problem. Suppose then that for the next few moments nothing goes on in my consciousness which could be regarded as the 'stuff' of my thought about that problem, and suppose that after those few moments I come out with the answer. I may then be said to have thought about it in an imageless way just as in the sleep case. However I was not asleep and we may suppose that there was a continuous flow of conscious experience throughout the period, though none of it was my thinking of the problem. If this is what is meant by imageless thinking it poses no special problem. It simply means that there are cerebral processes which have no reflection at the time of their going on in consciousness and which end in a cerebral process which is reflected in consciousness as the consciousness of a problem solved. Yet it is doubtful if this is what is meant by imageless thought.

(5) If this is not what is meant, it would seem that by 'imageless thinking' must be meant an experience neither of types (1), (2) or (3), nor an experience of anything describable as imagery. Some of the experiences in which such imageless thinking consists will presumably be experiences which constitute assent to

various propositions, constitute in fact belief experiences in a sense at least close to that with which we have been concerned all along.

But what are the direct objects of these experiences, or (what is the same thing) what is their intrinsic character? Maybe they are certain feelings of tension and strain the physical basis of which is perhaps unknown; perhaps they are certain inner feelings which we have no vocabulary to describe.

Now although I talked of a qualitative sense of 'image' above (pp. 227–9) as opposed to various senses of 'image' which applied to particulars in virtue of something other simply than their intrinsic character, it seems clear that we have not really fixed by this word any such definite quality that one can press the question with regard to any such nameless feeling whether it is imagy or not. Perhaps rather what I called the qualitative sense of 'image', was one in which it marked a definite qualitative contrast which holds between certain visual particulars, between certain auditory particulars, and so on. Images, in this qualitative sense, are the members of some such recognized group of experiential particulars which contrast with other members in this sort of way, the other members being called sense-data. The nameless feelings of which we are now talking may belong to no such group within which this contrast holds, and so the question whether they are images or data, in a qualitative sense, has no definite answer. Some find it natural to report the thought which consists in these feelings imageless, while others do not.

If thinking, and hence presumably believing (as an occurrence) can consist in the experiencing of these nameless feelings, the questions arise about such experiences which we have asked about the experience of images, and to some extent about the experience of words, as to how they can be directed on to various objectives, or be fitted to intend various facts. There is no reason why we should expect an essentially different answer in their case than in that of these others. The answers given in the case of these others then suggest the following possibilities.

(i) The nameless feelings may have little or no resemblance to the things which they are beliefs about, but they may produce emotional responses just such as experience of the things would have produced. That is, they act as substitutes for the things in that they are specified as though they were those things. The substitute-mentalist will say that in that case they are belief experiences on a par with image belief experiences. The imagist-mentalist will say that they do indeed constitute one way in which a belief may be said to become conscious, but that the consciousness is not so full and satisfactory as in the case of imagistic belief experiences. In short, they will call forth comments parallel to those upon the possibility of a purely verbal belief experience.

We may ask how such a nameless feeling universal comes to be treated as would the universal which figures in the objective which is believed. The answer to this question, which probably turns upon obscure cerebral connections, need not really concern us, but one possibility is of interest, namely that these nameless feelings are in fact regularly called forth by objects of the kind they serve as experiences of belief in, and are in this way associated with the objects.

(ii) This is of interest because it draws our attention to the possibility that the nameless feelings are really specification properties occurring in cases of belief in the absence of what they normally specify. This has already been recognized as a possible type of belief experience of a somewhat incomplete kind, and it has also been recognized, what is implicit in what we have just said, that once one gets away from the image belief case, it is often a somewhat arbitrary matter whether a belief experience be said to consist in a specification property for the thing believed in occurring in its absence, and followed by further specification properties, or whether it be said to be a substitute for the thing believed in, specified by other experiences in its place (see this chapter, pp. 322–3).

(iii) Another possibility is that there really is a definite resemblance between the nameless feeling and the thing believed in, that it really is in some way a mimic of the thing believed in, (perhaps so to speak in a different medium) and in virtue of that resemblance it acts as a substitute for the thing believed in, and is greeted with specification experiences for that thing. It may even be that the mind has the habit of imitating the things it comes across, when they are absent, in a different medium according to relatively constant habits of representation. Someone whose imagery was entirely tactile might have his own way of imitating visual data in the tactile medium. Likewise someone might have a regular way of imitating sense-data in a nameless medium which could hardly be described as either a datal or a corresponding imagy medium.

It may be said that this last possibility is really simply the possibility of a rather unobvious kind of image believing. That is indeed precisely the point I want to make. At least I want to point out that the possibilities, and indeed the actualities, are so rich, that one cannot neatly classify them into imagist cases of belief experiences, and others. Thus people who honestly and carefully report that they have no imagery may in fact have belief experiences which approach very closely to, or even satisfy, the description of a belief come in to full consciousness according to imagist-mentalism.

(iv) We may just remark on a fourth and less interesting role which these nameless feelings might play. They might be the signs that certain things were believed in one or other of the dispositional senses we have mentioned, without themselves amounting to belief experiences. They would indeed be signs which no-one ever was in a position to interpret, but they might still be linked by definite laws with certain states of belief. In short they might have pragmatic meaning in the sense in which linguistic utterances such as do not amount to belief experiences do.

(v) Another possibility is that during periods of time at which a man might be said to be thinking he experiences certain nameless feelings which however have no sort of variety corresponding to the variety of things about which behavioural criteria (such as the public tasks the organism was girding itself for) would suggest his thoughts were occupied. The brain would be a machine performing an immense number of different tasks the noise of which did not however alter according to the tasks it was performing, or at least only altered with certain very broad and gross changes in the type of task performed. Thus the feelings experienced could hardly be called symbols of the things thought of, since they would remain the same almost whatever was thought of.

There may be phases of thought which answer to something like this account. There may be a feeling of intense strain which occurs when certain intellectual feats are engaged in which have just the same character whatever the details of the feat. This may very often be what people refer to as imageless thought. A man whose private and inactive meditations were confined to this sort of thing would never enjoy anything but the very dimmest approach to what we are calling a conscious belief, except possibly when he was using public objects (or rather their appearances) as symbols of absent situations. (The imagist-mentalist, incidentally, should not deny the possibility of a *full* belief experience in which one kind of sense-datum symbolizes a different but similar kind of sense-datum.)

The view taken by the imagist-mentalist of imageless thinking, if the term can be used here, which falls under one of headings (1)–(4) should be clear from preceding sections. Apart from type (4), each of these may contain something which approaches fairly near a full consciousness of what is thought about, though it will be fairly unusual for it to do so. If imageless thinking is supposed to be something other than what falls under (1)–(4), it is hard to see how it can fail to fall under (5). Granted it is an experience (and the only alternative seems to be (4)), it must be an experience with some intrinsic character.

Some people may have a rich variety of nameless feelings without recognizing the fact, because they are too word-dominated to recall the nameless when thinking about thinking. My impression is that my own experience contains a rich store of nameless feelings which play their part in thought, and act as symbols of things absent. Some of these hover on the verge of being visual images, or images of some recognized modality. Some even seem to hover between two such modalities. Others are perhaps somatic sensations of certain kinds, or even images of such, the qualitative contrast being very vague between these two. A person who had feelings of this nameless sort, even the ones which hovered on the verge of being images of a recognized modality, but who never, or hardly ever, had images of a more definite kind, might describe himself as imageless. But it is clear that such a person might not only have belief experiences of the kind dwelt on by the substitute-mentalist with the nameless feelings acting as symbols of the things believed in but that resemblance of one sort and another might hold between the nameless feelings and the things they symbolized, so that these belief experiences in fact answer to the criteria of the imagist-mentalist. It is worth remarking that even words as experienced privately by each man, especially image words, may in a curious way take on qualities akin to the qualities of that which they symbolize.

This shows that the division between those belief experiences given a privileged status by imagist-mentalism, and those ones which substitute-mentalism would put on a par with them is rather a matter of degree than an absolute one. The question whether someone has imagery in the sense required by imagist-mentalism in those who can be said to have relatively complete belief experiences turns out finally to be somewhat vague.

For imagist-mentalism to be acceptable its claims must be pitched in some such key as this. It describes something which it calls a complete belief experience, or a belief come to full consciousness. Such experiences are very rare, and, moreover, even when they come only a small part of the objective which it would naturally occur to us to describe as being believed is really presented to this full consciousness. Only a divine being could bring to unitary consciousness all the claims which are made by any ordinary sentence to which we assent. Still, experiences which do not satisfy this ideal may approach more or less nearly to this ideal. Perhaps there is no one dimension in which their comparative approach to the ideal, may be charted, and some may come nearer in one way, others in another way. On the whole the ideal is approached most closely by cases in which images of the most definite sort are before the mind, but cases such as those the substitute-mentalist dwells on, including certain linguistic cases, may also approach quite closely to the ideal. Indeed the distinction between the two as just noticed is far from sharp. Closeness to the ideal is to be measured primarily by two factors, the closeness of the resemblance between the symbolizing object and the object symbolized, and the extent to which specifying properties for the thing symbolized are transferred to the thing symbolizing. Granted that no experience of belief in an ordinary matter of fact ever quite answers to the ideal, all that the imagist-mentalist can really claim is that when it is appropriate to say of someone that he is really making himself conscious of just what it is that he believes to be the case regarding a certain subject matter, it is because some quite close approach to this ideal has been made. This can happen even in the case of people who might regard themselves as not given to imagery, if their 'imageless thought' is of type 5(iii).

6 BELIEVING AND CONCEIVING

It may have struck the reader as an objection to imagist-mentalism as a theory of believing that its description of a belief experience is just as applicable to the state of one entertaining an idea as a fiction as to the state of one entertaining an idea as a truth. If the reader turns back to the description earlier in this chapter of the experiences which a man might enjoy in reading an auto-biography when he really brings home the meaning of what he is reading to himself, he may be struck, or may have already been struck, at the equal applicability of this description to experiences likely to be enjoyed in the reading of a novel. Indeed just because novels are books which involve more concrete detail and less abstraction than most other books, what we have called a belief experience is particularly likely to go on in reading a novel.

Briefly, the answer to this is that if we consider the experience enjoyed moment by moment as someone reads a novel it very often is one of believing in the actualness of what is described. What distinguishes the situation from that in which we read a book of supposed fact is that there is a great fund of disbelief ready to well up at any moment. One example of this is our tendency if the feelings aroused by the novel are too unpleasant to remind ourselves that it is 'only a story'. To utter such words as these to oneself is to stimulate a state of disbelief in the story. The fact that, where the story is one which we would hate to be true, doing this alleviates our distress, rather supports our identification of belief with the reacting to imagery, or to some-thing else playing the same role, as if it actually were the thing believed in. Reminding ourselves thus to disbelieve in the story does seem to be a matter of prompting oneself not to feel about the images as one would about the corresponding actualities, if they were being experienced.

The situation is complicated by the fact that we may continue to believe in the general characterization of human life offered by the novelist even when we do not believe that those very incidents took place. But to go into that point further would take us too far afield into the psychology of literature. The point to insist on here is that though one's experience when reading a novel may in fact be a belief experience, it is balanced by a tendency to disbelieve in the story, and it is this latter tendency which will be the more powerful once the reading is over. A connected point is this: When we read what we take to be fact we are likely to start believing in the existence of situations not directly described in the book, but which consist in the holding of certain relations between those situations and other situations. That is, everything that we read as fact takes its place as part of one vast picture and we are ready to experience pictures of the relations between any two elements in that one vast picture. When we read something as fiction, even while our experience may be in a way an experience of belief in the picture it presents, we are not likely to experience belief in relations holding between the elements of that picture and the elements of any other picture. Of course what I have called one vast picture into which the elements of everything one reads as fact are fitted is not experienced by human minds as a totality, but it is a truth about a large number of the pictures that they put before their minds that their ideal relations one to another are such that they are fitted to go together to make up such a picture.

Another point is this. From the point of view of a behaviourist analysis of belief, (the importance of which the imagist-mentalist quite acknowledges) the reader presumably does not believe in the incidents of the fiction. If this be granted, though the experience may indeed be in its intrinsic nature a belief experience, it cannot be described as a behaviouristically conceived belief come to consciousness, as other belief experiences can be. Now one of the things which makes an individual consciousness the consciousness *of a particular organism* is the fact that for the most part its belief experiences are the (behaviouristically conceived) beliefs of that organism come to consciousness. This is therefore an important role for belief experiences to play and it is one which the belief experiences aroused by explicit fiction do not play.

Actually it seems that usually there is some modification of the emotions induced when what is read is acknowledged fiction. There is surely something rather peculiar about the distress and joy normally induced by fiction which contrasts with the feelings evoked by reality, or by what is taken as a symbol for reality.

Still it is doubtless often the case that the experiences enjoyed when reading fiction are, so far as their intrinsic nature goes, belief experiences. If they are denied the title it must be in virtue of their relations to things other than themselves, not in virtue of their intrinsic nature.

An opponent of imagist-mentalism might infer from this not that the experiences are in virtue of their intrinsic nature belief experiences, but that whether an experience is a belief experience is not a matter of its intrinsic nature but of its relation to things outside it.

If the point goes no further than this it requires only a fairly modest modification of imagist-mentalism. The imagist-mentalist can say that what he has done is to describe the intrinsic nature of a kind of experience which, unless it stands in certain relations to experiences which are in appropriate relations to events outside it, will be a belief experience. It will be a belief experience, that is unless there is a predominating tendency, in the mind which enjoys it, to have similar experiences which contradict it. It is a belief experience, provided these relations do not hold, though whether or not it is the belief of a certain organism come to consciousness depends on further factors still.

Perhaps the imagist-mentalist should make this qualification in his doctrine as so far advanced. But the point is largely terminological, and does not affect the question whether the imagist-mentalist has adequately analysed the sort of experience one has when one brings home to oneself how one really thinks things are.

It is not strictly true, in any case, that for the imagist-mentalist the question whether an experience is a belief experience or not, rests entirely upon its intrinsic nature.[1] It is only that it is so to speak more of a matter of its intrinsic nature than if the qualification just mentioned be incorporated into imagist-mentalism.

What must be noted finally in connection with this discussion of fiction is that the imagist-mentalist is in effect committed to the Spinozistic view that believing is not conceiving plus something else, but that believing is the basic mode of conceiving, and that conceiving without believing, and other sorts of experience which are directed on an objective, are modified forms of believing. However, it is less apt to say that believing is merely conceiving in the absence of any conceiving of the opposite, than to say that mere conceiving is believing inhibited by an equal propensity, or at least by a propensity which constitutes a real rival, to believe

[1] Cf. Chapter IX, section 6.

the opposite. We have also considered the nature of one other propositional attitude, or rather experience, that of desiring and its close associate willing, and tried to chart its relation to believing. Such propositional experiences also we have regarded as believing modified in a certain way.

We have not aimed to give an account of propositional experiences in general, still less of propositional attitudes. In spite of the prominence of images in our discussion we have not set out to chart the different senses of 'imagining'. 'Imagining', we may remark here, often means 'supposing' or 'conceiving'. The discussion of this section points the way to an account of such experiences as we might describe in this way, as belief experiences which are immediately checked by a greater weight of belief experiences pointing the opposite way.

Imaging, that is the experience of particulars which are imagy in quality, must be sharply distinguished from imagining in any such senses as those above. The imagist-mentalist might be said to identify the experience of believing with the experience of imagining, where this is not checked by contrary imaginings (though it is better to explain imagining by reference to believing rather than *vice versa*) but he certainly cannot be said to identify believing with imaging, with the mere experience of imagy particulars which resemble the things he is said to believe in. These imagy particulars must be felt about as though they were the things they resemble for an experience of believing to take place. The fullest belief experience will be one in which the objects of direct experience both resemble the things said to be believed in, and are felt about as these things would be. But provided this latter condition is met the resemblance may dwindle away altogether, and the experience still qualify as a belief experience. Nonetheless the greater the resemblance, the more we may be said to have brought consciously to mind the true nature of the absent situation in the existence of which we are said to believe.

INDEX

International Library of Philosophy & Scientific Method

Editor: Ted Honderich

List of titles, page two

International Library of Psychology Philosophy & Scientific Method

Editor: C K Ogden

List of titles, page six

ROUTLEDGE AND KEGAN PAUL LTD
68 Carter Lane London EC4

International Library of Philosophy and Scientific Method
(*Demy 8vo*)

Allen, R. E. (Ed.)
Studies in Plato's Metaphysics
Contributors: J. L. Ackrill, R. E. Allen, R. S. Bluck, H. F. Cherniss, F. M. Cornford, R. C. Cross, P. T. Geach, R. Hackforth, W. F. Hicken, A. C. Lloyd, G. R. Morrow, G. E. L. Owen, G. Ryle, W. G. Runciman, G. Vlastos
464 pp. 1965. (2nd Impression 1967.) 70s.

Armstrong, D. M.
Perception and the Physical World
208 pp. 1961. (3rd Impression 1966.) 25s.
A Materialist Theory of the Mind
376 pp. 1967. (2nd Impression 1969.) 50s.

Bambrough, Renford (Ed.)
New Essays on Plato and Aristotle
Contributors: J. L. Ackrill, G. E. M. Anscombe, Renford Bambrough, R. M. Hare, D. M. MacKinnon, G. E. L. Owen, G. Ryle, G. Vlastos
184 pp. 1965. (2nd Impression 1967.) 28s.

Barry, Brian
Political Argument
382 pp. 1965. (3rd Impression 1968.) 50s.

Bird, Graham
Kant's Theory of Knowledge:
An Outline of One Central Argument in the *Critique of Pure Reason*
220 pp. 1962. (2nd Impression 1965.) 28s.

Brentano, Franz
The True and the Evident
Edited and narrated by Professor R. Chisholm
218 pp. 1965. 40s.

The Origin of Our Knowledge of Right and Wrong
Edited by Oskar Kraus. English edition edited by Roderick M. Chisholm. Translated by Roderick M. Chisholm and Elizabeth H. Schneewind
174 pp. 1969. 40s.

Broad, C. D.
Lectures on Physical Research
Incorporating the Perrott Lectures given in Cambridge University in 1959 and 1960
461 pp. 1962. (2nd Impression 1966.) 56s.

Crombie, I. M.
An Examination of Plato's Doctrine
1. Plato on Man and Society
408 pp. 1962. (3rd Impression 1969.) 42s.
II. Plato on Knowledge and Reality
583 pp. 1963. (2nd Impression 1967.) 63s.

2

International Library of Philosophy and Scientific Method
(*Demy 8vo*)

Day, John Patrick
Inductive Probability
352 pp. 1961. 40s.

Dretske, Fred I.
Seeing and Knowing
270 pp. 1969. 35s.

Ducasse, C. J.
Truth, Knowledge and Causation
263 pp. 1969. 50s.

Edel, Abraham
Method in Ethical Theory
379 pp. 1963. 32s.

Fann, K. T. (Ed.)
Symposium on J. L. Austin
Contributors: A. J. Ayer, Jonathan Bennett, Max Black, Stanley Cavell, Walter Cerf, Roderick M. Chisholm, L. Jonathan Cohen, Roderick Firth, L. W. Forguson, Mats Furberg, Stuart Hampshire, R. J. Hirst, C. G. New, P. H. Nowell-Smith, David Pears, John Searle, Peter Strawson, Irving Thalberg, J. O. Urmson, G. J. Warnock, Jon Wheatly, Alan White
512 pp. 1969.

Flew, Anthony
Hume's Philosophy of Belief
A Study of his First "Inquiry"
269 pp. 1961. (2nd Impression 1966.) 30s.

Fogelin, Robert J.
Evidence and Meaning
Studies in Analytical Philosophy
200 pp. 1967. 25s.

Gale, Richard
The Language of Time
256 pp. 1968. 40s.

Goldman, Lucien
The Hidden God
A Study of Tragic Vision in the *Pensées* of Pascal and the Tragedies of Racine.
Translated from the French by Philip Thody
424 pp. 1964. 70s.

Hamlyn, D. W.
Sensation and Perception
A History of the Philosophy of Perception
222 pp. 1961. (3rd Impression 1967.) 25s.

3

2*

International Library of Philosophy and Scientific Method
(Demy 8vo)

Kemp, J.
Reason, Action and Morality
216 pp. 1964. 30s.

Körner, Stephan
Experience and Theory
An Essay in the Philosophy of Science
272 pp. 1966. (2nd Impression 1969.) 45s.

Lazerowitz, Morris
Studies in Metaphilosophy
276 pp. 1964. 35s.

Linsky, Leonard
Referring
152 pp. 1968. 35s.

MacIntosh, J. J., and Coval, S. C. (Ed.)
The Business of Reason
280 pp. 1969. 42s.

Merleau-Ponty, M.
Phenomenology of Perception
Translated from the French by Colin Smith
487 pp. 1962. (4th Impression 1967.) 56s.

Perelman, Chaim
The Idea of Justice and the Problem of Argument
Introduction by H. L. A. Hart. Translated from the French by John Petrie
224 pp. 1963. 28s.

Ross, Alf
Directives, Norms and their Logic
192 pp. 1967. 35s.

Schlesinger, G.
Method in the Physical Sciences
148 pp. 1963. 21s.

Sellars, W. F.
Science, Perception and Reality
374 pp. 1963. (2nd Impression 1966.) 50s.

Shwayder, D. S.
The Stratification of Behaviour
A System of Definitions Propounded and Defended
428 pp. 1965. 56s.

Skolimowski, Henryk
Polish Analytical Philosophy
288 pp. 1967. 40s.

International Library of Philosophy and Scientific Method
(*Demy 8vo*)

Smart, J. J. C.
Philosophy and Scientific Realism
168 pp. 1963. (3rd Impression 1967.) 25s.

Smythies, J. R. (Ed.)
Brain and Mind
Contributors: Lord Brain, John Beloff, C. J. Ducasse, Antony Flew, Hartwig
Kuhlenbeck, D. M. MacKay, H. H. Price, Anthony Quinton and J. R. Smythies
288 pp. 1965. 40s.

Science and E.S.P.
Contributors: Gilbert Murray, H. H. Price, Rosalind Heywood, Cyril Burt,
C. D. Broad, Francis Huxley and John Beloff
320 pp. about 40s.

Taylor, Charles
The Explanation of Behaviour
288 pp. 1964. (2nd Impression 1965.) 40s.

Williams, Bernard, and Montefiore, Alan
British Analytical Philosophy
352 pp. 1965. (2nd Impression 1967.) 45s.

Winch, Peter (Ed.)
Studies in the Philosophy of Wittgenstein
Contributors: Hidé Ishiguro, Rush Rhees, D. S. Shwayder, John W. Cook,
L. R. Reinhardt and Anthony Manser
224 pp. 1969.

Wittgenstein, Ludwig
Tractatus Logico-Philosophicus
The German text of the *Logisch-Philosophische Abhandlung* with a new
translation by D. F. Pears and B. F. McGuinness. Introduction by
Bertrand Russell
188 pp. 1961. (3rd Impression 1966.) 21s.

Wright, Georg Henrik Von
Norm and Action
A Logical Enquiry. The Gifford Lectures
232 pp. 1963. (2nd Impression 1964.) 32s.

The Varieties of Goodness
The Gifford Lectures
236 pp. 1963. (3rd Impression 1966.) 28s.

Zinkernagel, Peter
Conditions for Description
Translated from the Danish by Olaf Lindum
272 pp. 1962. 37s. 6d.

International Library of Psychology, Philosophy, and Scientific Method

(*Demy 8vo*)

PHILOSOPHY

Anton, John Peter
Aristotle's Theory of Contrariety
276 pp. 1957. 25s.

Black, Max
The Nature of Mathematics
A Critical Survey
242 pp. 1933. (5th Impression 1965.) 28s.

Bluck, R. S.
Plato's Phaedo
A Translation with Introduction, Notes and Appendices
226 pp. 1955. 21s.

Broad, C. D.
Five Types of Ethical Theory
322 pp. 1930. (9th Impression 1967.) 30s.
The Mind and Its Place in Nature
694 pp. 1925. (7th Impression 1962.) 70s. See also Lean, Martin

Buchler, Justus (Ed.)
The Philosophy of Peirce
Selected Writings
412 pp. 1940. (3rd Impression 1956.) 35s.

Burtt, E. A.
The Metaphysical Foundations of Modern Physical Science
A Historical and Critical Essay
364 pp. 2nd (revised) edition 1932. (5th Impression 1964.) 35s.

Carnap, Rudolf
The Logical Syntax of Language
Translated from the German by Amethe Smeaton
376 pp. 1937. (7th Impression 1967.) 40s.

Chwistek, Leon
The Limits of Science
Outline of Logic and of the Methodology of the Exact Sciences
With Introduction and Appendix by Helen Charlotte Brodie
414 pp. 2nd edition 1949. 32s.

Cornford, F. M.
Plato's Theory of Knowledge
The Theaetetus and Sophist of Plato
Translated with a running commentary
358 pp. 1935. (7th Impression 1967.) 28s.

International Library of Psychology, Philosophy, and Scientific Method
(*Demy 8vo*)

Cornford, F. M. (*continued*)
Plato's Cosmology
The Timaeus of Plato
Translated with a running commentary
402 pp. Frontispiece. 1937. (5th Impression 1966.) 45s.

Plato and Parmenides
Parmenides' *Way of Truth* and Plato's *Parmenides*
Translated with a running commentary
280 pp. 1939. (5th Impression 1964.) 32s.

Crawshay-Williams, Rupert
Methods and Criteria of Reasoning
An Inquiry into the Structure of Controversy
312 pp. 1957. 32s.

Fritz, Charles A.
Bertrand Russell's Construction of the External World
252 pp. 1952. 30s.

Hulme, T. E.
Speculations
Essays on Humanism and the Philosophy of Art
Edited by Herbert Read. Foreword and Frontispiece by Jacob Epstein
296 pp. 2nd edition 1936. (6th Impression 1965.) 40s.

Lazerowitz, Morris
The Structure of Metaphysics
With a Foreword by John Wisdom
262 pp. 1955. (2nd Impression 1963.) 30s.

Lodge, Rupert C.
Plato's Theory of Art
332 pp. 1953. 25s.

Mannheim, Karl
Ideology and Utopia
An Introduction to the Sociology of Knowledge
With a Preface by Louis Wirth. Translated from the German by Louis Wirth
and Edward Shils
360 pp. 1954. (2nd Impression 1966.) 30s.

Moore, G. E.
Philosophical Studies
360 pp. 1922. (6th Impression 1965.) 35s. See also Ramsey, F. P.

International Library of Psychology, Philosophy, and Scientific Method
(*Demy 8vo*)

Ogden, C. K., and Richards, I. A.
The Meaning of Meaning
A Study of the Influence of Language upon Thought and of the Science of Symbolism
With supplementary essays by B. Malinowski and F. G. Crookshank
394 pp. 10th Edition 1949. (6th Impression 1967.) 32s.
See also Bentham, J.

Peirce, Charles, *see* Buchler, J.

Ramsey, Frank Plumpton
The Foundations of Mathematics and other Logical Essays
Edited by R. B. Braithwaite. Preface by G. E. Moore
318 pp. 1931. (4th Impression 1965.) 35s.

Richards, I. A.
Principles of Literary Criticism
312 pp. 2nd Edition. 1926. (17th Impression 1966.) 30s.

Mencius on the Mind. Experiments in Multiple Definition
190 pp. 1932. (2nd Impression 1964.) 28s.

Russell, Bertrand, *see* Fritz, C. A.; Lange, F. A.; Wittgenstein, L.

Smart, Ninian
Reasons and Faiths
An Investigation of Religious Discourse, Christian and Non-Christian
230 pp. 1958. (2nd Impression 1965.) 28s.

Vaihinger, H.
The Philosophy of As If
A System of the Theoretical, Practical and Religious Fictions of Mankind
Translated by C. K. Ogden
428 pp. 2nd edition 1935. (4th Impression 1965.) 45s.

Wittgenstein, Ludwig
Tractatus Logico-Philosophicus
With an Introduction by Bertrand Russell, F.R.S., German text with an English translation en regard
216 pp. 1922. (9th Impression 1962.) 21s.
For the Pears-McGuinness translation—*see page 5*

Wright, Georg Henrik von
Logical Studies
214 pp. 1957. (2nd Impression 1967.) 28s.

International Library of Psychology, Philosophy, and Scientific Method
(*Demy 8vo*)

Zeller, Eduard
Outlines of the History of Greek Philosophy
Revised by Dr. Wilhelm Nestle. Translated from the German by L. R. Palmer
248 pp. 13th (revised) edition 1931. (5th Impression 1963.) 28s.

PSYCHOLOGY

Adler, Alfred
The Practice and Theory of Individual Psychology
Translated by P. Radin
368 pp. 2nd (revised) edition 1929. (8th Impression 1964.) 30s.

Eng, Helga
The Psychology of Children's Drawings
From the First Stroke to the Coloured Drawing
240 pp. 8 colour plates. 139 figures. 2nd edition 1954. (3rd Impression 1966.) 40s.

Koffka, Kurt
The Growth of the Mind
An Introduction to Child-Psychology
Translated from the German by Robert Morris Ogden
456 pp 16 figures. 2nd edition (revised) 1928. (6th Impression 1965.) 45s.

Principles of Gestalt Psychology
740 pp. 112 figures. 39 tables. 1935. (5th Impression 1962.) 60s.

Malinowski, Bronislaw
Crime and Custom in Savage Society
152 pp. 6 plates. 1926. (8th Impression 1966.) 21s.

Sex and Repression in Savage Society
290 pp. 1927. (4th Impression 1953.) 30s.
See also Ogden, C. K.

Murphy, Gardner
An Historical Introduction to Modern Psychology
488 pp. 5th edition (revised) 1949. (6th Impression 1967.) 40s.

Paget, R.
Human Speech
Some Observations, Experiments, and Conclusions as to the Nature, Origin, Purpose and Possible Improvement of Human Speech
374 pp. 5 plates. 1930. (2nd Impression 1963.) 42s.

Petermann, Bruno
The Gestalt Theory and the Problem of Configuration
Translated from the German by Meyer Fortes
364 pp. 20 figures. 1932. (2nd Impression 1950.) 25s.

International Library of Psychology, Philosophy, and Scientific Method
(*Demy 8vo*)

Piaget, Jean
The Language and Thought of the Child
Preface by E. Claparède. Translated from the French by Marjorie Gabain
220 pp. 3rd edition (revised and enlarged) 1959. (3rd Impression 1966.) 30s.

Judgment and Reasoning in the Child
Translated from the French by Marjorie Warden
276 pp. 1928. (5th Impression 1969.) 30s.

The Child's Conception of the World
Translated from the French by Joan and Andrew Tomlinson
408 pp. 1929. (4th Impression 1964.) 40s.

The Child's Conception of Physical Causality
Translated from the French by Marjorie Gabain
(3rd Impression 1965.) 30s.

The Moral Judgment of the Child
Translated from the French by Marjorie Gabain
438 pp. 1932. (4th Impression 1965.) 35s.

The Psychology of Intelligence
Translated from the French by Malcolm Piercy and D. E. Berlyne
198 pp. 1950. (4th Impression 1964.) 18s.

The Child's Conception of Number
Translated from the French by C. Gattegno and F. M. Hodgson
266 pp. 1952. (3rd Impression 1964.) 25s.

The Origin of Intelligence in the Child
Translated from the French by Margaret Cook
448 pp. 1953. (2nd Impression 1966.) 42s.

The Child's Conception of Geometry
In collaboration with Bärbel Inhelder and Alina Szeminska. Translated from the French by E. A. Lunzer
428 pp. 1960. (2nd Impression 1966.) 45s.

Piaget, Jean, and Inhelder, Bärbel
The Child's Conception of Space
Translated from the French by F. J. Langdon and J. L. Lunzer
512 pp. 29 figures. 1956. (3rd Impression 1967.) 42s.

Roback, A. A.
The Psychology of Character
With a Survey of Personality in General
786 pp. 3rd edition (revised and enlarged 1952.) 50s.

Smythies, J. R.
Analysis of Perception
With a Preface by Sir Russell Brain, Bt.
162 pp. 1956. 21s.

International Library of Psychology, Philosophy, and Scientific Method
(*Demy 8vo*)

van der Hoop, J. H.
Character and the Unconscious
A Critical Exposition of the Psychology of Freud and Jung
Translated from the German by Elizabeth Trevelyan
240 pp. 1923. (2nd Impression 1950.) 20s.

Woodger, J. H.
Biological Principles
508 pp. 1929. (Re-issued with a new Introduction 1966.) 60s.

PRINTED BY HEADLEY BROTHERS LTD 109 KINGSWAY LONDON WC2 AND ASHFORD KENT